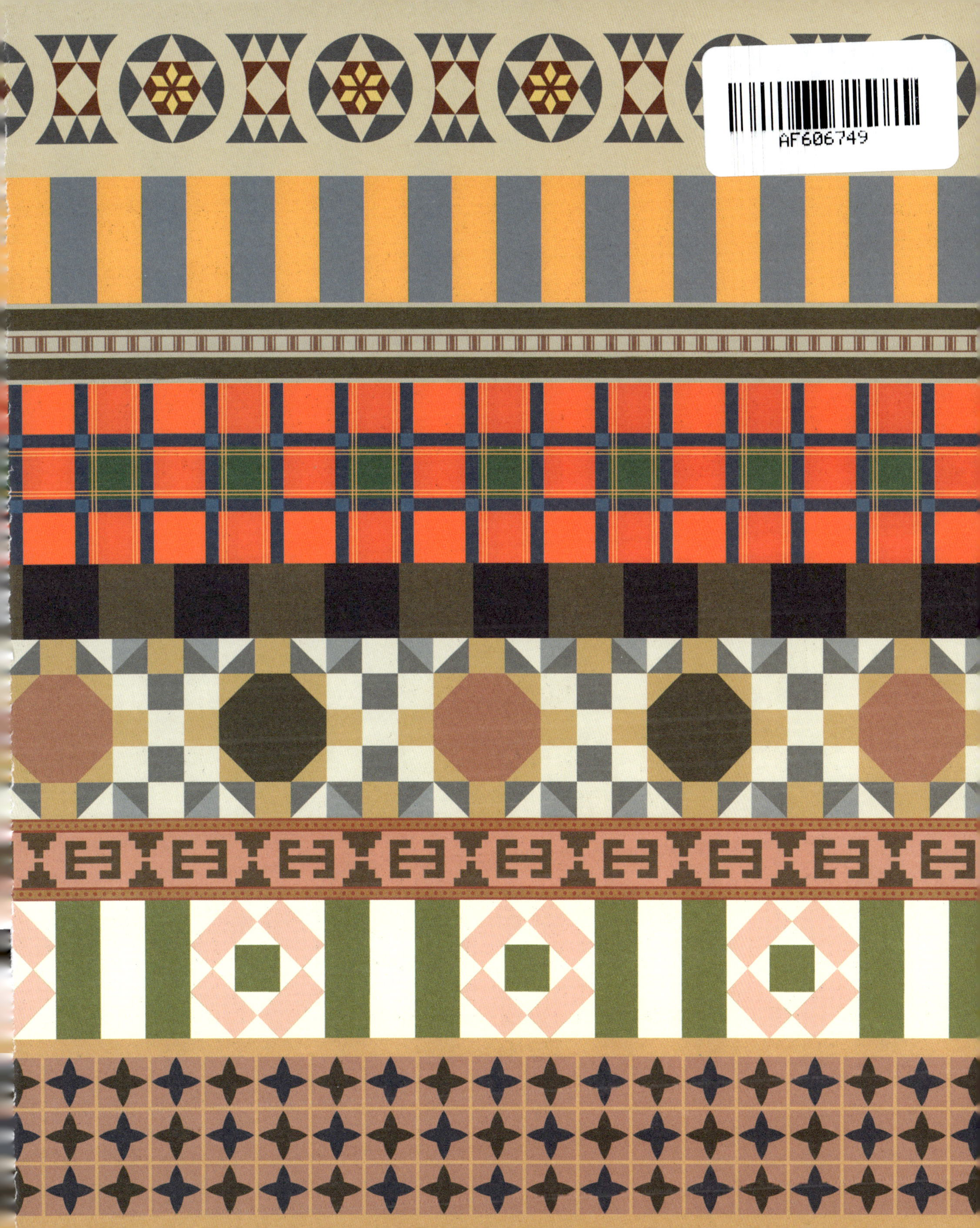

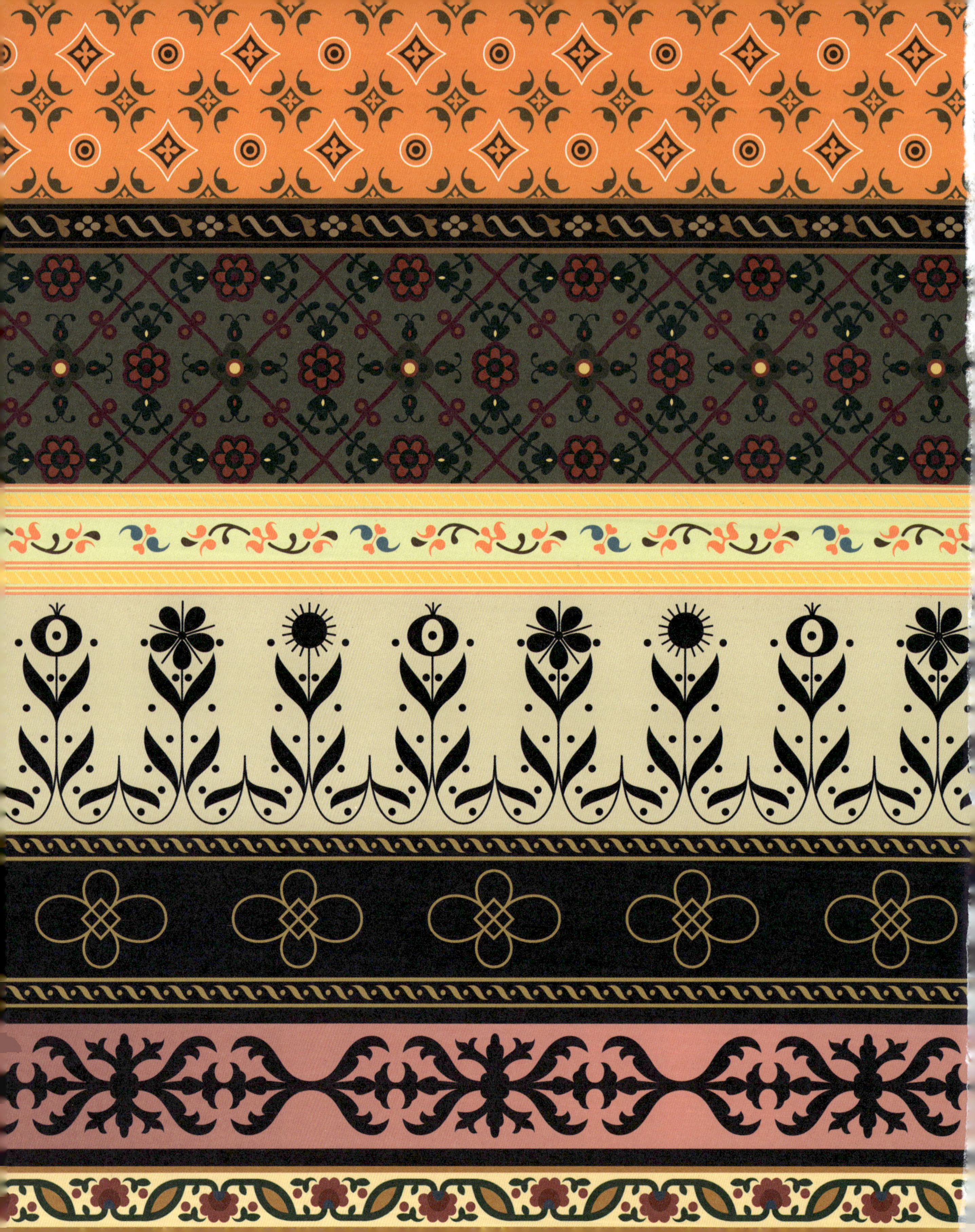

PATTERNS IN ART

 Inquiries should be addressed to Abbeville Press, 655 Third Avenue, New York, NY 10017. The text of this book was set in Novel Sans. Printed in China. First edition 10 9 8 7 6 5 4 3 2 1 · ISBN 978-0-7892-1340-2 Library of Congress Cataloging-in-Publication Data available upon request · For bulk and premium sales and for text adoption procedures, write to Customer Service Manager, Abbeville Press, 655 Third Avenue, New York, NY 10017, or call 1-800-ARTBOOK. Visit Abbeville Press online at www.abbeville.com.

· For the English-language edition: copy editor, Sheila Berg; production manager, Louise Kurtz · First published in the United States of America in 2019 by Abbeville Press, 655 Third Avenue, New York, NY 10017 ·

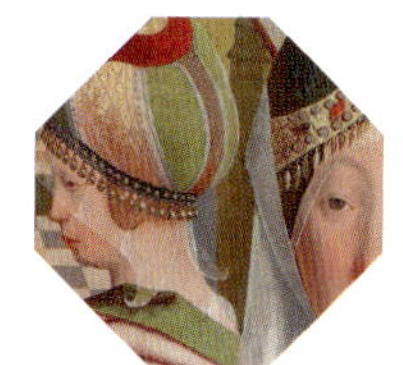

PATTERNS IN ART

A closer look at the Old Masters

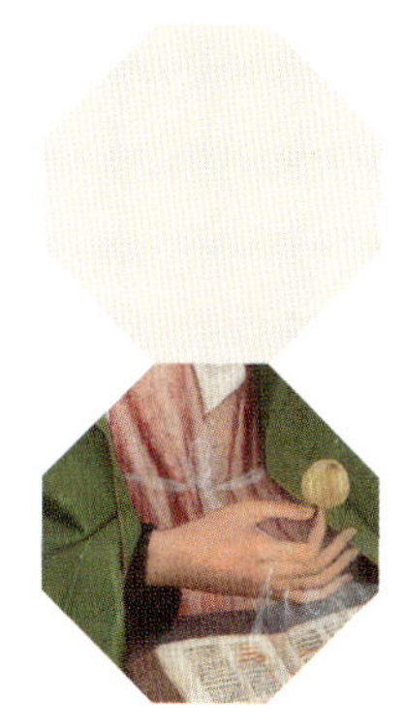

Francesca Leoneschi with
illustrations by **Giovanna Ferraris**
text by **Silvia Lazzaris**

Abbeville Press Publishers
New York London

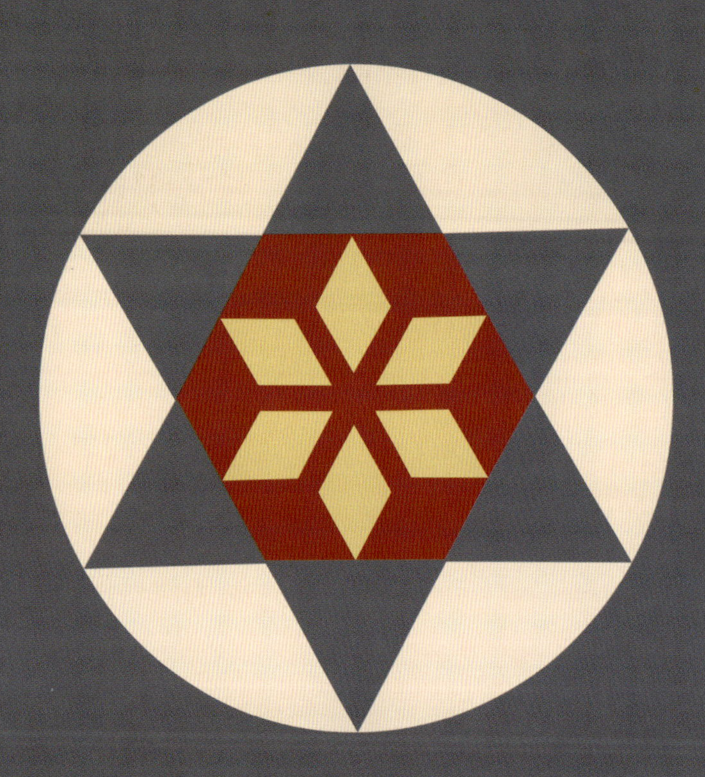

I cherish small details. I am fascinated by the geometric patterns of ceiling moldings, I am mesmerized by the intricate designs of bird nests. Walking around museums, galleries, or art collectors' homes, I can look at paintings so intently that I get lost in the embroidery of a figure's clothing, the veins of a leaf, or the tiles of a floor. I find that exciting and strange stories tend to hide behind these often overlooked elements.

I started to collect interesting details from paintings a long time ago. Whenever I noticed that a piece of art showed some exciting feature, I would take a picture of it. After deconstructing a painting in this way, by focusing solely on some of its intricate features, I would feel the urge to reassemble its parts into a new form. A couple of years ago, I started to think about how I might translate this interest into the creation of something tangible. The result is the book that you now have in your hands. The patterns in this book constitute a synthesis of my way of looking at paintings. Contained within it are motifs and colors from over four centuries of art history. Through this book, I hope to celebrate these decorative elements and highlight their enduring value.

The text of this book also takes a different approach than other works of art history. Sometimes you will still find references to an artist's brushstrokes or use of light. However, most of the time you will read stories about people, their societies, and their costumes. For example, we encounter the trade in fake pearls in 17th-century Italy; the use of art to foster cultural assimilation in Spain's New World colonies; and the only professional woman painter in the United States in the 19th century.

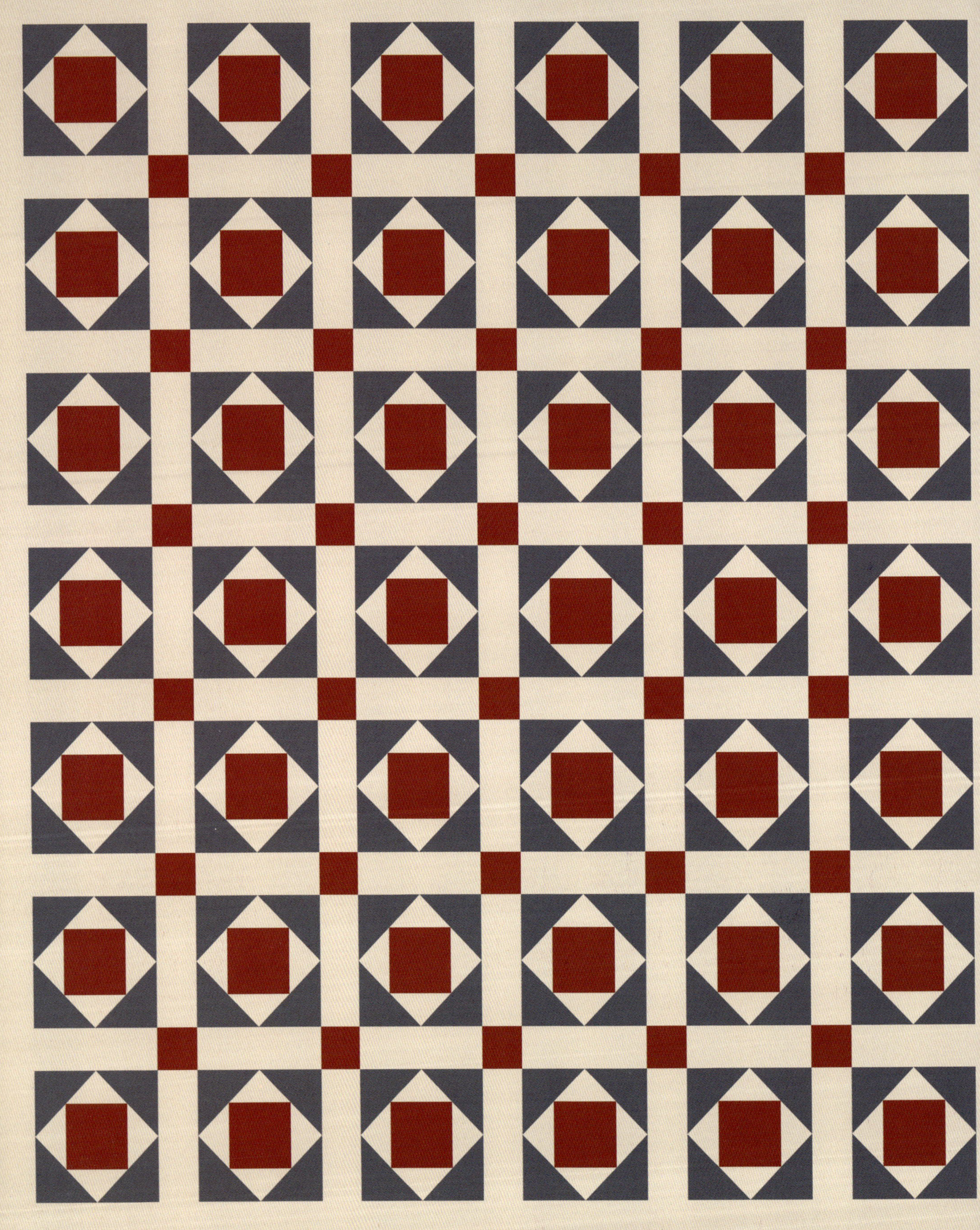

C 13
M 16
Y 27
K 0

C 18
M 84
Y 84
K 42

C 64
M 44
Y 38
K 35

Above all, my coauthors and I have chosen paintings for this book that are rich in meticulously delineated patterns. We have also selected the works in these pages from museums that have made part of their collections accessible online and available to use commercially as part of the public domain. Despite our attempts to include artworks with a broad range of provenances and styles, the paintings that most suited these criteria were from Western artists who lived from the 14th to the 19th century. We have tried to maintain a balance between religious and secular paintings, although accomplishing such an objective was not easy: it is not uncommon for the most beautiful floor tiles represented in art to appear under the feet of the Virgin Mary.

For now, with the help of this book, I hope to provide you with a new and somehow different set of eyes to look at art. I hope you will enjoy this adventure as much as we did.

Francesca Leoneschi

C 19
M 62
Y 56
K 8

C 50
M 39
Y 38
K 20

C 43
M 27
Y 25
K 5

C 15
M 32
Y 59
K 3

C 10
M 9
Y 16
K 0

C 56
M 47
Y 87
K 44

C 98
M 63
Y 47
K 47

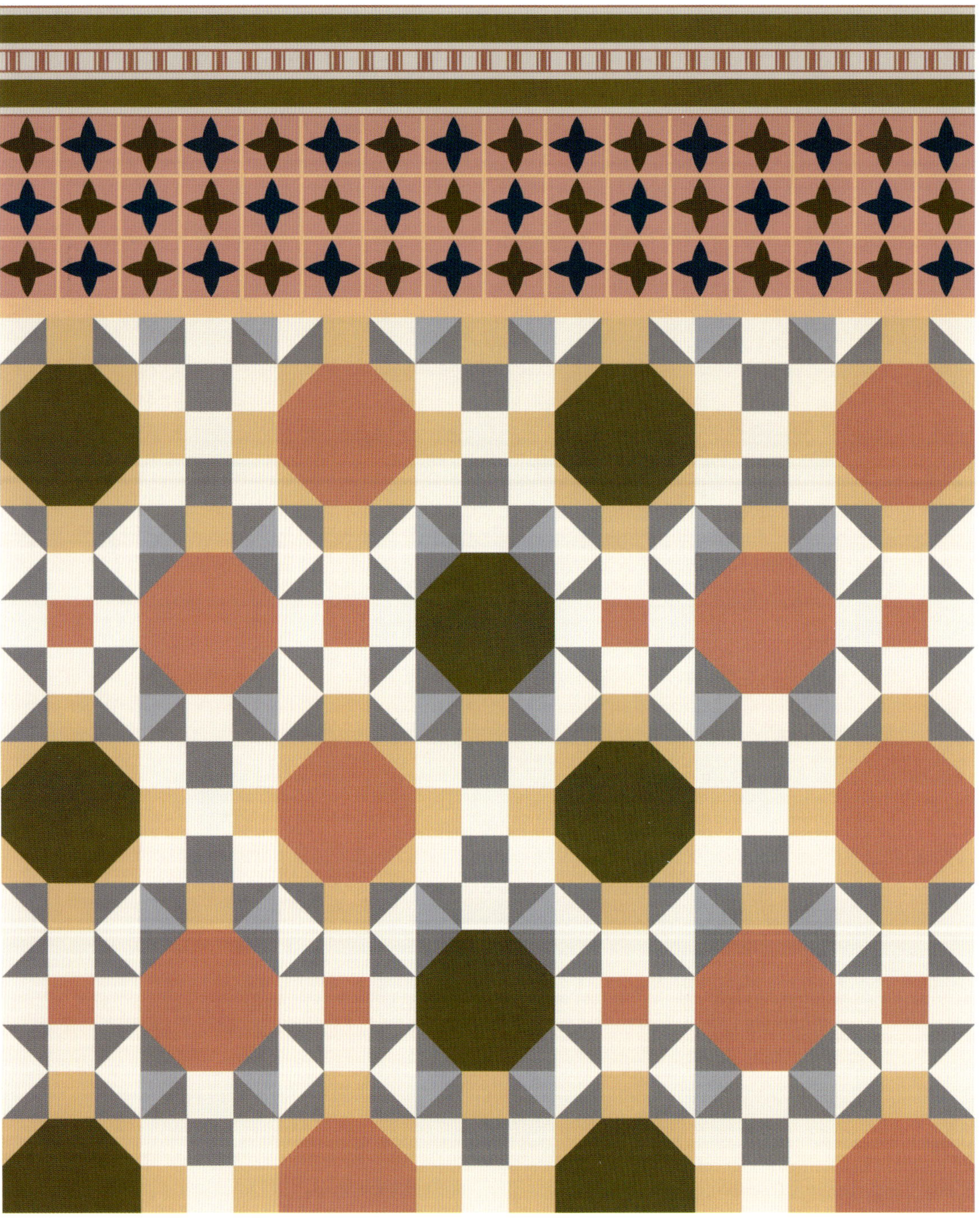

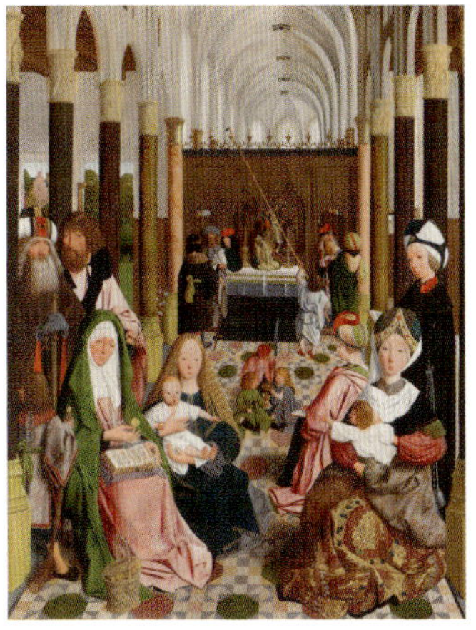

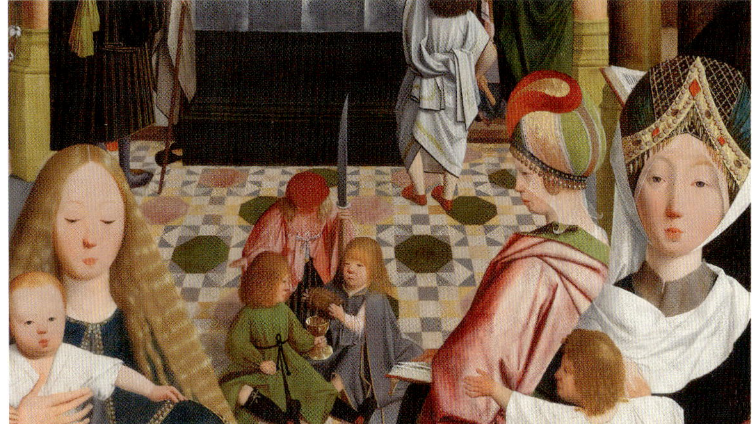

Workshop of Geertgen tot Sint Jans
The Holy Kinship

circa 1495
Rijksmuseum, Amsterdam

The Holy Kinship was a widely depicted subject in Christian art in the 15th and 16th centuries, especially in Germany and the present-day Netherlands. The kinship consists of Jesus's relatives from his mother Mary's extended family. Scenes like the one depicted in this painting by Geergen tot Sint Jans were based on the late medieval belief that Saint Anne, the Virgin Mary's mother, had three husbands. From each of these marriages a daughter was born: Mary, mother of Christ, and her two half sisters, mothers of three apostles. Here, Mary is depicted holding Jesus just to the left of center, and farther left is Saint Anne, holding a book and a flower. Behind the two women stand their husbands, Joachim and Saint Joseph, the latter holding a lily branch to Mary as a symbol of her chaste conception. To the right sits Saint Elizabeth, Mary's cousin, with her son John the Baptist. Three young cousins of Jesus are shown playing farther down the center of the aisle, pouring wine into a chalice. These cousins will later become his disciples, and the wine is a reference to the Eucharist. Farther into the background, on the altar, a sculpture shows Abraham's sacrifice of Isaac, a symbol of God's foreknowledge of the sacrifice of Jesus.

C 5
M 81
Y 79
K 15

C 47
M 32
Y 57
K 26

C 13
M 16
Y 27
K 0

C 18
M 84
Y 84
K 42

C 64
M 44
Y 38
K 35

C 6
M 15
Y 60
K 0

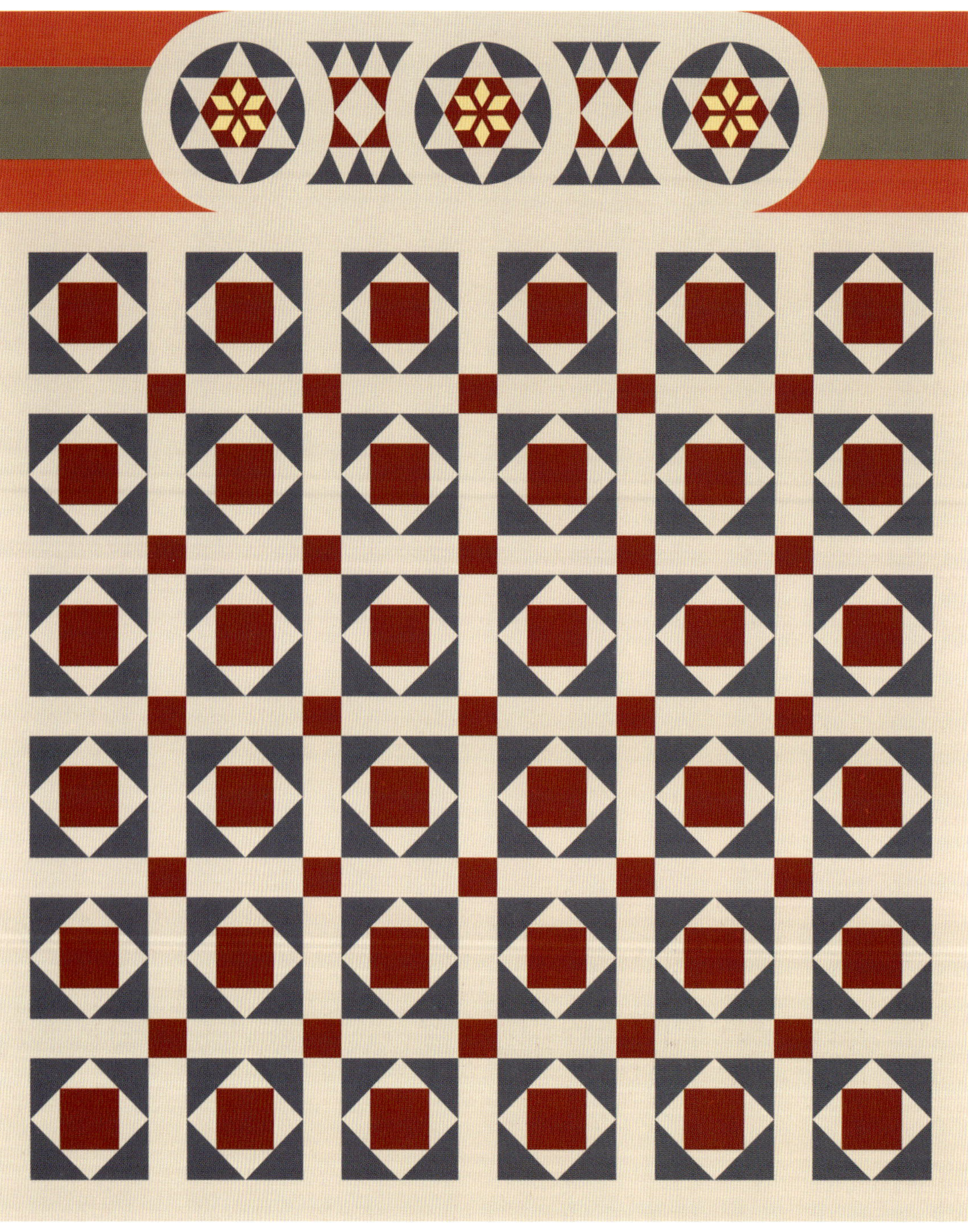

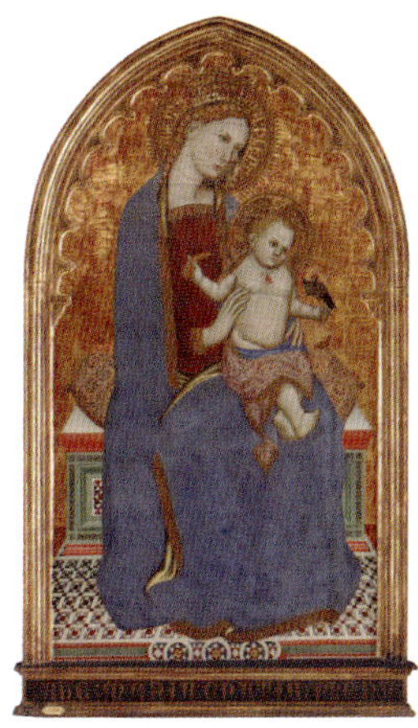

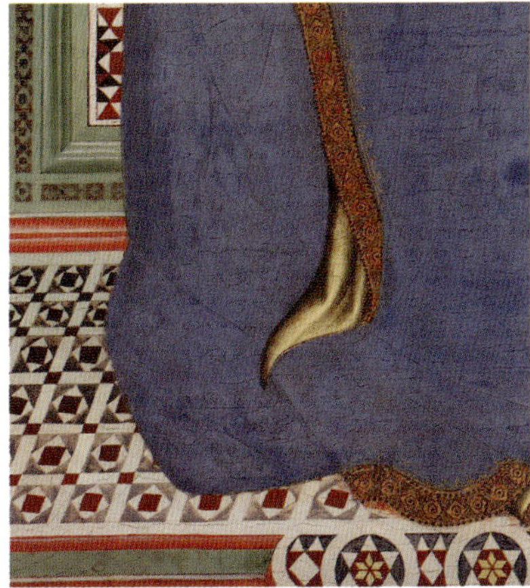

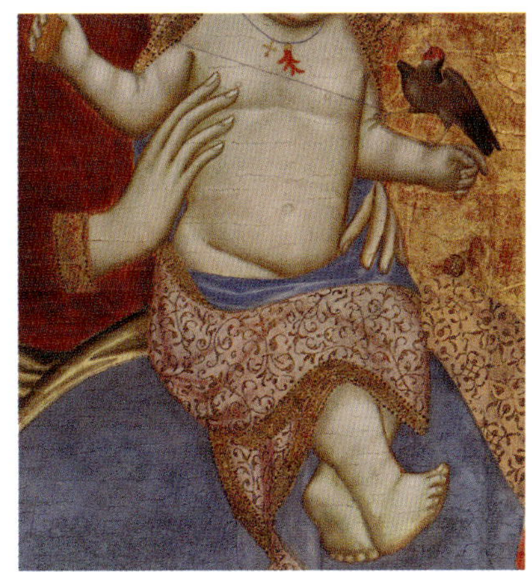

Cecco di Pietro
Virgin and Child Playing with a Goldfinch and Holding a Sheaf of Millet

1379
SMK National Gallery of Denmark, Copenhagen

Cecco di Pietro is an artist who was active in Italy in the late 14th century. His work is characterized by stylized figures, as well as a lack of depth and perspective. It also makes frequent use of symbolism, which is readily apparent in this painting. Of the symbols in this Madonna with Child, perhaps the most well known is the goldfinch that the child is holding in his left hand. In depictions of Christ as an infant, he is often represented with a goldfinch in his hand, foreshadowing his own passion, since goldfinches eat the seeds of the thistle, whose thorns were used to make Christ's crown. According to Christian legend, a goldfinch was also among the three birds—along with a robin and a chaffinch—that, moved by Christ's anguish, detached all of the thorns from his crown, which left each of them wounded and permanently speckled with blood. The imagery and symbolism of Cecco di Pietro's painting are set against a backdrop filled with gold, which represents the holy realm of Heaven.

C 13
M 16
Y 27
K 0

C 18
M 84
Y 84
K 42

C 64
M 44
Y 38
K 35

C 18
M 43
Y 41
K 6

C 36
M 52
Y 94
K 38

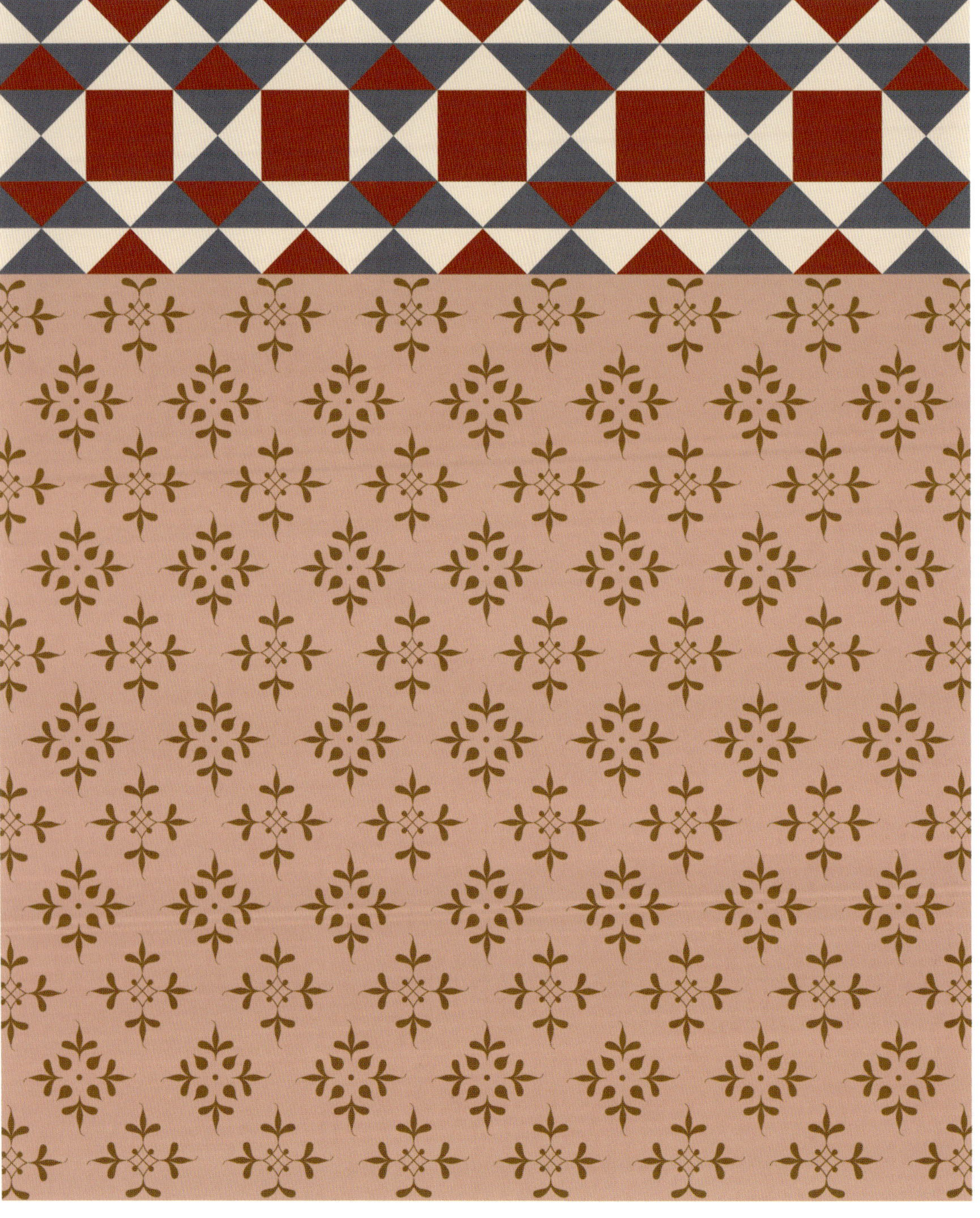

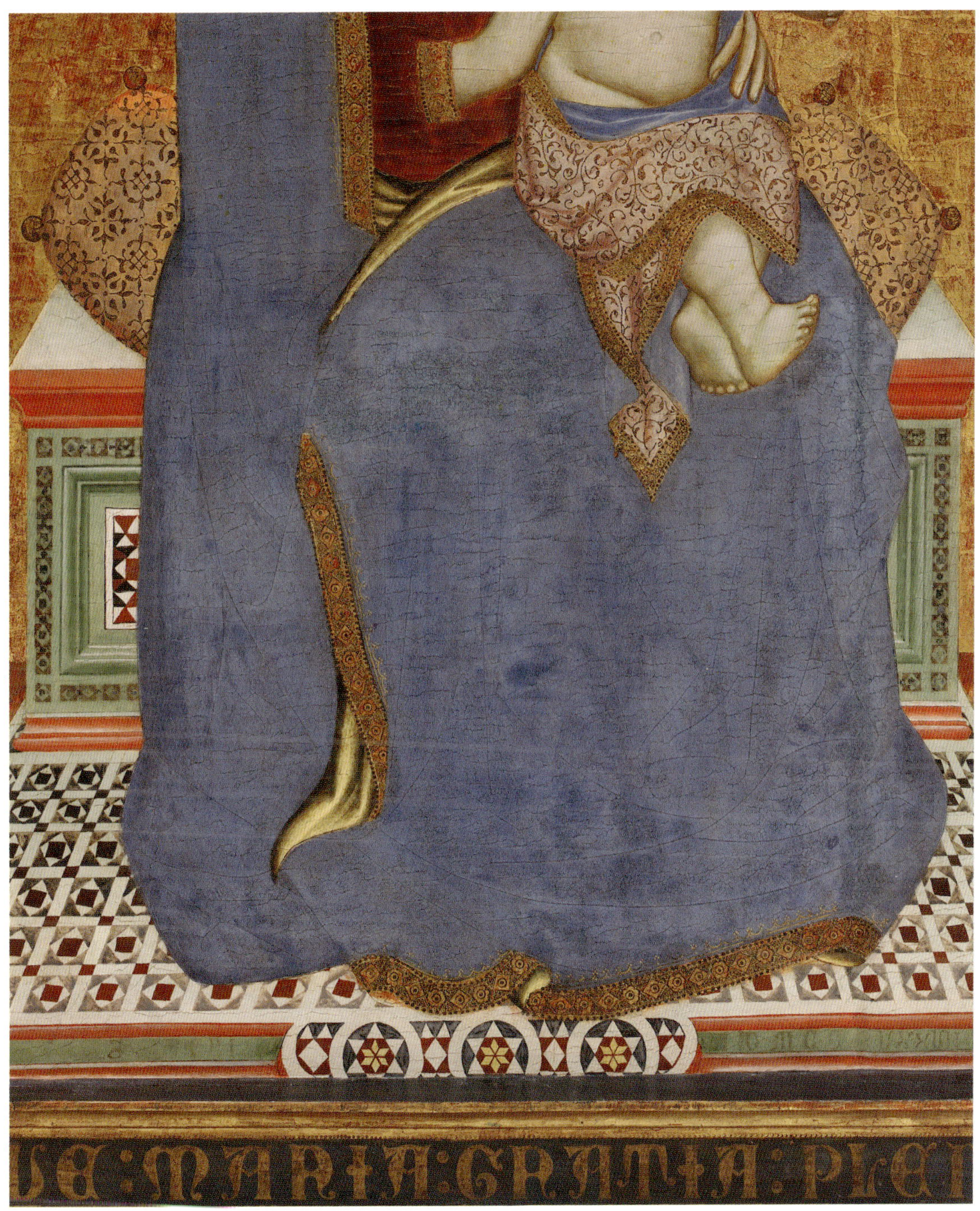
MARIA:GRATIA:

C 60
M 52
Y 58
K 73

C 2
M100
Y 91
K 0

C 84
M 23
Y 85
K 29

C 5
M 0
Y 38
K 0

C 0
M 29
Y 97
K 0

C 0
M 88
Y 99
K 0

C100
M 62
Y 33
K 31

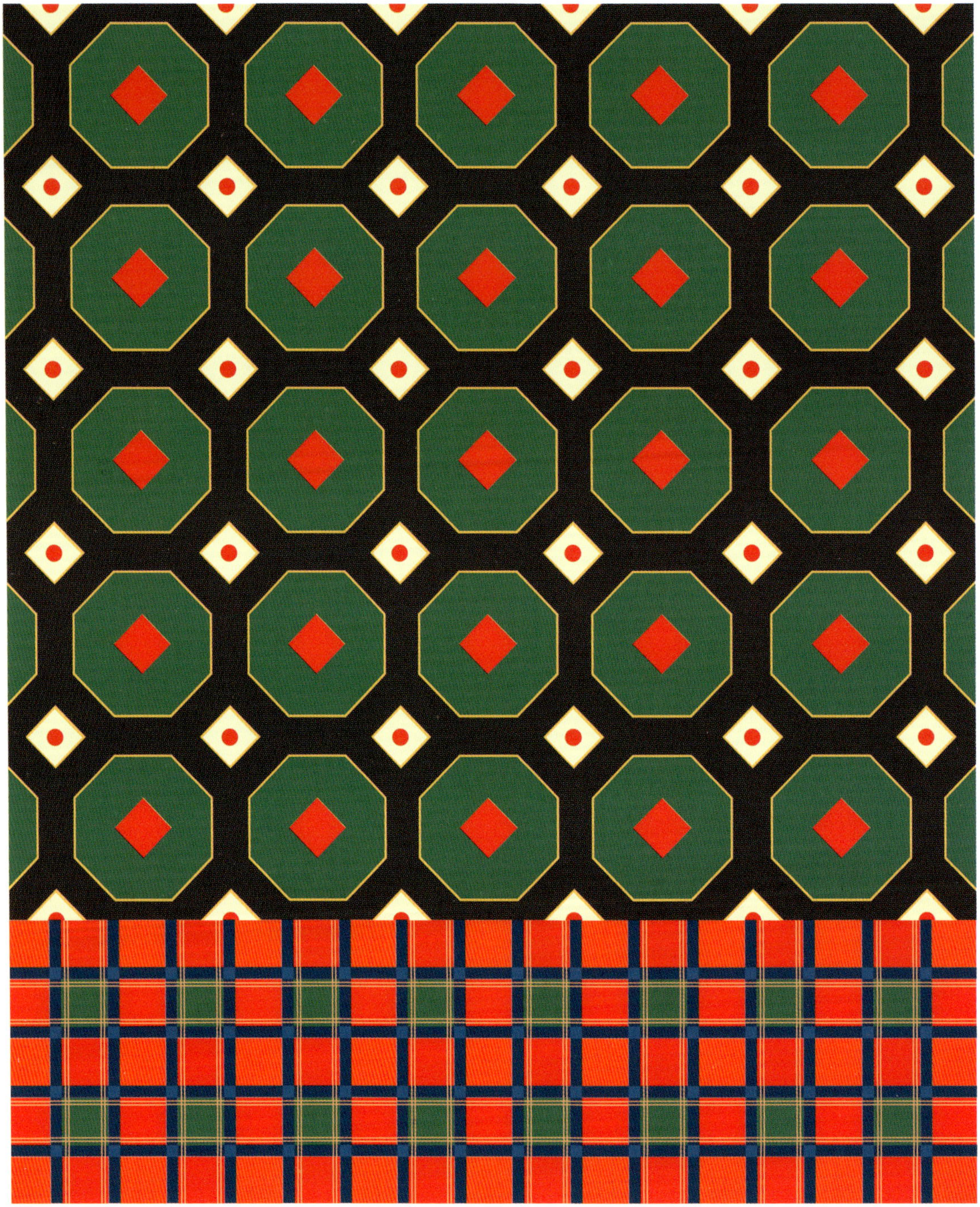

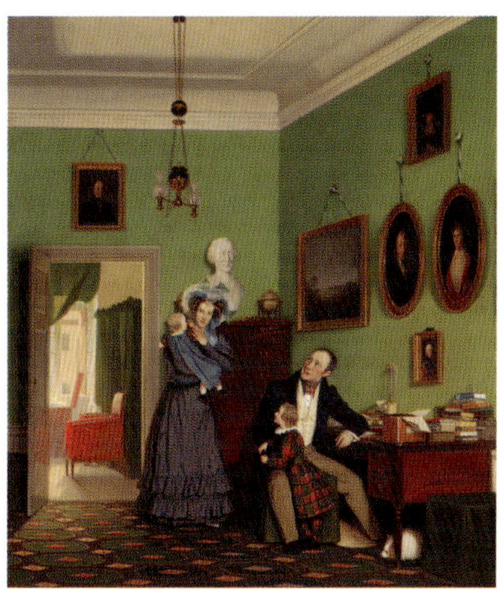

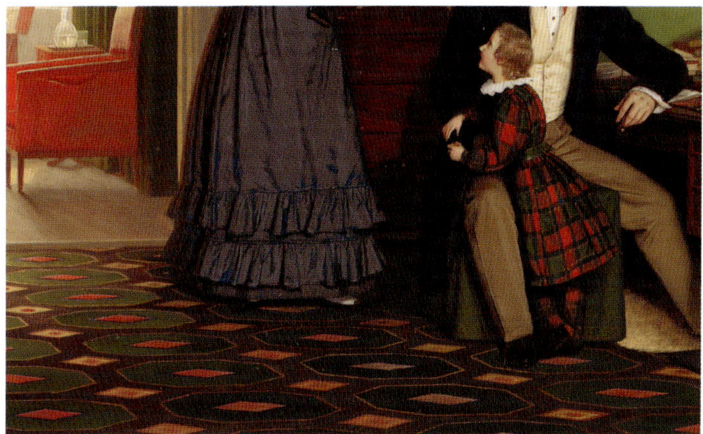

Wilhelm Bendz
The Waagepetersen Family

1830
SMK National Gallery of Denmark, Copenhagen

Christian Waagepetersen, represented here in his studio with his family, was the leading wine merchant in Copenhagen in the early 19th century. He was also the main supplier to the Danish royal court. Looking closely, you can see a portrait of the Danish king, Frederik VI, above the books on the mahogany desk.

The Waagepetersens opened the doors of their home in Store Stranstraede to the most prominent musicians, painters, sculptors, and intellectuals of their time. Among the frequent attendees at these informal gatherings was Wilhelm Ferdinand Bendz, a promising young artist who painted this portrait at the age of twenty-six, only two years before his premature death. As patrons of the arts and sciences, the Waagepetersens supported many musicians and supplied research equipment to universities. So deep was their love of music that they named their children Mozart, Haydn, and Beethoven. Perhaps their passion for science is also why Mr. Waagepetersen has a small green frog in a glass cylinder on the desk.

C 19
M 13
Y 93
K 54

C 0
M 32
Y 91
K 17

C 0
M 99
Y 71
K 29

C 93
M 41
Y 20
K 61

C 39
M 40
Y 74
K 44

C 75
M 64
Y 59
K 75

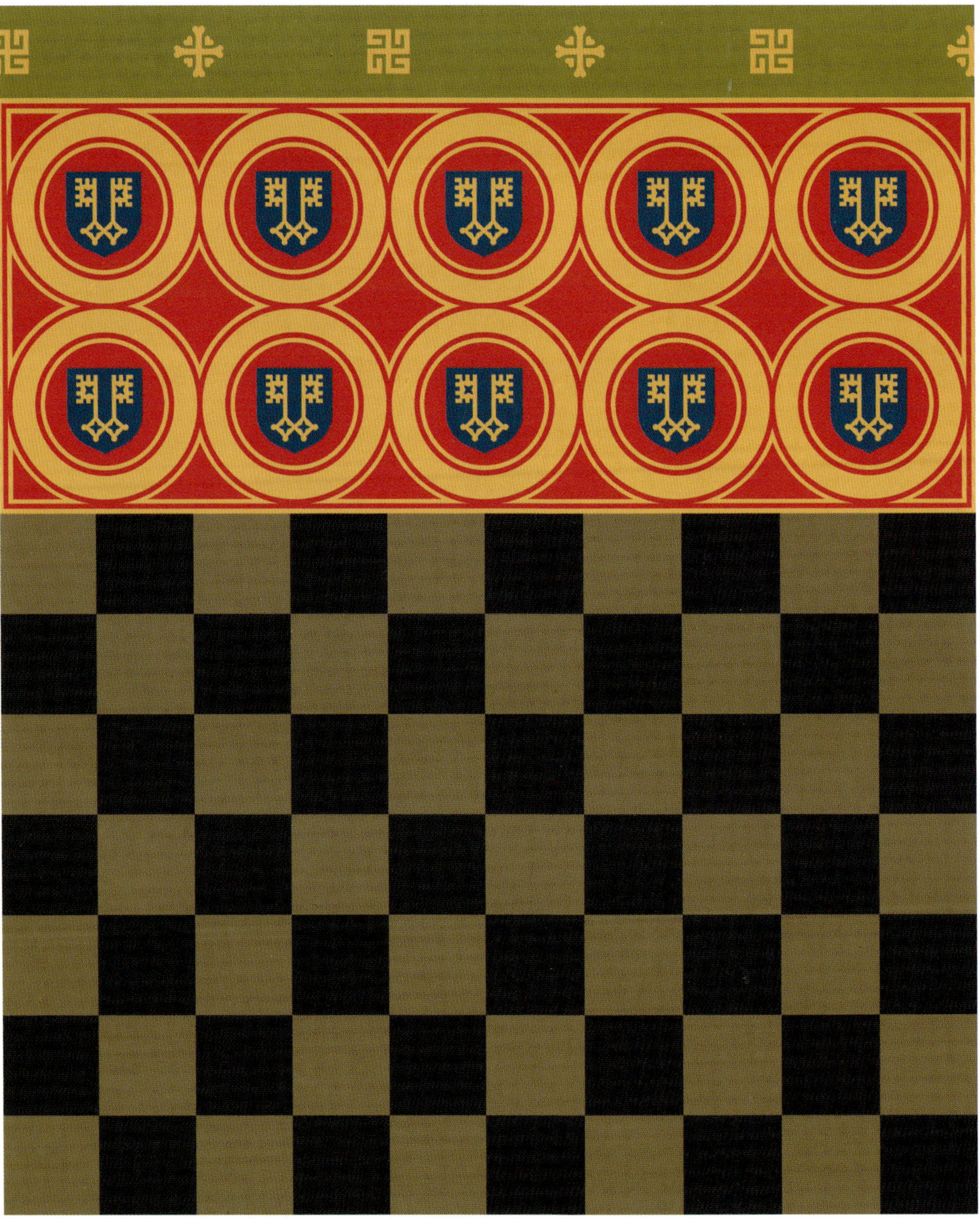

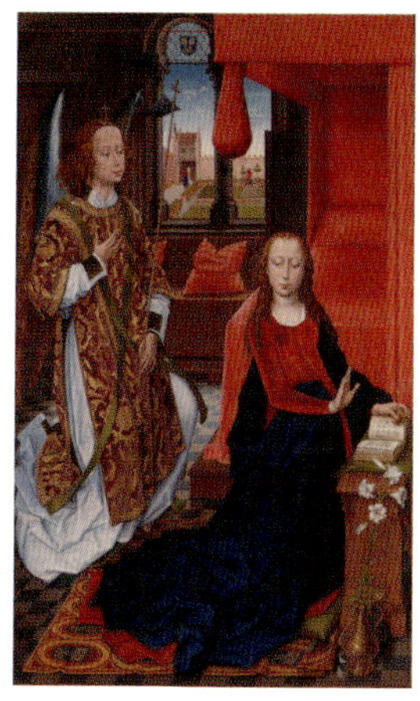
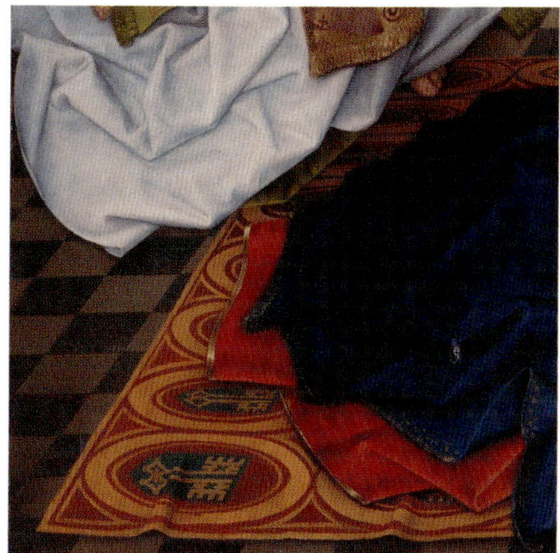
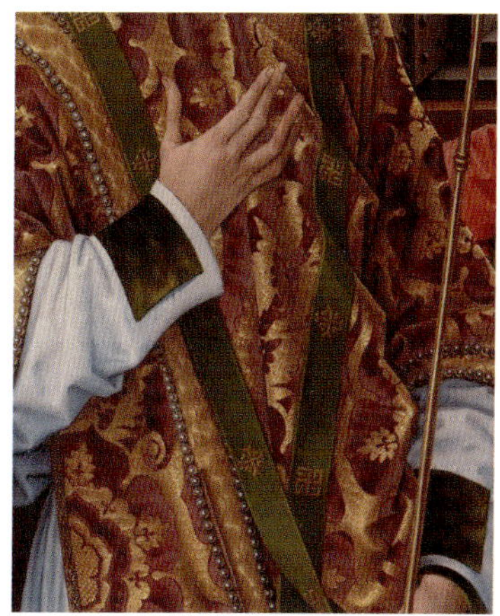

Hans Memling
The Annunciation

circa 1465–1470
The Metropolitan Museum of Art, New York

This Annunciation is one of the largest that has survived into the modern era. It was realized collaboratively by Rogier van der Weyden, who designed the composition, and Hans Memling, his apprentice, who carried out the actual painting. Interestingly, researchers have applied infrared reflectography to this piece, which revealed the underlying preparatory drawings. In this version of the Annunciation, both the Virgin Mary and the angel Gabriel are portrayed as having Dutch facial features and complexions. A painstaking attention to detail is evident in all parts of the painting, as is common in early Netherlandish art. If we look closely, we can see the angel Gabriel's tiny toes showing from beneath his robe. The scene outside the window depicts what seems to be a Dutch castle or fortress with classical columns surrounding a *hortus conclusus*, or enclosed garden, which is a symbolic attribute of the Virgin Mary.

C 60
M 41
Y 24
K 6

C 3
M 34
Y 85
K 0

C 45
M 28
Y 95
K 14

C 6
M 29
Y 20
K 0

C 2
M 0
Y 11
K 0

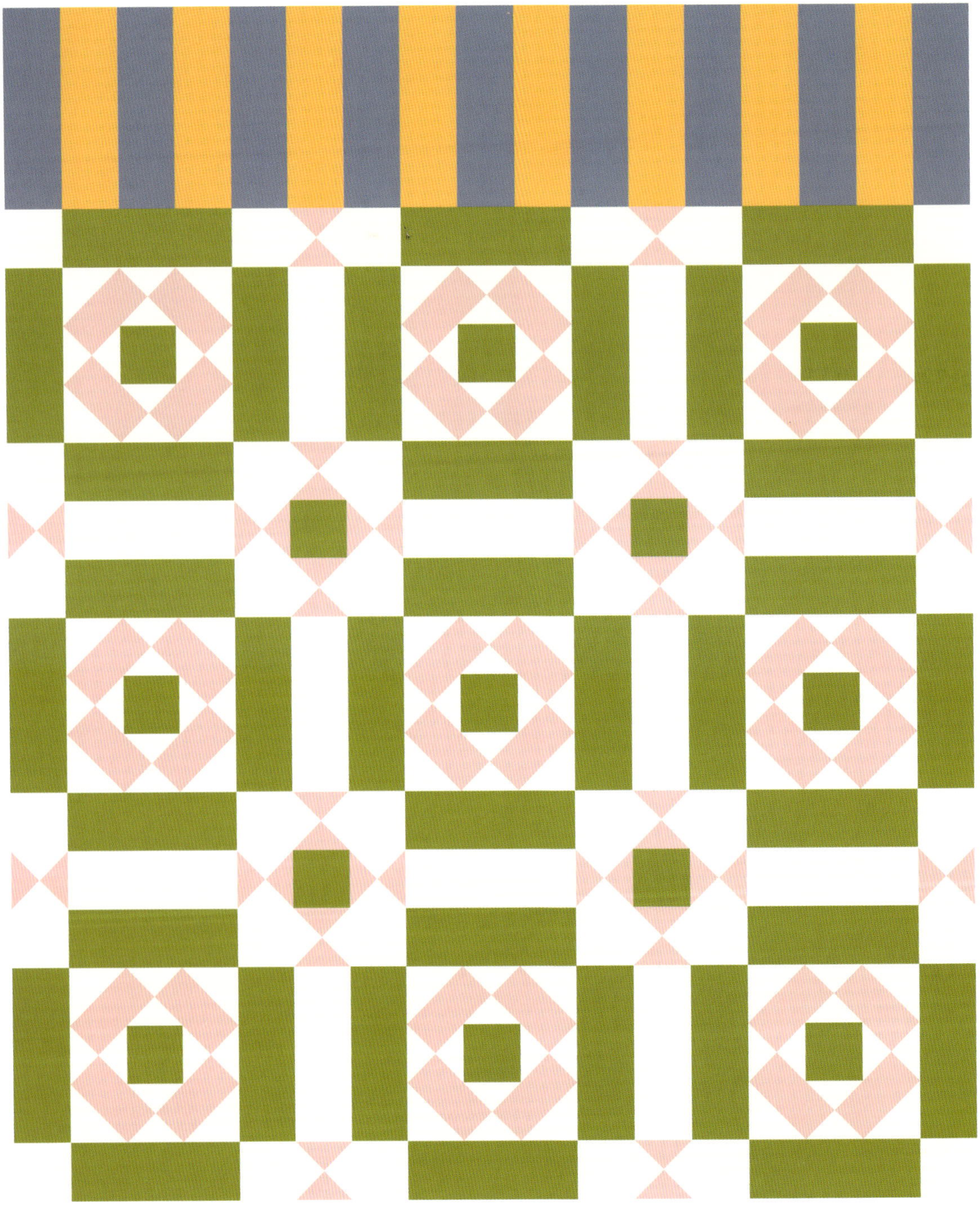

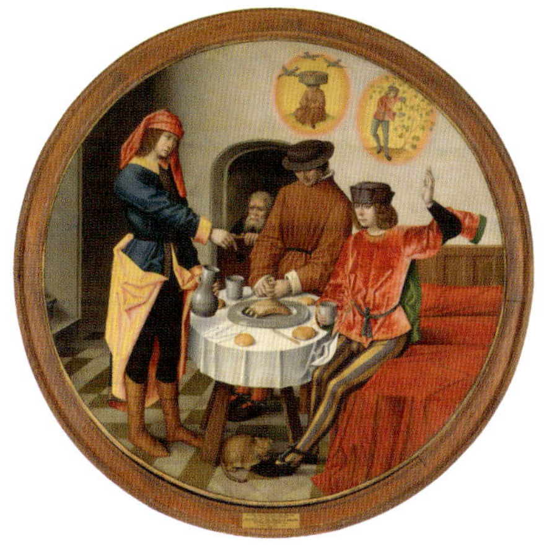
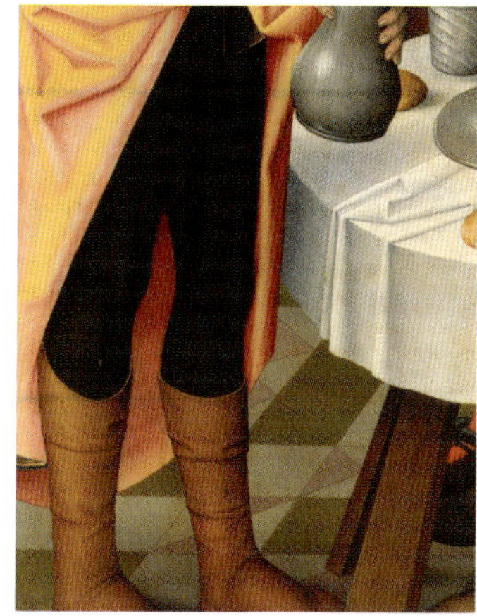
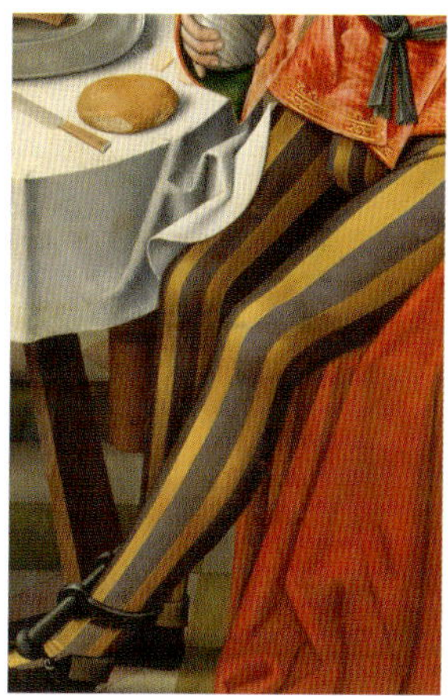

Master of the Story of Joseph
Joseph Interpreting the Dreams of His Fellow Prisoners

circa 1500
The Metropolitan Museum of Art, New York

The style of this modest painting is highly representative of the many unknown artists who worked in Brussels and were inspired by the painter Roger van der Weyden. Based on the clothing portrayed here, the painting can be dated to around 1500. This work tells a story taken from chapter 40 of Genesis, in which Joseph, here standing on the left of the table, interprets the dreams of two officials—the chief cupbearer and the chief baker—who had been imprisoned with him by Pharaoh. Joseph's interpretation of the cupbearer's dream is favorable, and the cupbearer is restored to his post in just three days. Joseph's interpretation of the baker's dream, however, is unfavorable. He will be hung in three days. Despite the somewhat somber subject, the artist delightfully depicts the setting and the subjects' garments, in particular the shimmering yellow of the vest that Joseph wears draped over his belt, as well as the velvet texture of the red shirt of the right-hand prisoner, upon whose foot a little cat is resting.

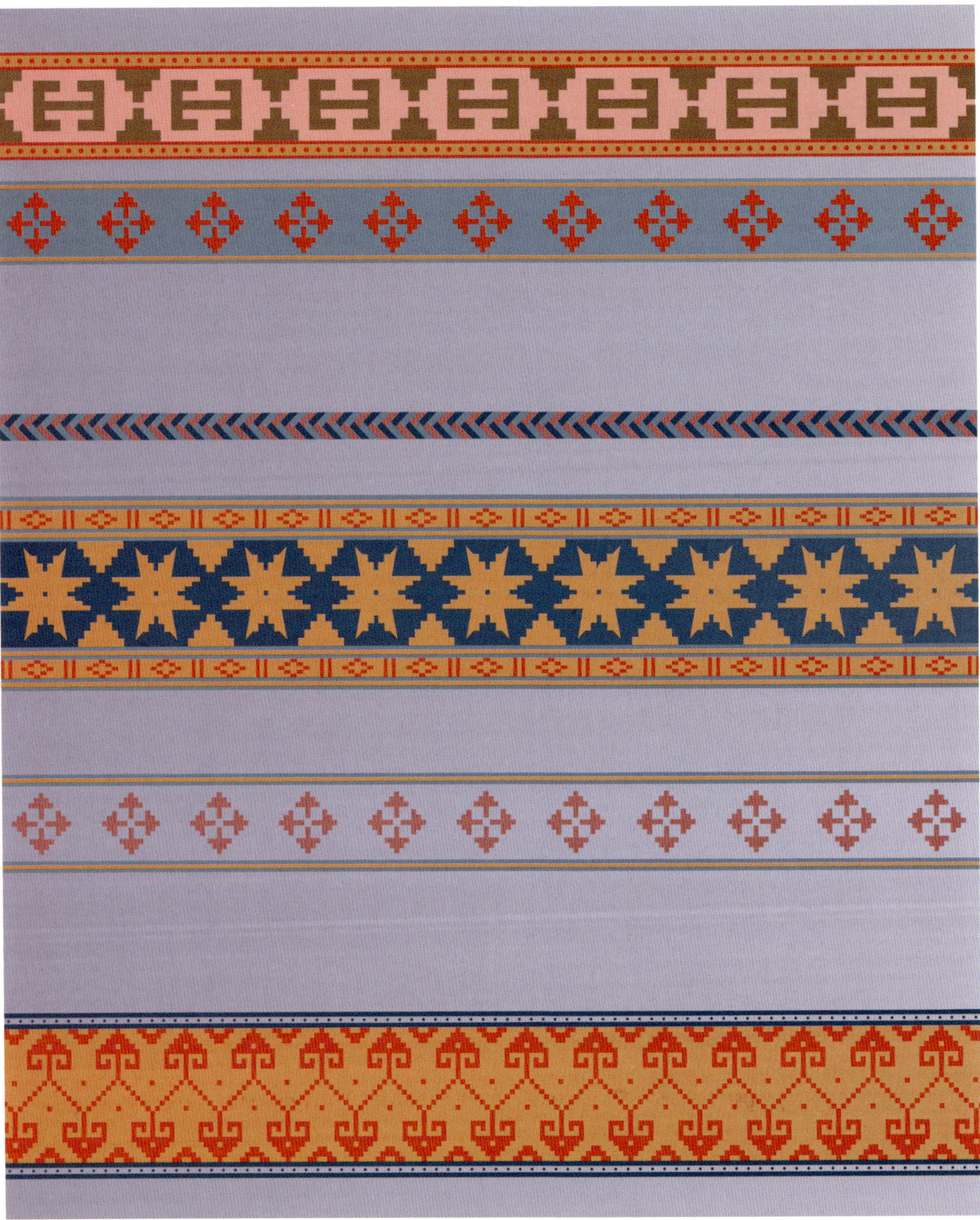

C 46
M 33
Y 12
K 0

C 71
M 37
Y 27
K 11

C 94
M 57
Y 36
K 29

C 18
M 54
Y 85
K 8

C 18
M 92
Y 100
K 10

C 24
M 70
Y 51
K 18

C 35
M 52
Y 76
K 39

C 11
M 53
Y 38
K 0

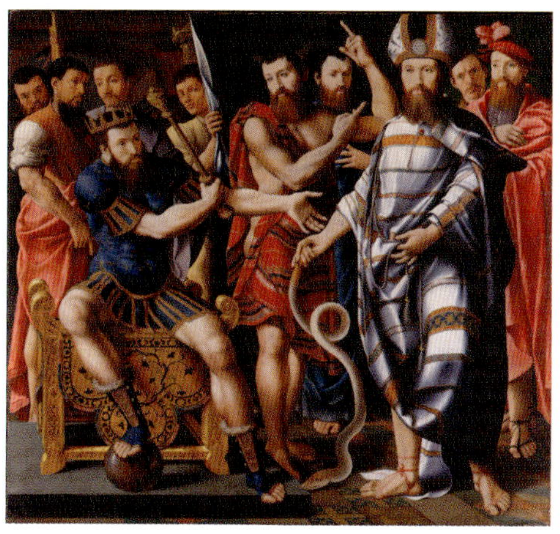

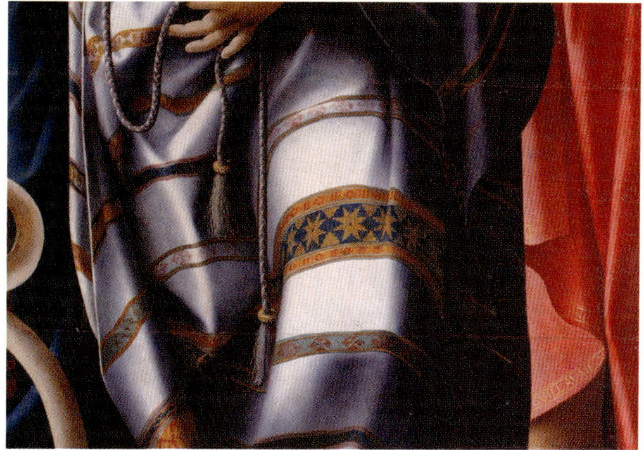

Master of the Dinteville Allegory
Moses and Aaron before Pharaoh

1537
The Metropolitan Museum of Art, New York

The Dinteville brothers were important members of the 16th-century French court. In this painting by a Netherlandish or French painter whose identity is still unknown, the brothers are depicted acting out a passage from Exodus. Aaron and Moses have just asked Pharaoh's permission for the Israelites to depart Egypt. Moses's rod transforms into a snake, signifying that God is on their side. This allegorical painting takes on an almost satirical tone, however, since at the time of its painting the Dinteville family had fallen out of favor with King Francis I, depicted here as Pharaoh. The subjects' garments are very richly decorated, representing a combination of Hellenistic and modern styles. The entire scene takes place in the foreground, with the backdrop consisting only of a green velvet curtain and a Roman triumphal arch. Carved at the top left corner is François de Dinteville's motto, "Virtuti fortuna comes" (Fortune is the companion of virtue).

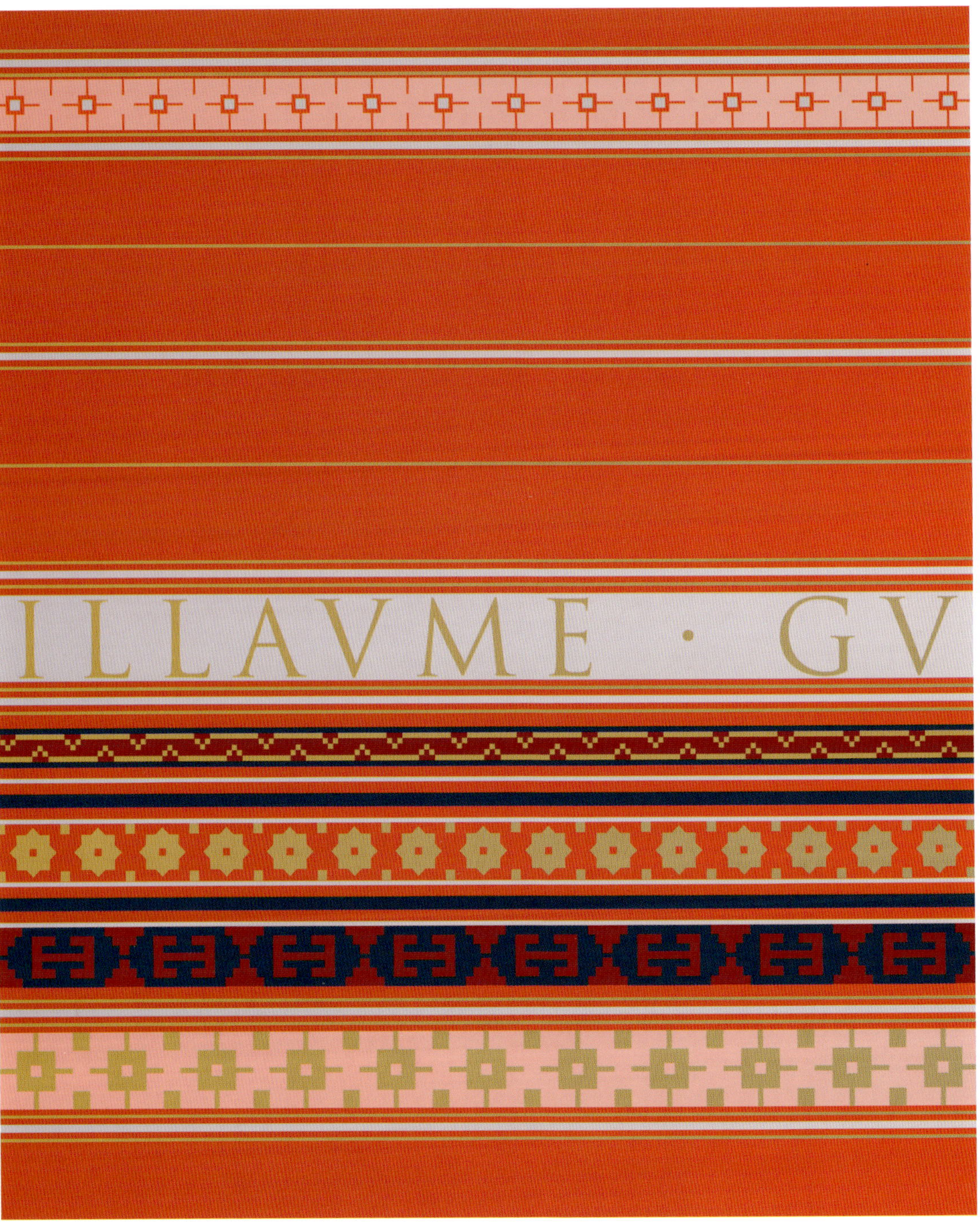

C 13
M 91
Y 100
K 9

C 19
M 38
Y 83
K 14

C 100
M 66
Y 41
K 48

C 24
M 100
Y 91
K 44

C 10
M 51
Y 35
K 0

C 27
M 26
Y 19
K 0

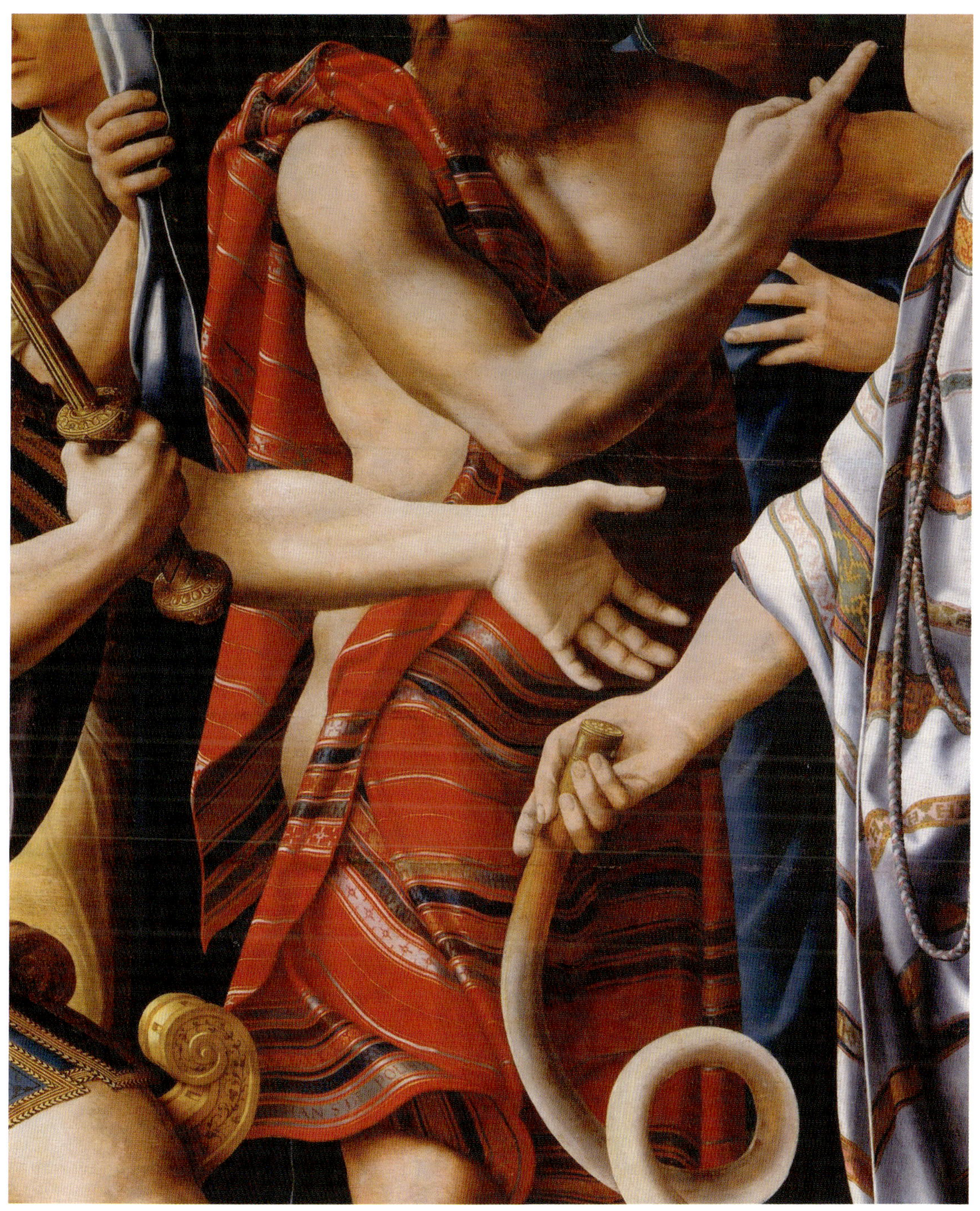

C 95
M 49
Y 41
K 36

C 9
M 45
Y 83
K 0

C 22
M 65
Y 73
K 17

C 0
M 0
Y 0
K100

C 82
M 37
Y 35
K 20

C 0
M 50
Y 97
K 0

C 19
M 53
Y 58
K 9

C 21
M 22
Y 37
K 0

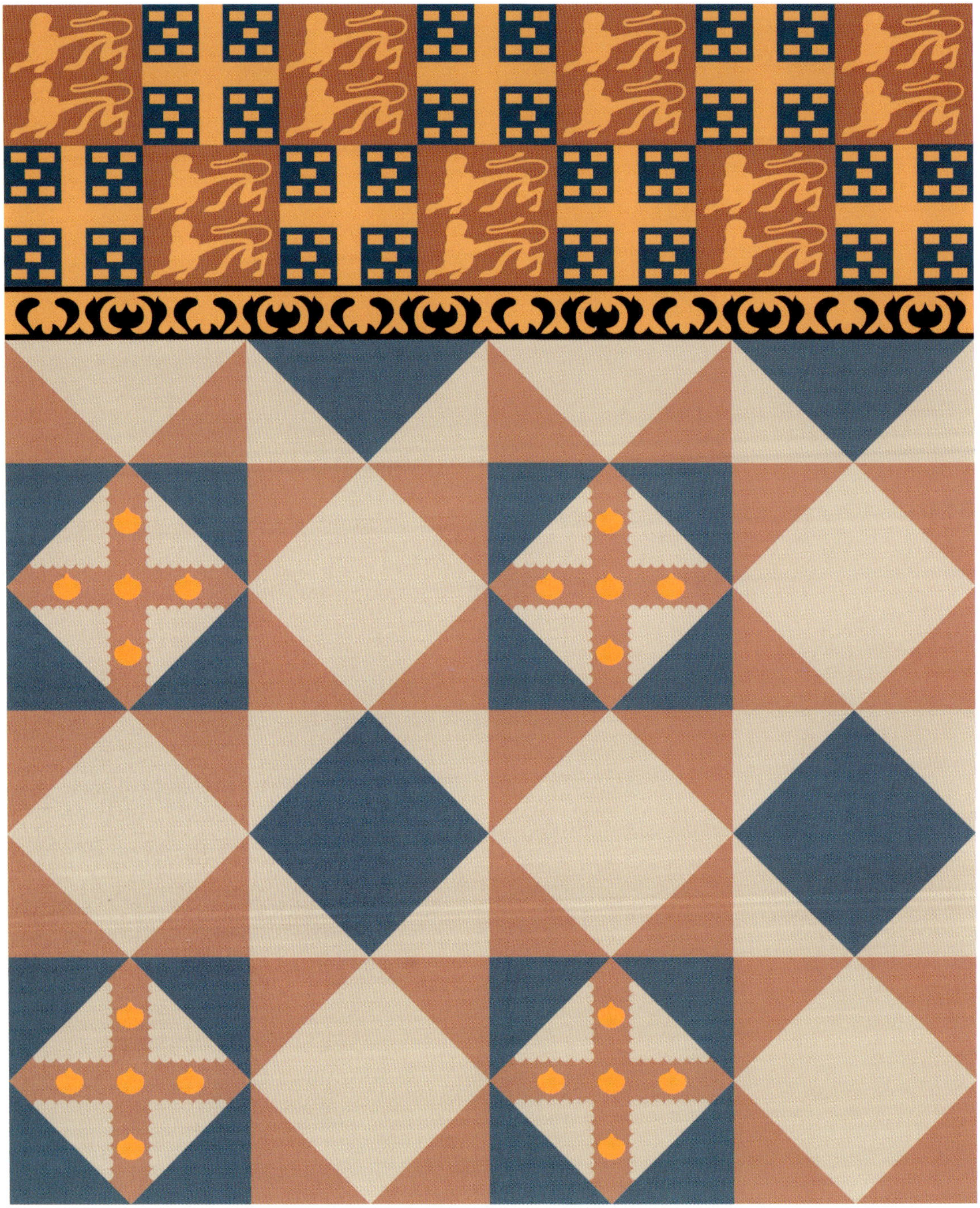

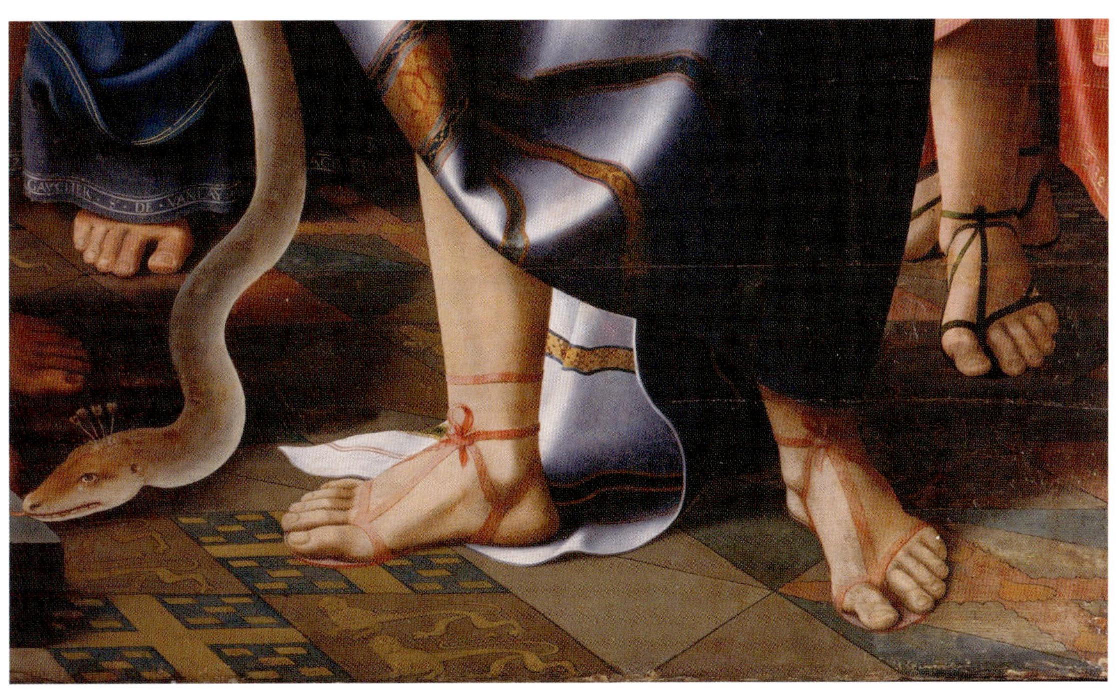
DE

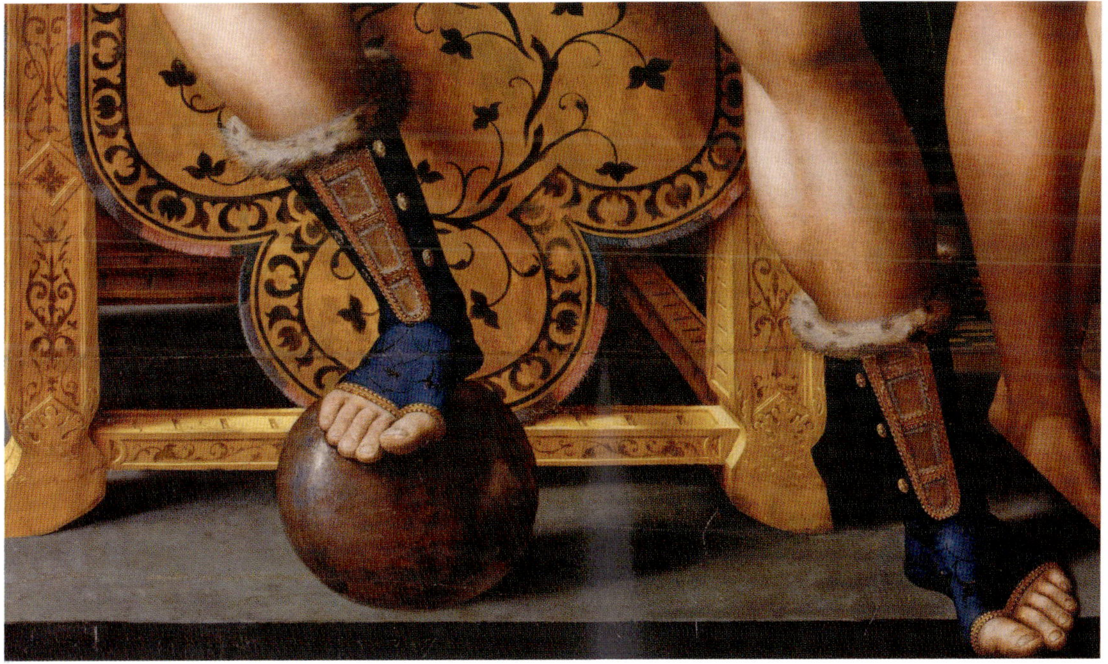

C 91
M 36
Y 78
K 56

C 20
M 35
Y 92
K 0

C 0
M 77
Y 100
K 0

C 70
M 58
Y 52
K 71

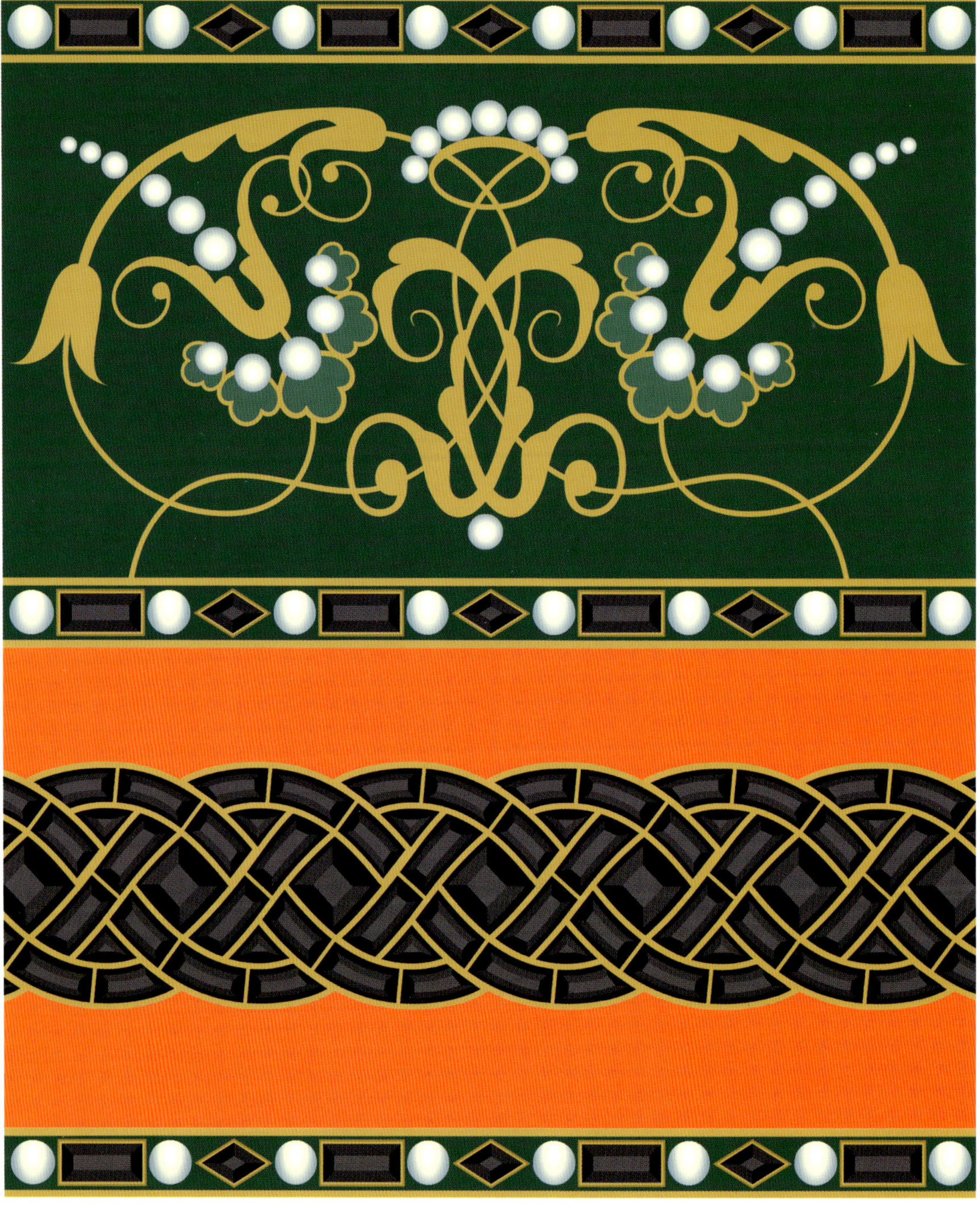

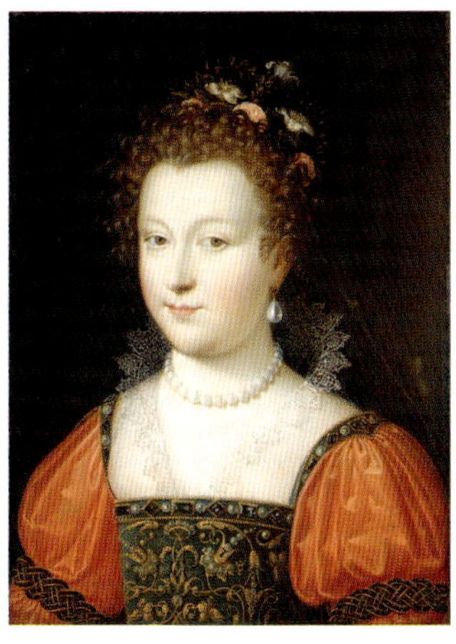

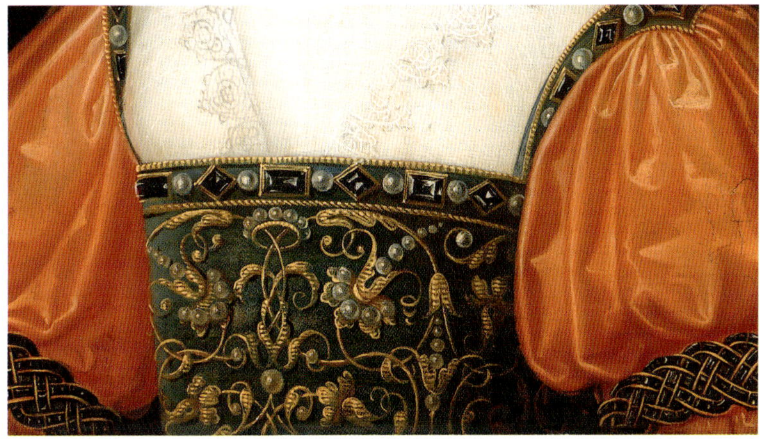

Anonymous
Portrait of a Woman
(previously identified as Queen Elizabeth I)

1550–1574
Rijksmuseum, Amsterdam

It is unknown who painted this portrait, which was produced in Fontainebleau, a French town southeast of Paris. The subject is also mysterious. Although the woman was initially identified as Queen Elizabeth I, this theory was later dismissed. However, in addition to the subject's slight facial resemblance to Elizabeth, many details of her self-presentation recall the queen of England, such as the bust positioned slightly to the left, the curly reddish hair adorned with flowers, the jewelry and ruffs, and the embroidered cloth of the dress. Was the woman deliberately trying to look like Queen Elizabeth? We cannot possibly answer this question, but we do know that Elizabeth had become a style icon for many women of her time. In 1597, in fact, a royal proclamation was issued dictating in minute detail what people of different social classes could and could not wear, ultimately creating a sartorial social pyramid. Accordingly, apparel was often used to create the deceptive appearance of belonging to a higher social class—a ruse often employed by prostitutes.

C 29
M 75
Y 82
K 29

C 19
M 45
Y 84
K 6

C 68
M 43
Y 57
K 39

C 6
M 8
Y 24
K 0

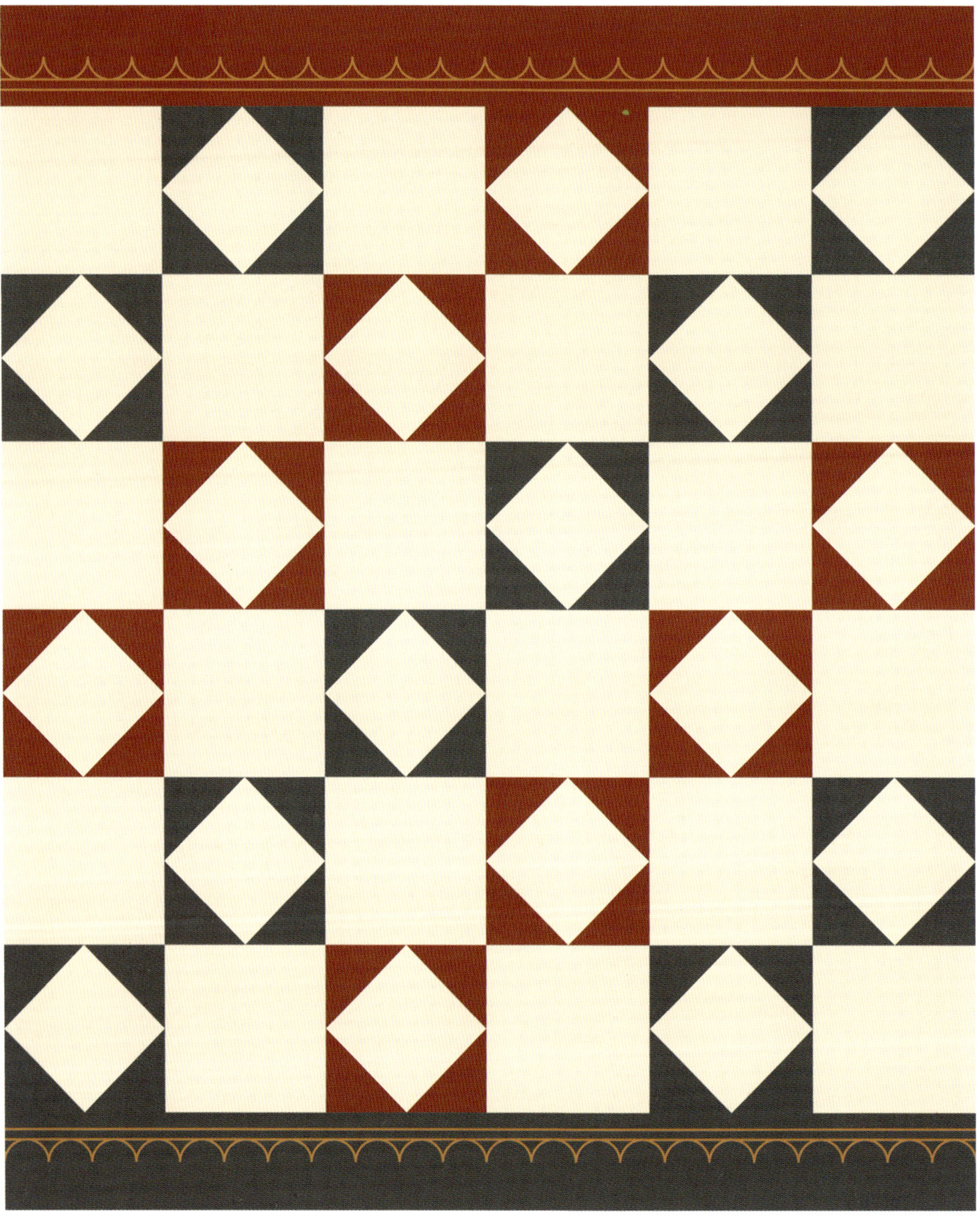

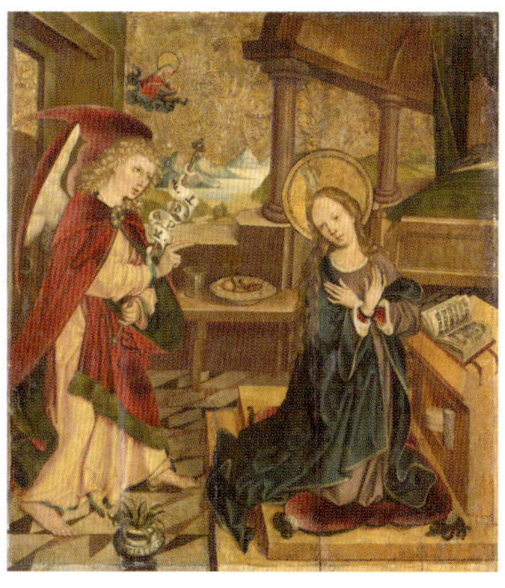

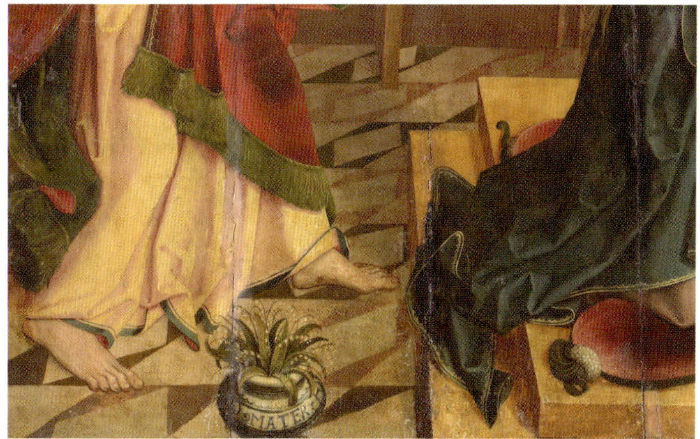

Master of the Salem Altar
The Annunciation

1490–1510
Rijksmuseum, Amsterdam

The Annunciation is one of the most frequently portrayed subjects of Christian art and the archangel Gabriel's announcement to the Virgin Mary that she will conceive the son of God. The first known artistic renderings of the Annunciation are from 4th-century Roman catacombs. In this painting by the German master of the Salem Altar, likely part of an altarpiece depicting scenes from the life of the Virgin, Mary is portrayed in her bedroom kneeling on regal pillows. She turns to the archangel Gabriel as he interrupts her prayer to bring the holy news. Mary's bedroom seems to be surrounded by a natural landscape, with a depiction of God in the upper left corner directing the scene. In the bottom left we can see a vase with the word *mater* (mother) painted on it, in which a small plant is symbolically flourishing.

C 12
M 15
Y 35
K 0

C 0
M 0
Y 0
K100

C 62
M 41
Y 51
K 31

C 17
M 45
Y 92
K 6

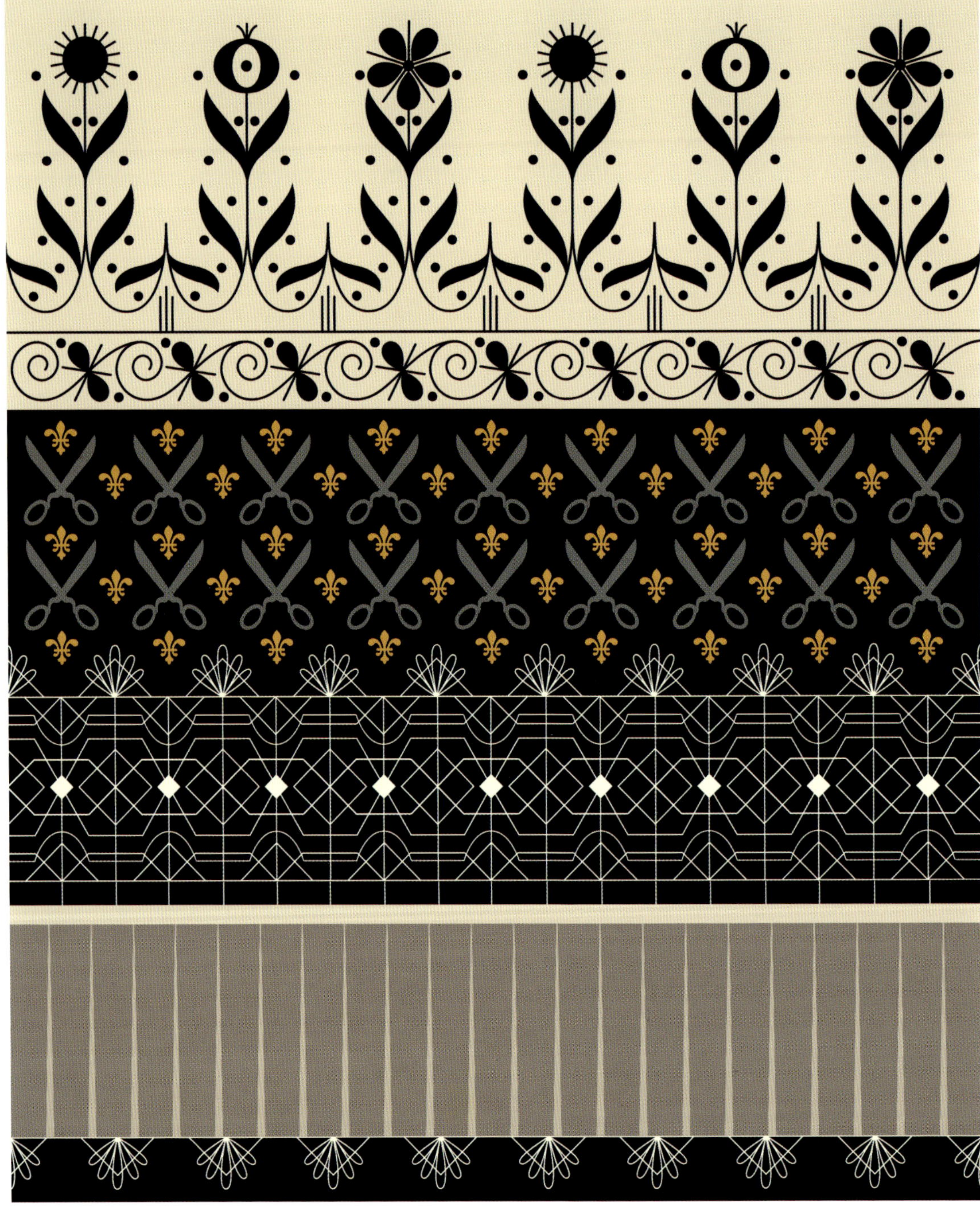

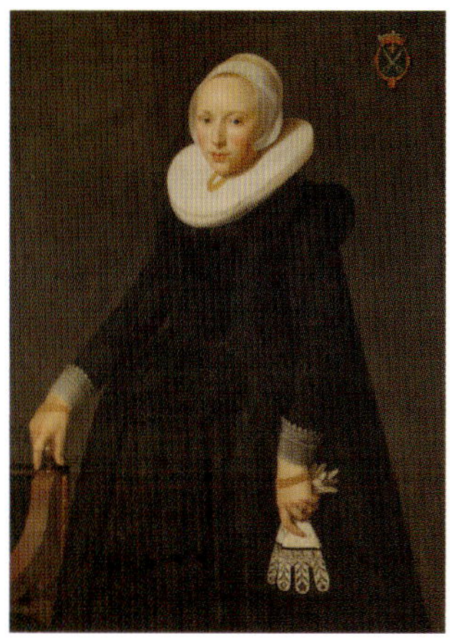

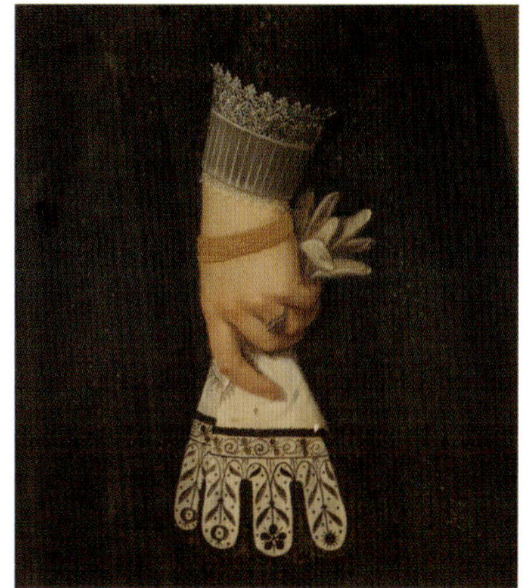

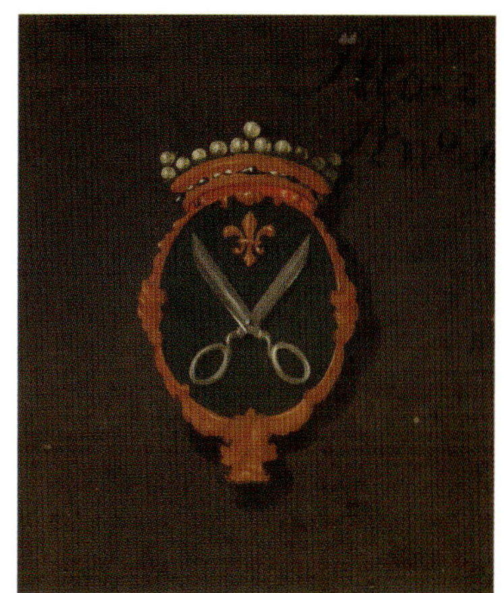

Anonymous
Portrait of Trijntje Tijsdr van Nooij

1631
Rijksmuseum, Amsterdam

Trijntje Tijsdr van Nooij was the wife of Reinier Ottsz Hinloopen, a Dutch merchant from Hoorn. In this portrait by an anonymous painter, Trijntje is standing next to a chair against a plain backdrop with the family coat of arms in the upper right-hand corner. The viewer's attention is drawn to the white gloves held in her left hand, decorated with floral and geometric patterns. Decorated and embroidered gloves started to appear in portraits of women in the late 17th century as a symbol for marriage, as they were a mandatory gift that the groom gave to his bride-to-be during their engagement. These gloves were then supposed to be put on display during the time that elapsed between the engagement and the wedding ceremony. Many varieties of preciously embroidered wedding gloves are found in paintings of this time. The gloves depicted here, however, are of a more modest kind and might not even have symbolized marriage.

C 13
M 87
Y 99
K 16

C 12
M 38
Y 78
K 5

C 60
M 49
Y 47
K 65

C 25
M 95
Y 82
K 51

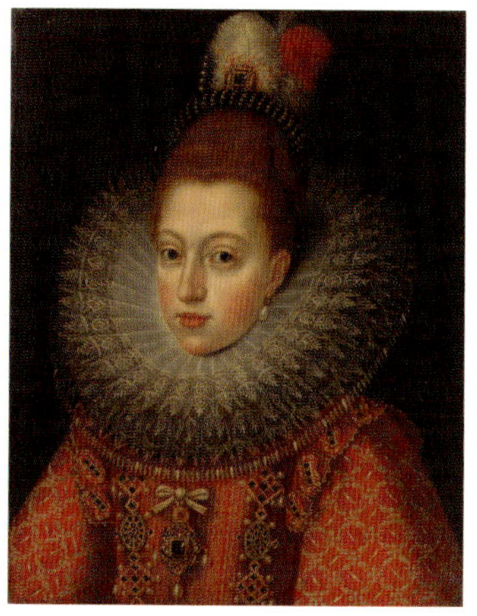

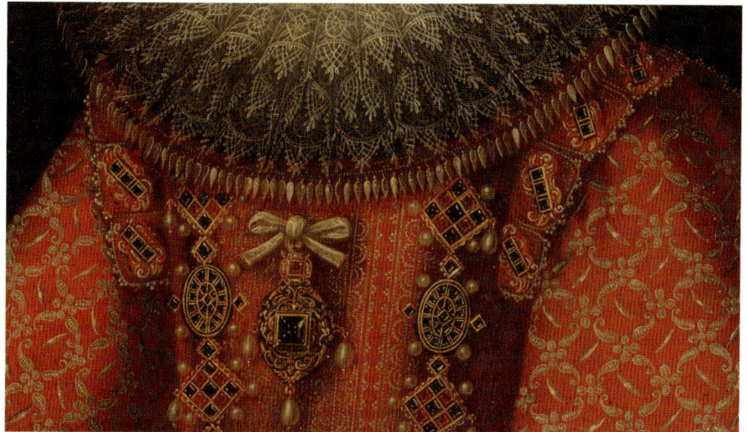

Workshop of
Frans Pourbus the Younger
Portrait of Margaret of Austria, Consort of Philip III

circa 1600
Rijksmuseum, Amsterdam

In this painting by Frans Pourbus the Younger, Margaret of Austria is portrayed in rich garments, with an elaborately patterned embroidered dress and a wide ruff. Margaret became queen consort of Spain and Portugal by marrying her cousin, King Philip III, at the age of fifteen. Although she died only nine years later, after bearing eight children, she managed to become a very influential figure in the Spanish court. A keen patron of the arts, she was known to be astute and skillful in dealing with the social dynamics of her husband's court. Together with a circle of other women, she held significant influence over the king, with whom she had a genuinely affectionate and close relationship. The portrait of Margaret is by Frans Pourbus the Younger, a Flemish artist trained by his father, Frans Pourbus the Elder. Pourbus the Younger painted portraits of the high society of his time and tended to place his subjects against plain monochromatic backdrops, similar to the one seen here.

C 2
M 11
Y 64
K 0

C 20
M 25
Y 75
K 9

C 9
M 84
Y 100
K 13

C 62
M 32
Y 85
K 35

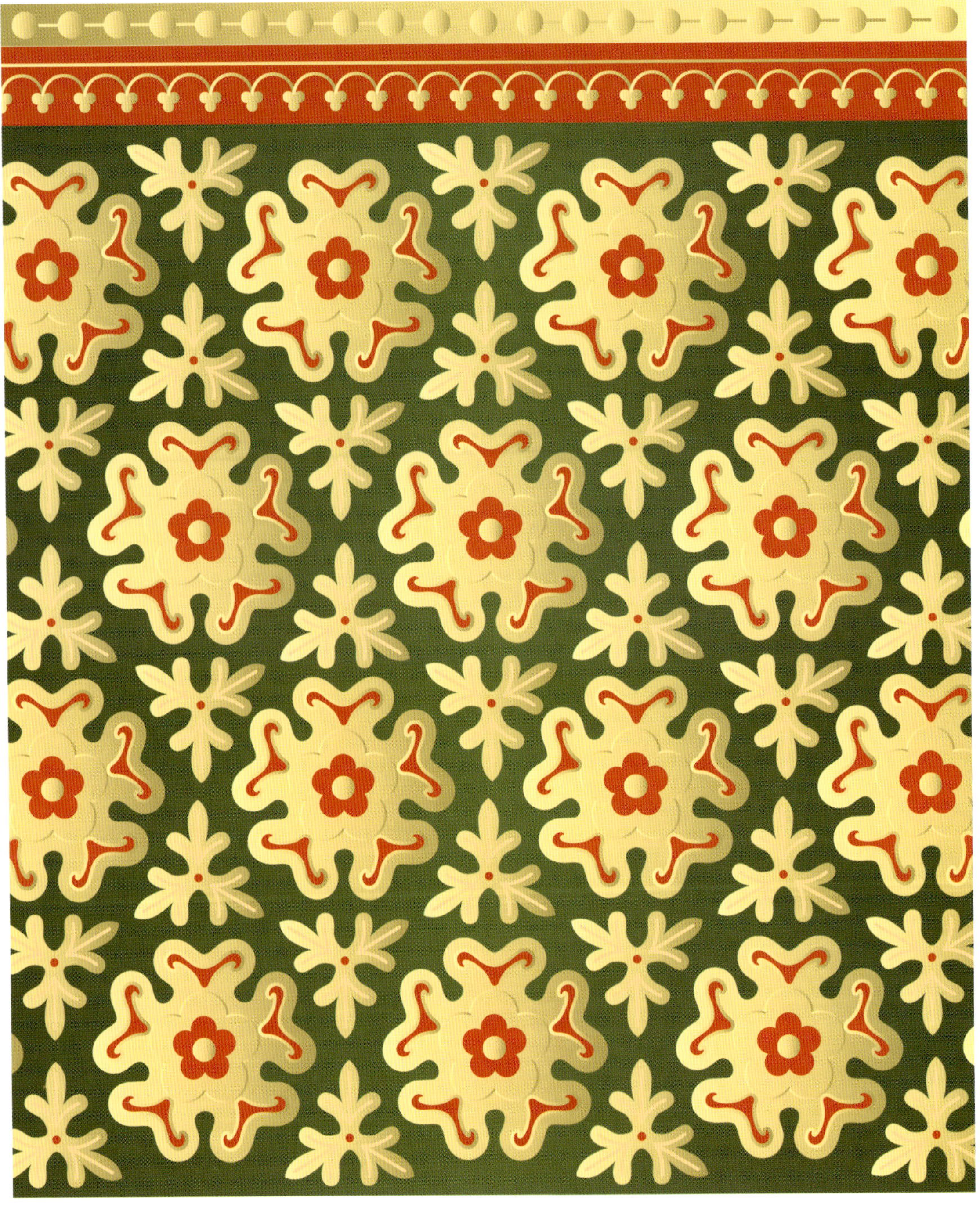

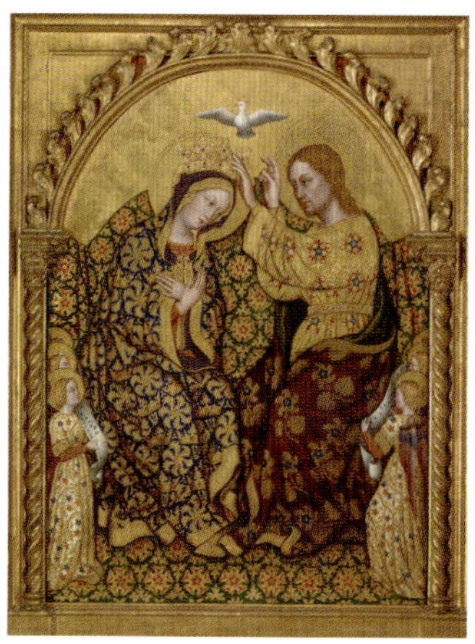

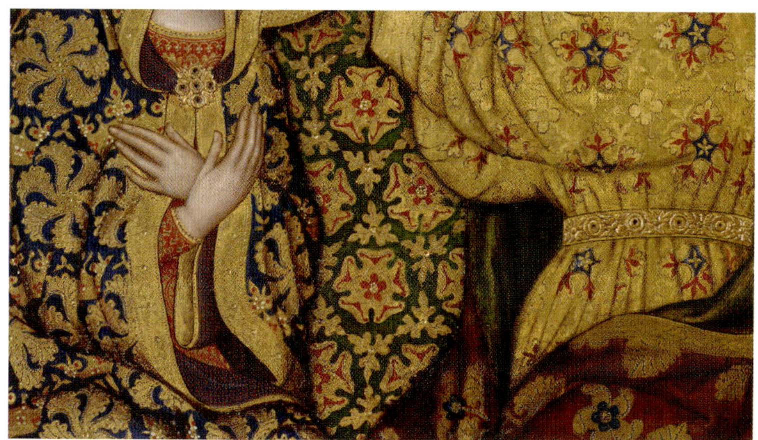

Gentile da Fabriano
Coronation of the Virgin

circa 1420
The J. Paul Getty Museum,
Los Angeles

At the peak of his artistic career, Gentile da Fabriano was commissioned to paint this scene for his hometown. The painter created a sumptuous, textured effect, using tempera and gold leaf to masterfully transform the wooden panel into a tapestry-like surface. Complex patterns and elaborate materials in the clothing and floor create harmonious contrasts, outlined by the flowing lines of the robes. A close inspection reveals that the bottom of the scene is framed by six angels holding scrolls with detailed musical notations. The words written underneath the musical notations are from the fifth chapter of the Book of Revelation. Golden crowns are also visible in the patterns of the Virgin's robe. Depictions of Christ crowning and blessing the Virgin at the same time were common in Tuscany, where the artist spent most of his career.

C 5
M 13
Y 58
K 0

C 22
M 28
Y 73
K 15

C 18
M 77
Y 89
K 33

C 92
M 67
Y 18
K 7

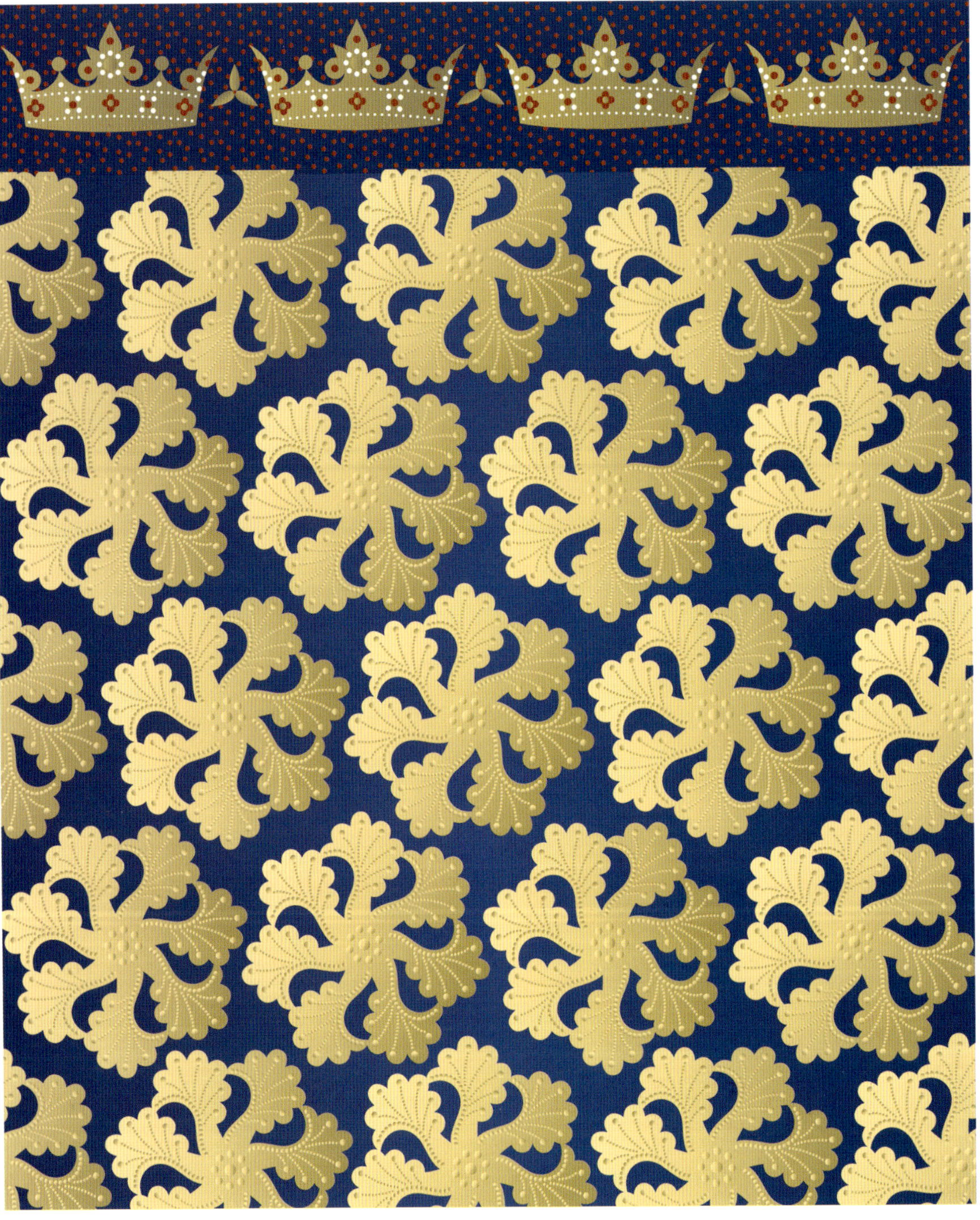

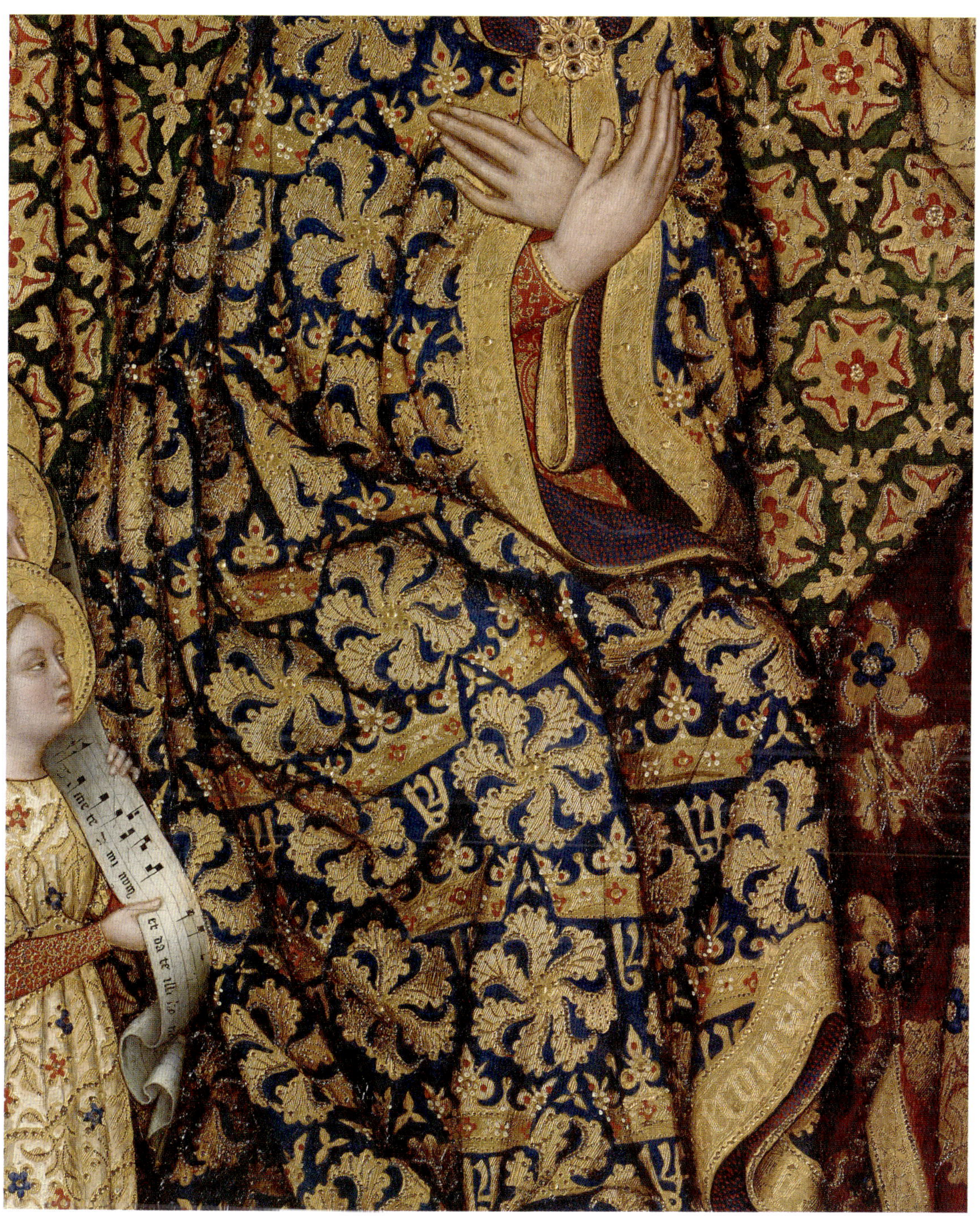
me te mi num
et da te illi

C 8
M 14
Y 49
K 0

C 17
M 24
Y 67
K 2

C 20
M 76
Y 94
K 19

C 91
M 66
Y 11
K 0

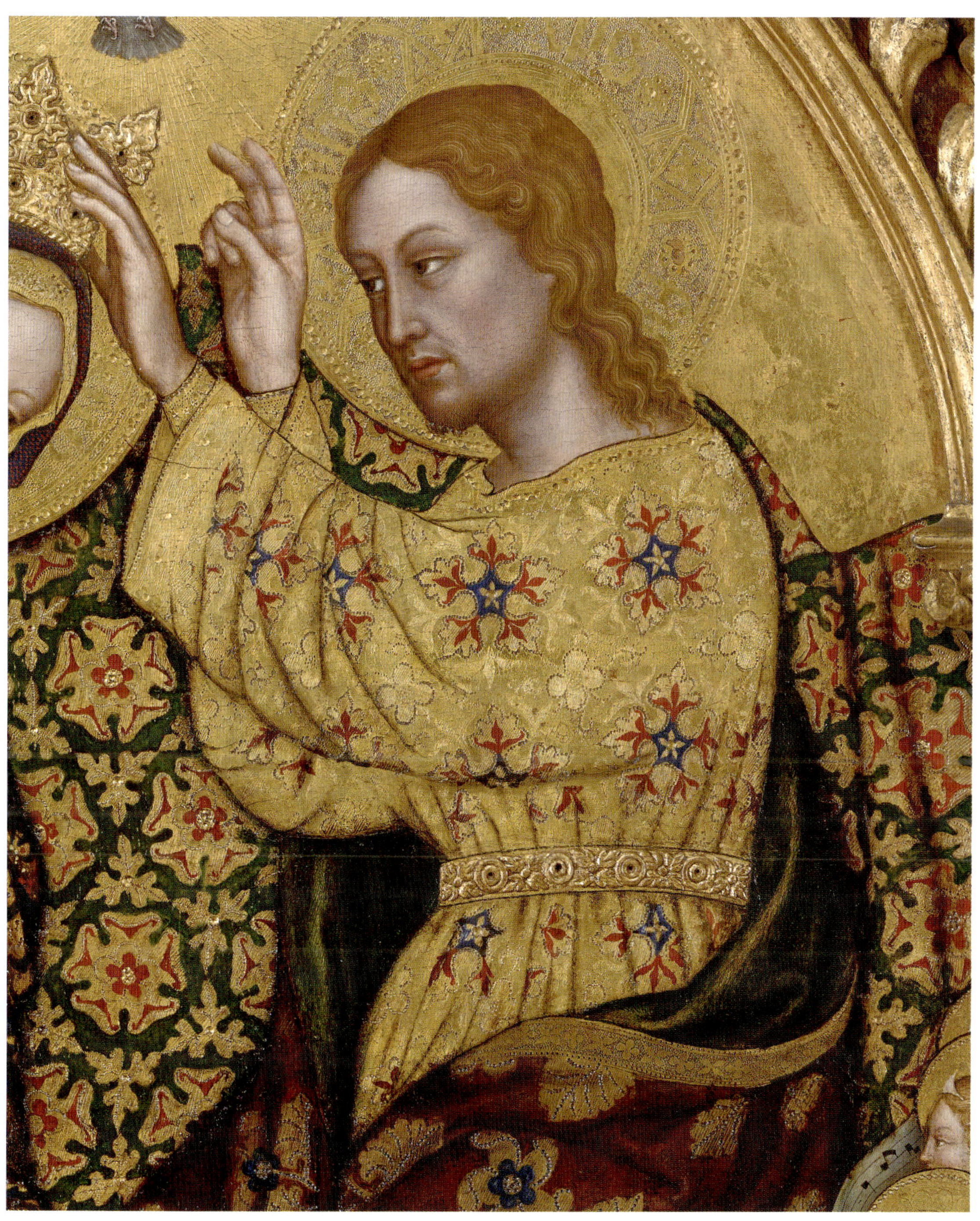

C 8
M 12
Y 43
K 0

C 22
M 28
Y 72
K 15

C 16
M 82
Y 100
K 16

C 16
M 89
Y 82
K 28

C 87
M 80
Y 25
K 32

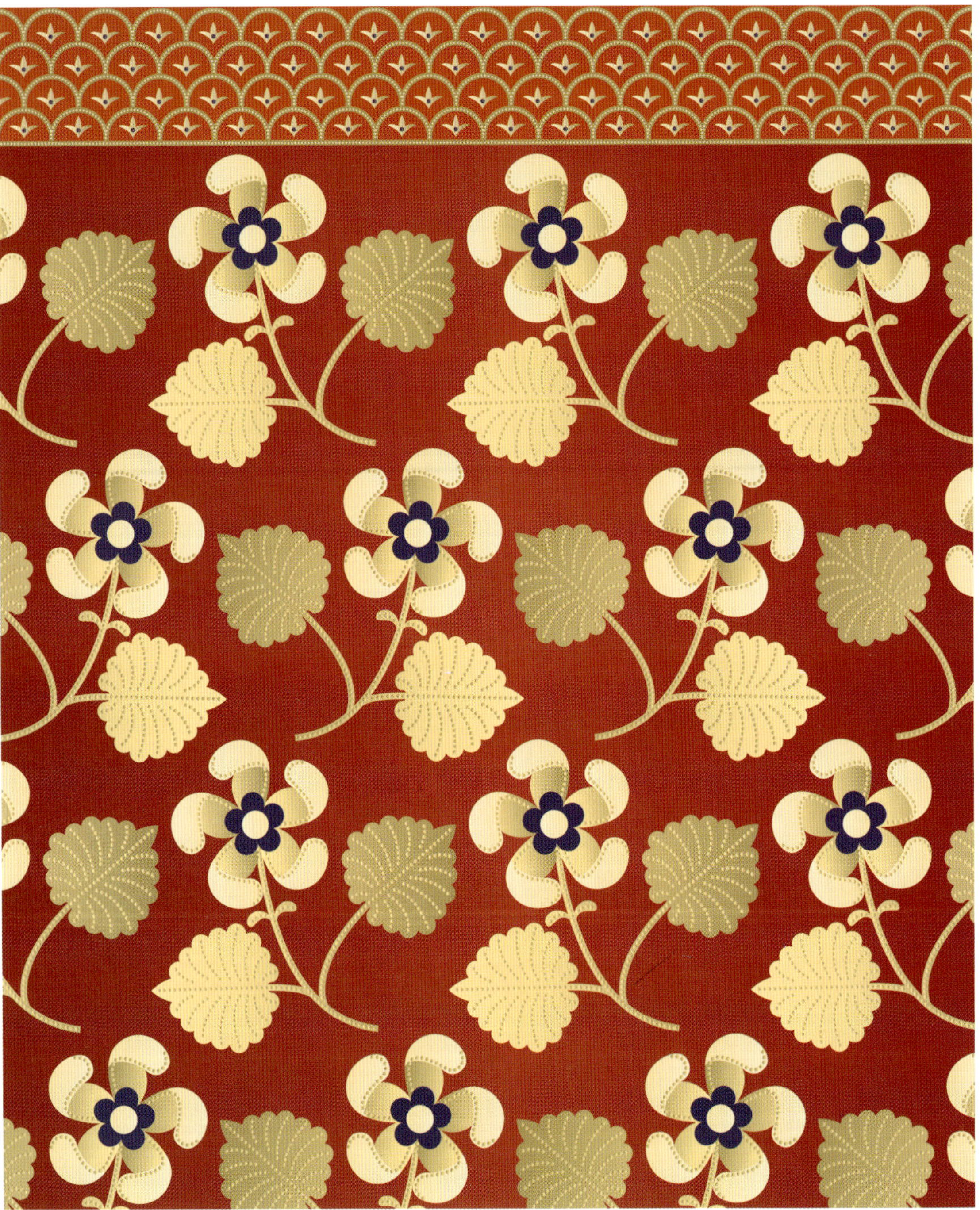

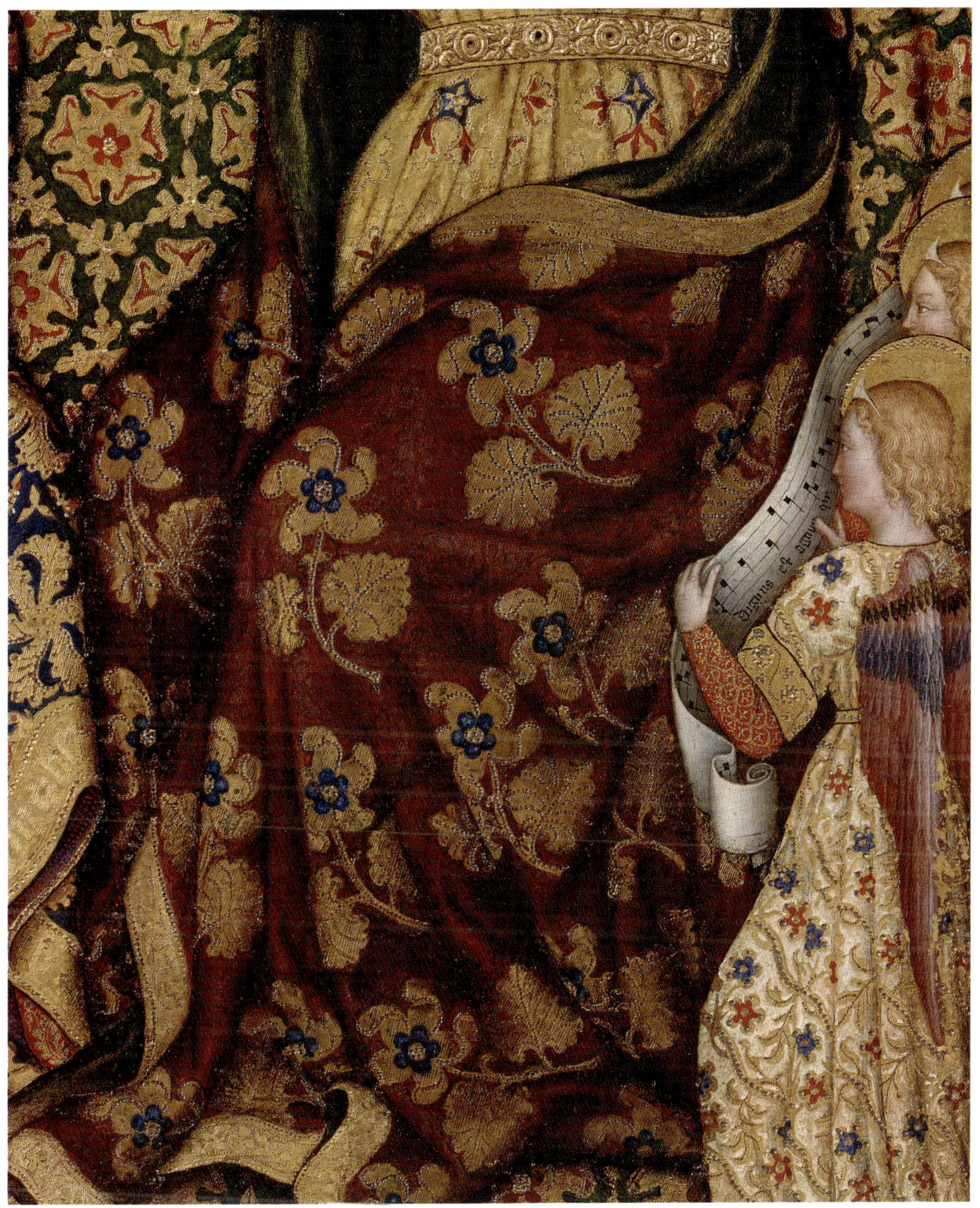
Dignus et agnus qui

C 35
M 47
Y 75
K 57

C 28
M 44
Y 76
K 42

C 20
M 37
Y 67
K 26

C 6
M 13
Y 30
K 0

C 15
M 87
Y 78
K 30

C 84
M 60
Y 34
K 41

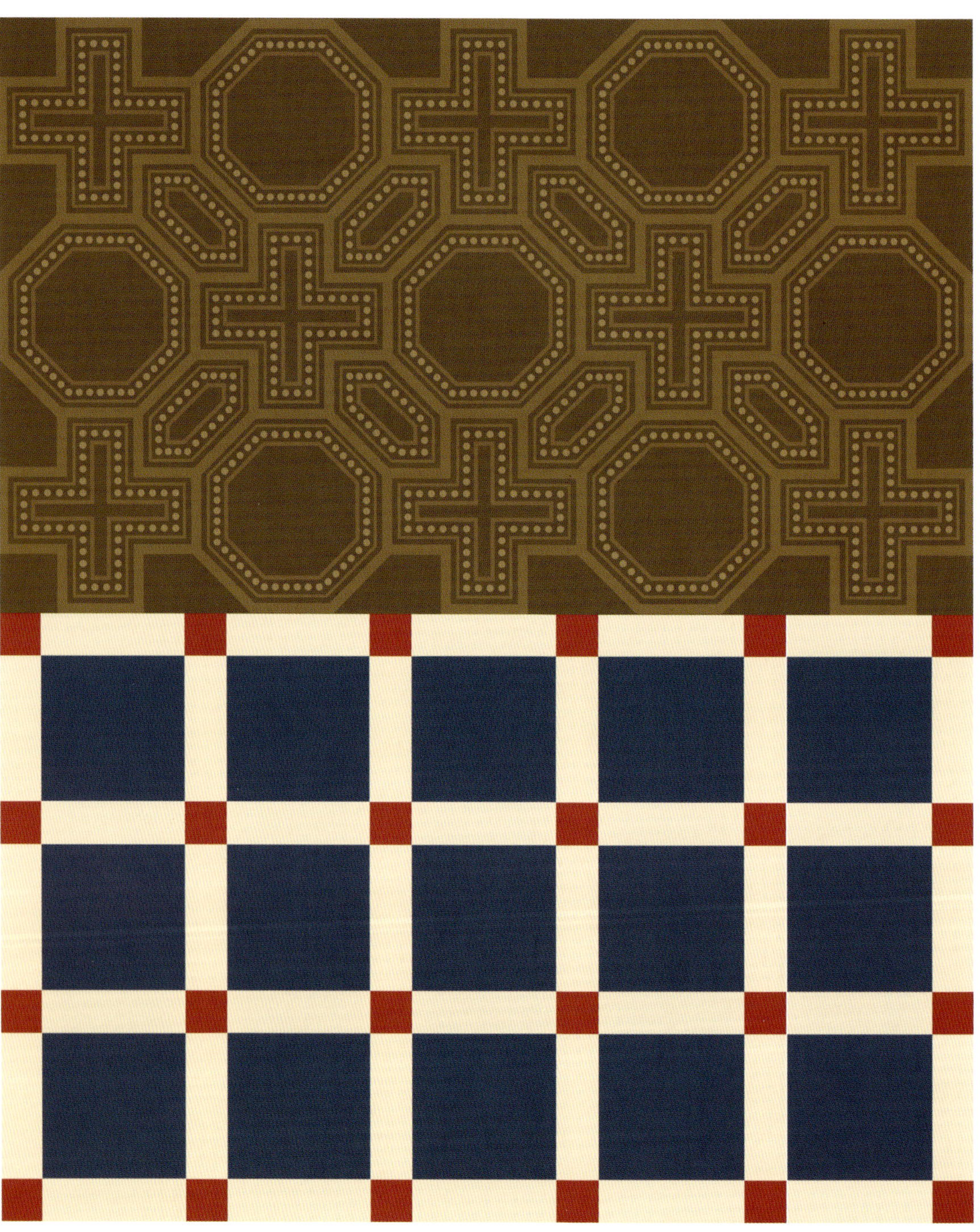

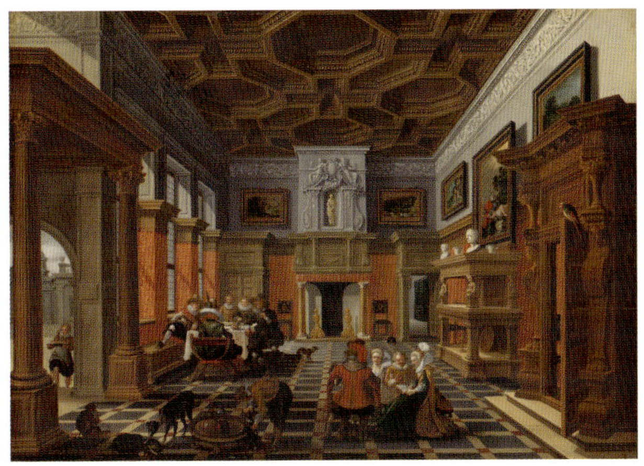

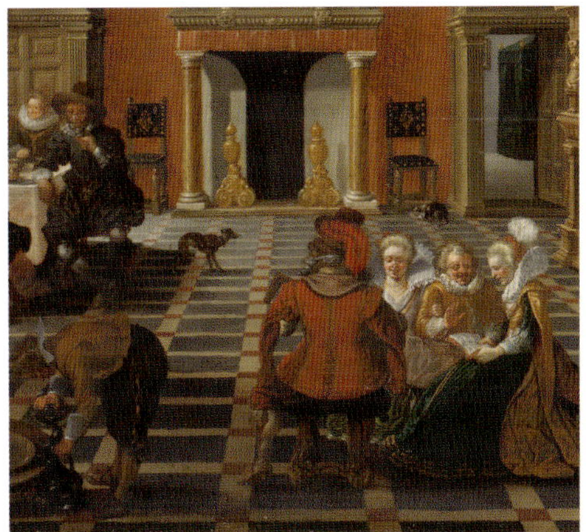

Bartholomeus van Bassen
Interior with a Company

1622–1624
Rijksmuseum, Amsterdam

Bartholomeus van Bassen, an architect and painter working in Delft in the 17th century, realized this work in collaboration with his colleague Esaias van de Velde. Van Bassen painted the interior: a fictional rendering of a grand and stylish residence inspired by the work of the architect Hans Vredeman de Vries, who was famous for his publications on ornaments and perspective. De Vries's numerous publications had a great deal of influence on many painters' artistic representation of space, such as the nature of the perspectival grid paving, the quantity of architectural elements, and the location of the vanishing point. Van de Velde then worked on the figures: a company of elegant people entertaining themselves in the vast space of the room, surrounded by servants, dogs, cats, paintings, a monumental chimneypiece, and an elaborate wooden ceiling. A parrot overlooks the scene from the top of a door.

C 66
M 61
Y 56
K 71

C 21
M 15
Y 37
K 0

C 10
M 76
Y 95
K 10

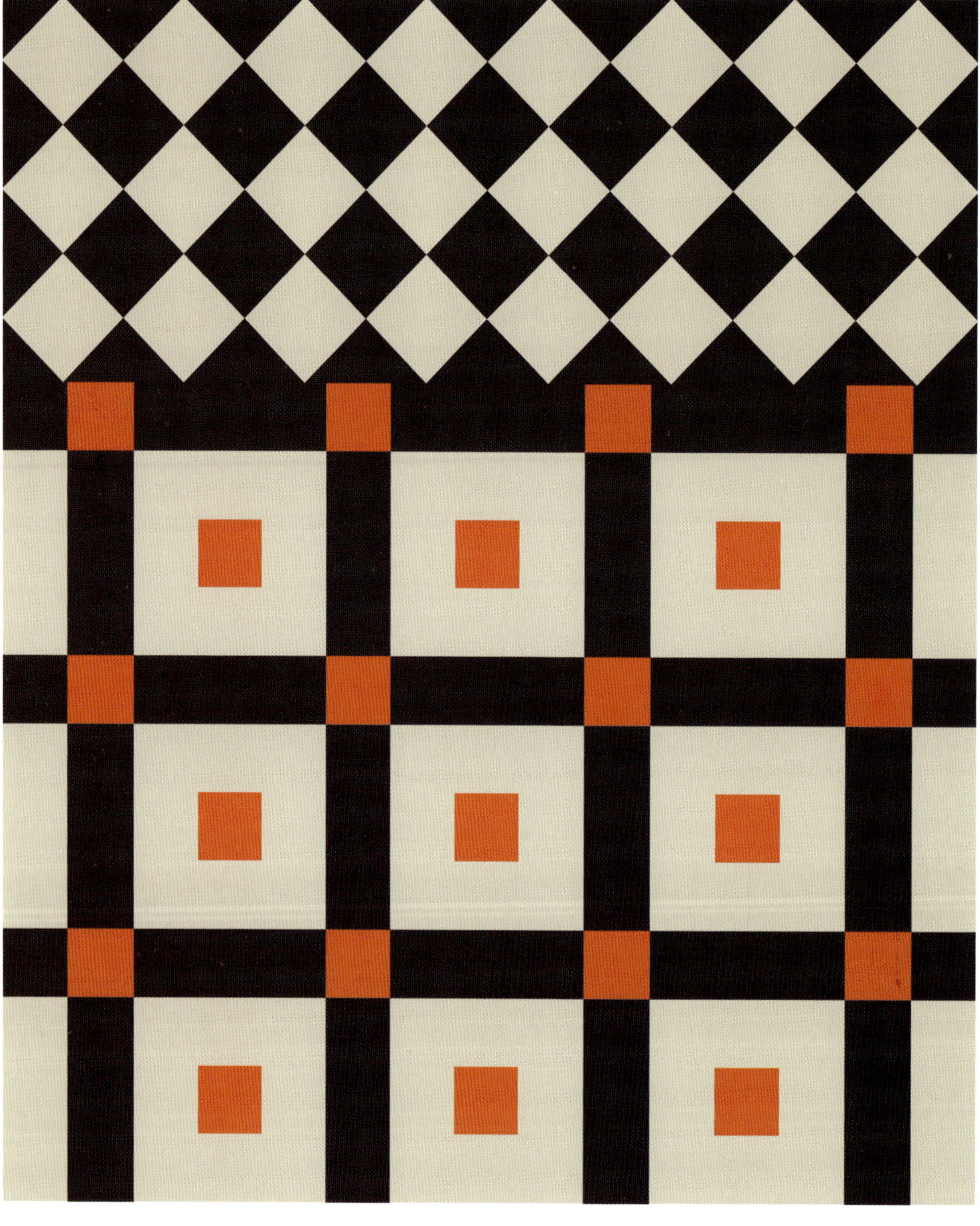

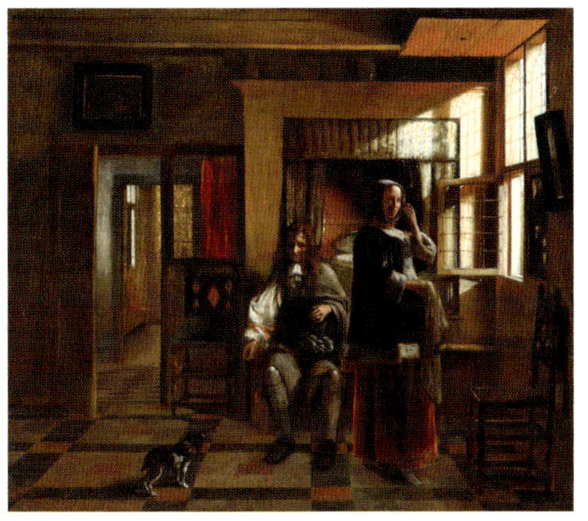

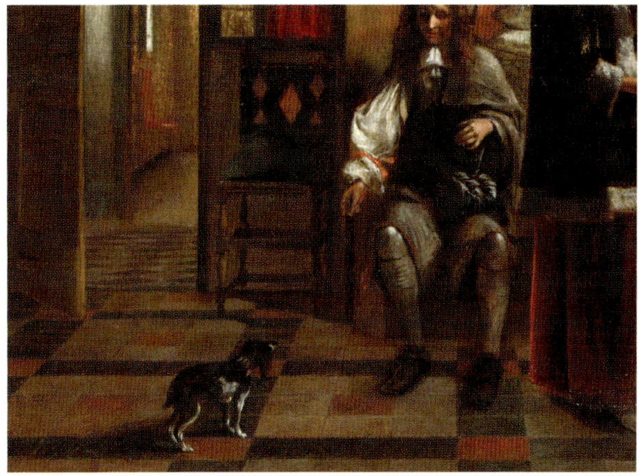

Pieter de Hooch
Interior with a Young Couple

circa 1662–1665
The Metropolitan Museum of Art, New York

Quiet scenes of family life, usually depicted in wealthy Dutch interiors, were de Hooch's specialty. There was in fact a taste, in the 17th-century Netherlands, for paintings that depicted episodes from daily life: although they seemed to show nothing of great importance, in reality these paintings portrayed love and the virtues of domestic life. This painting is a great example of the artist's skill in rendering subtle shifts in the light that emanates from doors and windows—an ability that was well appreciated by the collectors of the time. In this morning scene, a couple seems to be placidly composing themselves in their bedroom. The woman could either be looking out the window or adjusting her scarf while gazing into a mirror on the wall just next to it. The man awaits her while sitting and beckoning to their dog.
De Hooch captures and conveys the couple's serenity and ease superbly. Beyond the door, we can see a different pattern of floor tiles and some gilt-leather wall hangings.

C 16
M 31
Y 93
K 4

C 0
M 0
Y 0
K100

C 5
M 71
Y 91
K 0

C 9
M 15
Y 33
K 0

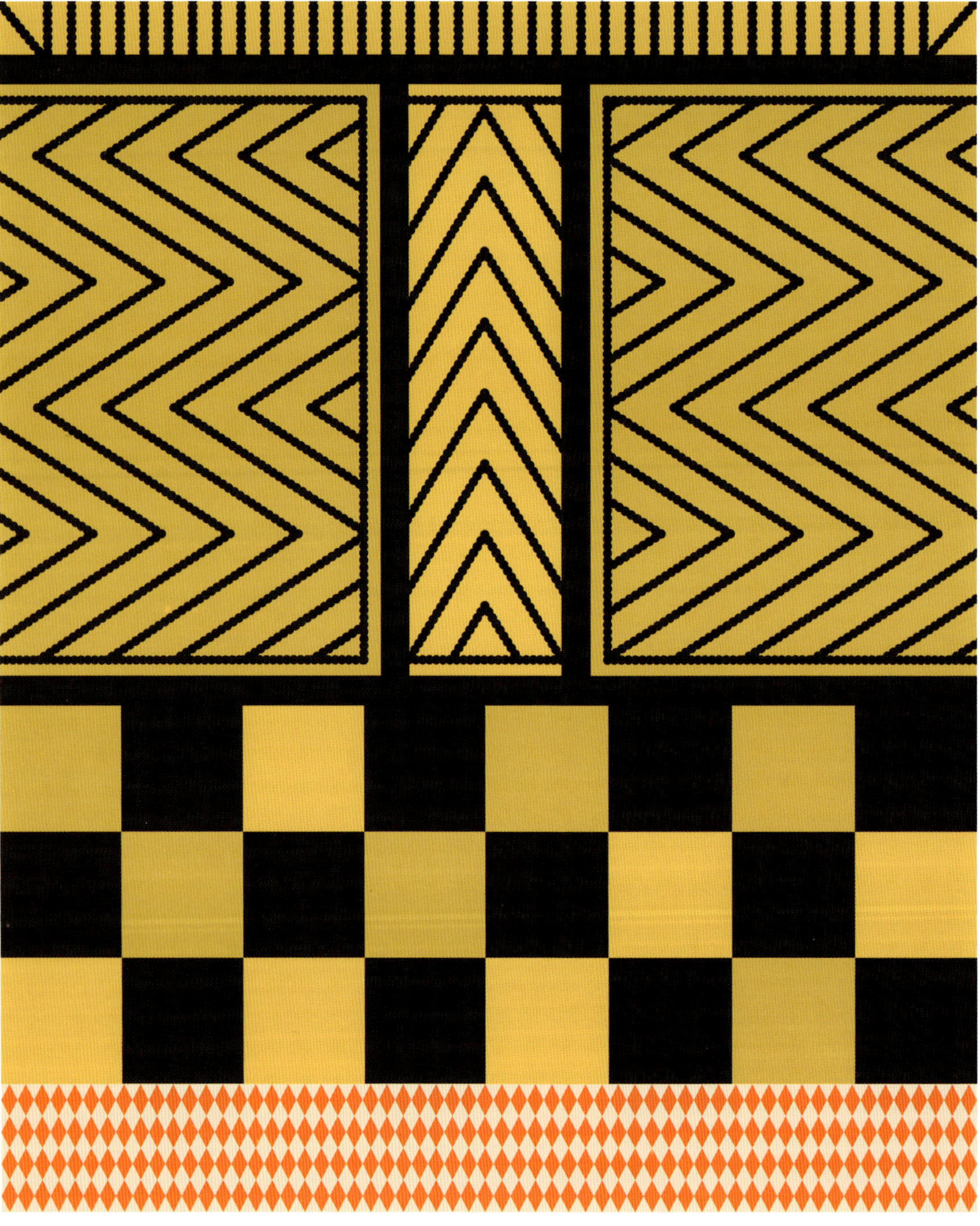

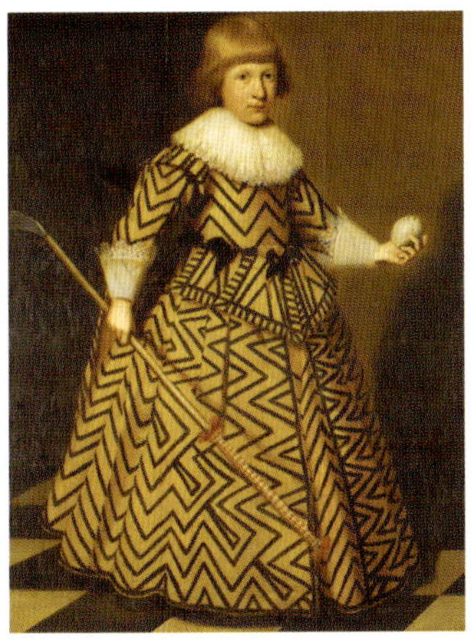

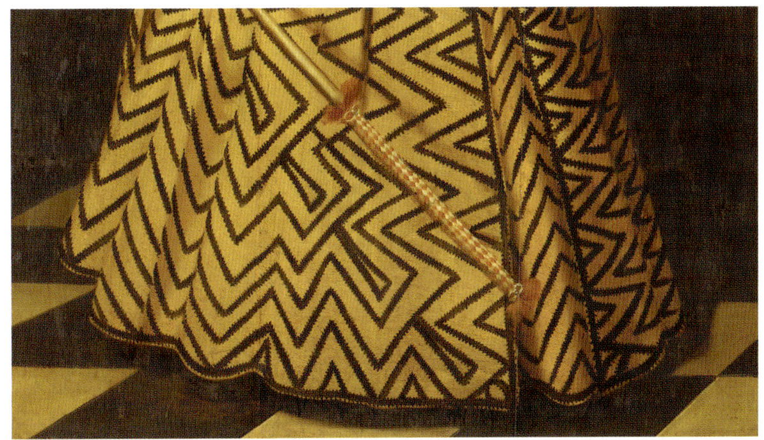

Wybrand de Geest
Portrait of a Boy with a Kolf Club

1631
Rijksmuseum, Amsterdam

Although this painting is ostensibly a portrait of a boy, the real subject is perhaps the boy's outstanding dress. The gold and black zigzag pattern of this long garment perfectly coordinates with the pattern of the floor tiles, the boy's hair, and the backdrop colors, creating a consistent and smooth color palette throughout. In his right hand, the boy holds a kolf club—called a *kliek* from the Scottish word *cleek*—with a wooden shaft and a lightweight iron head. In his left hand, he holds a sajet ball, a soft woolen ball used to play kolf, a 17th-century court game that was an early ancestor of modern golf. In the Netherlands at the time, most boys wore skirts, and would be allowed to start wearing their first breeches at the age of seven. Wybrand de Geest was famous in the art world of his time. After he spent years refining his technique in Rome, his fellow Dutch painters gave him the nickname "Frisian Eagle," because of the speed with which he produced his art.

C 29
M 36
Y 56
K 17

C 19
M 58
Y 60
K 7

C 18
M 24
Y 32
K 2

C 24
M 28
Y 35
K 5

C 38
M 25
Y 34
K 5

C 24
M 36
Y 72
K 13

C 31
M 91
Y100
K 47

C 59
M 62
Y 75
K 79

C 29
M 36
Y 56
K 17

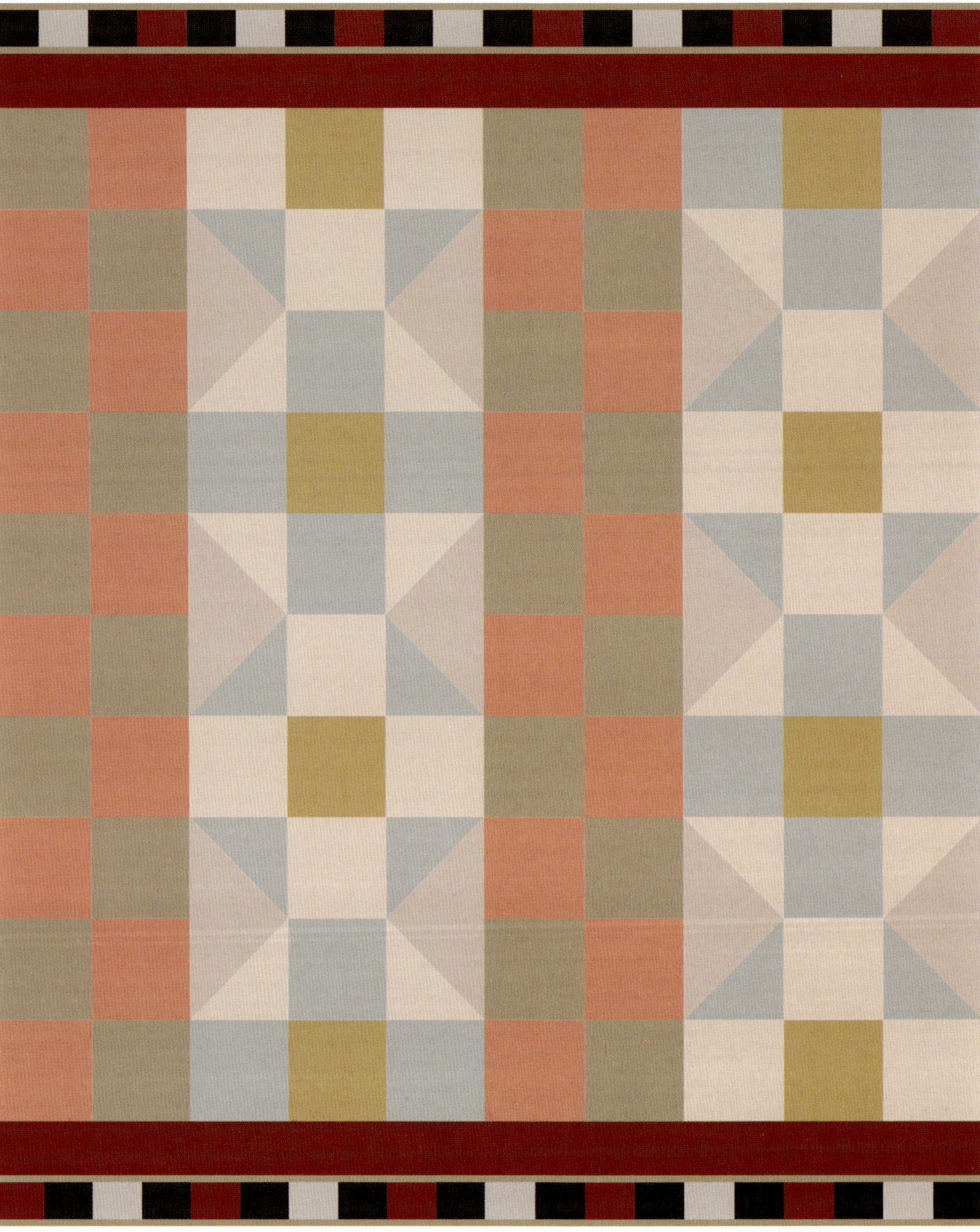

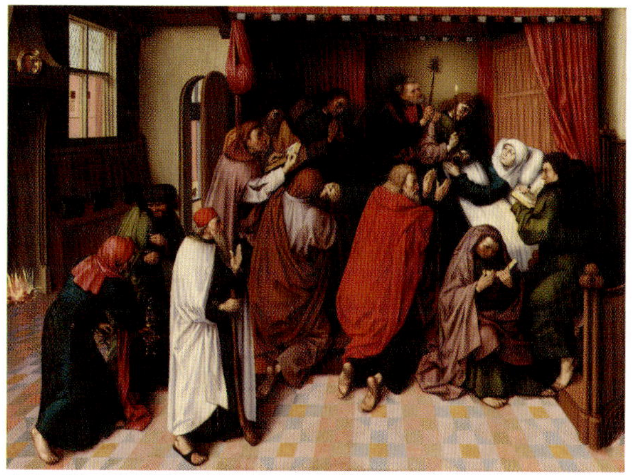

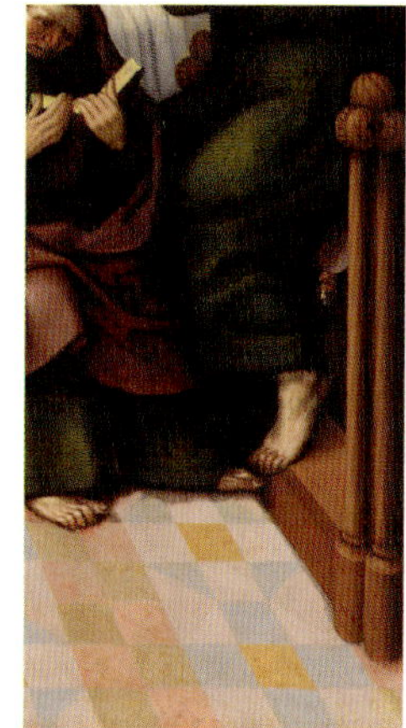

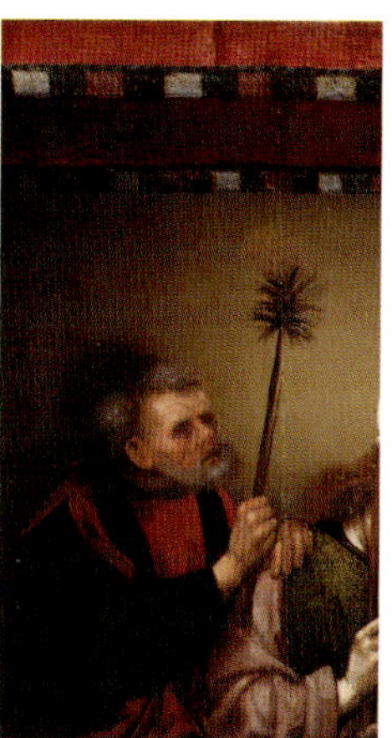

Master of the Amsterdam Death of the Virgin
The Death of the Virgin

circa 1500
Rijksmuseum, Amsterdam

The Bible never discusses the death of the Virgin Mary. However, by the 5th century, one particular anecdote began to circulate widely, in which the twelve apostles left their missionary activities around the world and miraculously gathered to be present at Mary's deathbed. This scene became a common subject in works of art, and was painted by such artists as Mantegna, Caravaggio, and Rembrandt. This 16th-century depiction was realized by a minor Dutch painter whose life is surrounded by mystery and whose artistic attributions have often been debated by critics. In this piece, we see Peter ready to bless the Virgin Mary with holy water while the other apostles pray intensely and read scripture in preparation for her departure. The figures are small, with disproportionately small heads and hands in comparison to their large torsos covered in drapery. Interestingly, all of the depictions of the death of Mary from the late Middle Ages represent the scene in contemporary domestic settings instead of historically accurate ones.

C 18
M 39
Y 78
K 8

C 20
M 42
Y 83
K 11

C 18
M 97
Y 100
K 15

C 84
M 73
Y 45
K 60

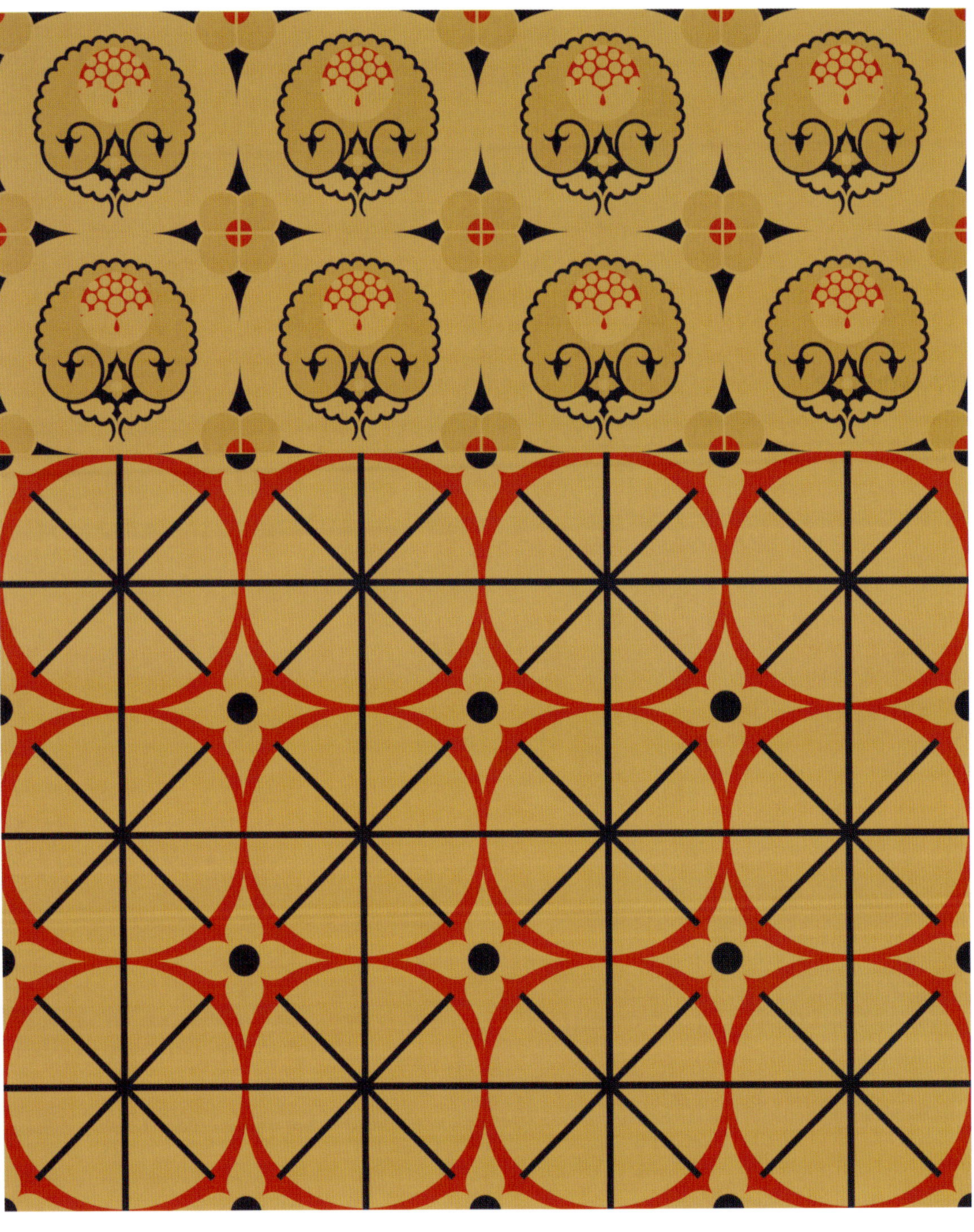

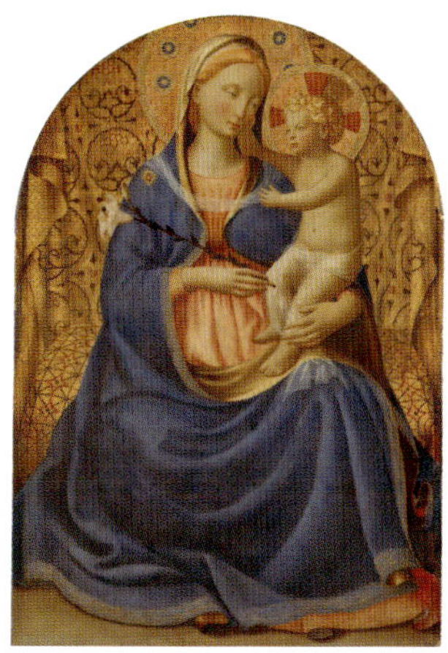

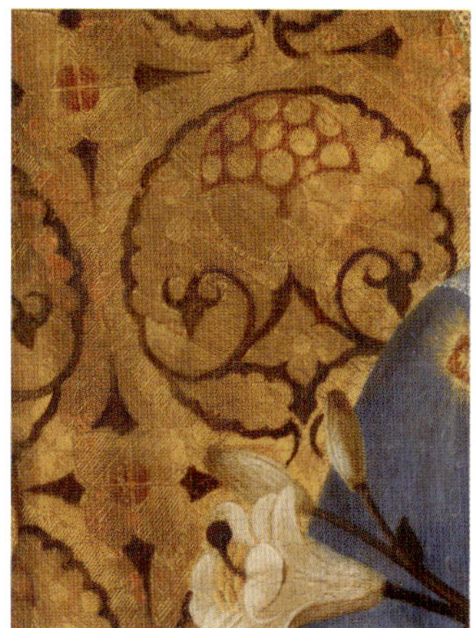

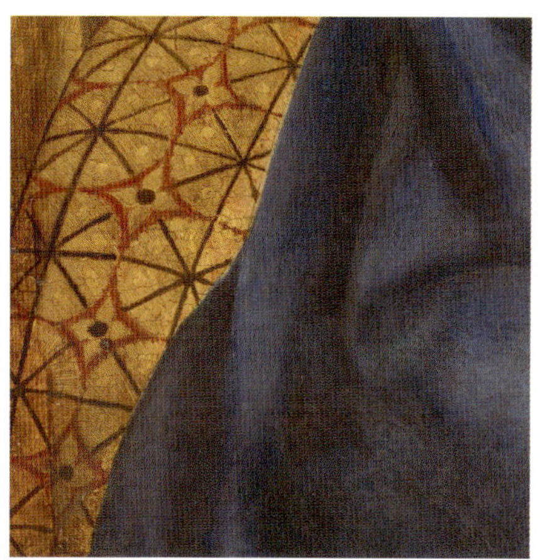

Fra Angelico
Madonna of Humility

circa 1440
Rijksmuseum, Amsterdam

Fra Angelico was a Dominican monk. Working inside his monastery, he enjoyed some degree of freedom from the strict rules of the Florentine painters' guild. His Madonna of Humility is an example of his freedom to experiment: the strong realism and use of solid forms are mixed with a certain degree of sweetness in the representation of the subjects. Their halos merge perfectly with the complex golden pattern of the backdrop, while the reddish golden hair creates a consistent palette throughout. We notice that the only colors used are red, blue, and gold. A bright element appears on the right shoulder of the Virgin's robe: perhaps a brooch representing the rising star. On the brocade robe, we can also see a pattern representing thistle flowers, a fairly typical motif in the materials imported from the East by Florentine textile traders.

C 25
M 63
Y 82
K 10

C 10
M 35
Y 65
K 0

C 0
M 0
Y 0
K100

C 31
M 84
Y100
K 28

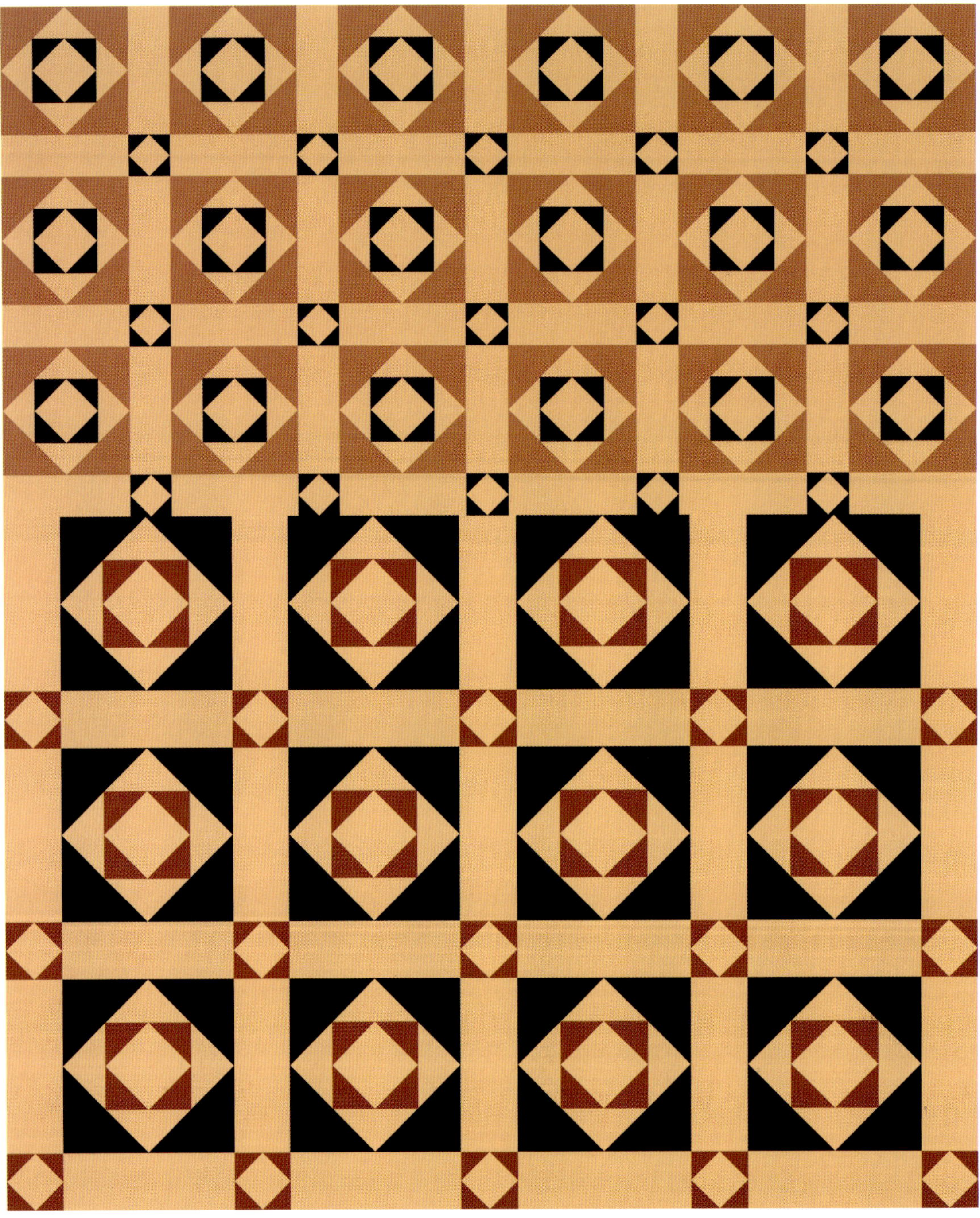

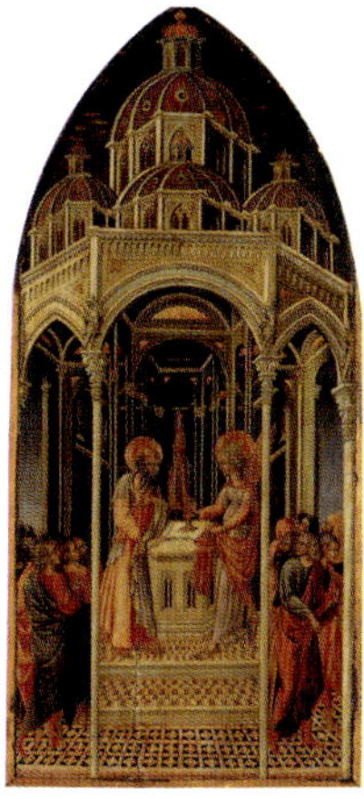

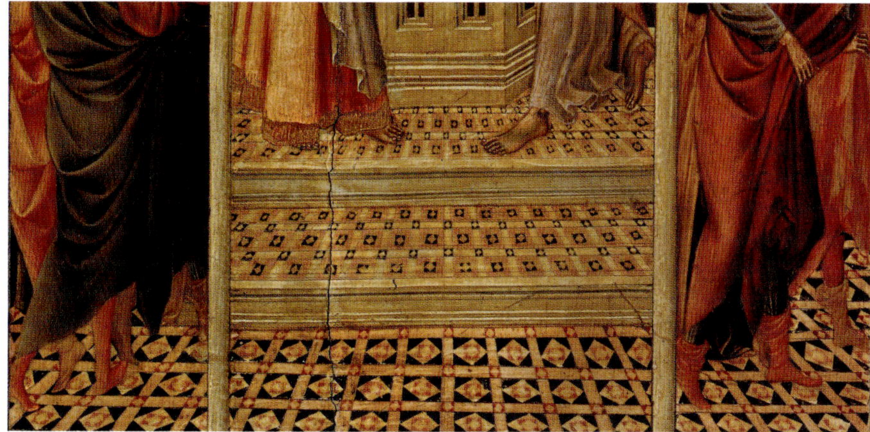

Giovanni di Paolo
The Annunciation to Zacharias

circa 1455–1460
The Metropolitan Museum of Art, New York

The Annunciation to Zacharias is the first scene of a series by Giovanni di Paolo narrating the life of Saint John the Baptist. The angel Gabriel on the right, depicted with slightly feminine facial traits, reveals to Zacharias that he and his wife, a couple fairly advanced in age, are expecting a baby; Zacharias's incredulity is very skillfully rendered. The painter enjoyed playing with symmetries and contrasts to create harmony and variation in the composition. The main figures, at the center of the scene, are wrapped in brightly colored draperies with alternating tones. The light blue vest of the angel contrasts with the golden orange of the cloak, and the same colors are then inverted in Zacharias's clothes. The same color contrast is seen between the standing figures on the sides of the main subjects. When we look closely, we see that the men standing on the left side are facing away from us, whereas those on the right are facing toward us.

C 36
M 29
Y 17
K 10

C 0
M 25
Y 73
K 0

C 76
M 39
Y100
K 35

C 8
M 56
Y 93
K 4

C 35
M 47
Y 68
K 36

C 00
M 00
Y 00
K100

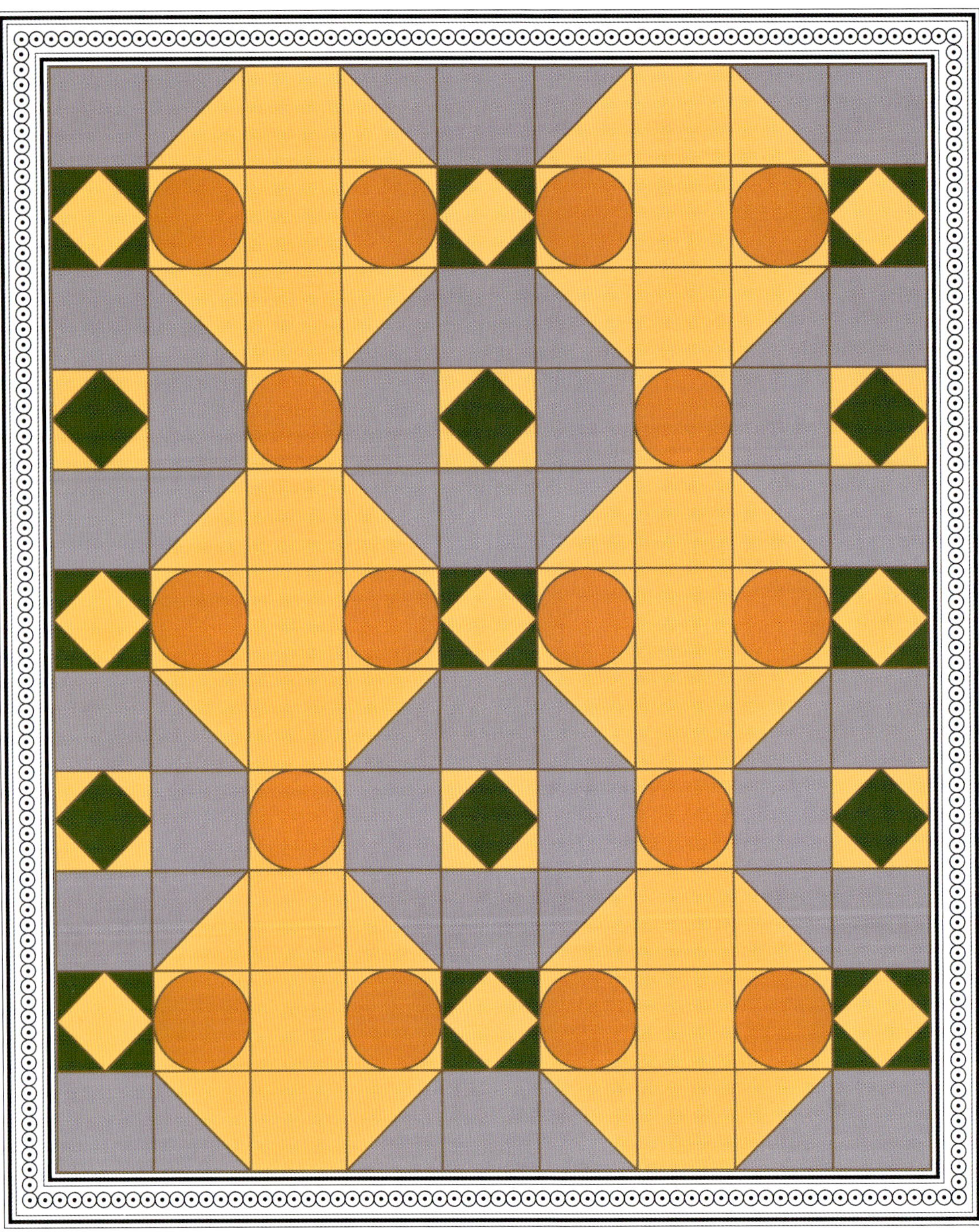

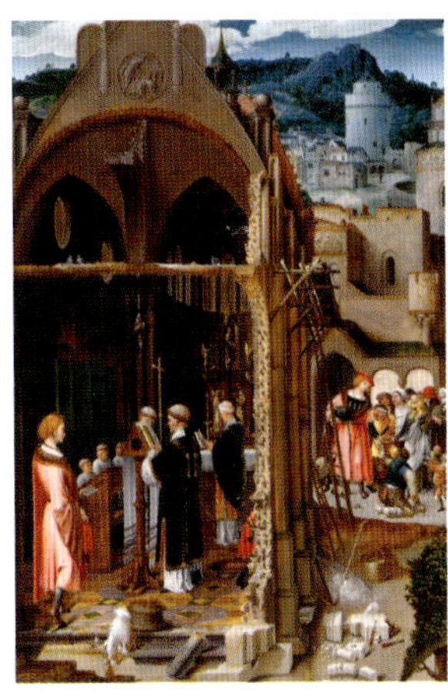

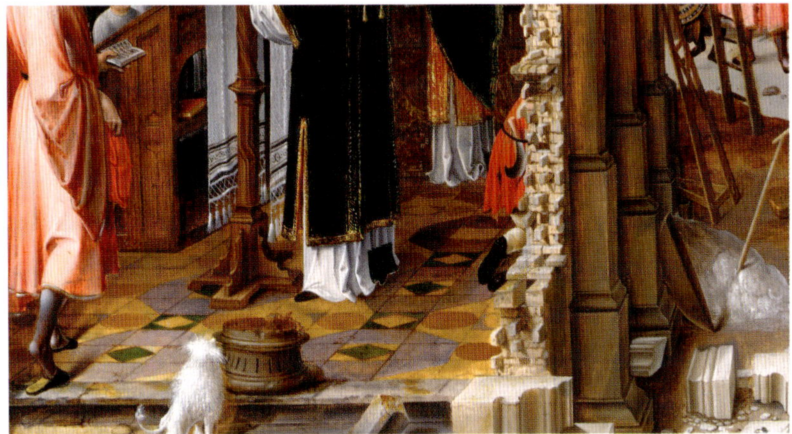

Netherlandish Painter
A Sermon on Charity
(possibly the Conversion of Saint Anthony)

16th century
The Metropolitan Museum of Art,
New York

This painting, whose meaning is as much debated as the identity of the painter, is a compelling illustration of the contrast between the ways that biblical humanists and traditional Christians interpret sacred texts. Christian humanism, a reform movement that emerged during the Renaissance, deemed "acting out the life of Christ" morally superior to participating in codified church rituals. In this painting, the painter depicts charity, one of the moral obligations championed by the humanists, in two very different ways. On the left, traditional churchgoers listen to a sermon about charity in a church. On the right, however, humanists are out in the street practicing charity through active intervention. The unfinished wall could symbolize a church that needs to reform itself. Another contrast can be seen in the sudden switch between the bright, saturated colors in the foreground and the cold, blue background.

C100
M 63
Y 48
K 55

C 0
M 23
Y 74
K 0

C 13
M 56
Y 68
K 0

C 18
M 99
Y 91
K 12

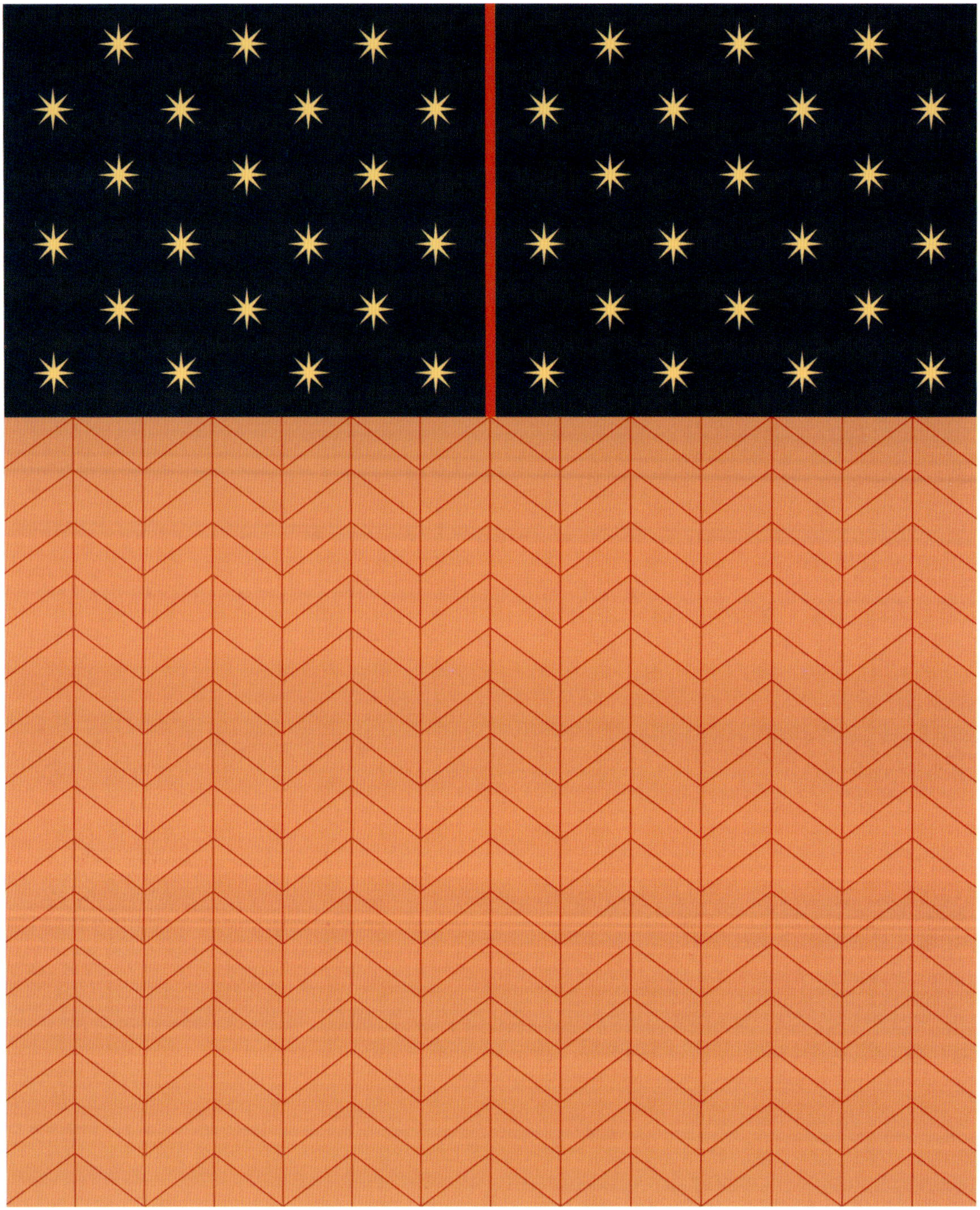

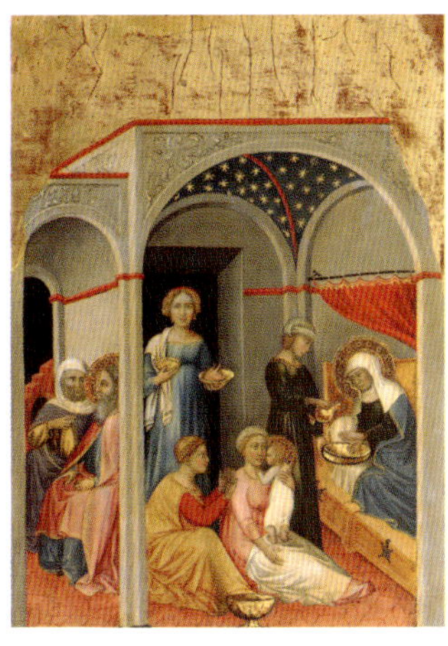

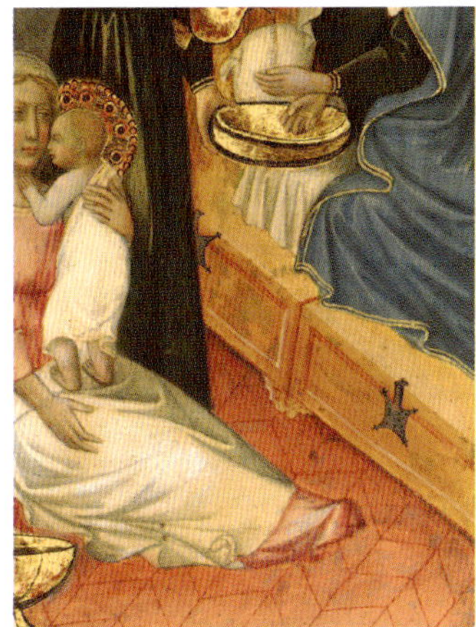

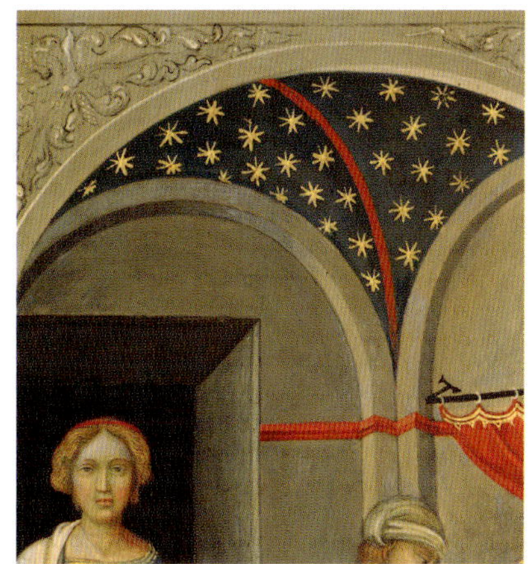

Andrea di Bartolo
The Nativity of the Virgin

circa 1400–1405
National Gallery of Art, Washington

Andrea di Bartolo depicts the newborn Mary as a very special infant who can already stand up on her own. Her mother and other women greet her in a warm domestic environment, while her father is waiting outside the room in the company of another man. Our attention, however, is drawn to the standing woman who has just entered the room, holding a dish of chicken while looking straight into our eyes. Not only does Andrea di Bartolo masterfully convey a sense of intimacy by packing the figures closely together, but he also manages to create great spatial depth. The division of the rooms, the vase in the foreground, the black background beyond the room's doors: every detail contributes to expanding the space. The refined use of color and the delicately traced lines reveal di Bartolo's fidelity to the style of 14th-century Siena, where he ran a workshop together with his father.

C 60
M 43
Y 91
K 38

C 36
M 92
Y 69
K 60

C 29
M 25
Y 48
K 7

C100
M 81
Y 36
K 31

C 19
M 17
Y 39
K 2

C 53
M 28
Y 21
K 4

C 37
M 23
Y 21
K 3

C 36
M 15
Y 12
K 0

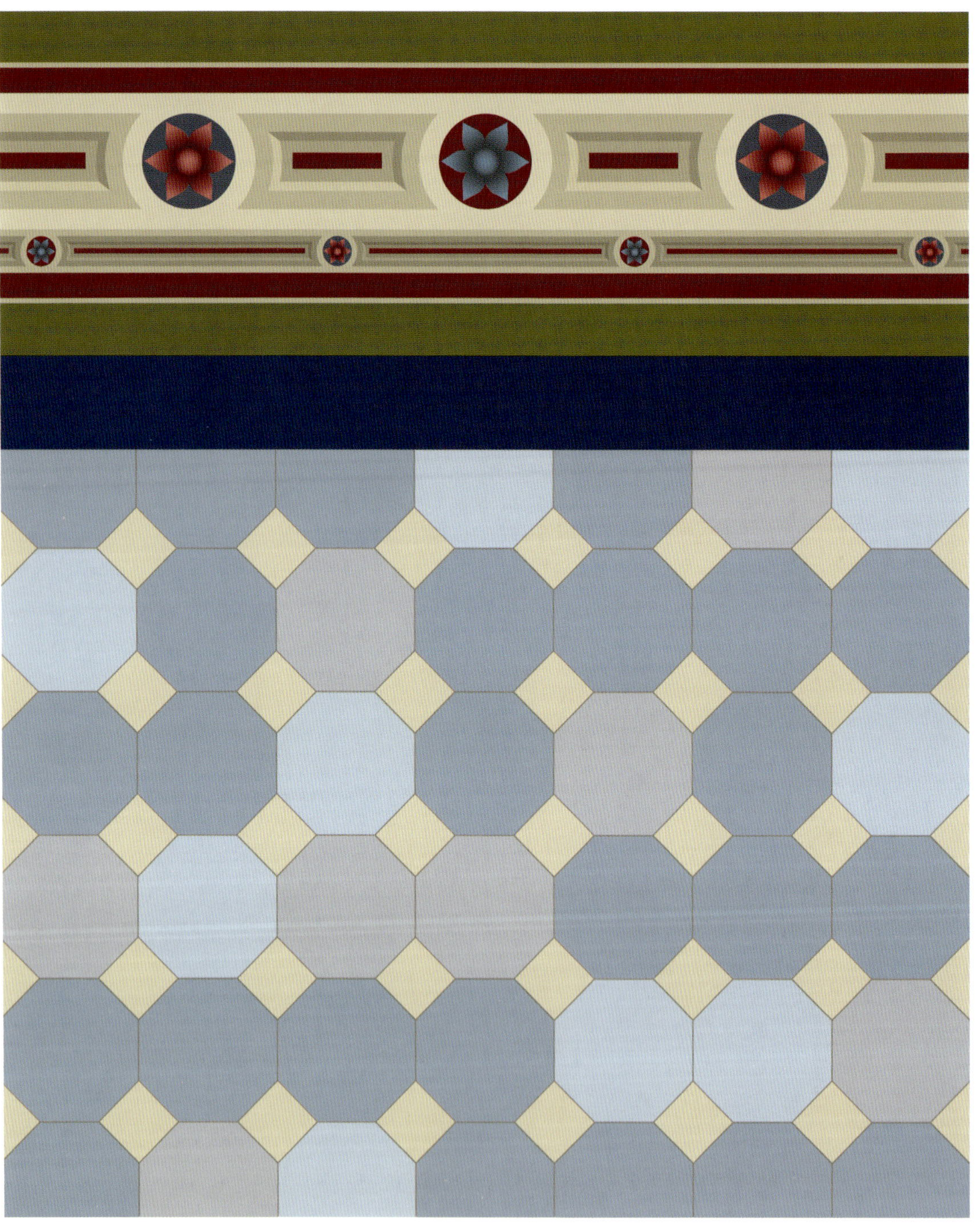

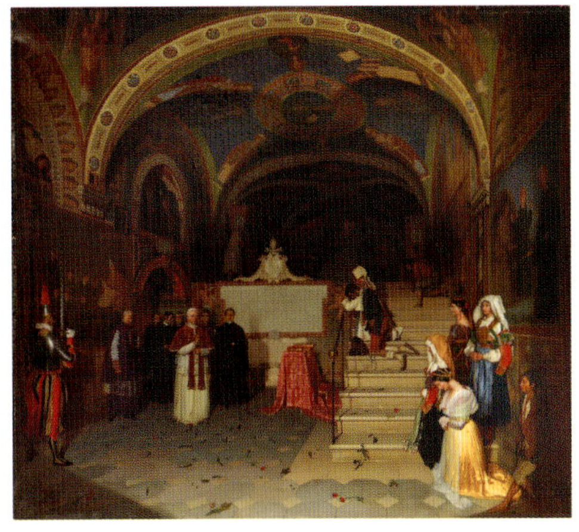

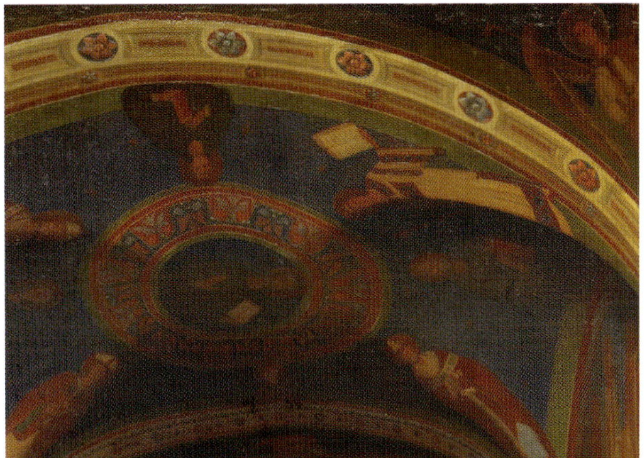

Jean-François Montessuy
Pope Gregory XVI Visiting
the Church of San Benedetto at Subiaco

1843
The Metropolitan Museum of Art,
New York

This painting is considered the first masterpiece by Jean-François Montessuy, and it is with this work that he successfully established himself at the Paris Salon in 1844. Reports of the Salon noted that this work generated high praise for Montessuy. In particular, his depiction of the woman in blue costume on the right was widely commended. Montessuy depicts Pope Gregory XVI entering the Monastery of San Benedetto, built during the Middle Ages as a pilgrimage site. He emerges in the Lower Basilica of the monastery through the Sacro Speco, the cave where Saint Benedict supposedly lived as a hermit around AD 500. The artist masterfully reproduced the 14th-century frescoes that can be found in the church, which depict stories from Saint Benedict's life.
Gregory XVI was a controversial pontiff. He encouraged missionary activity abroad, and in 1839 he even issued an apostolic letter against the Atlantic slave trade, soliciting all Christian nations to "turn away from the inhuman slave trade of Negroes and all other men." However, he was also a conservative and traditionalist pope. Ultimately, his harsh opposition to many modernizing reforms, as well as his financial extravagance, made him unpopular in the Papal States and around Europe.

C 83
M 63
Y 45
K 61

C 51
M 30
Y100
K 28

C 12
M 82
Y 92
K 40

C 15
M 61
Y 67
K 22

C 43
M 38
Y 45
K 34

C 4
M100
Y 00
K 00

C 56
M 38
Y100
K 37

C 19
M 30
Y 92
K 21

C 38
M 44
Y 67
K 36

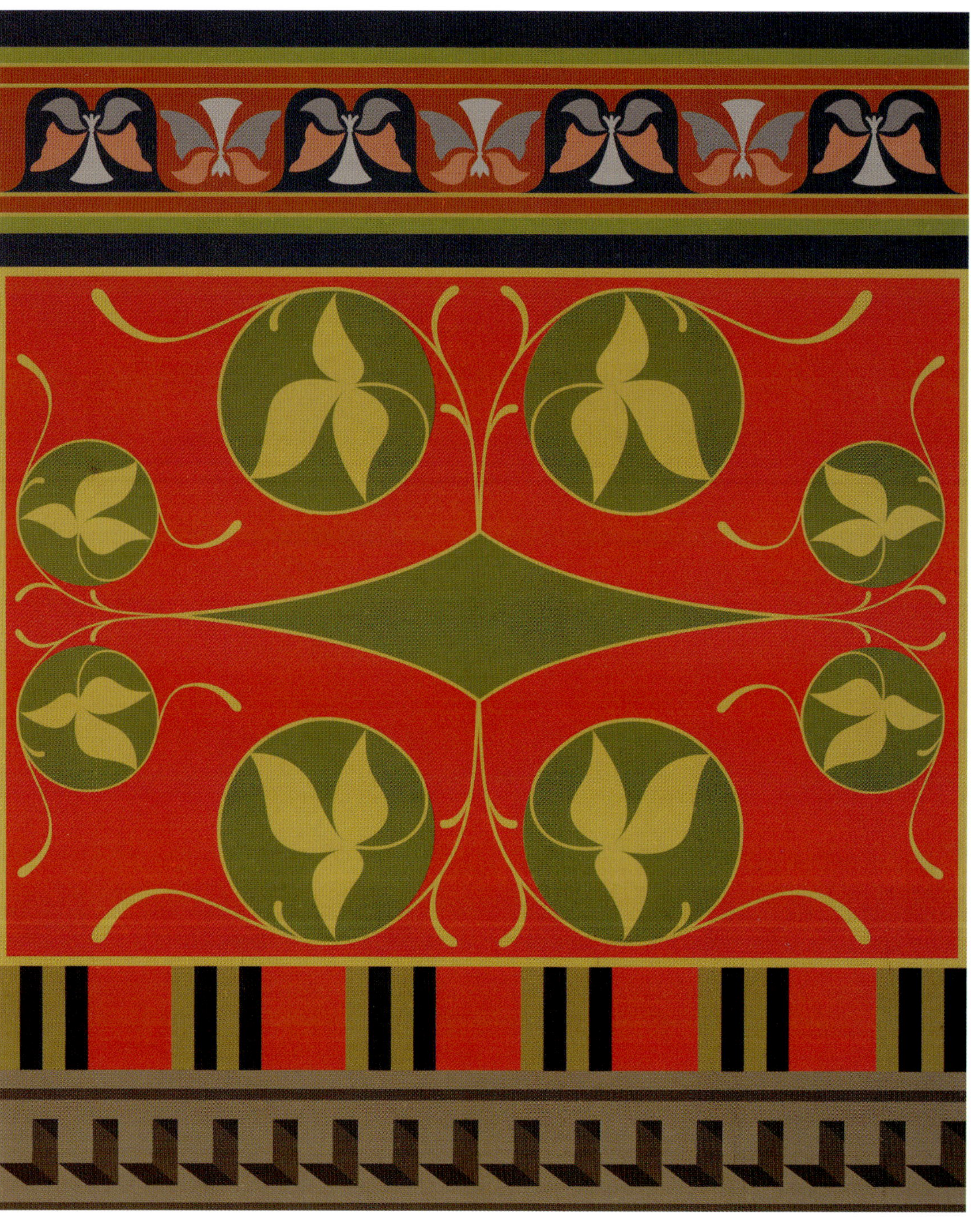

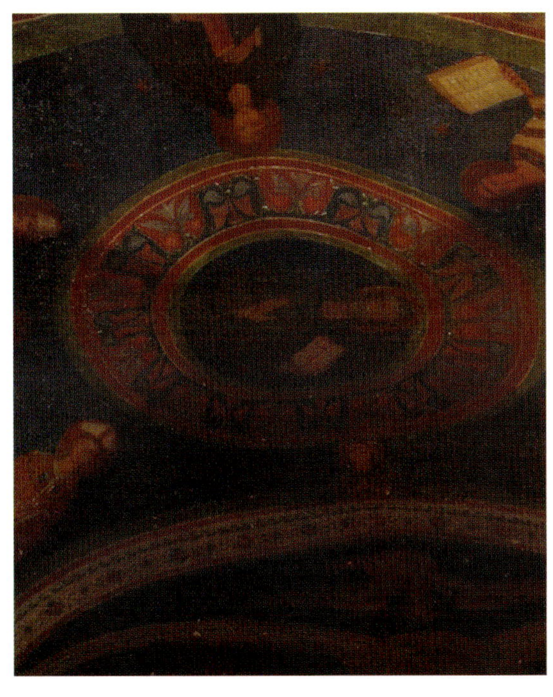
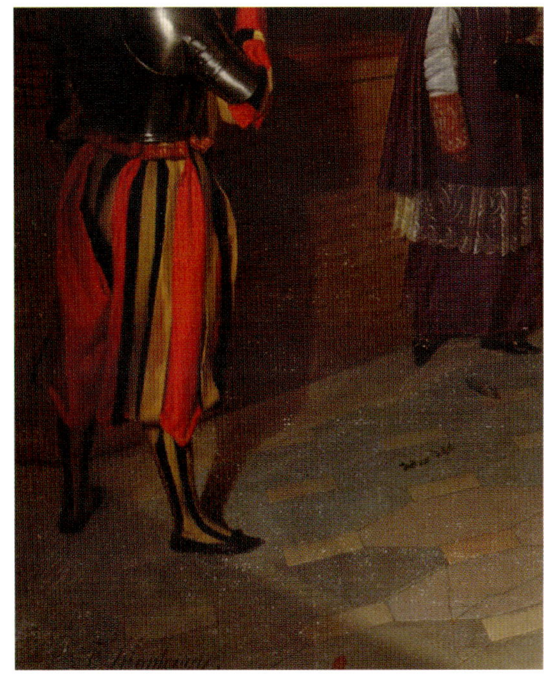
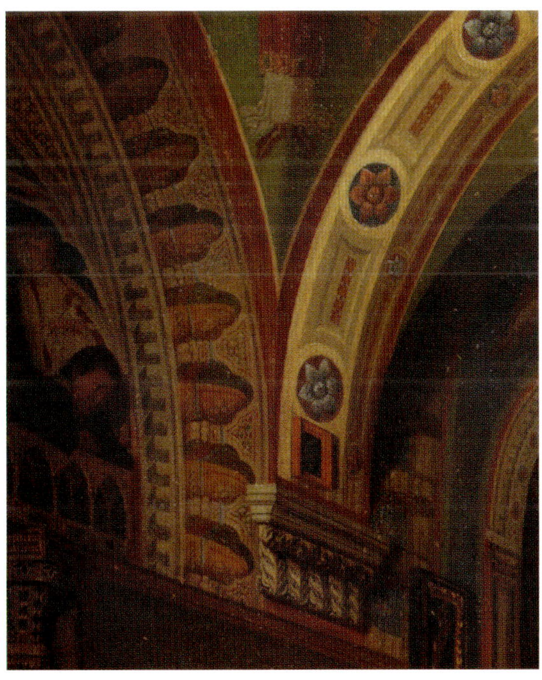
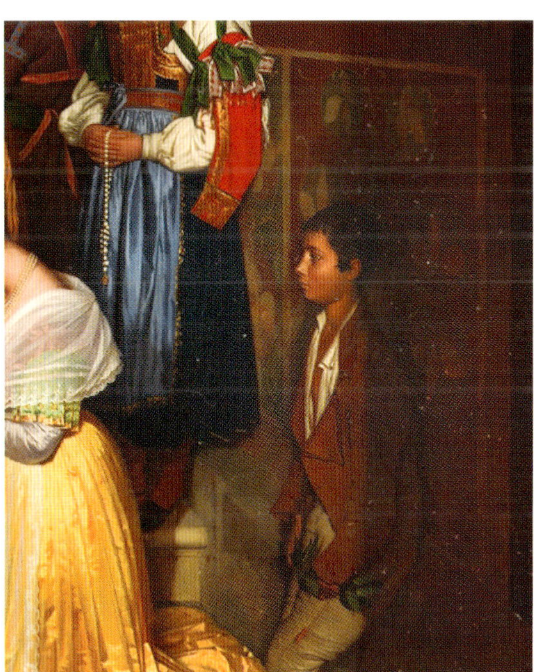

C 89
M 69
Y 35
K 24

C 13
M 44
Y 99
K 0

C 0
M 85
Y 99
K 0

C 11
M 95
Y100
K 0

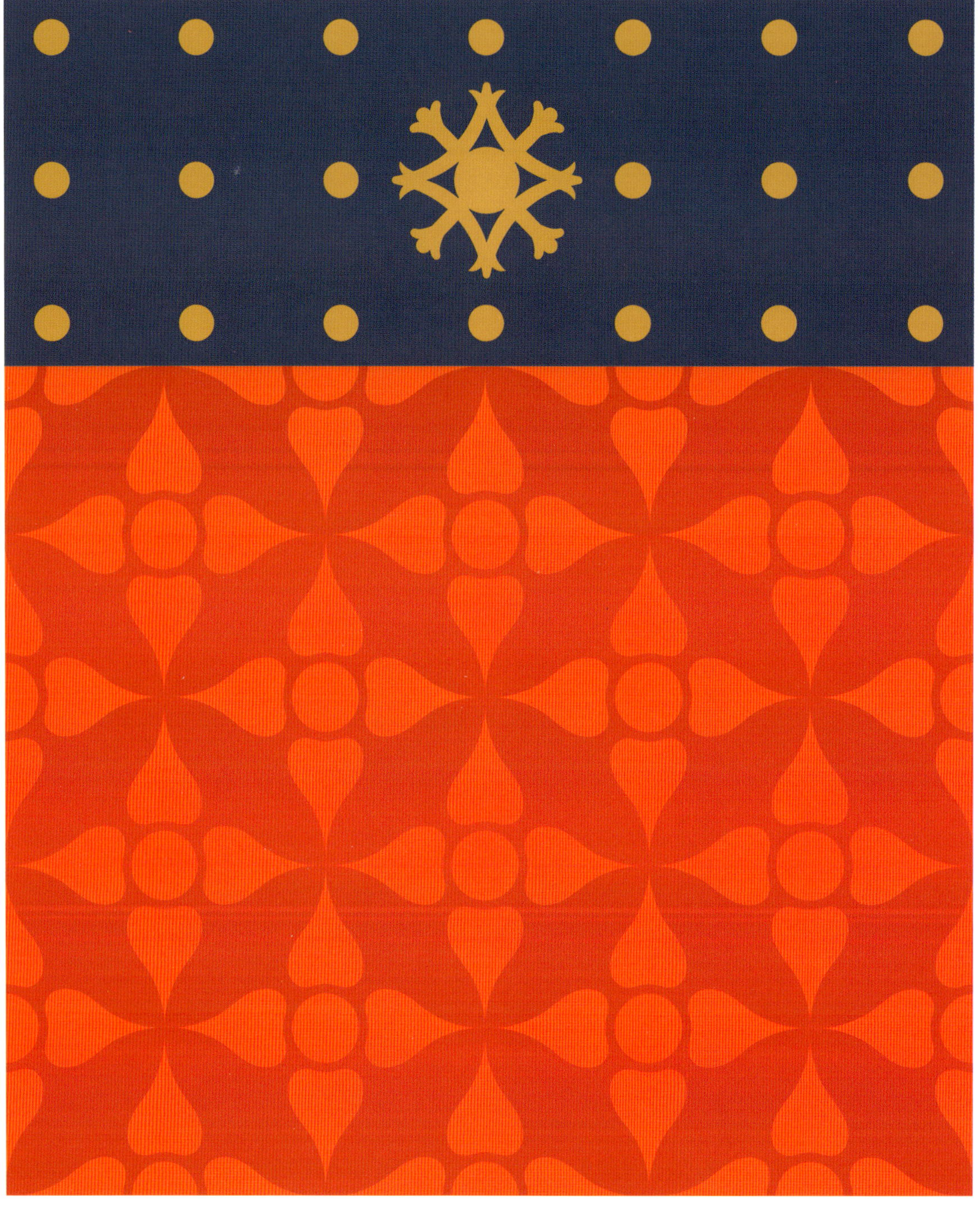

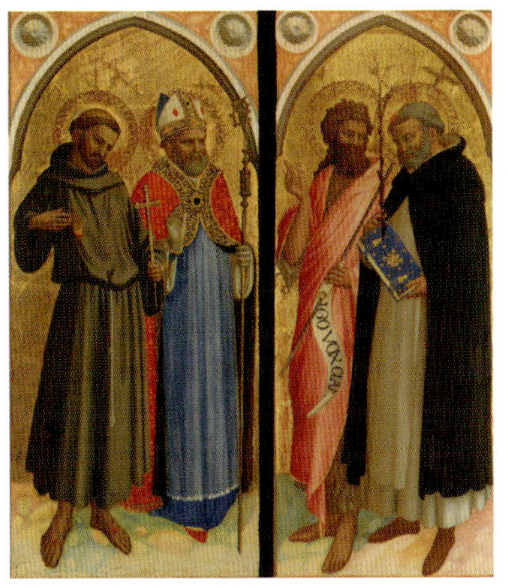

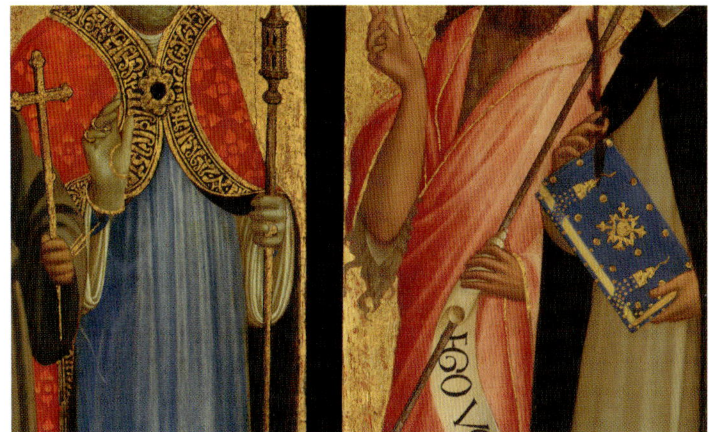

Fra Angelico
Saint Francis and a Bishop Saint;
Saint John the Baptist and Saint Dominic

late 1420s
The J. Paul Getty Museum,
Los Angeles

These two panels, painted by Fra Angelico, were used as wings of an altarpiece and depict four saints with clearly identifiable attributes. Saint Francis can be recognized on the left panel by the stigmata on his hands, side, and feet. Also visible are two of the three knots tied in the rope around his waist—symbols of the Franciscan religious vows of chastity, poverty, and obedience. An unknown bishop saint, richly dressed, stands next to him. The right panel depicts Saint John the Baptist, holding a scroll on which is written "Ego vox clamantis in deserto" (I am the voice crying in the wilderness). This phrase is repeated throughout the Bible to refer to a warning not heeded. To the right of Saint John the Baptist stands Saint Dominic, who is holding a lily and a Gospel book. Fra Angelico, who was perhaps inspired to become a painter by admiring Masaccio at work, was also one of the first to adopt his innovative naturalism. Although these panels have a traditional gold-leaf background, Fra Angelico employs color and shading in a way that conveys the subjects' natural expressions and grace.

C 20
M100
Y 88
K 51

C 0
M 23
Y 73
K 26

C 94
M 52
Y 37
K 42

C 12
M 87
Y 72
K 16

C 18
M 12
Y 26
K 0

C 7
M 36
Y 82
K 0

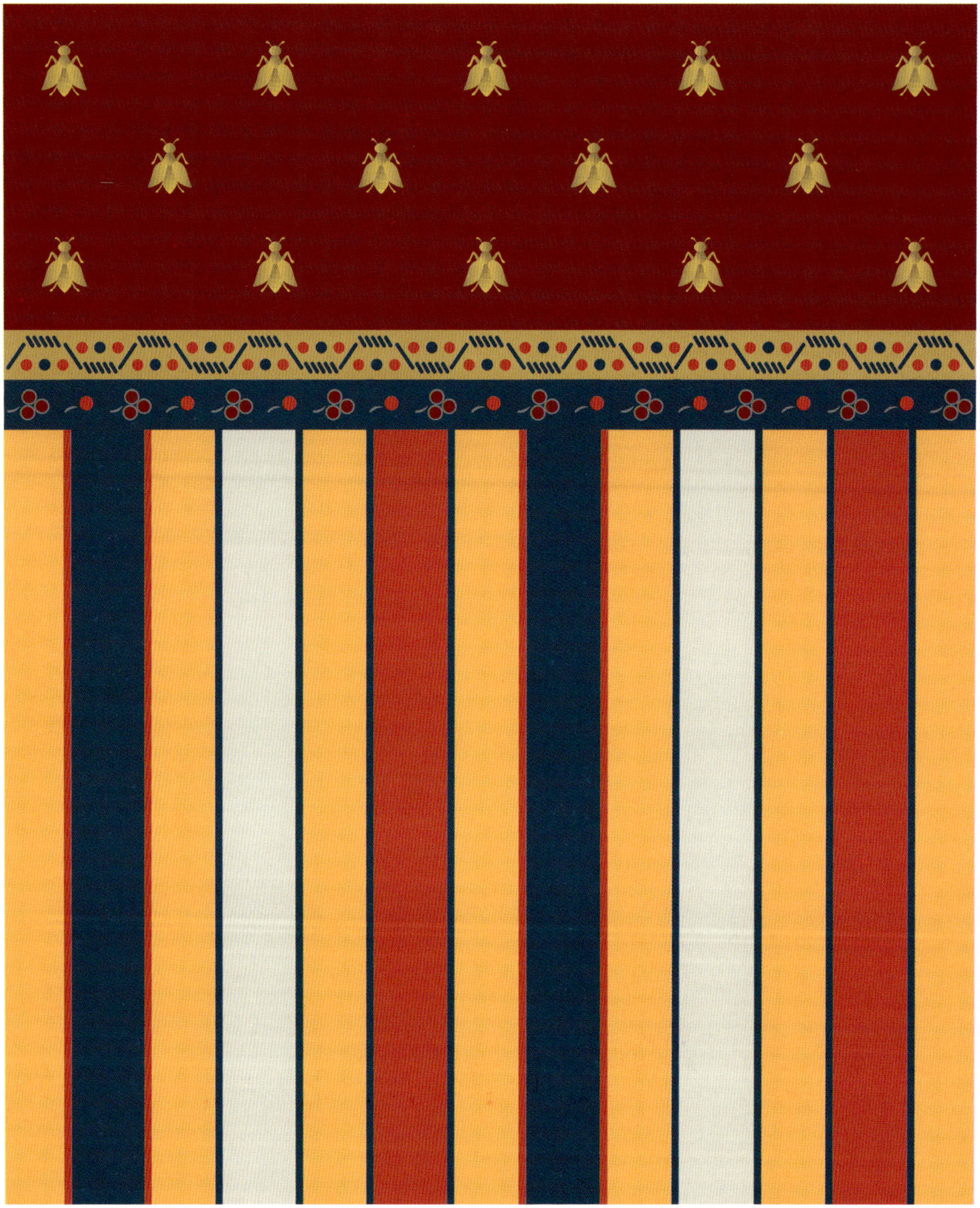

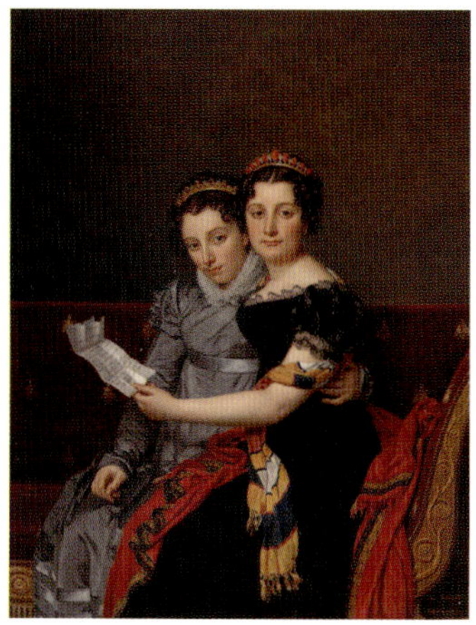

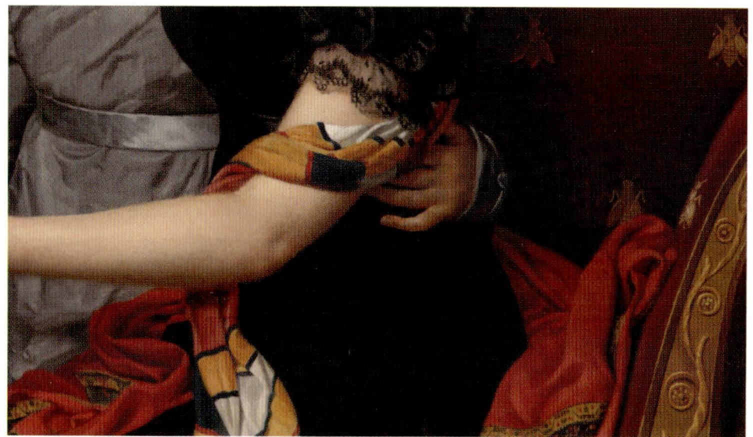

Jacques-Louis David
Portrait of the Sisters Zénaïde and Charlotte Bonaparte

1821
The J. Paul Getty Museum, Los Angeles

Jacques-Louis David, a renowned French political painter during Napoleon's reign, was forced to flee to Brussels after the emperor's fall. David completed this portrait in Brussels in 1821, depicting the sisters Zénaïde and Charlotte Bonaparte, Napoleon's nieces, who were also exiled together with their mother. Their father, Joseph Bonaparte, went to the United States, where he purchased an estate on the Delaware River near Bordentown, New Jersey. In this painting, the two sisters are immortalized reading a letter from their father. The painter's realism even allows us to see that the letter was sent from Philadelphia. David adeptly portrays the intimacy of the two sisters and is able to delicately convey their different personalities. Zénaïde, the elder sister, sophisticated and elegantly dressed, looks at the viewer with confidence while holding both the letter and her sister in a protective manner. In contrast, Charlotte, who is more modestly dressed, holds her sister tightly and with a certain shyness. Both sisters would marry cousins from the Bonaparte family. By the time this painting was completed, Charlotte was about to leave Brussels to join her father for three years in the United States. Zénaïde also visited him there.

C 9
M 11
Y 18
K 0

C 0
M 0
Y 0
K100

C 42
M 41
Y 13
K 0

C 7
M 25
Y 63
K 0

C 56
M 32
Y 38
K 19

C 17
M 67
Y 62
K 2

C 18
M 40
Y 58
K 13

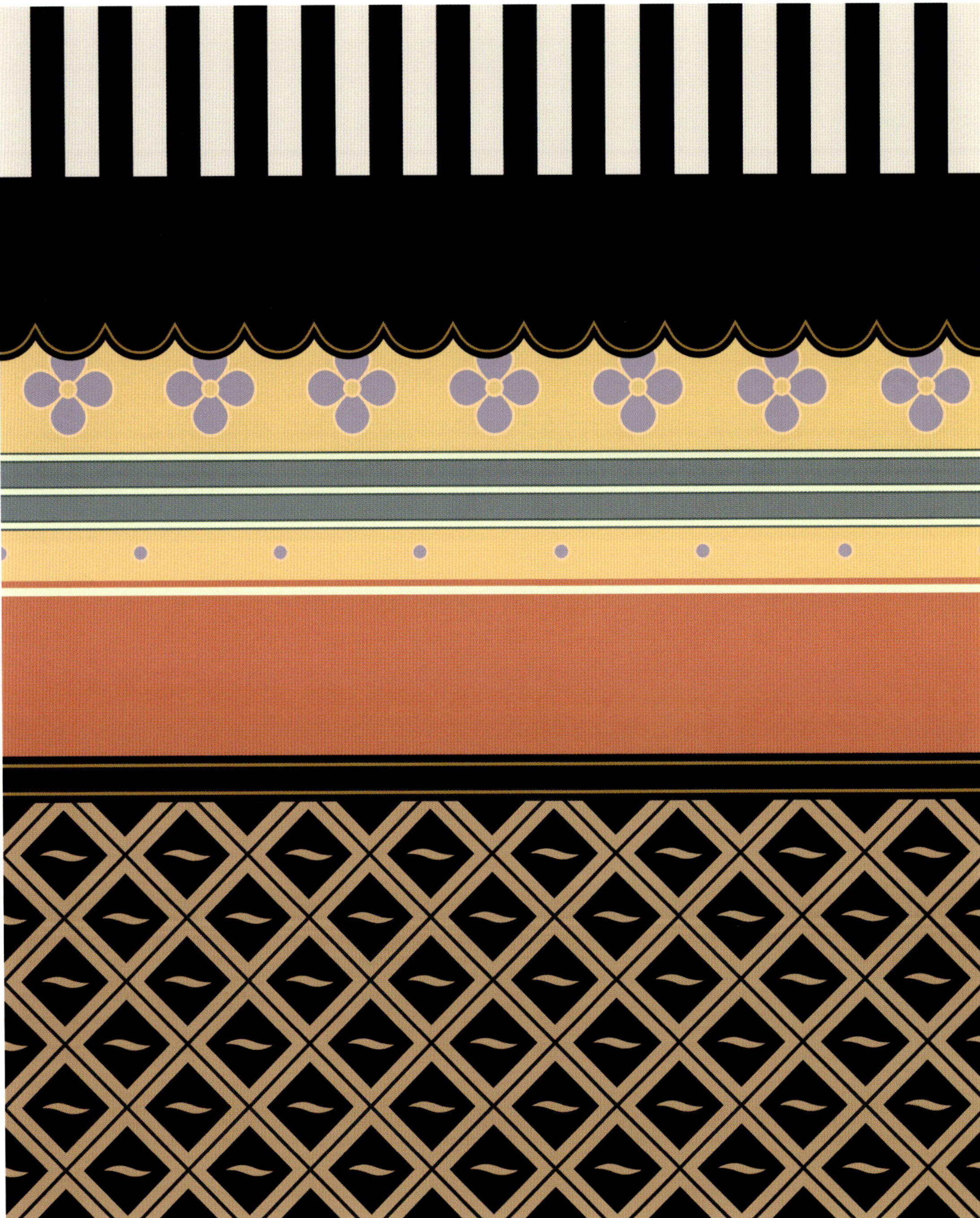

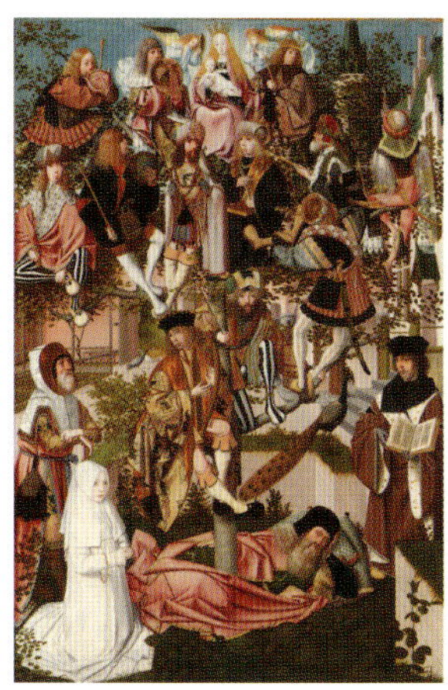

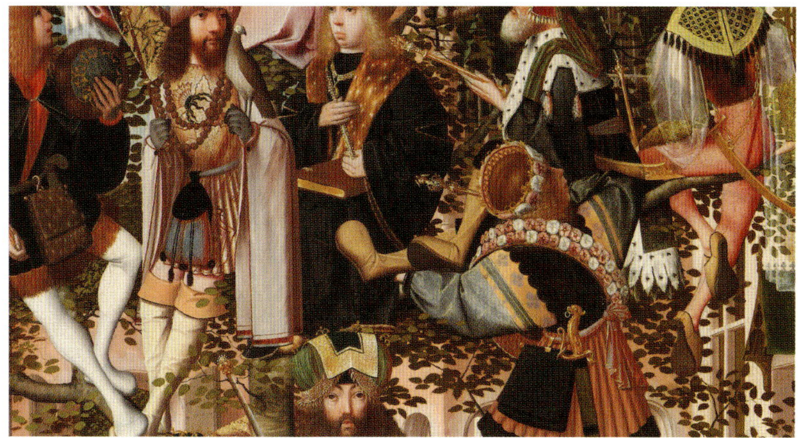

Circle of Geertgen tot Sint Jans
The Tree of Jesse

circa 1500
Rijksmuseum, Amsterdam

The Tree of Jesse was a popular theme in the Middle Ages and particularly in 15th- and 16th-century German art. The subject is inspired by the Book of Isaiah, in which Jesse, the father of King David, is described as the root of a family tree. It is perhaps the first historical use of a family tree to describe genealogical relations. In this early 16th-century painting by an artist in the circle of Geertgen tot Sint Jans, the tree is depicted in a manner not encountered elsewhere. The trunk of the tree grows out of Jesse, and large figures of Christ's ancestors perch in its branches, with the Virgin Mary and Jesus sitting at the top. The kneeling nun dressed in white had been painted over with an extension of the brick wall until 1932, when the overpainting was removed. Whether this painting was done by Geertgen tot Sint Jans or by someone belonging to his circle is still unknown, mostly because of the uncertainty surrounding the date of the artist's death.

C 4
M 7
Y 13
K 0

C 3
M 28
Y 16
K 0

C 0
M 0
Y 0
K100

C 79
M 56
Y 33
K 28

C 19
M 74
Y 83
K 24

C 11
M 39
Y 56
K 2

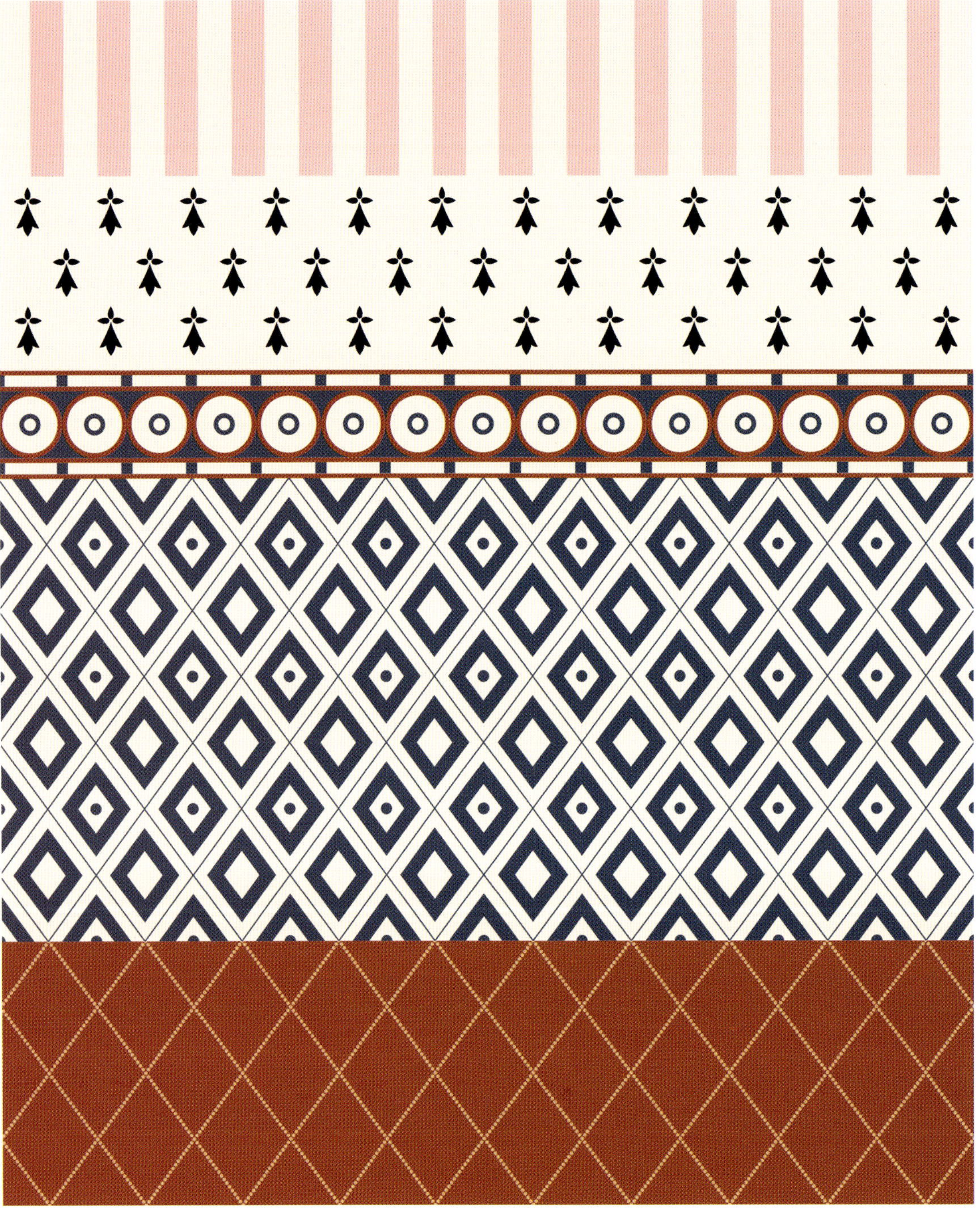

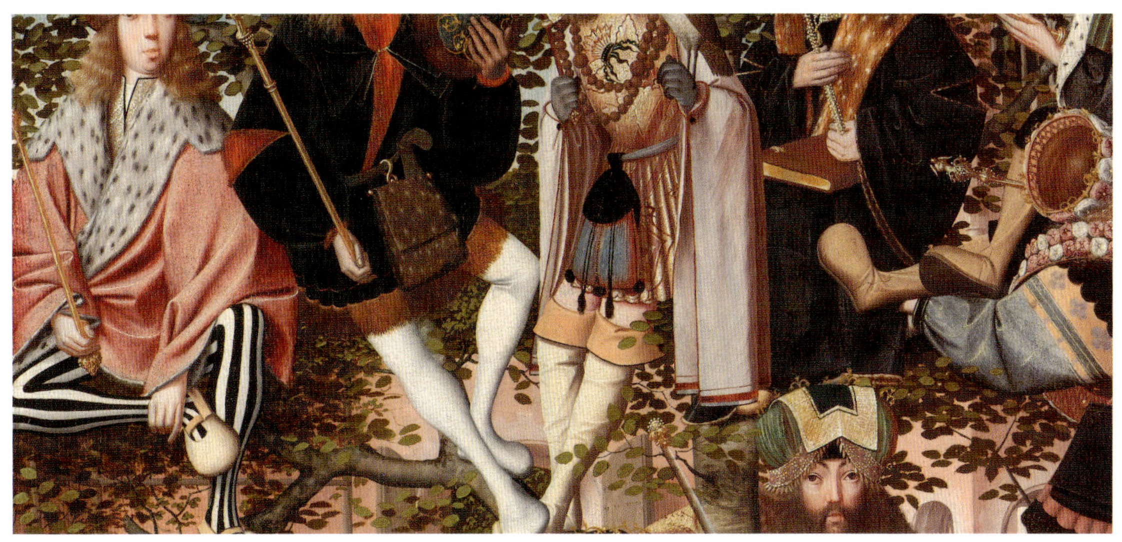

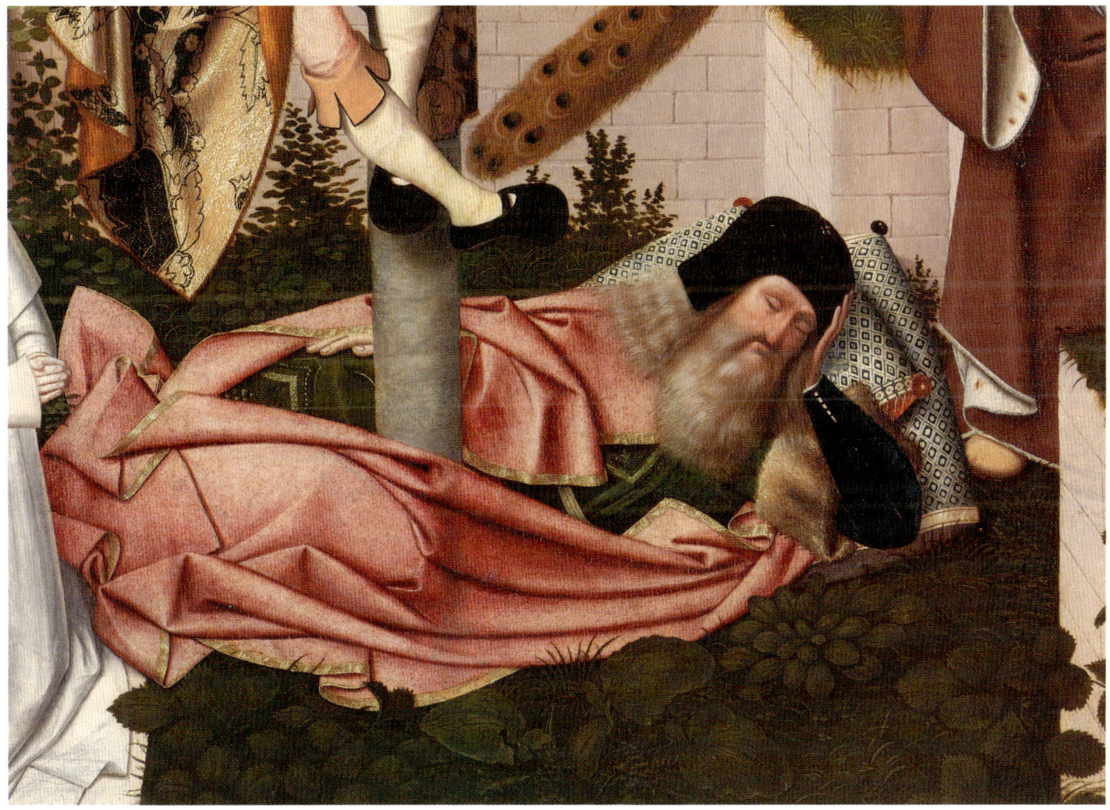

C 6
M 93
Y 96
K 0

C 20
M 35
Y 78
K 9

C 93
M 47
Y 56
K 64

C 6
M 83
Y 92
K 0

C 99
M 53
Y 37
K 31

C 83
M 31
Y 24
K 6

C 51
M 23
Y 21
K 0

C 26
M 0
Y 0
K 0

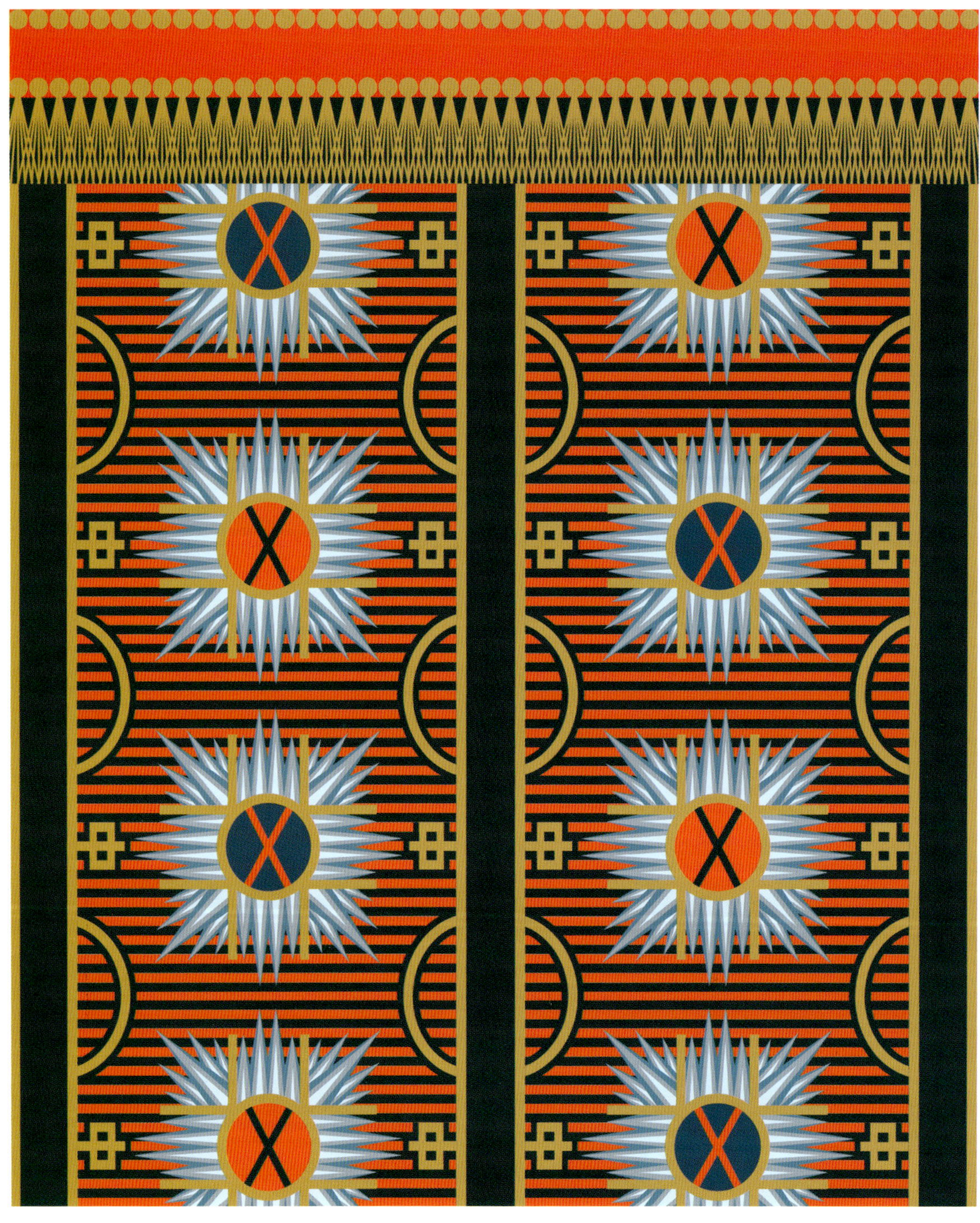

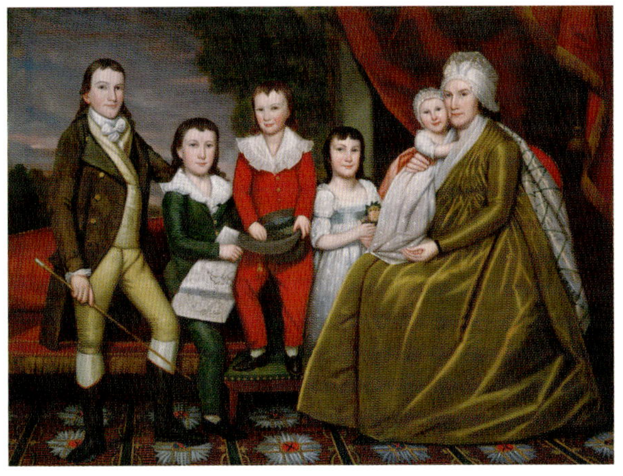

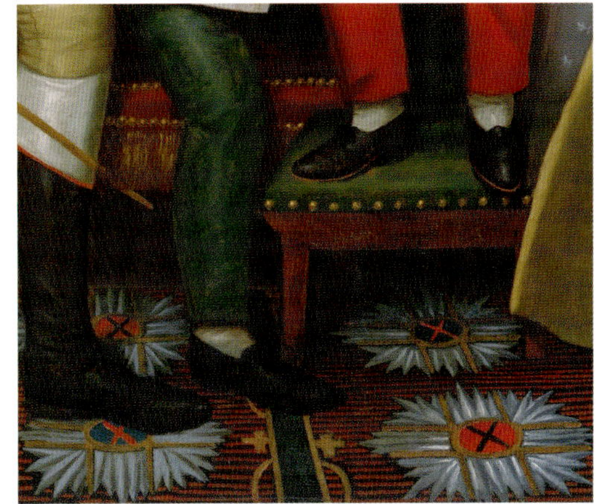

Ralph Earl
Mrs. Noah Smith and Her Children

1798
The Metropolitan Museum of Art, New York

This group portrait, painted by Ralph Earl in Vermont, is perhaps the pinnacle of Earl's ambition as an artist. It depicts Chloe Burall Smith and her five children on a canvas more than 7 feet (2 m) wide and about 5 feet (1.6 m) high. Chloe Burrall Smith was the wife of Noah Smith, who served as a justice of the Vermont Supreme Court. They had eight children together, but the five depicted here are the only ones who survived into adulthood. Ralph Earl was a known loyalist to Britain during the American Revolution and was accused of treason by his fellow citizens in Connecticut. In 1778, he fled to London, where he studied with Benjamin West. Seven years later, he returned to America and spent the remainder of his career traveling throughout New England to find portrait and landscape commissions. Earl depicted textiles in a very lifelike way in his paintings, and although he simplified his style to accord with the taste of his rural patrons, we can still see rich details in the textiles here.

C 0
M 0
Y 0
K100

C 16
M 62
Y 38
K 7

C 2
M 10
Y 22
K 0

C 51
M 19
Y 28
K 0

C 82
M 33
Y 36
K 22

C 5
M 29
Y 98
K 0

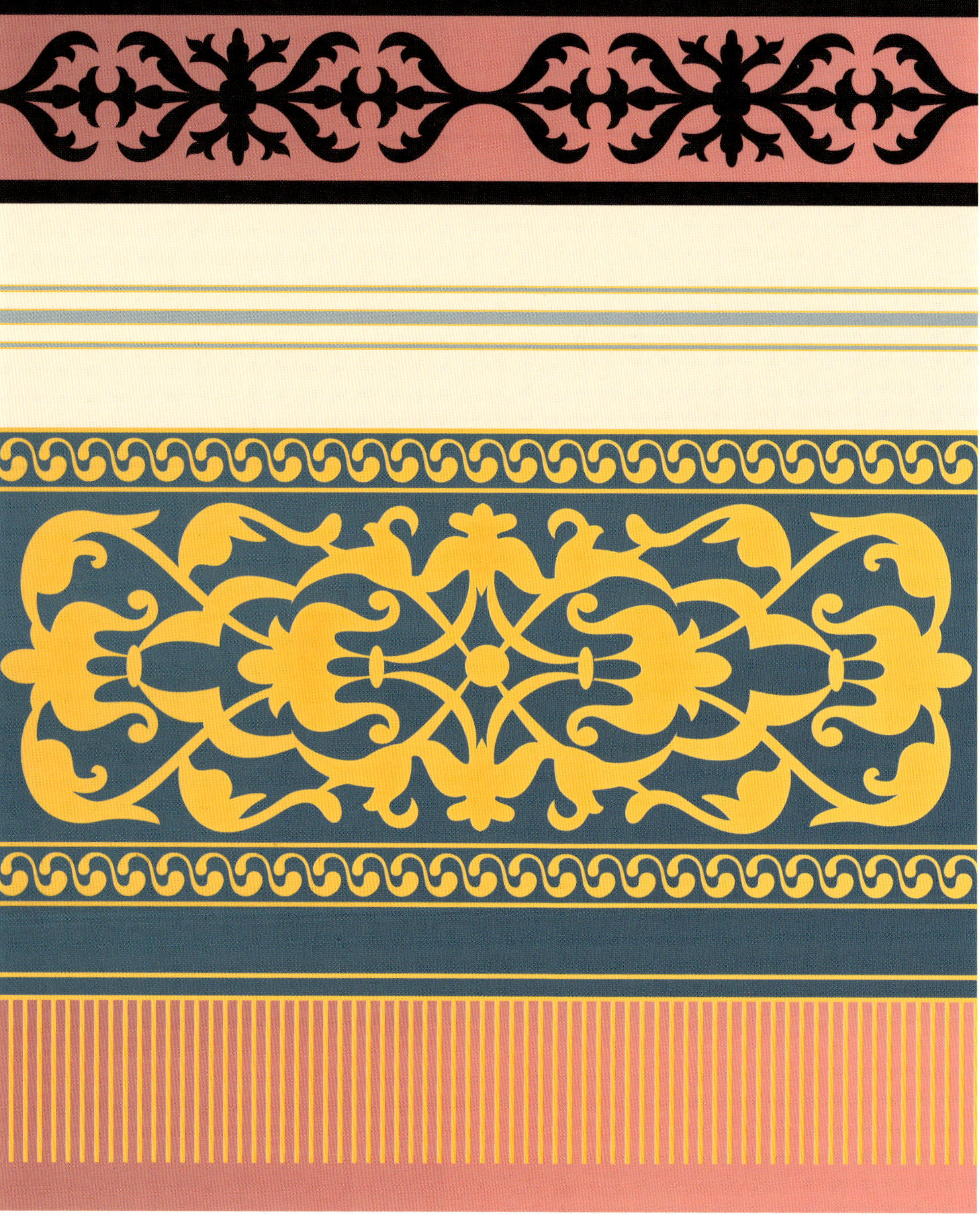

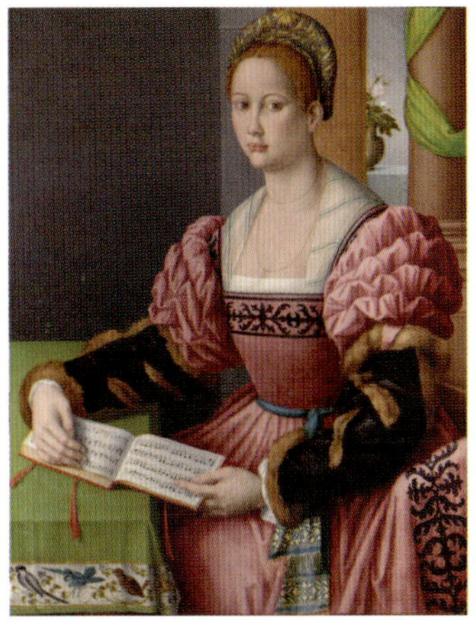

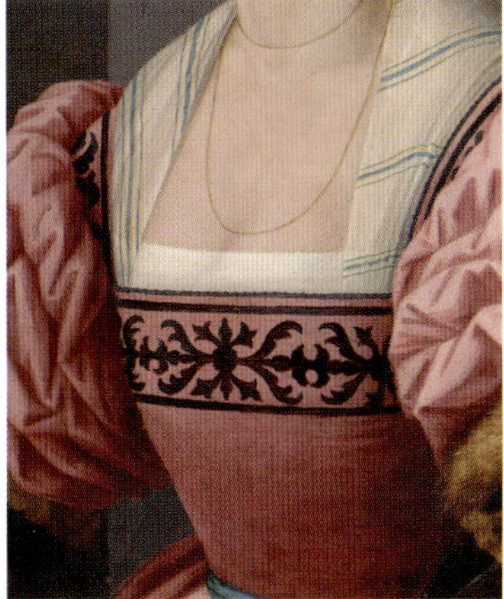

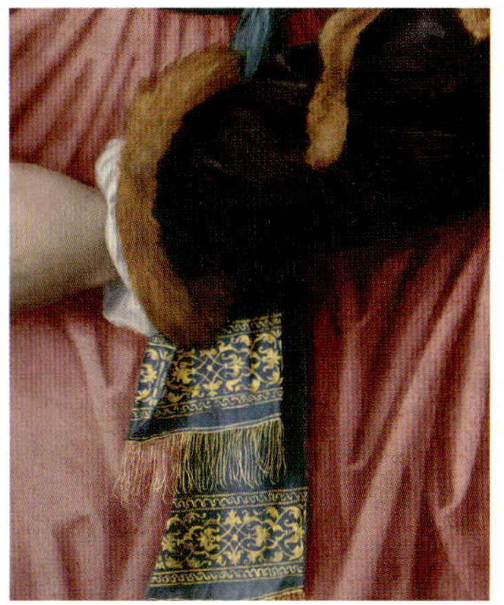

Bachiacca
Portrait of a Woman with a Book of Music

circa 1540–1545
The J. Paul Getty Museum, Los Angeles

Francesco Ubertini, better known as Bachiacca, was famous in Medici Florence not only for his paintings but also for creating a variety of luxury items. Together with his brother, Bachiacca created tapestries, fabrics, and zoological illustrations for the Medici court. This painting brings together the artist's many skills, from the intricate textile designs of the subject's dress, to the three colored birds carefully painted on the edge of the tablecloth. The same zoological design was found in fabrics produced by the artist. The combination of vivid, dissonant colors, such as the green of the tablecloth and the pink of the dress, was probably inspired by Agnolo Bronzino's portraits of the Medici family. From the clothing, education, and poise of the unidentified woman, we can conclude that she was almost certainly an aristocrat. She may have belonged to the Frescobaldi, a family of bankers who once owned the painting. Bachiacca's surprising and eclectic craftsmanship, however, kept him from reaching the fame he perhaps deserved, as his works could not be consistently attributed to a particular category of art.

C 16
M 97
Y 97
K 0

C 0
M 0
Y 0
K100

C 25
M 56
Y 97
K 11

C 7
M 23
Y 46
K 0

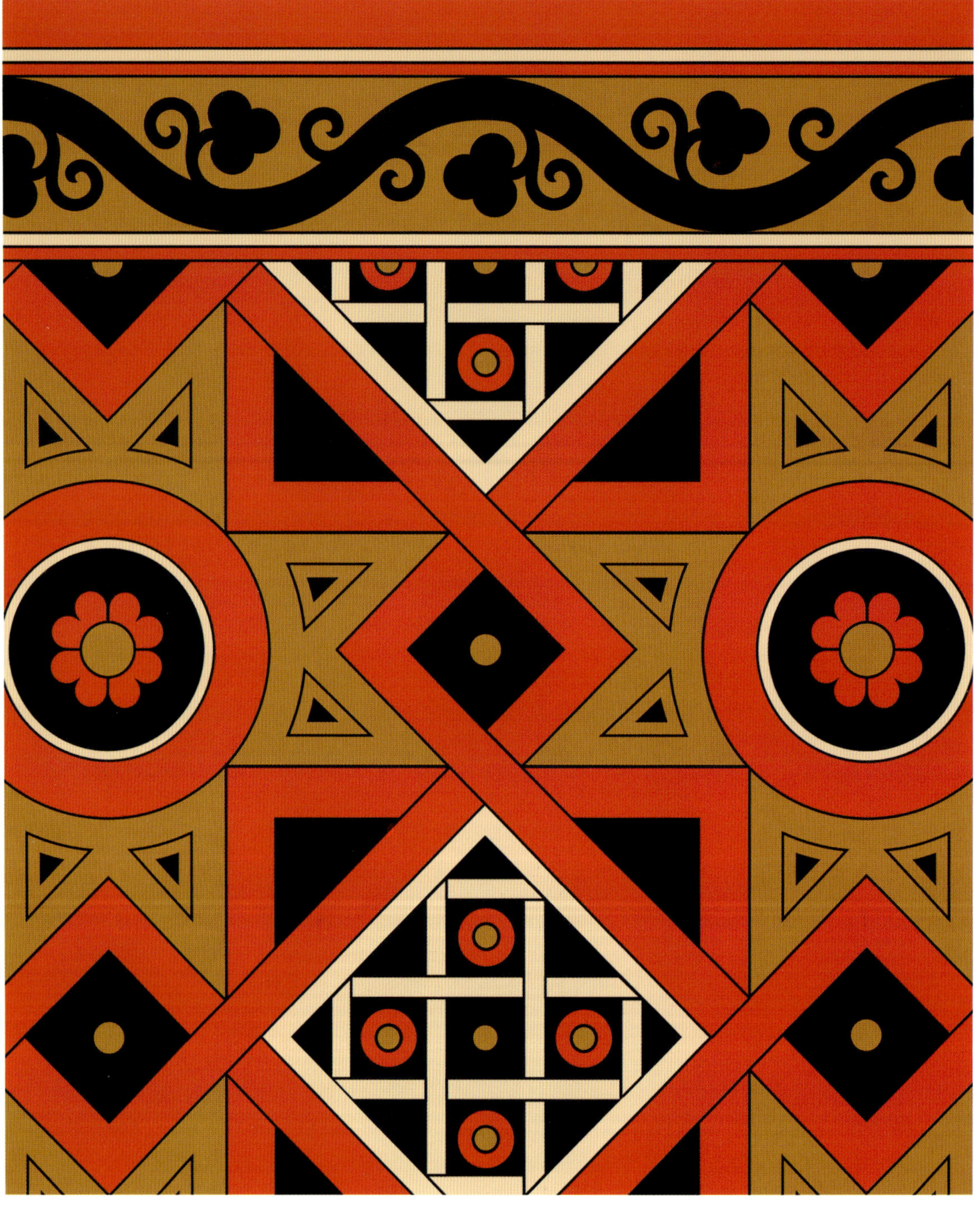

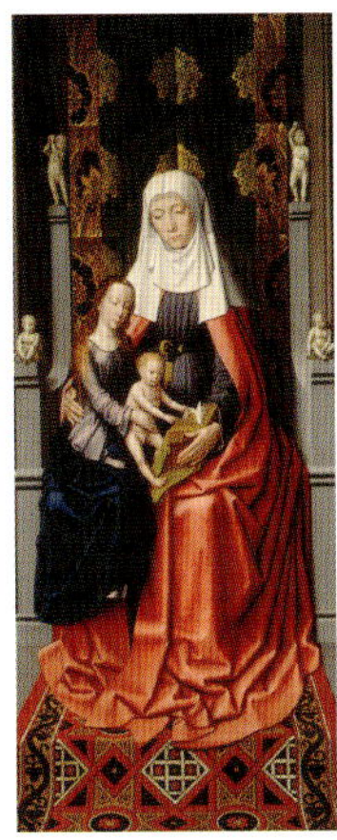

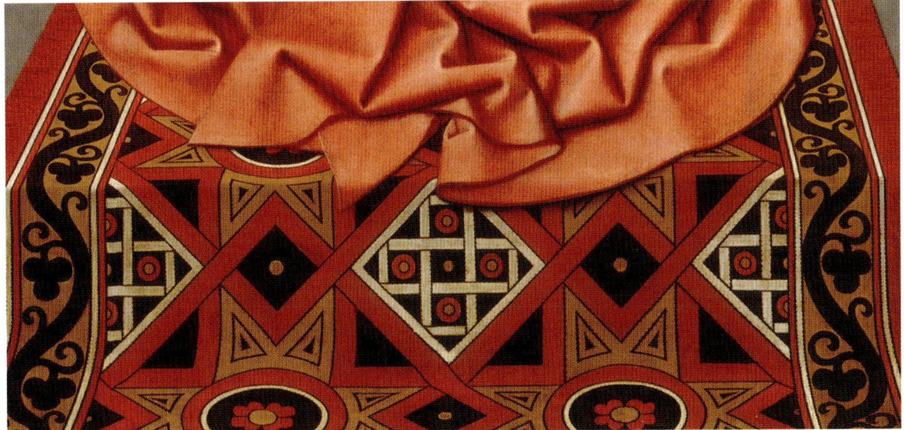

Gerard David
The Saint Anne Altarpiece:
Saint Anne with the Virgin and Child

circa 1500–1520
National Gallery of Art, Washington

Around 1520, the workshop of Gerard David produced an altarpiece consisting of nine panels. This painting is its central scene. It depicts the Virgin Mary's mother, Saint Anne; Mary herself; and the infant Christ. The setting and clothes depicted are extremely sumptuous and rich. When the nine panels are arranged as they should be, the perspective lines of the floor tiles, platform, and Oriental carpet converge perfectly on Saint Anne's heart. The painting was produced for export to either Italy or Spain, but the questionable quality of the work has led to doubts as to whether it was actually executed by David or by an apprentice in his workshop. The motif of the Virgin holding Christ as she turns the pages of a book can be found in other paintings by David, as well as in many paintings of Hans Memling's circle, to which David belonged. When it was first displayed almost five hundred years ago, the giant size of the panel—more than 7 feet (2 m) in height—must have left quite an impression on its viewers.

C 16
M 48
Y 35
K 11

C 19
M 74
Y 96
K 13

C 0
M 28
Y 67
K 0

C 8
M 42
Y100
K 0

C 2
M 92
Y 96
K 0

C 58
M 39
Y 37
K 22

C 99
M 76
Y 49
K 67

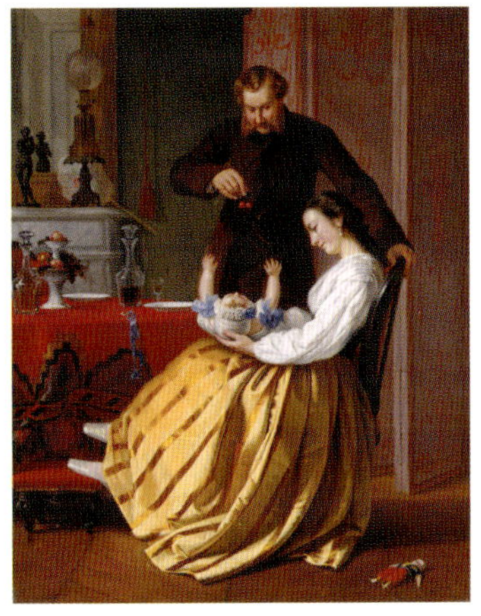

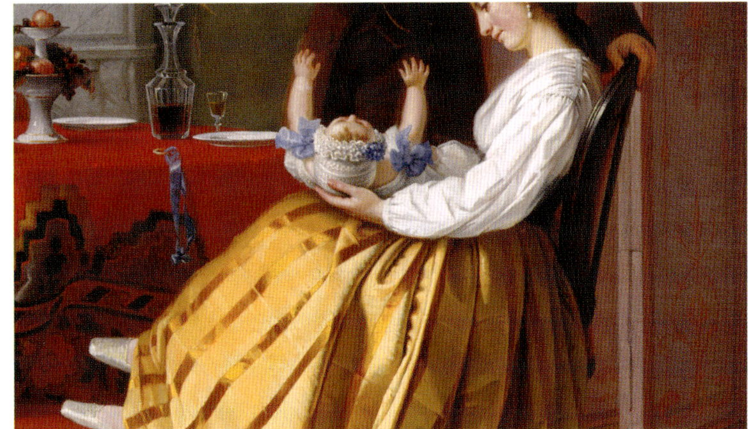

Lilly Martin Spencer
Conversation Piece

circa 1851–1852
The Metropolitan Museum of Art,
New York

This is a scene of everyday tranquility. At the end of a meal a mother holds and looks at her baby, while a smiling father entertains him with a bunch of cherries. This is the kind of scene favored by Lilly Martin Spencer, who is both the painter and the subject of this work. Spencer, the only known professional woman painter in 19th-century America, often used herself and her family members as models for her domestic scenes. In a time when women painted as a hobby, Spencer was encouraged by her highly educated family to make painting a profession and earn some fame. During a time of economic hardship, she was in fact the only member of her family to bring home an income. Spencer's work is characterized by exquisite detail and color in the clothing and textiles, and her detailed representations of everyday objects (such as the Limoges compote and the Carcel lamp) give us a glimpse into the prevailing taste of the time in America.

C 6
M 16
Y 75
K 0

C 0
M 0
Y 0
K100

C 10
M 31
Y 99
K 0

C 49
M 22
Y 30
K 2

C 5
M 5
Y 24
K 0

C 82
M 41
Y 42
K 43

C 25
M 42
Y 98
K 20

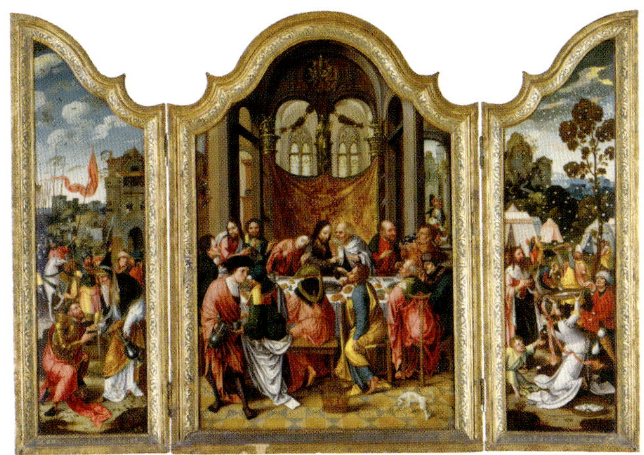

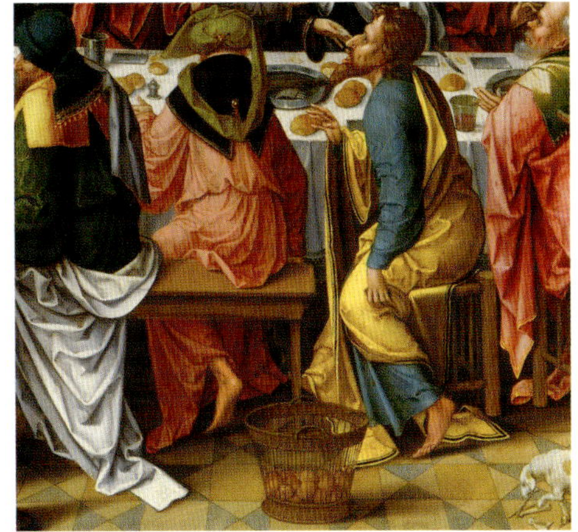

Netherlandish Painters
The Last Supper

1515–1520
The Metropolitan Museum of Art, New York

It is unclear how many artists worked on this altarpiece, but there is evidence of brushstrokes from at least three anonymous masters. These painters seem to belong to the Antwerp Mannerists—an early 16th-century school whose members remain largely anonymous since, for the most part, they did not sign their paintings.
The central panel represents the Last Supper, set in an extremely rich and sumptuous Renaissance structure. The scene is flanked by two scenes of people receiving food: on the left, Abraham is fed by a high priest, and on the right, Moses and the Israelites are fed by manna from heaven, a substance that miraculously fell from the sky. The painting exhibits meticulous attention to detail. From the banquet to the subjects' garments to the drapery and the decoration of the architectural space, every detail is represented with exquisite accuracy.

C 62
M 52
Y 49
K 51

C 0
M 17
Y 55
K 0

C 0
M 9
Y 21
K 0

C 24
M 36
Y 80
K 14

C 00
M 00
Y 00
K100

C 2
M 76
Y 91
K 0

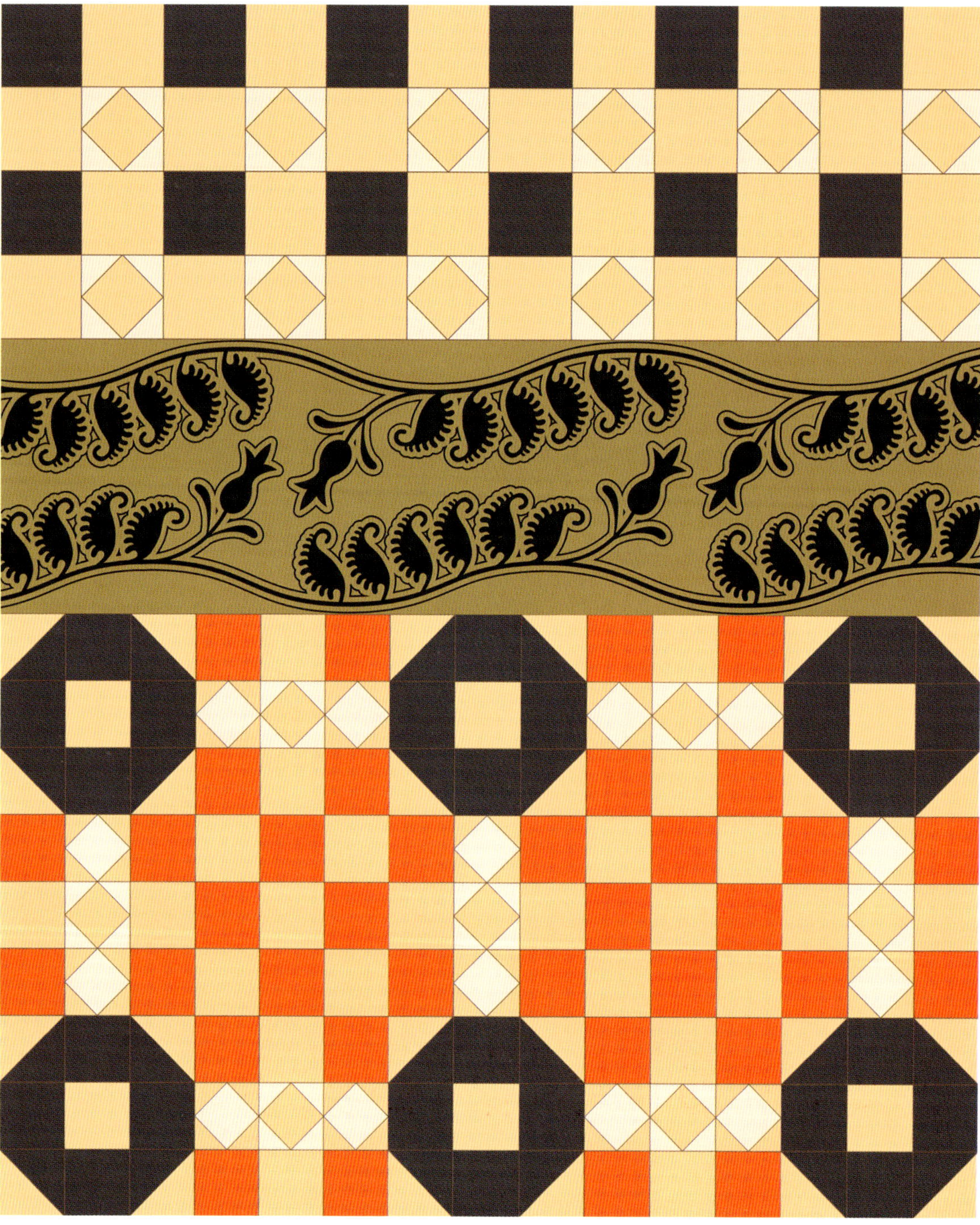

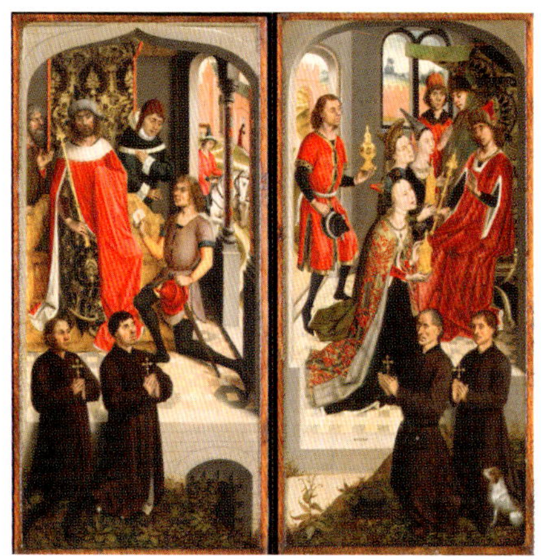

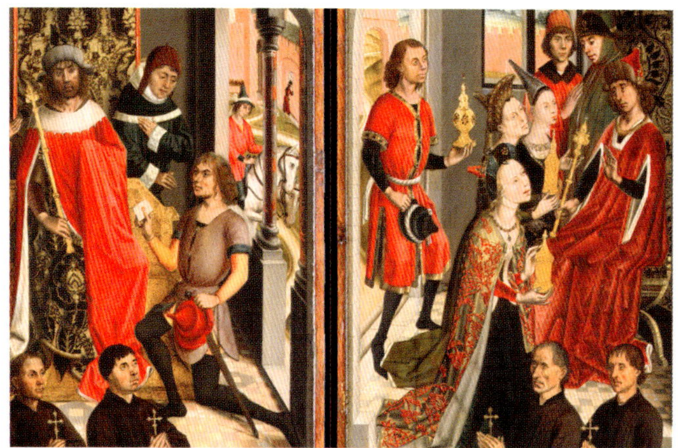

Master of
the Saint Barbara Legend
Abner's Messenger before David (?);
The Queen of Sheba Bringing Gifts
to Solomon

circa 1480
The Metropolitan Museum of Art,
New York

One of the most remarkable features of this work is the artist's extraordinary attention to detail. From the opulent decorations to the clothing and jewelry, the painter rendered material objects with an acute naturalism. This painting is set in a loggia, with an open view out onto a garden. The loggia's back windows also allow us to see what seems to be a defensive wall or castle. Although its setting is apparently expansive, this painting presents a crowded and somewhat chaotic composition of figures in a narrow space. Studies have revealed that this and other paintings attributed to the same artist could have been collaborative studio works. Whether the artist realized this painting with an assistant or collaborated with other Brussels masters, we should not be surprised. Most Netherlandish painters of the 15th and early 16th century led active workshops and met the high demand for their paintings with help from assistants and other masters' studios.

C 40
M 25
Y 22
K 0

C 75
M 36
Y 41
K 25

C 5
M 0
Y 7
K 0

C 38
M 26
Y 45
K 8

C 11
M 20
Y 49
K 0

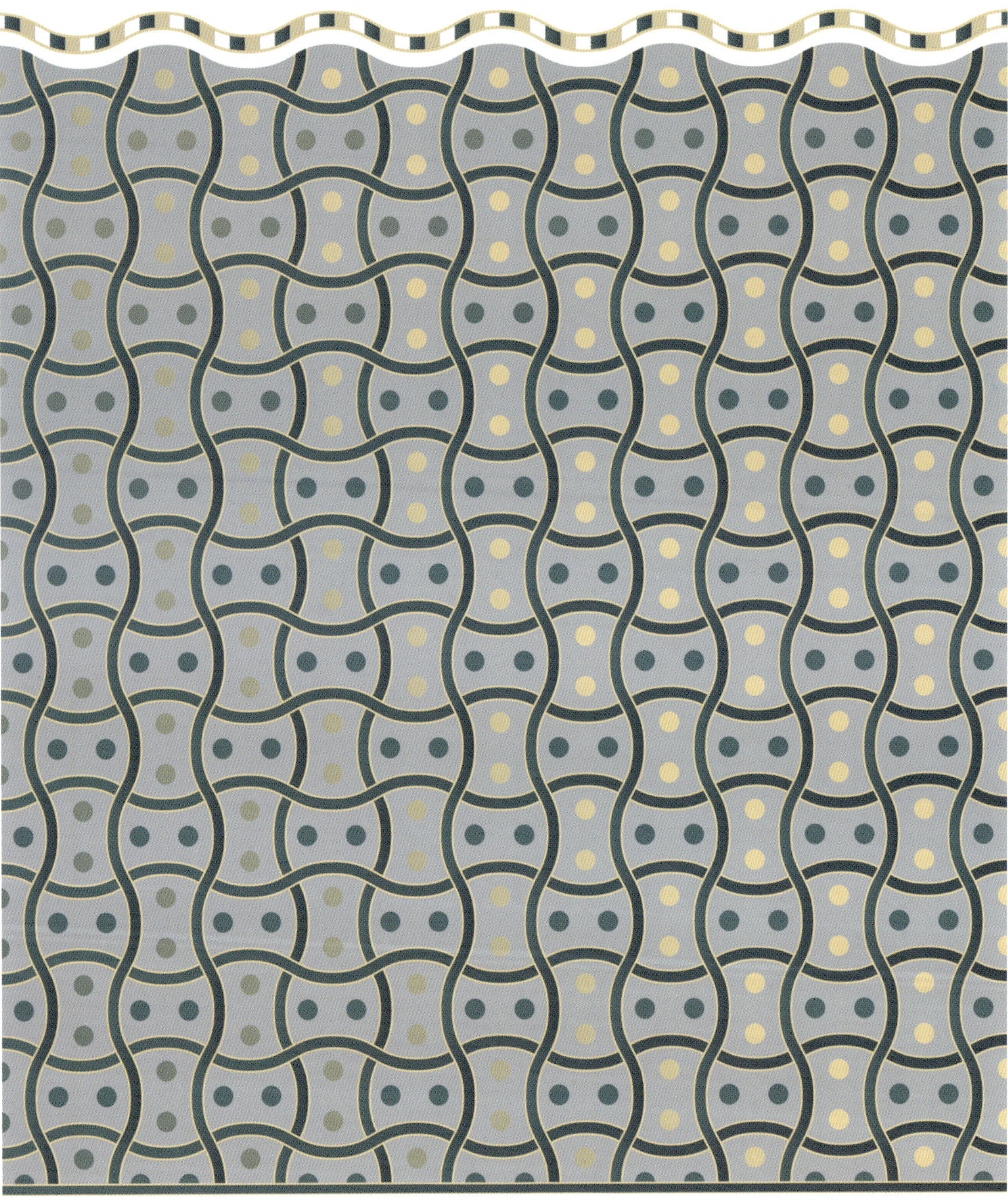

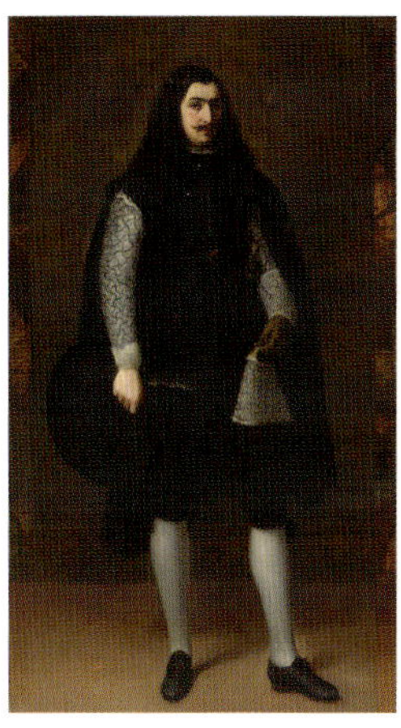

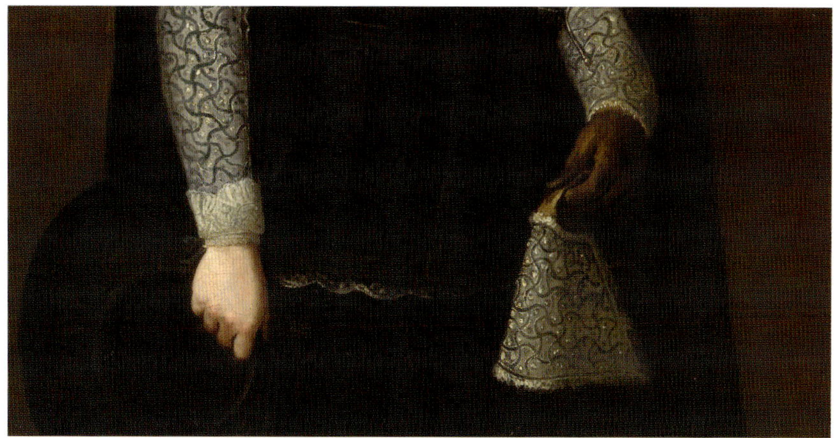

Bartolomé Estebán Murillo
A Knight of Alcántara or Calatrava

circa 1650–1655
The Metropolitan Museum of Art, New York

The subject of this portrait is likely to have been a knight of Alcántara or Calatrava, as he wears a pendant with the symbol of those military orders. In the 19th century, the knight was erroneously identified as Don Pedro Nuñez de Villavicencio, as it was later found that the painting was completed too early for him to have been the subject. The Order of Alcántara was founded to protect the city of that name in western Spain, which was taken from the Muslims in 1214. To defend this conquest, the king of Spain decided to resort to a military order, as the region was located on a border exposed to assault. The Knights of Alcántara became very wealthy from looting during this war, at the expense of their Muslim adversaries. This portrait has been attributed to Bartolomé Estebán Murillo, one of the most important painters in 17th-century Spain. In this painting, we can see evidence of Murillo's interest in secular themes, as well as his convincing Baroque naturalism, shown in the knight's natural facial expression.

C 0
M 0
Y 0
K 100

C 18
M 38
Y 94
K 0

C 24
M 64
Y 95
K 20

C 12
M 94
Y 94
K 14

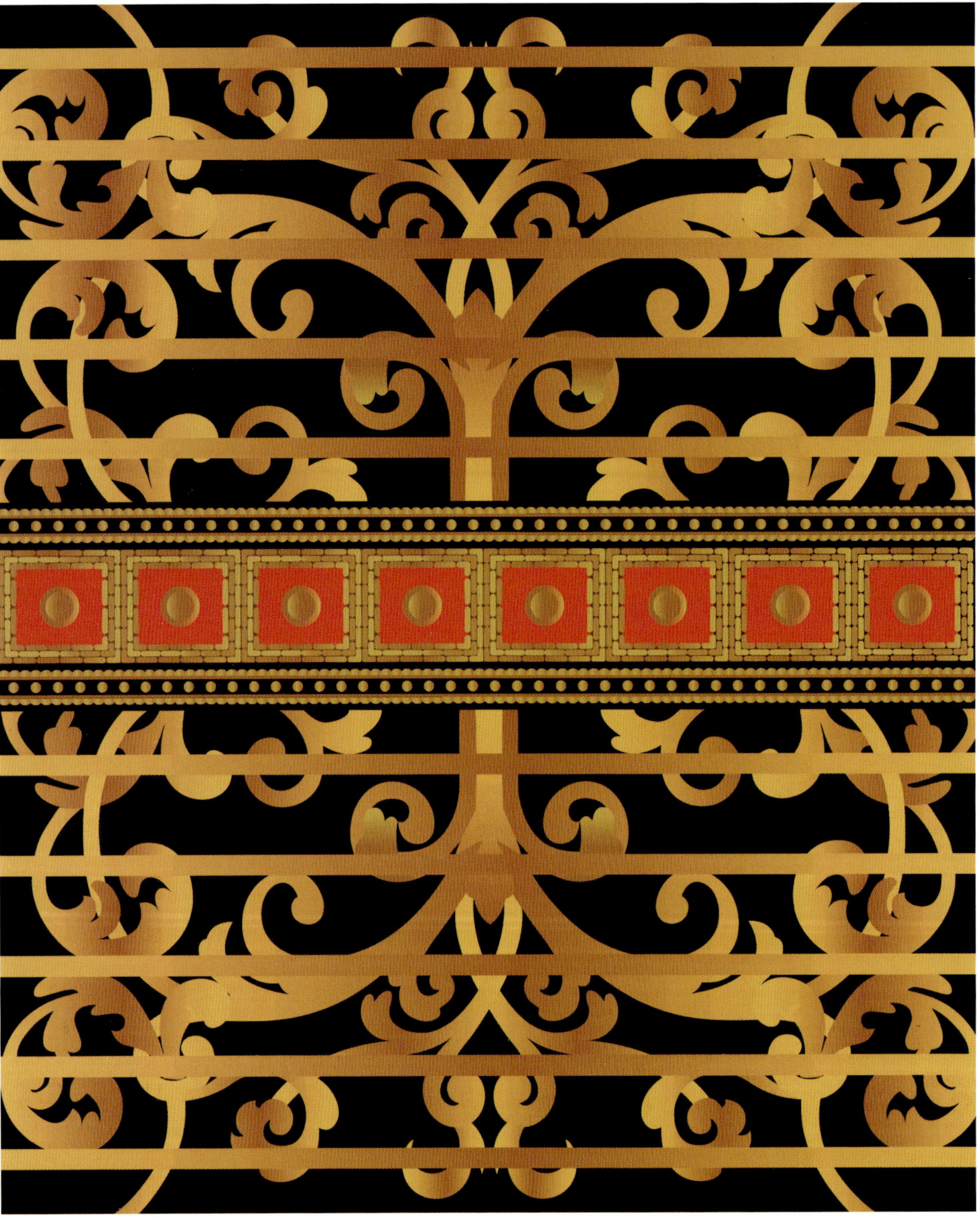

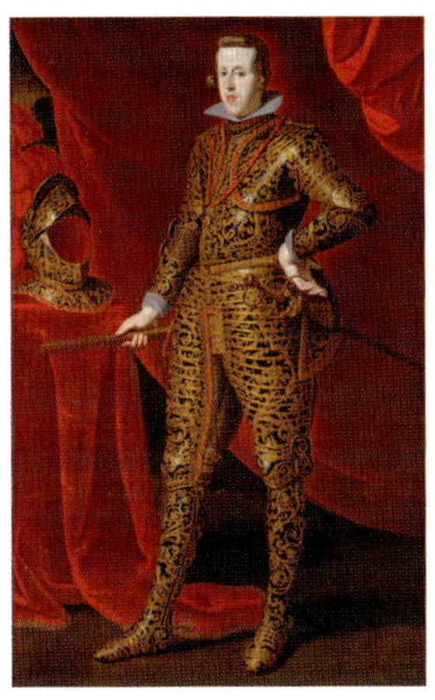

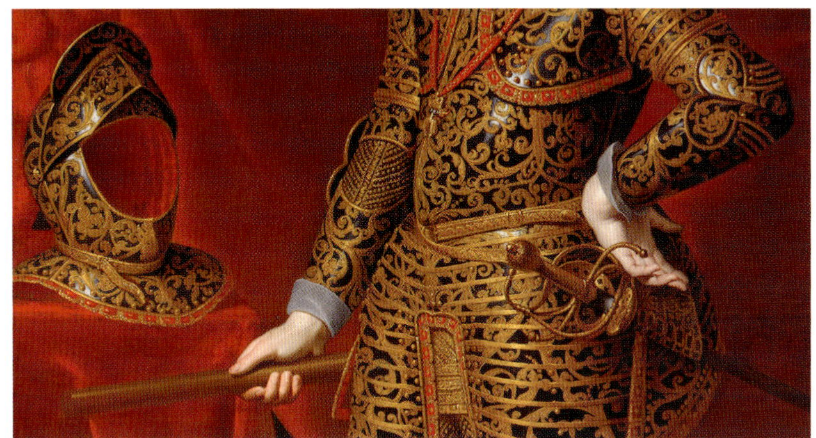

Gaspar de Crayer
Philip IV in Parade Armor

circa 1628
The Metropolitan Museum of Art,
New York

Gaspar de Crayer was one of the most eminent Flemish painters of his time. Although he was not considered by his contemporaries, or by historians of art, to be a man of profound genius, he was a great draftsman and an admirable colorist. De Crayer was a court painter to the governors of the southern Netherlands and painted several portraits of Philip IV. In this painting, the king of Spain is depicted in richly decorated Flemish cavalry armor. Just a few decades earlier, a change in taste and fashion had occurred that entailed a new acceptance of the human body, its shapes and physicality. In this period, new, tighter armor was produced in a way that would better display the contours of the wearer's form. Armor was often encrusted with gold and silver and decorated with fluting and etching, as we can see in this painting. There are many different accounts of Philip's personality. Victorian authors described him as a weak, debauched individual who deferred to others too much. On the contrary, his contemporaries perceived him as the model of Baroque kingship, and foreign visitors remained impressed by his poise, some even claiming that he was so impassive in public that he resembled a statue.

C 0
M 6
Y 37
K 0

C 55
M 50
Y 90
K 60

C 47
M 44
Y 99
K 38

C 0
M 56
Y 100
K 0

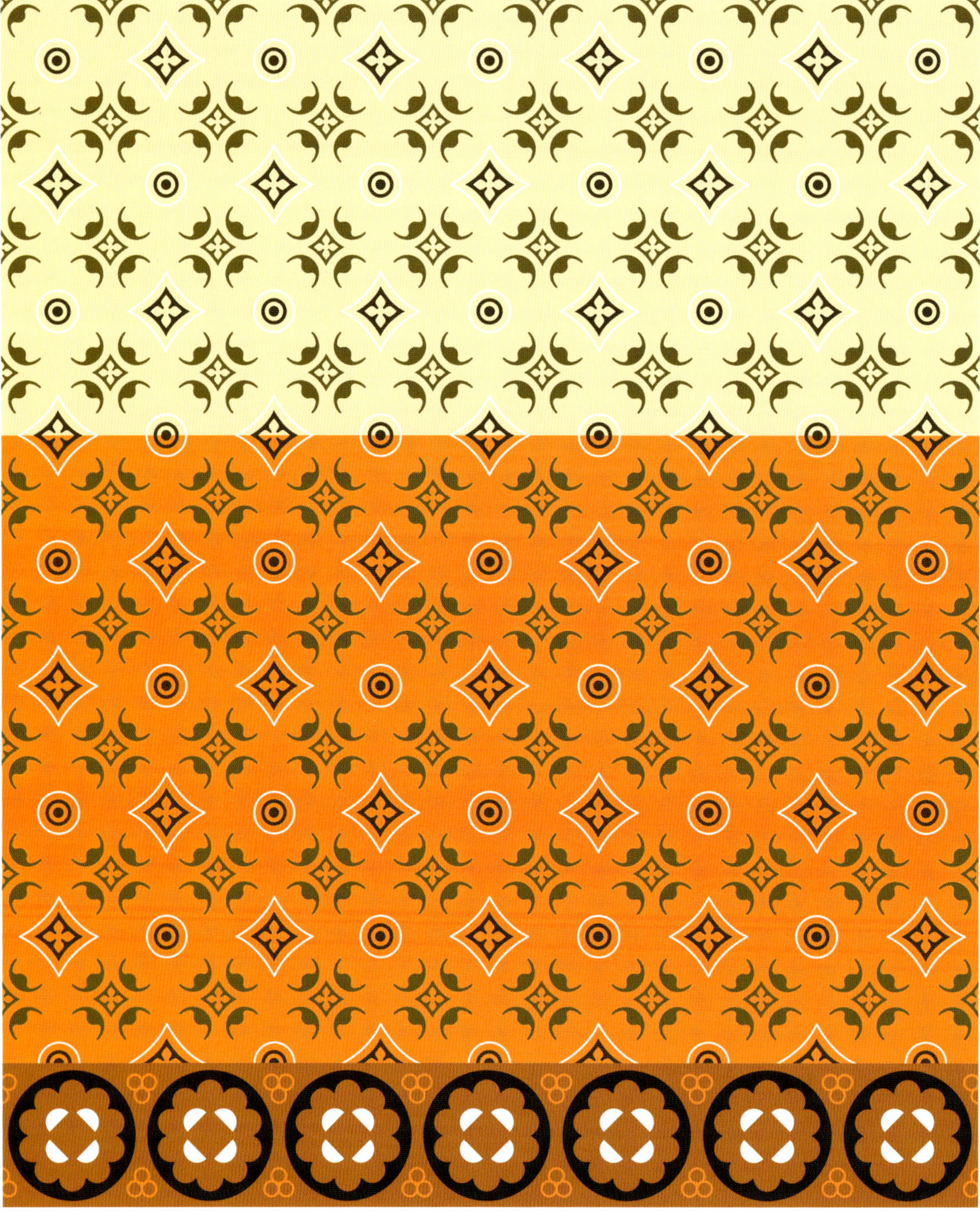

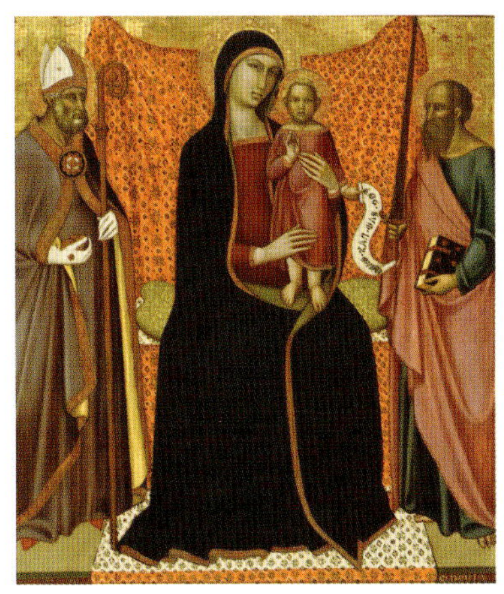

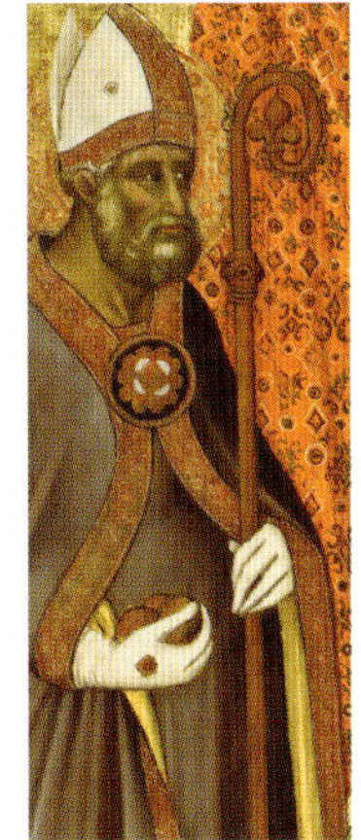

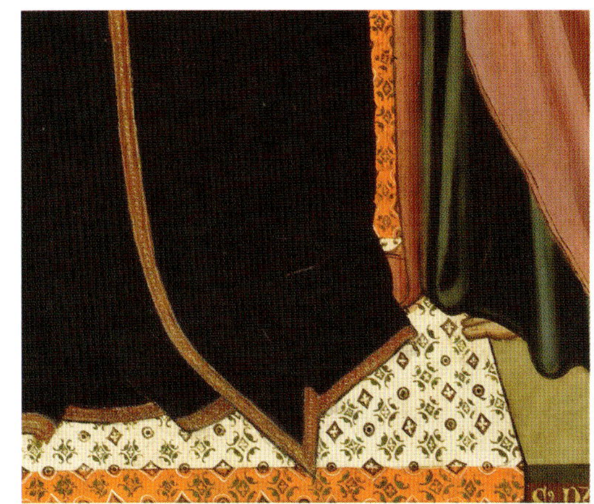

Luca di Tommè
Madonna and Child
with Saints Nicholas and Paul

circa 1370
Los Angeles County Museum of Art

Luca di Tommè was not an artistic innovator. He worked in Siena in the second half of the 14th century, and his main accomplishment seems to have been to sustain the decorative Sienese style, which survived well into the 15th century. Contemporary records suggest that Luca was a well-known, prolific, and respected artist. In this painting, the Virgin is sitting on a throne, holding a standing infant Christ who displays a scroll that reads "Ego sum lux mundi" (I am the light of the world). On the left, Saint Nicholas carries a crosier, the hooked staff that recalls a shepherd's crook, as the bishop is to be the shepherd of people. Saint Nicholas also holds three gold balls, representing the gold he gave to provide dowries for impoverished maidens. On the other side, Saint Paul holds a sword. This symbolizes both his past and his martyrdom. Although Saint Paul had initially persecuted Christians, he converted to Christianity and started to spread the word of God among the kings and people of Israel. As a result, he was decapitated with a sword by the Romans.

C 18
M 18
Y 79
K 13

C 9
M 20
Y 68
K 2

C 68
M 25
Y 68
K 25

C 54
M 86
Y 36
K 75

C 58
M 42
Y 13
K 3

C 0
M 90
Y 67
K 6

C 0
M 5
Y 65
K 0

C 88
M 34
Y 62
K 59

C 8
M 0
Y 11
K 0

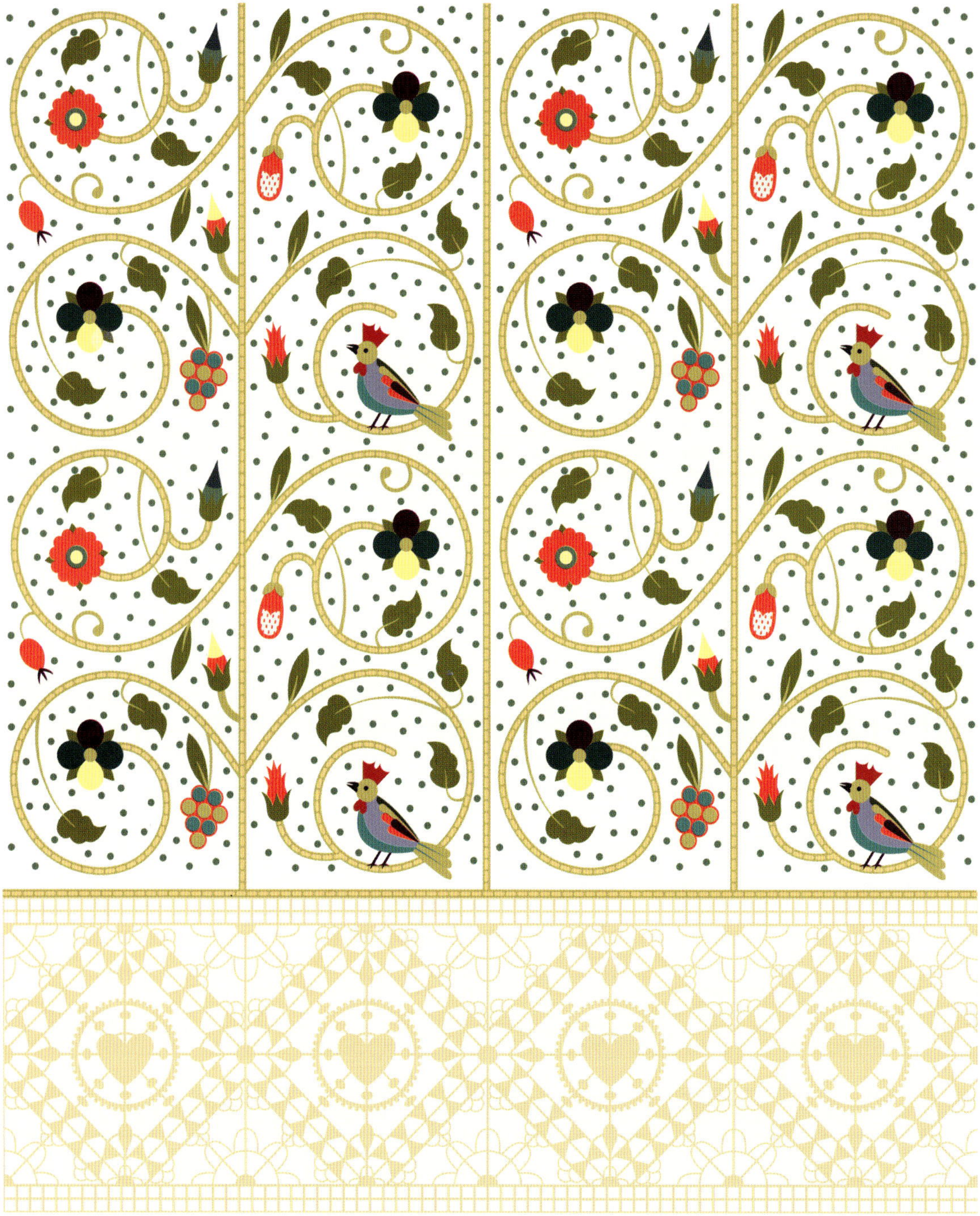

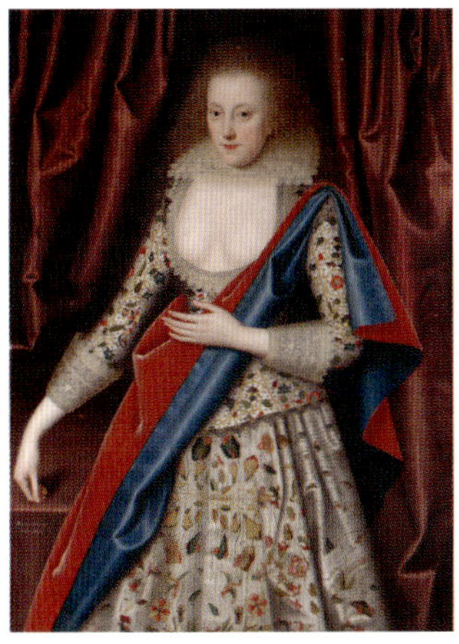

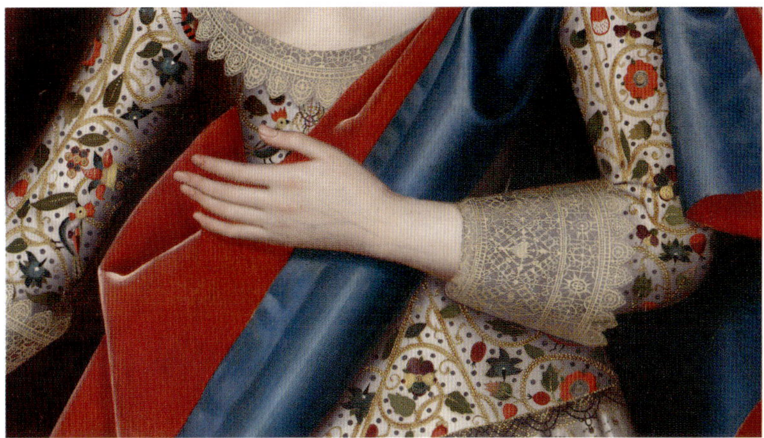

William Larkin
Portrait of a Young Lady, possibly Jane, Lady Thornhaugh

1617
Yale Center for British Art, New Haven

The portraits that this artist painted for the members of the court of King James I of England have become invaluable records of fashion trends in the Jacobean era. Textiles, lace, jewelry, and embroidery, as well as curtains and carpets, are the true protagonists of the portraits completed by the so-called Curtain Master, who was only identified as William Larkin in 1969. Besides Larkin's brilliant attention to detail, a key feature of his work was the way he framed his subjects within draped silk curtains. Lady Thornhaugh's gown is an example of the playful textile patterns that were popular at the time. The gown is covered in fantastical flora and fauna, including insects, birds, and sea monsters diving in and out of the fabric. This is a clear example of the passage from a Renaissance style, inspired by classical antiquity, to a Baroque style, which was more variegated and full of ornaments and curves. Larkin's work marks in fact the last stage of a tradition of British portraiture in which the sitter was painted in a meticulously rendered environment, with each detail carefully delineated—from background to face, garments, and props.

C100
M 71
Y 56
K 72

C 16
M 91
Y 49
K 53

C 0
M 25
Y 75
K 0

C 0
M 1
Y 10
K 0

C 6
M 15
Y 33
K 0

C 13
M 76
Y 56
K 35

C 67
M 48
Y 46
K 62

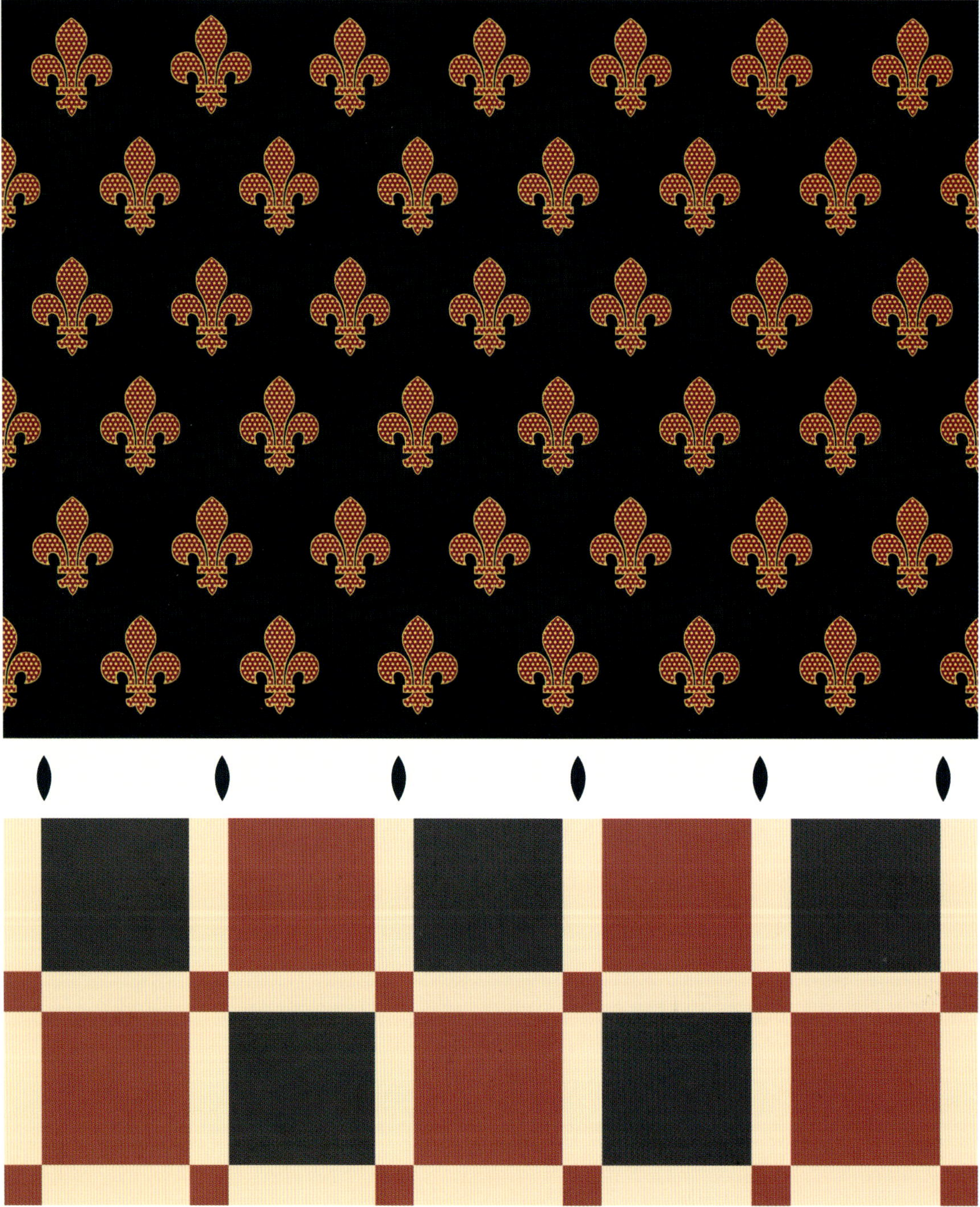

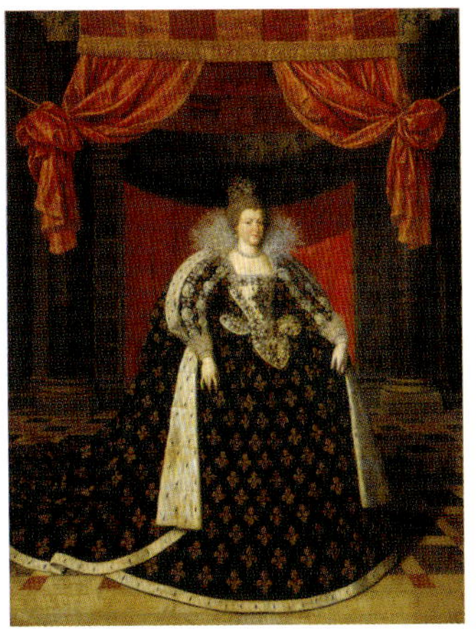

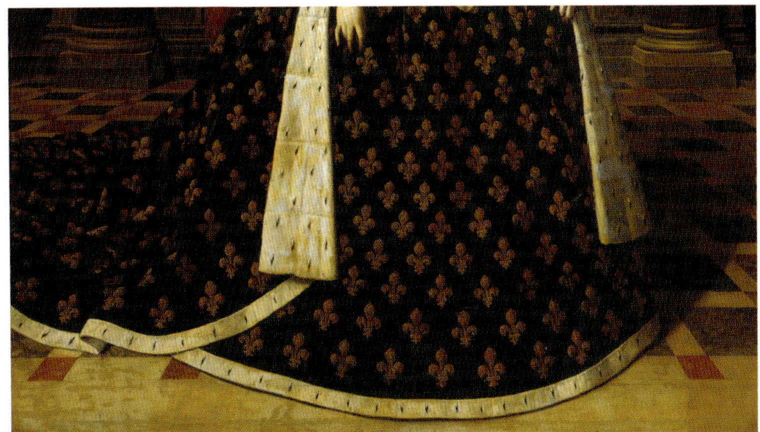

Workshop of
Frans Pourbus the Younger
Marie de' Medici,
Consort of Henry IV, King of France

1590–1620
Rijksmuseum, Amsterdam

This painting depicts the thirty-seven-year-old Marie de' Medici, second wife of King Henry IV of France, on the eve of her coronation in 1610. It is what some would consider a "parade portrait": the subject is dressed in ceremonial costume, showing off an unparalleled wealth of jewels, velvets, embroideries, ruffs, and silks. The backdrop is laden with palatial marble columns, tiles, and heavy draperies. The day after Marie's coronation, her husband was assassinated and she was made regent of her son. Some historians argue that she must have known about the king's assassination before it happened but did not do anything to prevent it. Marie was surely known for her ceaseless political intrigues, as well as for her vulgar quarrels with the numerous mistresses who shared her husband's bed. Indeed, her marriage to King Henry had never been a happy one, even from the very first day. Henry did not show up on the day of their wedding, which was attended by four thousand guests in Florence. The two were therefore married by proxy.

C 6
M 23
Y 41
K 0

C 18
M 45
Y 77
K 0

C 20
M 55
Y 88
K 0

C 83
M 56
Y 55
K 69

C 6
M100
Y 93
K 14

C 11
M 76
Y 58
K 0

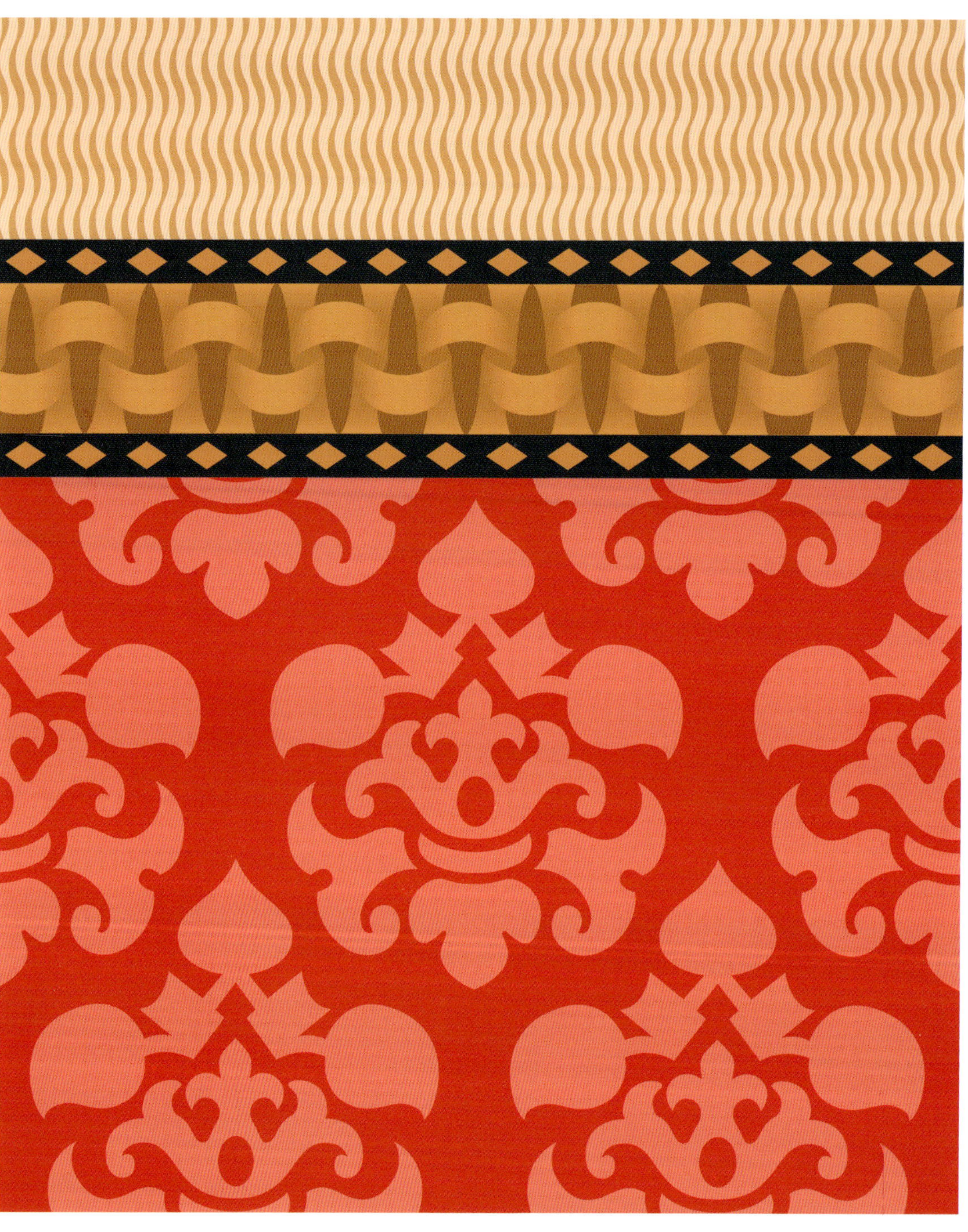

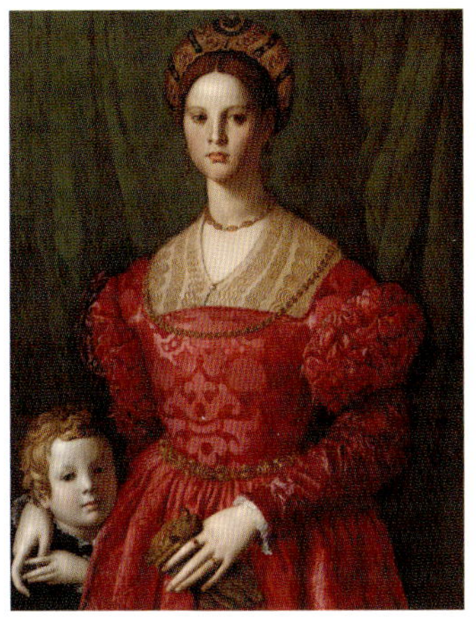

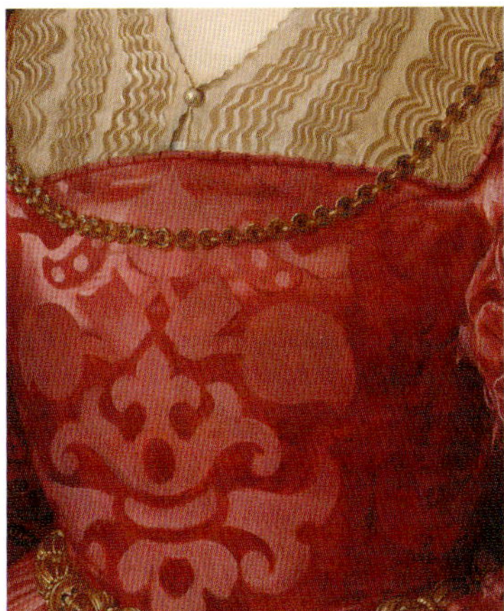

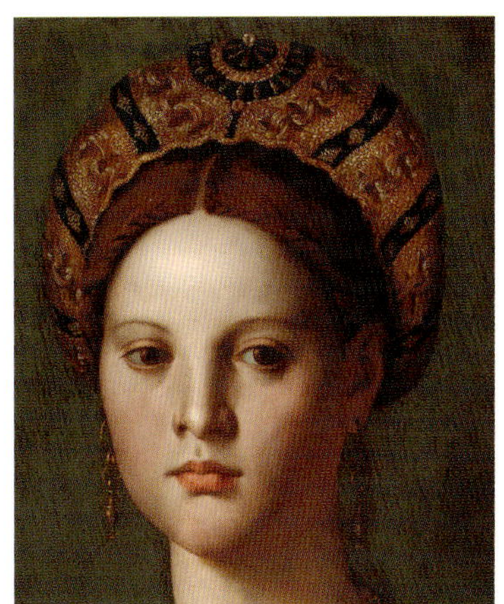

Agnolo Bronzino
A Young Woman and Her Little Boy

circa 1540
National Gallery of Art, Washington

A Young Woman and Her Little Boy is proof that in the hands of a master like Agnolo Bronzino oil paint can be used to almost the same effect as Photoshop to retouch an already existing image. Initially, the child was not meant to be part of the portrait, which explains why the woman occupies most of the available space. Only during a later, second round of painting was the boy added. When he returned to the painting, Bronzino also decided to update the young woman's attire to keep up with the fashion of the time. He added her gloves, enlarged and added details to her headdress, and widened the sleeves of her richly decorated dress.
As Bronzino was the official portraitist to Cosimo de' Medici, the noblewoman represented here is likely to be a member of his court. This theory about her identity is also strengthened by her expensive-looking attire, as well as by her static and calm pose. Bronzino was known for his depictions of cool, unemotional women, which influenced the course of court portraiture throughout Europe for more than a century.

C 0
M 95
Y 75
K 25

C 20
M 49
Y 92
K 13

C 15
M 37
Y 42
K 0

C 40
M 30
Y 25
K 3

C 61
M 48
Y 85
K 64

C 10
M 18
Y 38
K 0

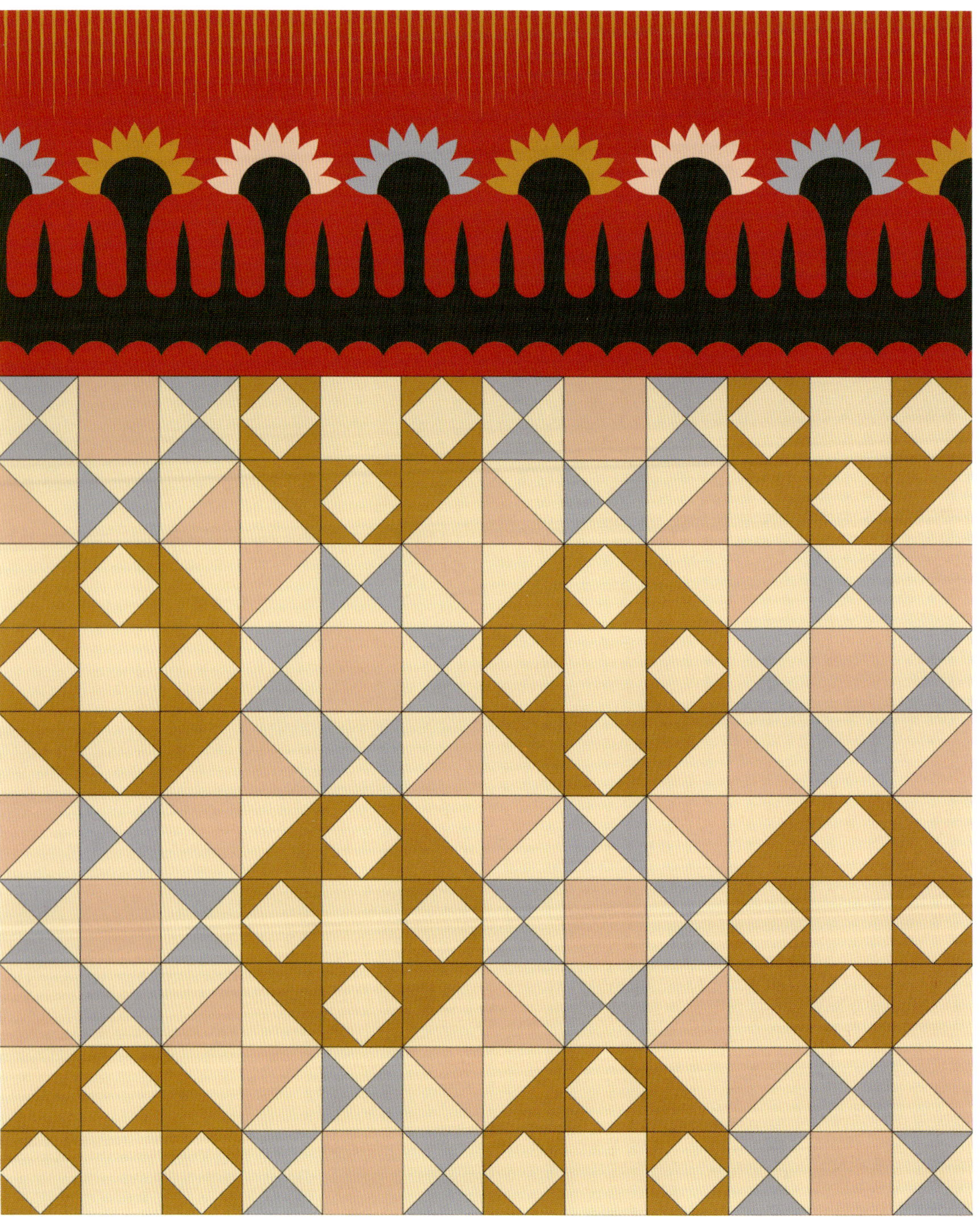

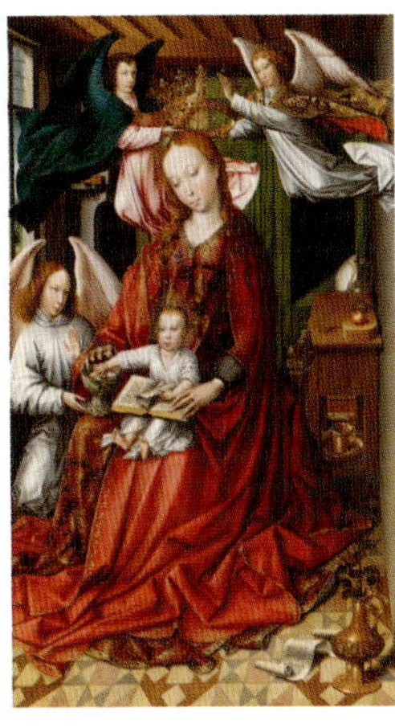 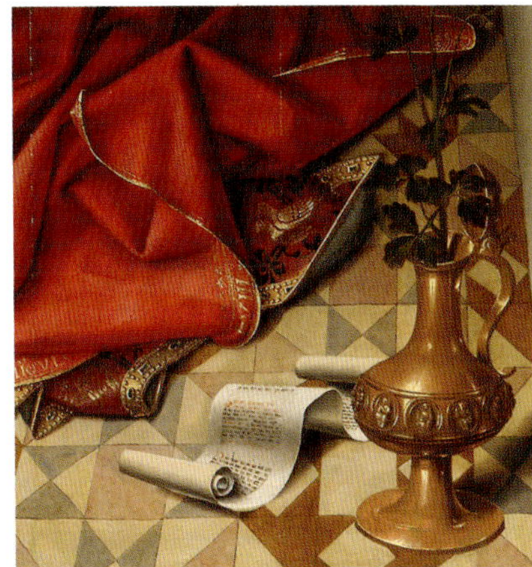 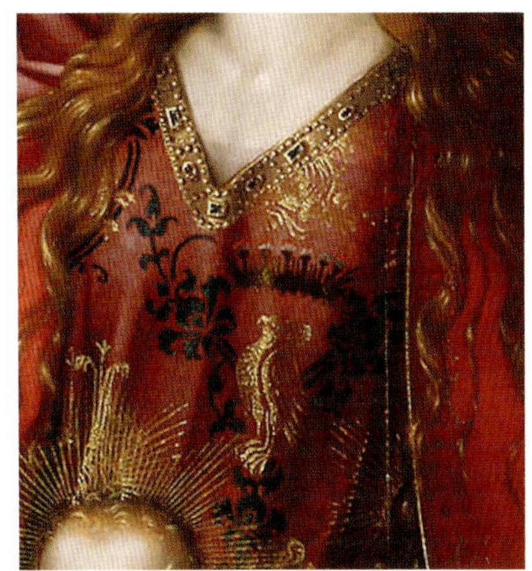

Colyn de Coter
Virgin and Child Crowned by Angels

1490–1495
The Art Institute of Chicago

One of the most remarkable features of Colyn de Coter's work is his attempt to emphasize both the human and the divine aspects of Christ's nature. In this painting, for example, the infant Christ already seems to have adult facial expressions. He is humanized, however, through his infantile movements: with one hand he touches the book that his mother is holding, and with the other he reaches out to a bowl of fruit or flowers offered to him by an angel. Another interesting characteristic of de Coter's style is his claustrophobic treatment of space, which is clearly seen in the way that this traditional Netherlandish bedchamber is almost entirely filled by the figures who occupy it. The perspective is also exaggerated in order to show both the wooden ceiling and the tiled floor. De Coter was also very talented in reproducing little decorative elements, from tiles and ceiling beams to garments and furnishings. One remarkable example is the Virgin's red garment, decorated in gold and blue embroidery.

C 26
M 43
Y 59
K 20

C 58
M 35
Y 38
K 36

C 0
M 0
Y 0
K100

C 20
M 35
Y 85
K 7

C 64
M 41
Y 44
K 55

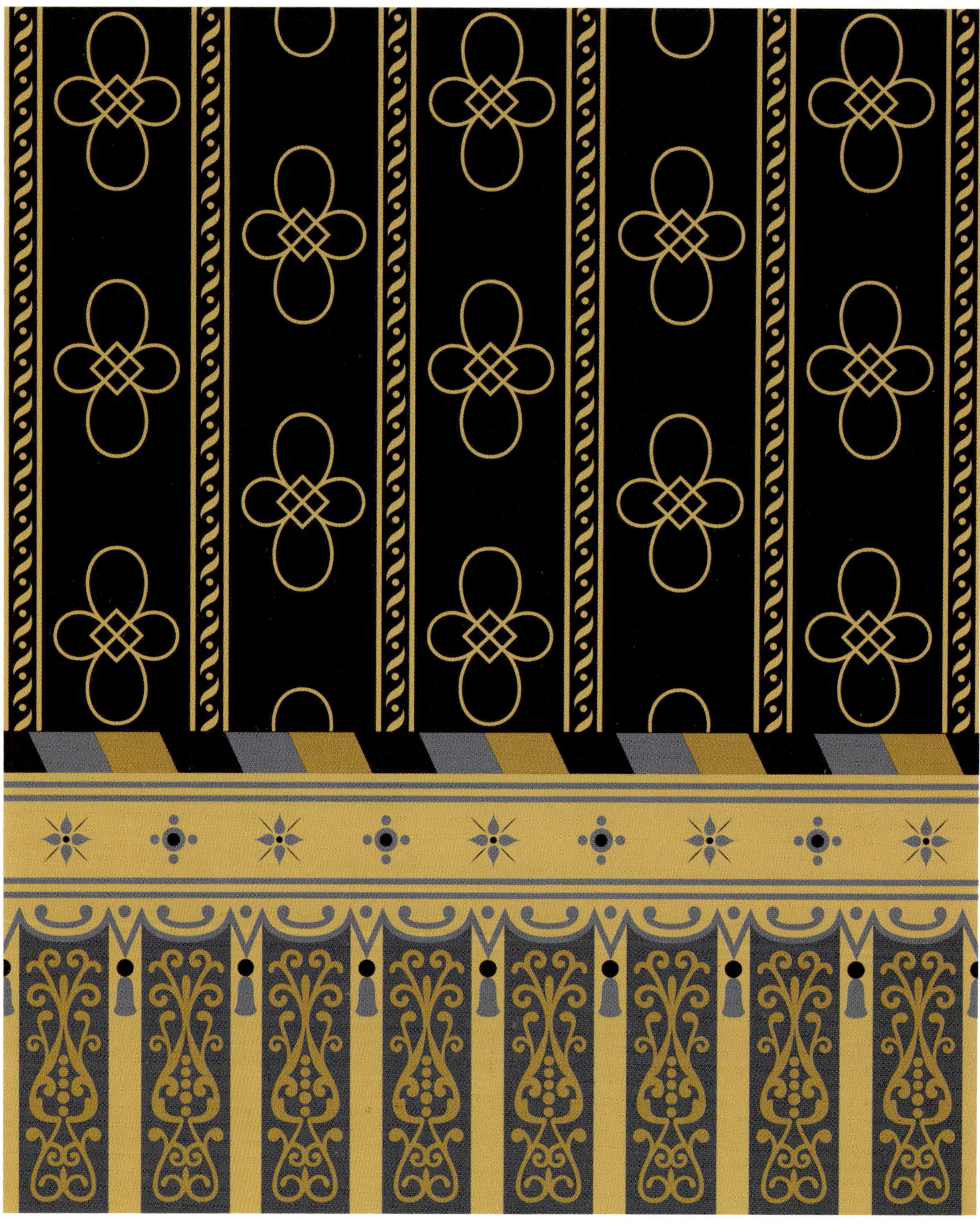

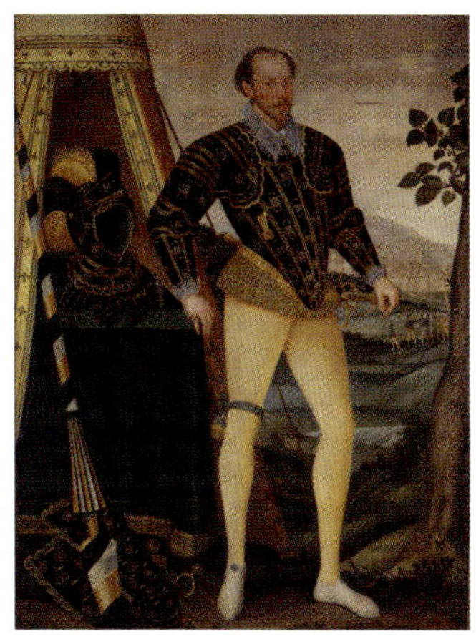

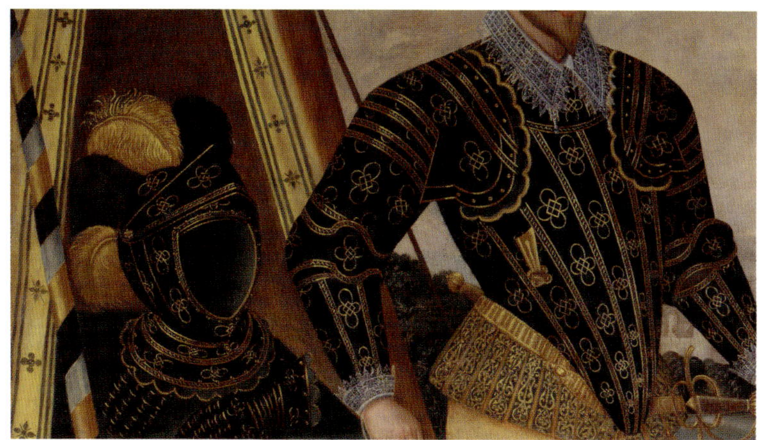

Daniël van den Queborne
Sir William Drury, of Hawstead, Suffolk

1587
Yale Center for British Art, New Haven

William Drury was an English statesman and soldier in the Elizabethan era. Part of a powerful family, Drury inherited a large piece of land in Suffolk where he hosted many important members of Queen Elizabeth's court. This included the queen herself, whom Sir William welcomed with a "costly and delicate dinner" in May 1578. Drury commissioned this portrait with the aim of promoting and assuring his honor and status, and to affirm the justness of his military appointment by Lord Willoughby after he had disobeyed some of Queen Elizabeth's orders. The aim of the painting is made clear by the Italian word *sconsolato*, meaning "afflicted," placed to the right of Sir William. The full-length painting depicts Sir William in ceremonial tournament armor, encrusted with gold decoration, conveying his elegance and athleticism. Drury also wears men's jewelry, including a ring on his right hand and a hoop earring. Earrings had become popular among male courtiers of the time, although they were mainly associated with maritime explorers and literary figures. A year later, Sir William would die in a duel in France.

C 24
M 22
Y 46
K 8

C 33
M 37
Y 65
K 29

C 12
M 36
Y 93
K 13

C 89
M 18
Y 64
K 17

C 44
M 53
Y 24
K 13

C 80
M 20
Y 37
K 11

C 24
M 9
Y 35
K 0

C 7
M 11
Y 68
K 0

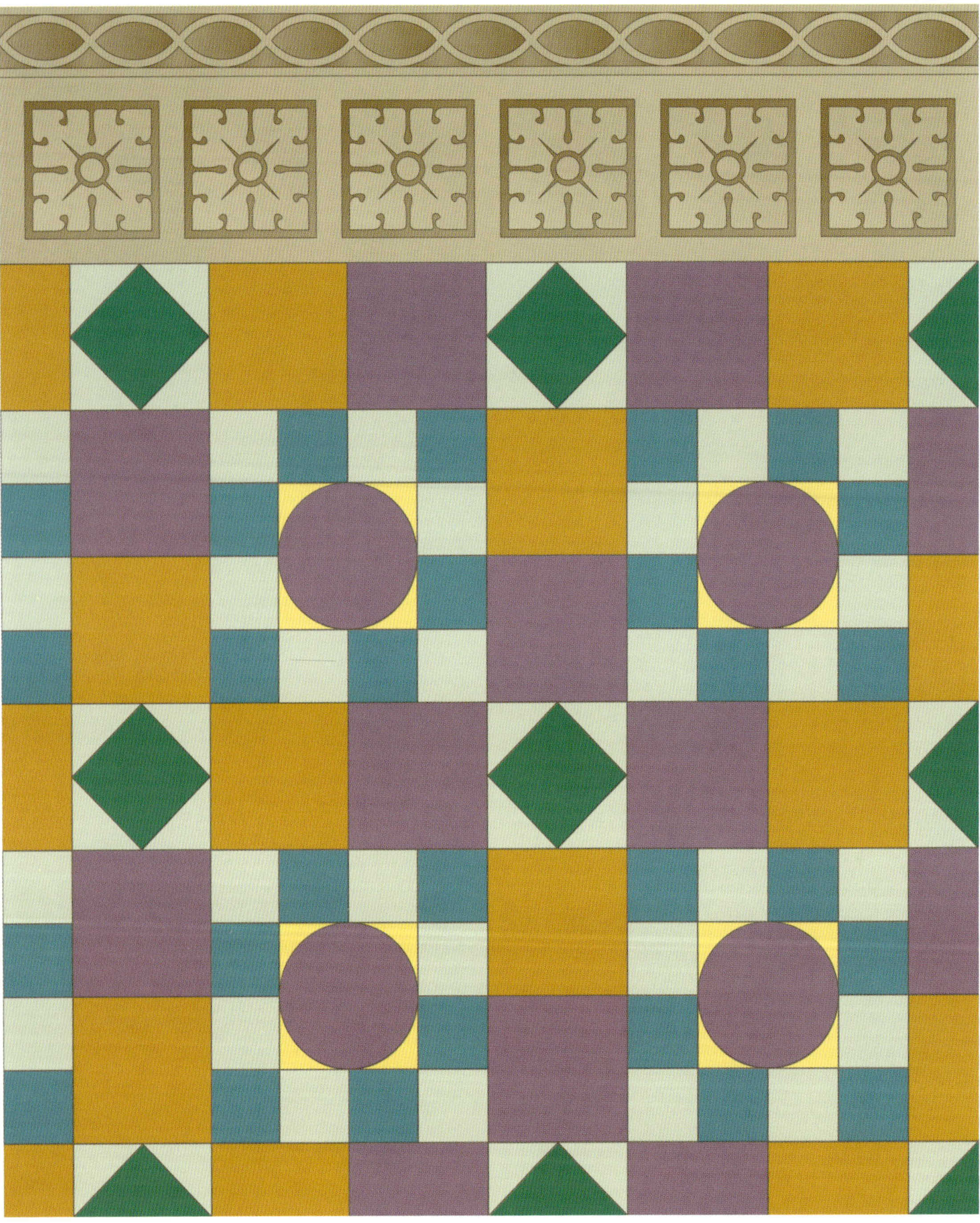

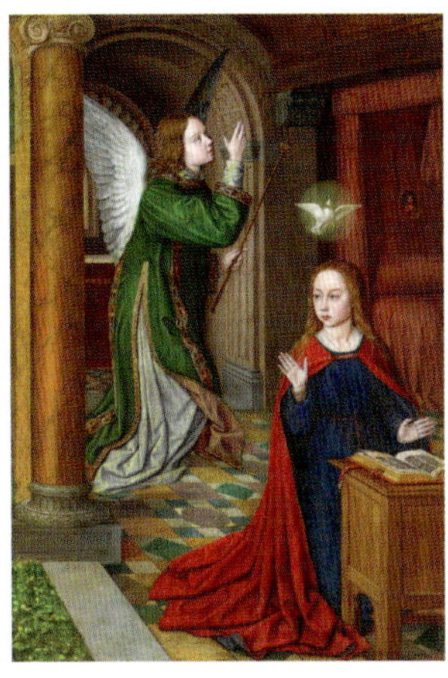

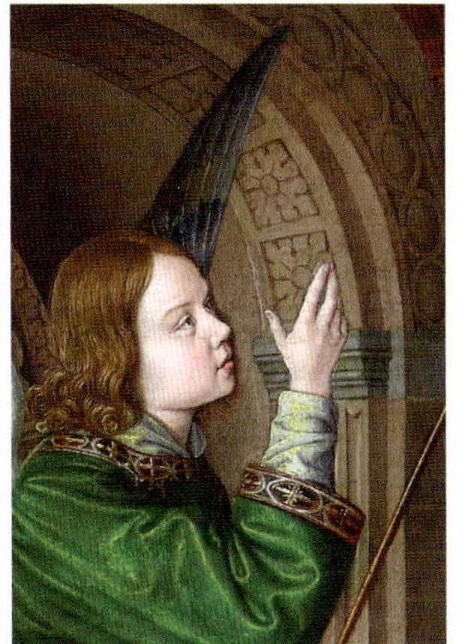

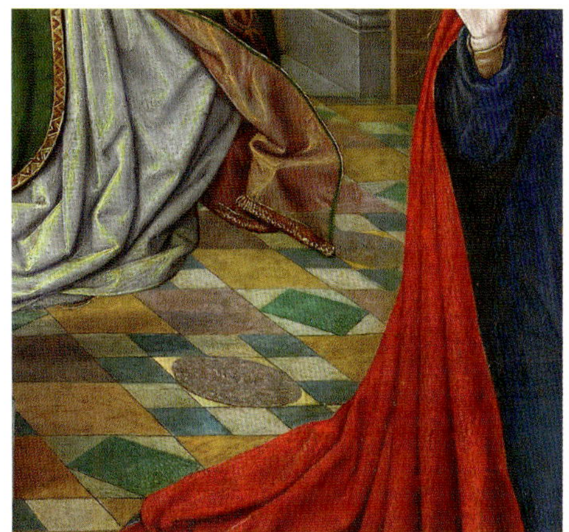

Jean Hey,
known as the Master of Moulins
The Annunciation

1490–1495
The Art Institute of Chicago

Jean Hey's style reflects both his Flemish origins and the French Renaissance artistic environment in which he lived and worked. This painting displays not only the intense naturalism and rich attention to detail typical of Flemish painting but also evidence of an emerging interest in antiquity that was a feature of Renaissance painting. This fascination with antiquity is most evident in the Italian bourgeois architecture of the room, which includes certain classical elements such as the column beside the angel. The Virgin and the angel meet in Mary's bedchamber, which opens onto a garden, as suggested by the grass depicted at the left bottom edge of the painting. This opening between indoor and outdoor environments was a key feature of Netherlandish art. The artist uses vibrant colors and depicts details in a way that only Flemish painters were able to achieve.
For example, the angel's wings are depicted with meticulous realism. The realism is complemented, however, with expressive gestures by the painting's subjects.
Hey also makes remarkable use of color to render a pale, uniform natural light that illuminates the whole room from outside.

C 31
M 35
Y 64
K 34

C 9
M 26
Y 61
K 3

C 0
M 0
Y 0
K100

C 0
M 2
Y 35
K 0

C 47
M 31
Y 91
K 34

C 54
M 38
Y 82
K 50

C 7
M100
Y 89
K 27

C 16
M 12
Y 61
K 0

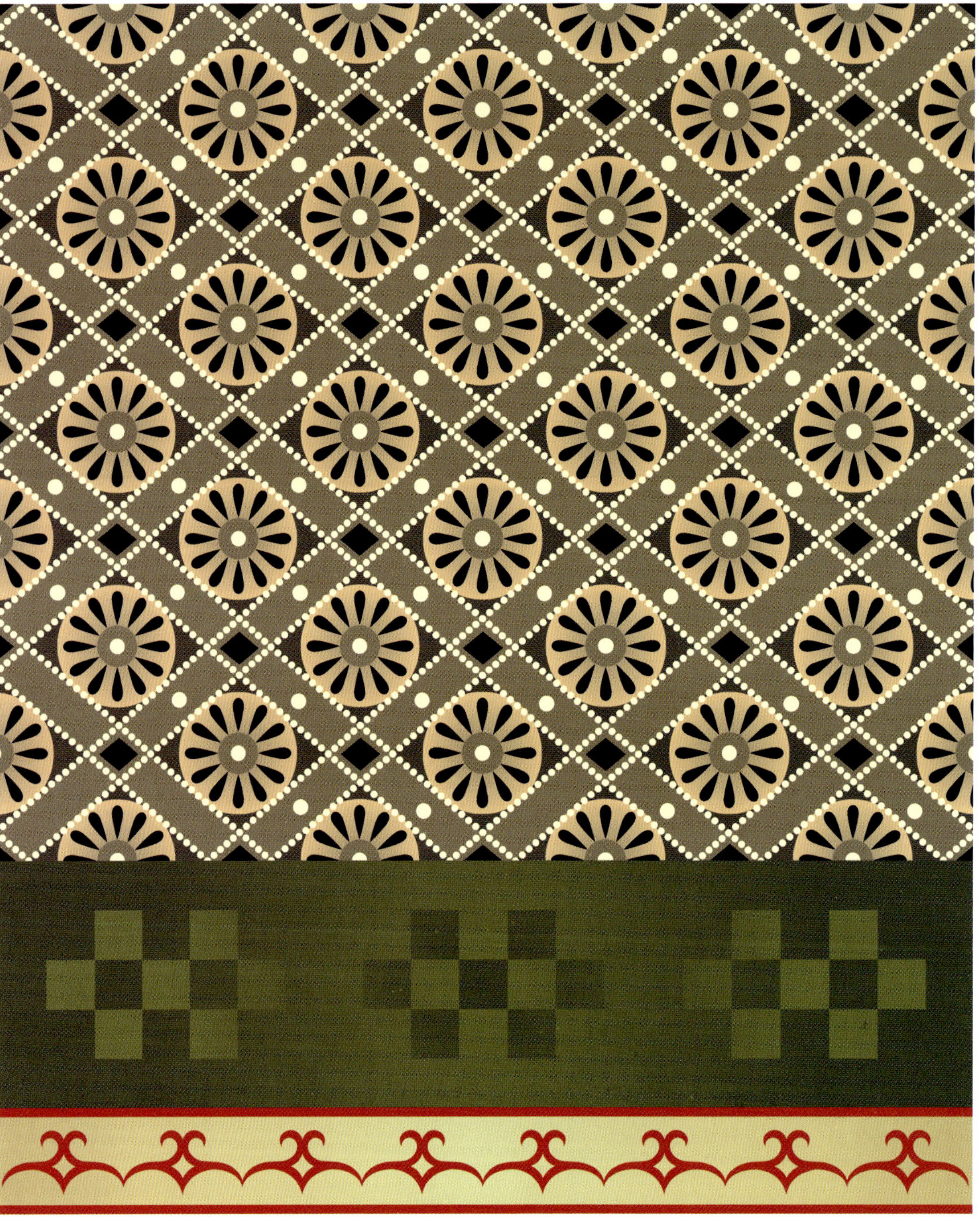

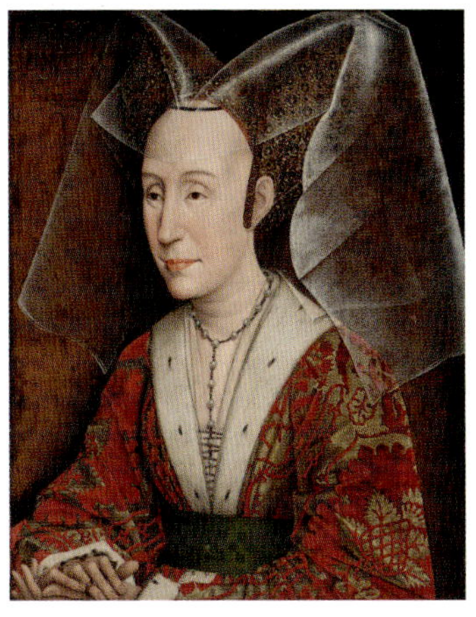

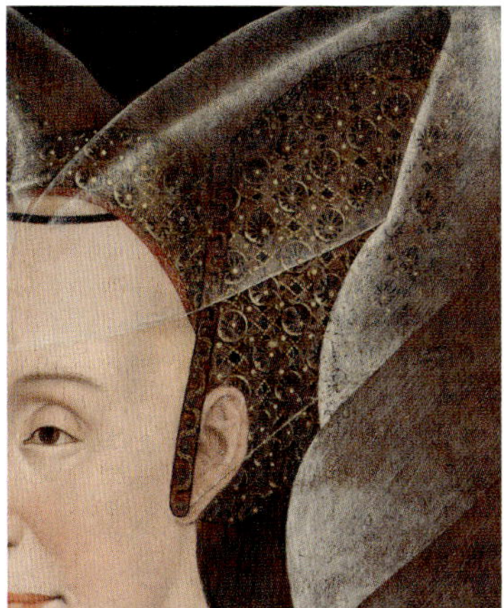

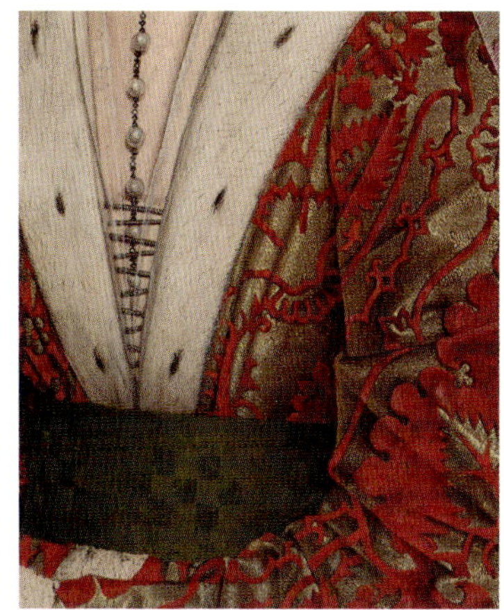

Workshop of
Rogier van der Weyden
Portrait of Isabella of Portugal

circa 1450
The J. Paul Getty Museum,
Los Angeles

This portrait depicts Isabella's hands crossed in a very delicate pose and gives her eyes an aura of silent superiority. Although we may imagine these traits to represent the noble bearing of Isabella of Portugal, Duchess of Burgundy, they should rather be attributed to the taste of the artist, an unknown painter from the workshop of Rogier van der Weyden. The artist never met Isabella but might have copied a now-lost portrait of her. The painter probably also took some liberties in representing the duchess's rich clothing. For example, her two sleeves have different patterns, which was uncommon at the time. Isabella of Portugal, third wife of Duke Philip the Good, was a refined and intelligent woman. At her father's wish, she received the same education as her brothers. She understood politics and spoke Latin, French, English, and Italian. Despite her significant influence on her husband, at one point during their marriage she decided to distance herself from Philip and the cruelty of his court. She established a parallel court in the castle of La Motte-au-Boi, where she welcomed the victims of her husband's politics.

C 7
M 74
Y 90
K 5

C 36
M 47
Y 74
K 52

C 46
M 14
Y 29
K 0

C 0
M 23
Y 56
K 0

C 0
M 66
Y 68
K 0

C 71
M 55
Y 54
K 76

C 5
M 54
Y 77
K 0

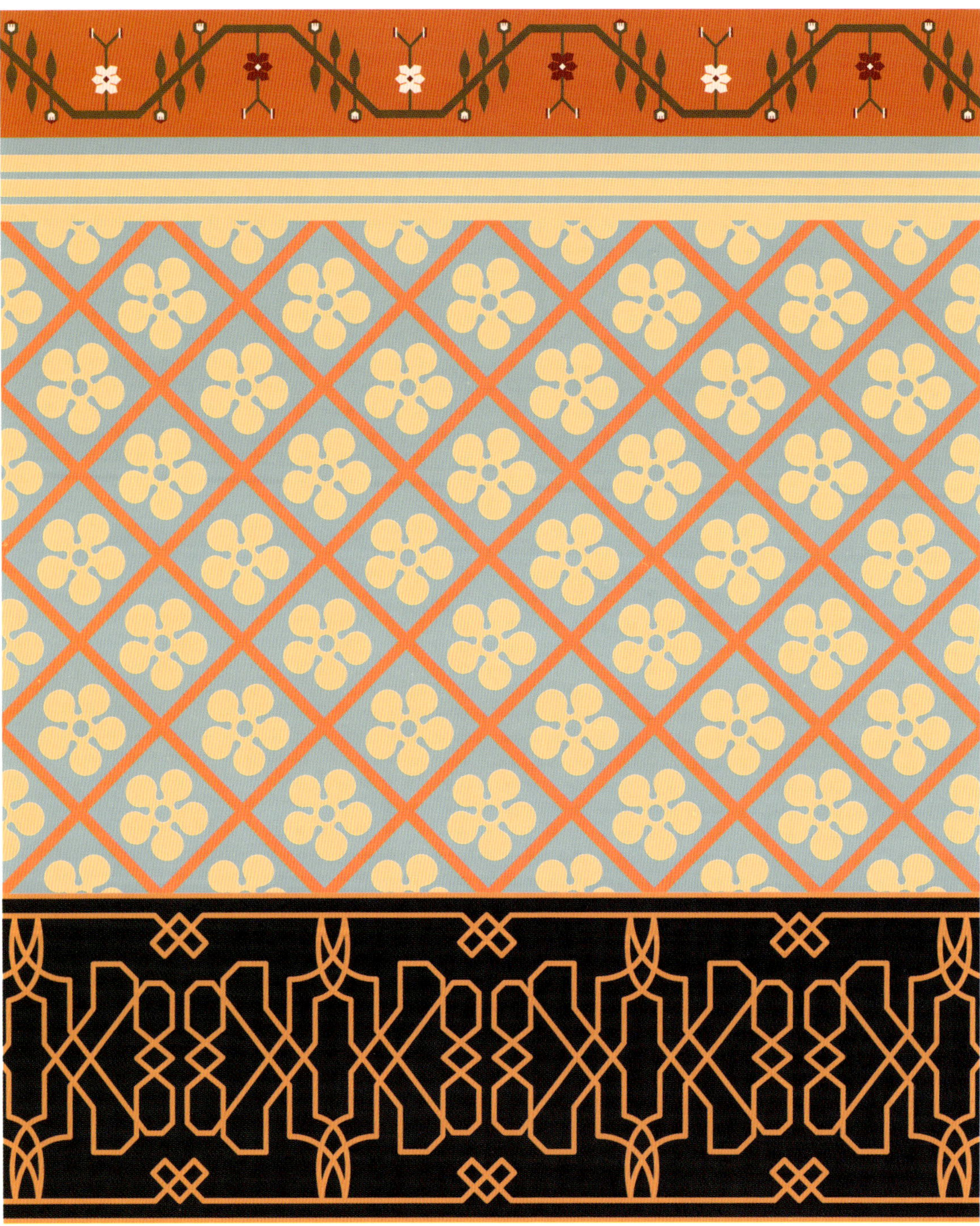

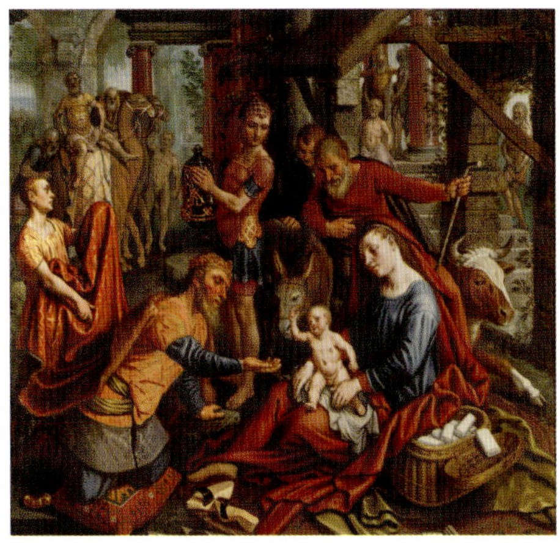
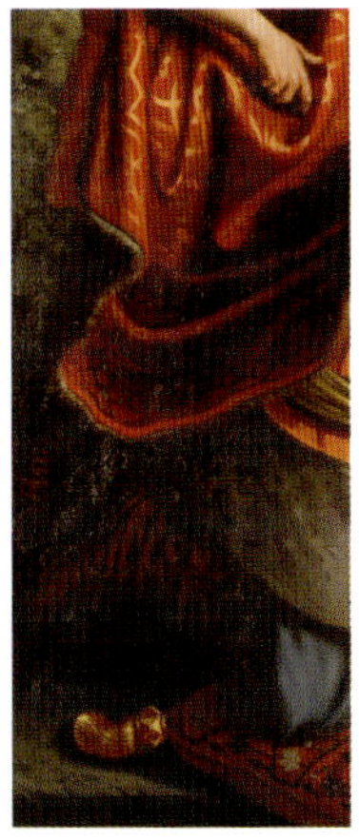
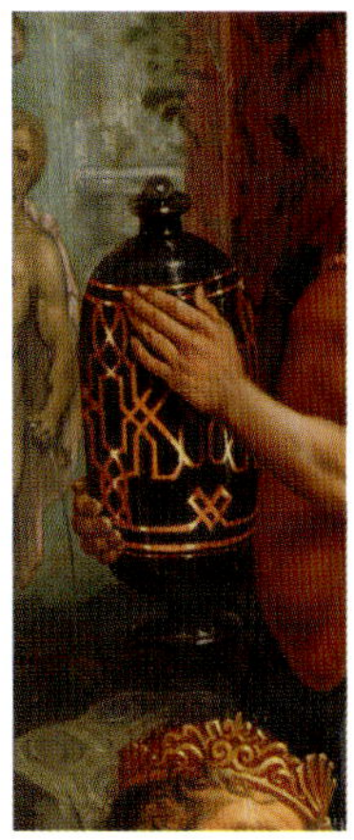
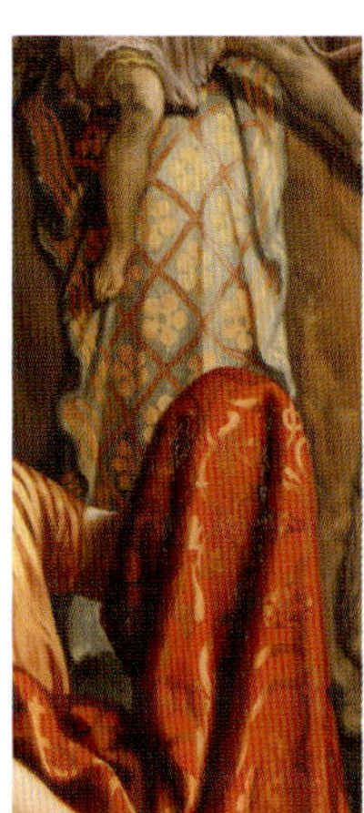

Pieter Aertsen
The Adoration of the Magi

circa 1560
Rijksmuseum, Amsterdam

One of the major features of Pieter Aertsen's work is his mixture of the sacred with the secular, often incorporating religious scenes in simple depictions of peasant life.
This piece is a clear example of Aertsen's narrative taste: he sets the scene in a space divided into two open views, and he populates foreground and background with figures belonging to different realms and epochs.

The main scene takes place in the foreground, and it represents the sacred episode of the Nativity. Here, the attention is on the details, such as the luxurious and colorful garments and the cushion on which one of the Magi is kneeling, as well as a pair of wooden clogs, typical Dutch shoes. The background, by contrast, is painted in paler tones and dominated by peasants witnessing the scene and wearing either nothing or classic robes. This panel belonged to one of the many altarpieces that Aertsen produced in the mid-16th century, most of which were destroyed while he was still alive. This happened during the "Beeldenstorm" (statue storm) of 1566, when Calvinist crowds destroyed a great deal of Catholic art as part of the Protestant Reformation.

C 0
M 7
Y 26
K 0

C 11
M 33
Y 80
K 0

C 15
M 46
Y 85
K 5

C 62
M 58
Y 32
K 31

C 0
M 16
Y 47
K 0

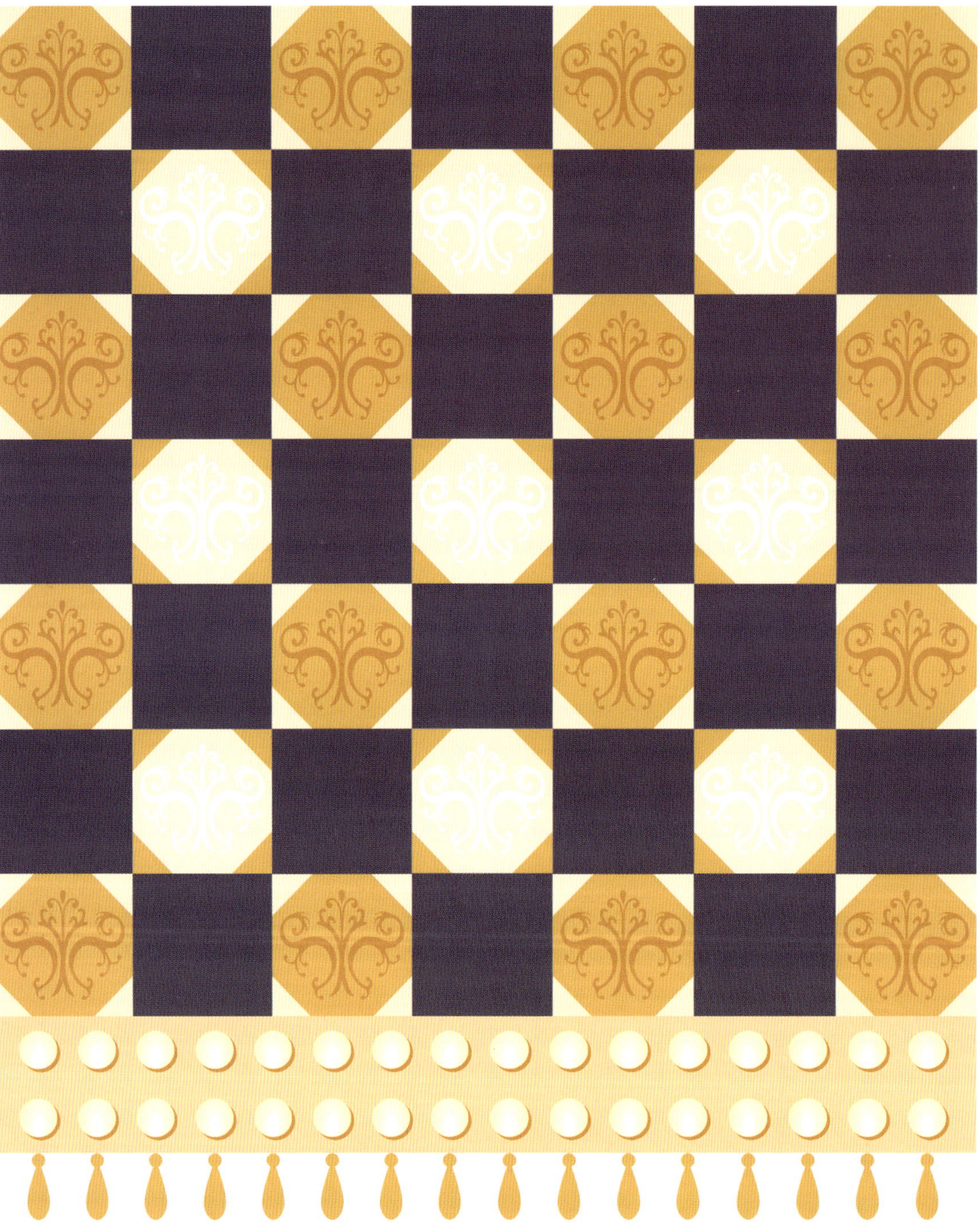

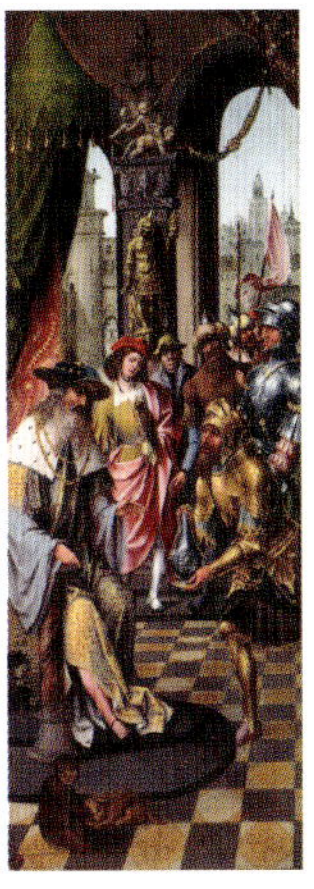

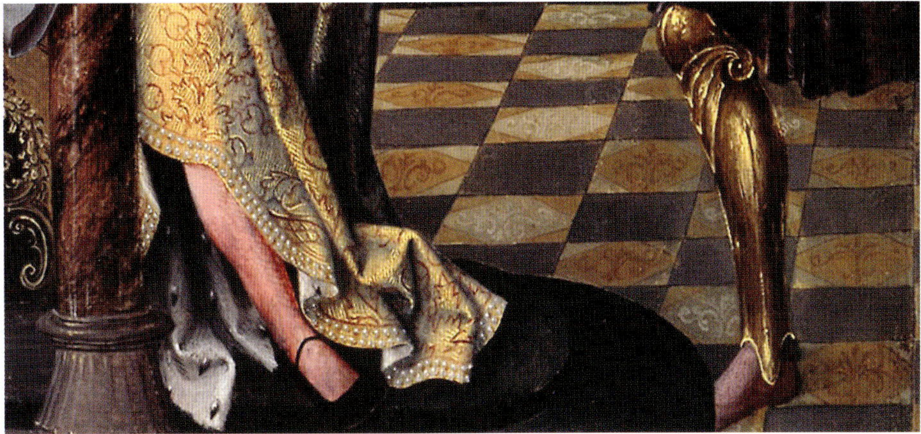

Antwerp Mannerist
King David Receiving
the Cistern Water of Bethlehem

1505–1525
The Art Institute of Chicago

This scene exemplifies the work of the Antwerp Mannerists, a group of largely anonymous artists whose paintings about with elaborate architecture, exotic elements, and luxury goods. The scene is set in a sumptuous palace loggia crowded with many eye-catching details, including richly decorated robes and armor. Most notable is King David's elaborate brocade with ermine fur, golden chains, and blue silk sleeves. Exotic elements include the monkey playing on the floor in the foreground, as well as the Middle Eastern facial features of the soldiers. This painting depicts the biblical episode in which King David expresses his desire to drink the water from the cistern by the gate of Bethlehem, then occupied by a garrison of Philistines. The men around him have faced injury and death to venture out among the Philistines and fulfill his desire. David is delighted by their act of devotion. However, he refuses to drink the water and pours it out before the Lord.

C 40
M 82
Y 68
K 39

C 0
M 28
Y100
K 5

C100
M 58
Y 29
K 49

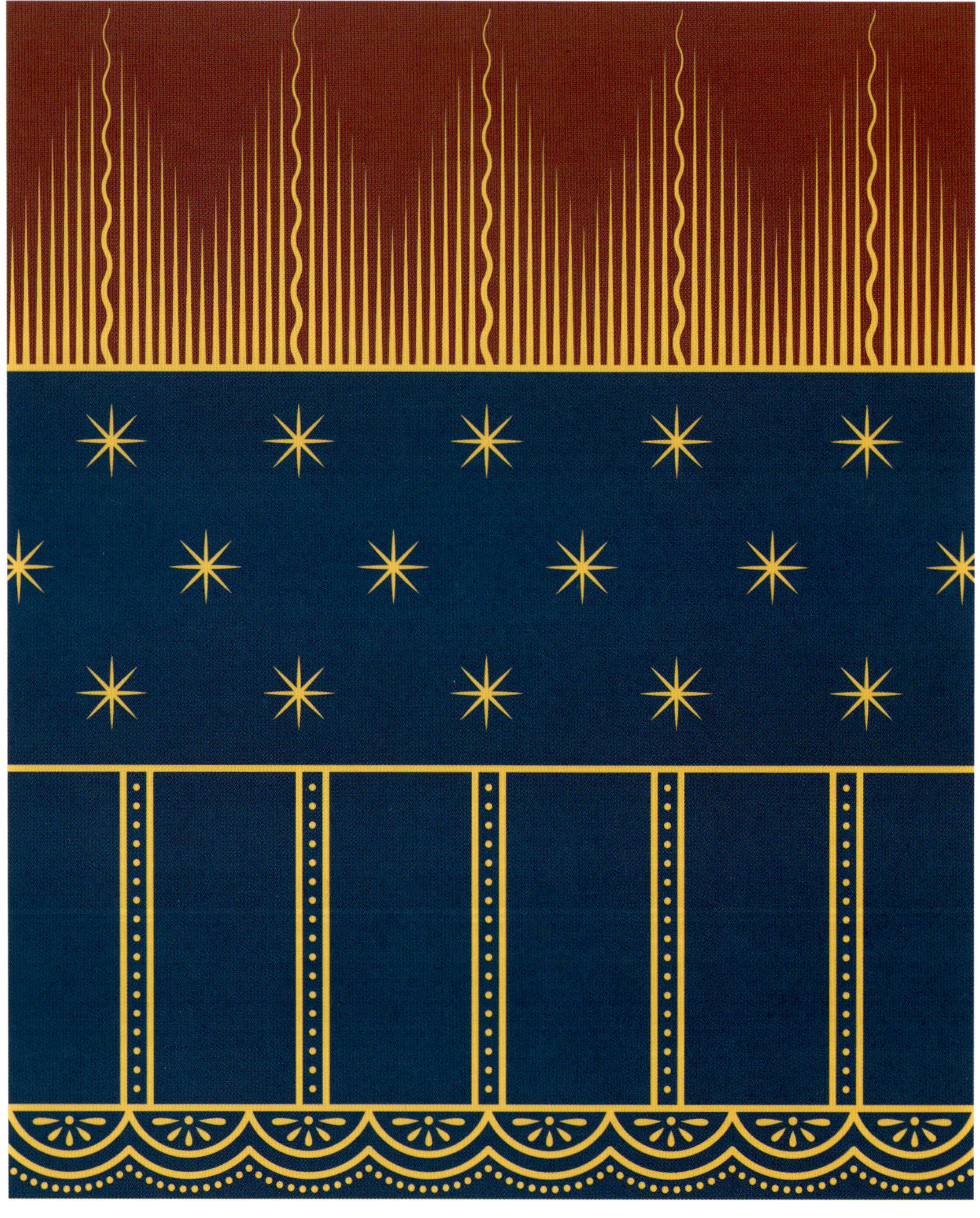

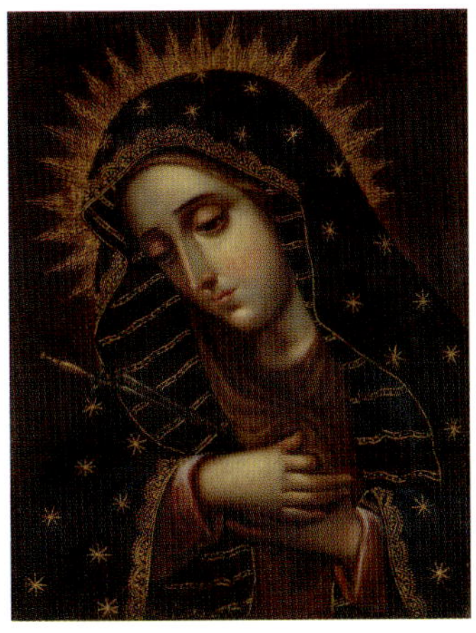

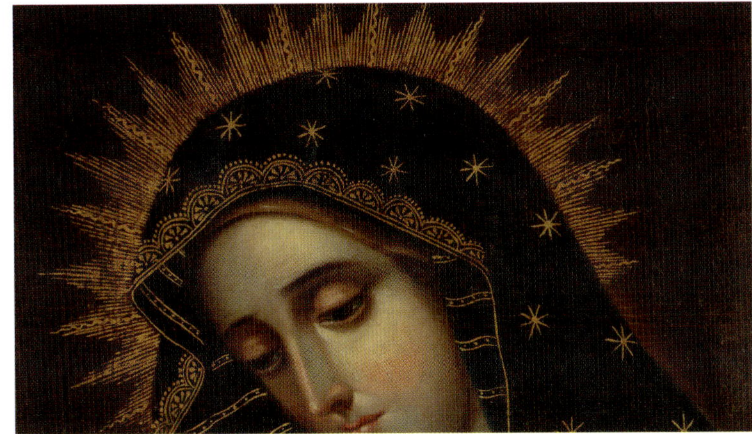

Anonymous
The Virgin of Sorrows

18th century
The Metropolitan Museum of Art, New York

This work is thought to have been painted by an unknown artist working in Mexico in the 18th century. It portrays the sorrow of Mary as a result of the crucifixion and death of Christ—a theme that became popular in Christian art around the 15th century. The main influence on the artist came from Spanish Baroque art, a style that was used as a way to reinforce Spain's dominance over its colonies. In fact, religious art proliferated in the Spanish colonies, contributing to the deep religious sentiment of their societies. The Virgin of Sorrows is here portrayed tilting her head and crying, with knives or daggers piercing her heart. She wears a dark blue garment with gold embroidery and has a golden aura that causes her to stand out from the dark tones of the background.

C 24
M 3
Y 0
K 0

C 35
M 7
Y 0
K 0

C 81
M 50
Y 14
K 2

C 96
M 62
Y 24
K 23

C 64
M 27
Y 85
K 22

C 5
M 25
Y 31
K 0

C 70
M 24
Y 18
K 2

C 12
M 7
Y 20
K 0

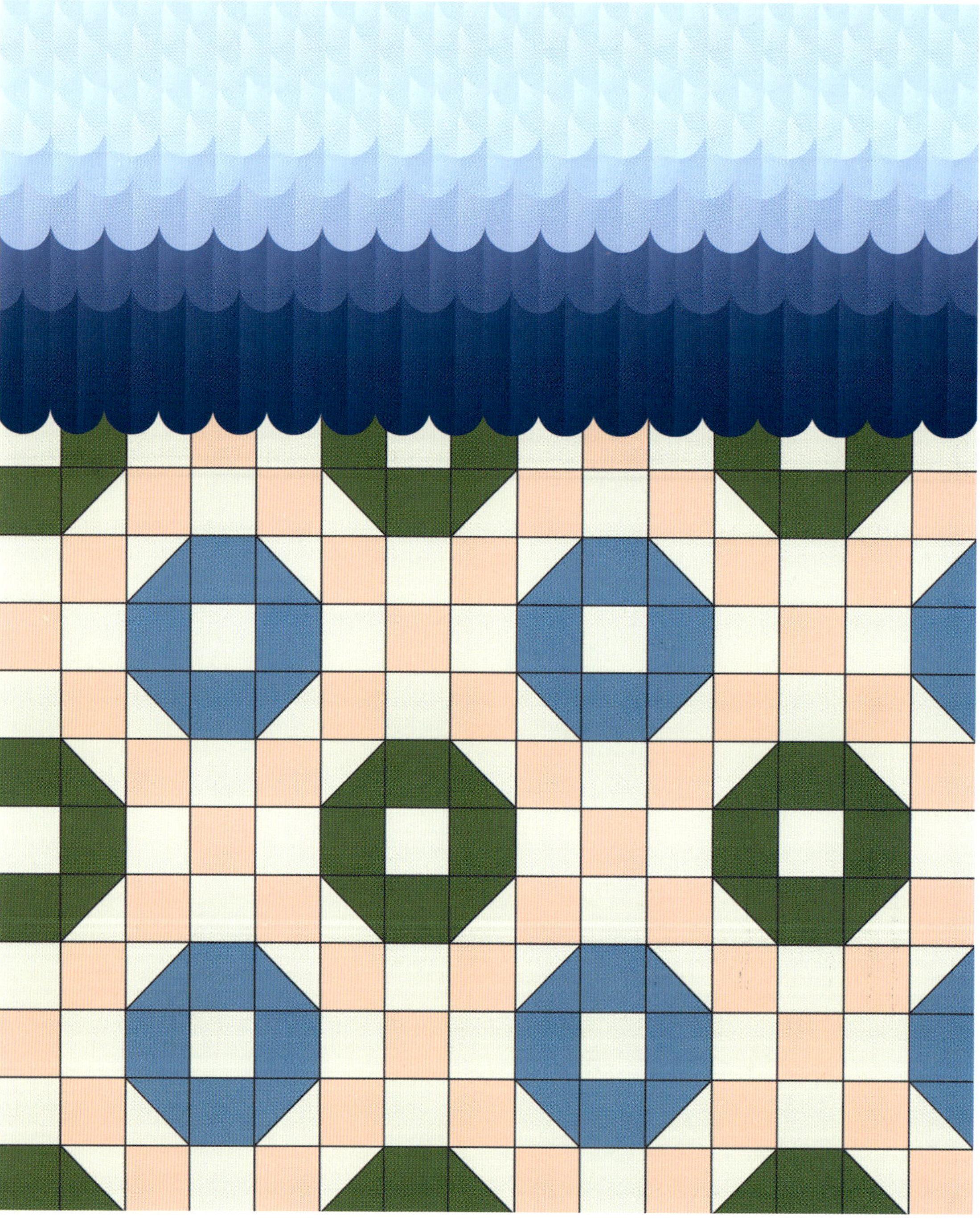

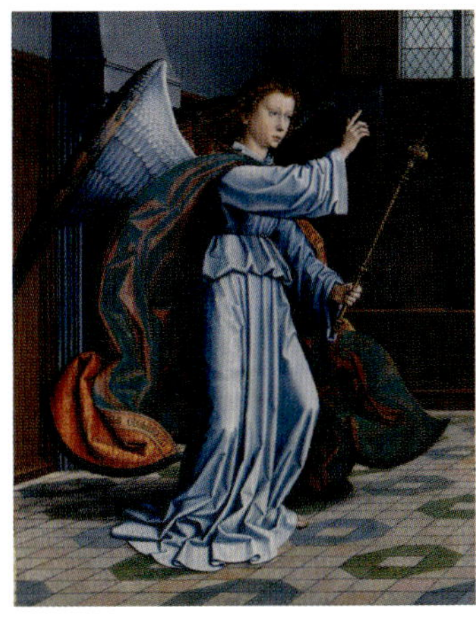
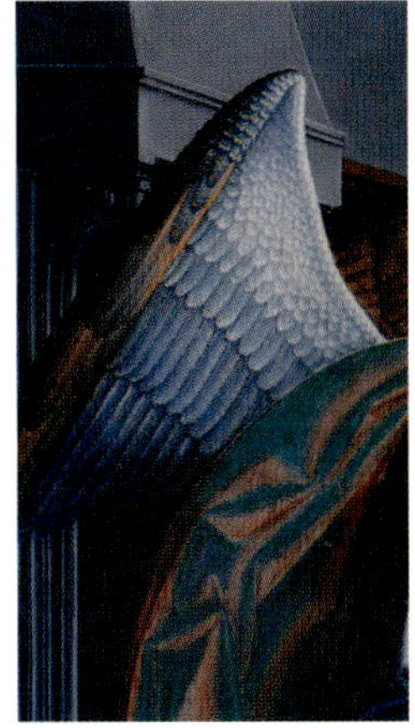
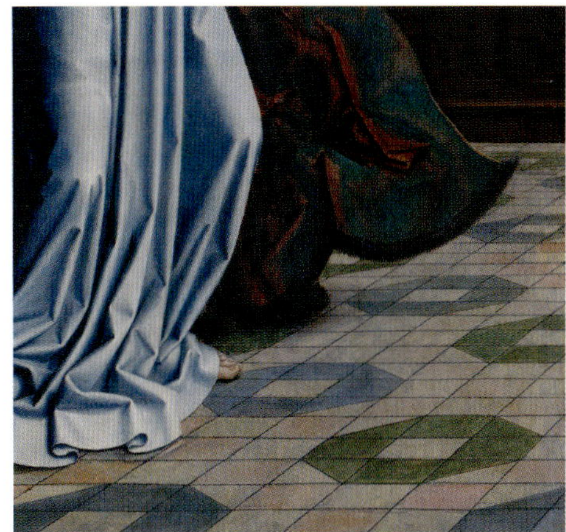

Gerard David
The Annunciation (left panel)

1506
The Metropolitan Museum of Art, New York

The Annunciation by Gerard David is doubtless one of the most important masterpieces of early Flemish art. It also represents the height of David's artistic ability, displaying his exceptional taste and skill with color. This was perhaps his greatest contribution to the larger circle of contemporary painters in Bruges. The pale blue, green, and pink colors of the walls and floor tiles create a perfectly delicate backdrop from which the angel stands out in his soft and shaded blue dress and color-changing cloak. The reddish-orange tone of the wooden Gothic panels also perfectly matches the color of Gabriel's hair and wings. The light, which strikes the angel from the front, creates shadows that convey a sense of movement on both the angel's garments and his grave features.
If we focus on the painting for a few moments, we can almost imagine Gabriel's landing from heaven to earth, and perhaps even hear the sound of the moving draperies and wings in the rather empty Flemish room.

C 72
M 35
Y 33
K 19

C 18
M 20
Y 75
K 0

C 2
M 1
Y 9
K 0

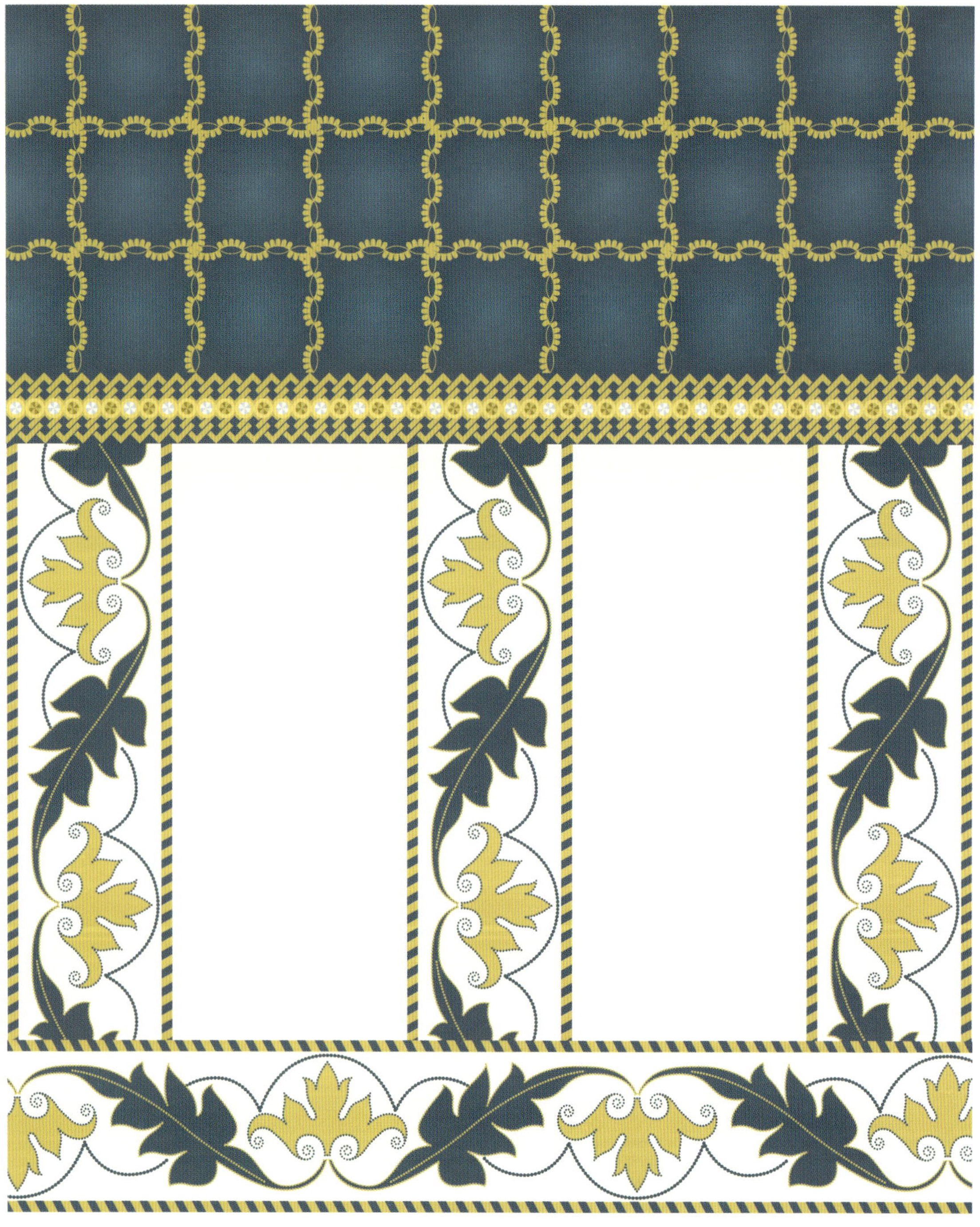

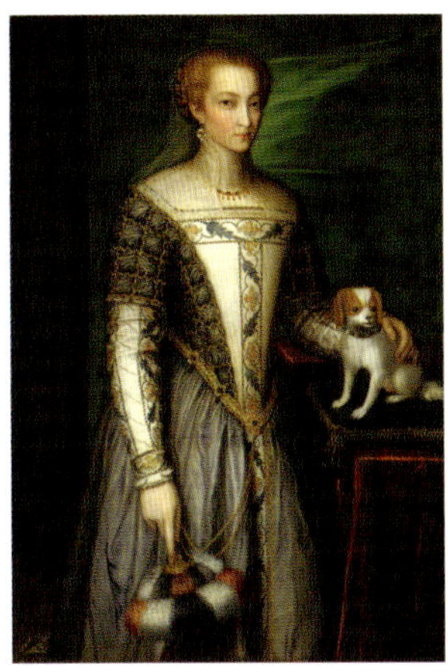

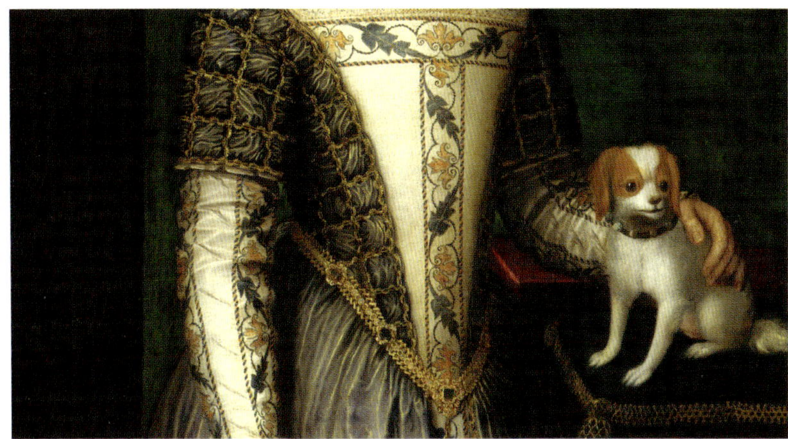

Bernardino Campi
Portrait of a Woman

late 1560s
The Metropolitan Museum of Art, New York

Renaissance portraits did not merely reproduce the sitter's likeness but often incorporated symbolic and idealized elements. Backgrounds, ornaments, and accessories—even animals—all played a role in representing the character, family values, and social class of the subject. It was not uncommon, for example, for members of aristocratic families to pose with their dogs, which symbolized loyalty. Small dogs like the one depicted in this painting are often found in portraits of women and children, whereas men would usually pose with dogs of a bigger size, often hunting dogs. The unknown woman represented here was most likely wealthy, given the luxurious fabric of her dress, perhaps a brocaded silk. The dress also matches the latest fashion of the time, which was heavily influenced by Spanish farthingales. In this style, the overall silhouette of the dress is made to look like an hourglass, with bum rolls worn underneath ever-growing gowns and inverted cone-shaped corsets.

C 24
M 41
Y 93
K 22

C 85
M 56
Y 53
K 69

C 14
M 68
Y 93
K 5

C 0
M 0
Y 18
K 0

C 87
M 36
Y100
K 42

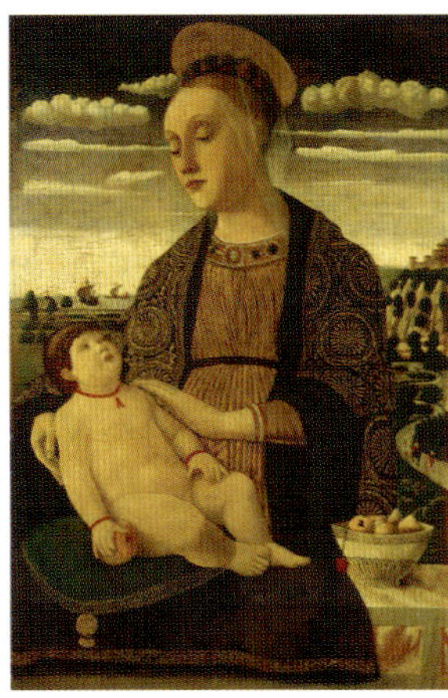

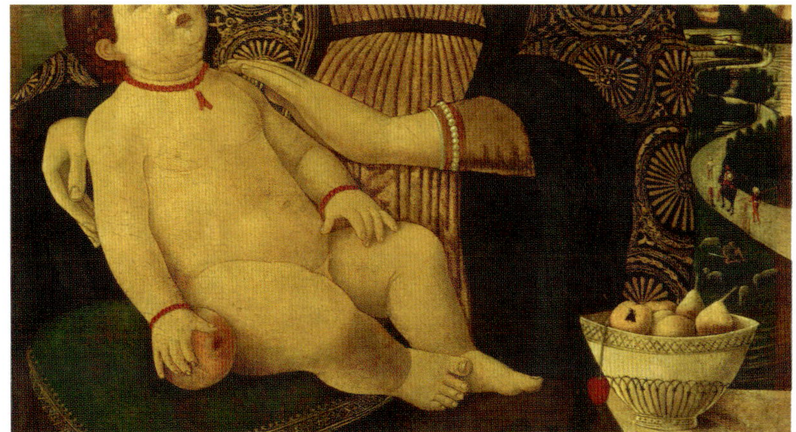

Francesco Benaglio
Madonna and Child

late 1460s
National Gallery of Art, Washington

Francesco Benaglio is remembered for having introduced his city, Verona, to the artistic language and innovations of the Renaissance. Beginning in the 1460s, he had started searching for a new pictorial vision, approaching painters active in Padua and central Italy to find inspiration. His five Madonnas are among the most remarkable results of the innovations he subsequently applied to his work. In this one, Benaglio makes use of foreshortening: the shapes look compressed and stylized, in some cases even sculpted. The face of the Virgin as well as the body of the infant Christ seem as if they are made out of porcelain. Geometric rigidity characterizes the figures in the foreground as much as the background landscape and castle. Benaglio is also known for having painted obscene frescoes on the facade of a palace belonging to the Sagramorso family, alongside a fellow painter, Martino; the artists were apparently commissioned by enemies of the Sagramorsos. Both men were arrested and sentenced to four months in prison.

C 80
M 62
Y 31
K 15

C 17
M 30
Y 92
K 0

C 53
M 28
Y 34
K 0

C 27
M 45
Y 89
K 5

C 4
M 13
Y 41
K 0

C 11
M 49
Y 39
K 0

C 3
M 2
Y 15
K 0

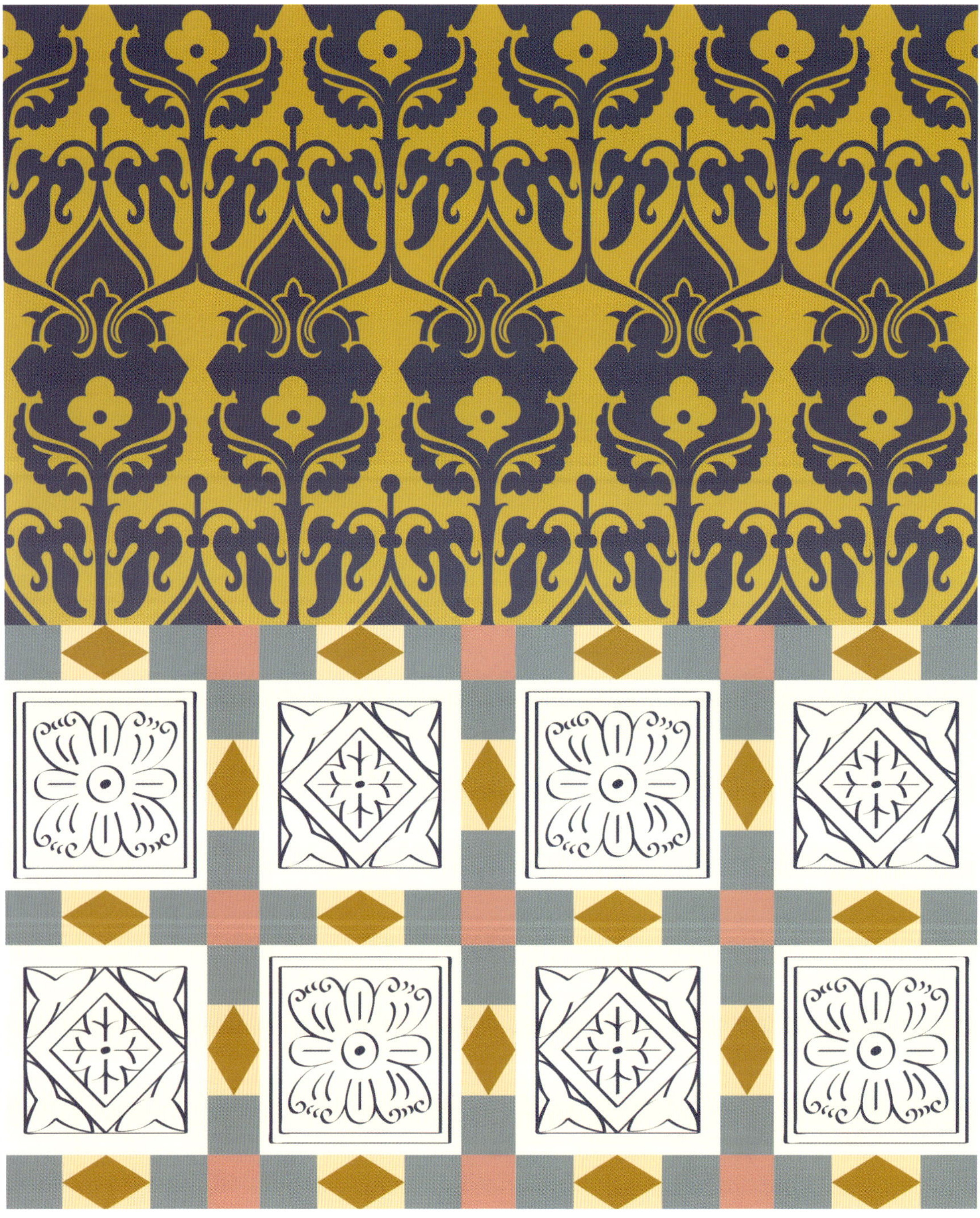

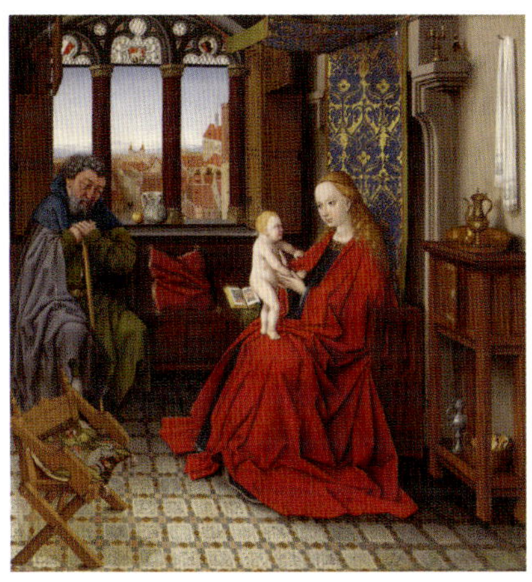

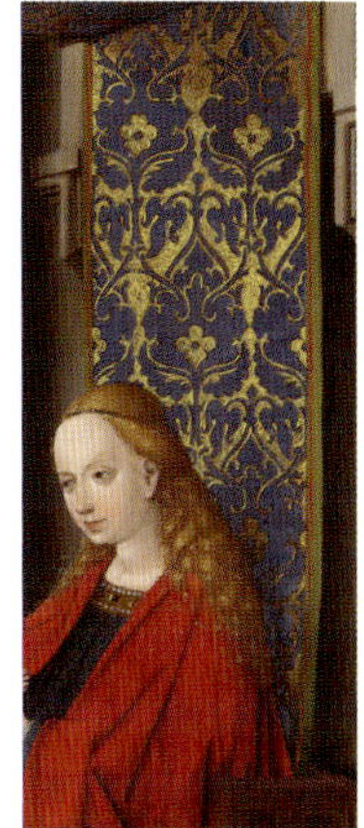

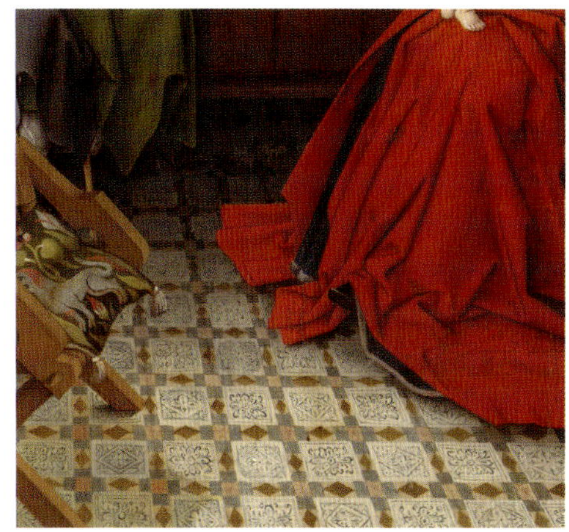

South German
Holy Family

1475
The Art Institute of Chicago

The Holy Family is represented here in a comfortable, luxurious interior characterized by a convincing treatment of space. The triple-arched window overlooks a townscape, dominated by an imposing Gothic church. The majolica pavement tiles show the unknown, likely southern German, artist's commitment to representing detail. Certain aspects of the composition, such as the Virgin's pose, suggest that the artist worked from pattern drawings based on the groundbreaking early Netherlandish masters like Rogier van der Weyden and Jan van Eyck. Other interesting and intricate patterns can be seen in the high canopy covering the Virgin's throne, as well as on the cover of the cushion placed on a small carved wooden chair, depicting a dog and floral motifs. In the middle pane of the window sits a lion in stained glass, probably the symbol of the donor's coat of arms.

C 0
M 20
Y 96
K 0

C 10
M 5
Y 44
K 0

C 0
M 68
Y 69
K 0

C 85
M 26
Y 30
K 20

C 35
M 48
Y 90
K 56

C 0
M 64
Y 79
K 4

C 20
M 10
Y 22
K 0

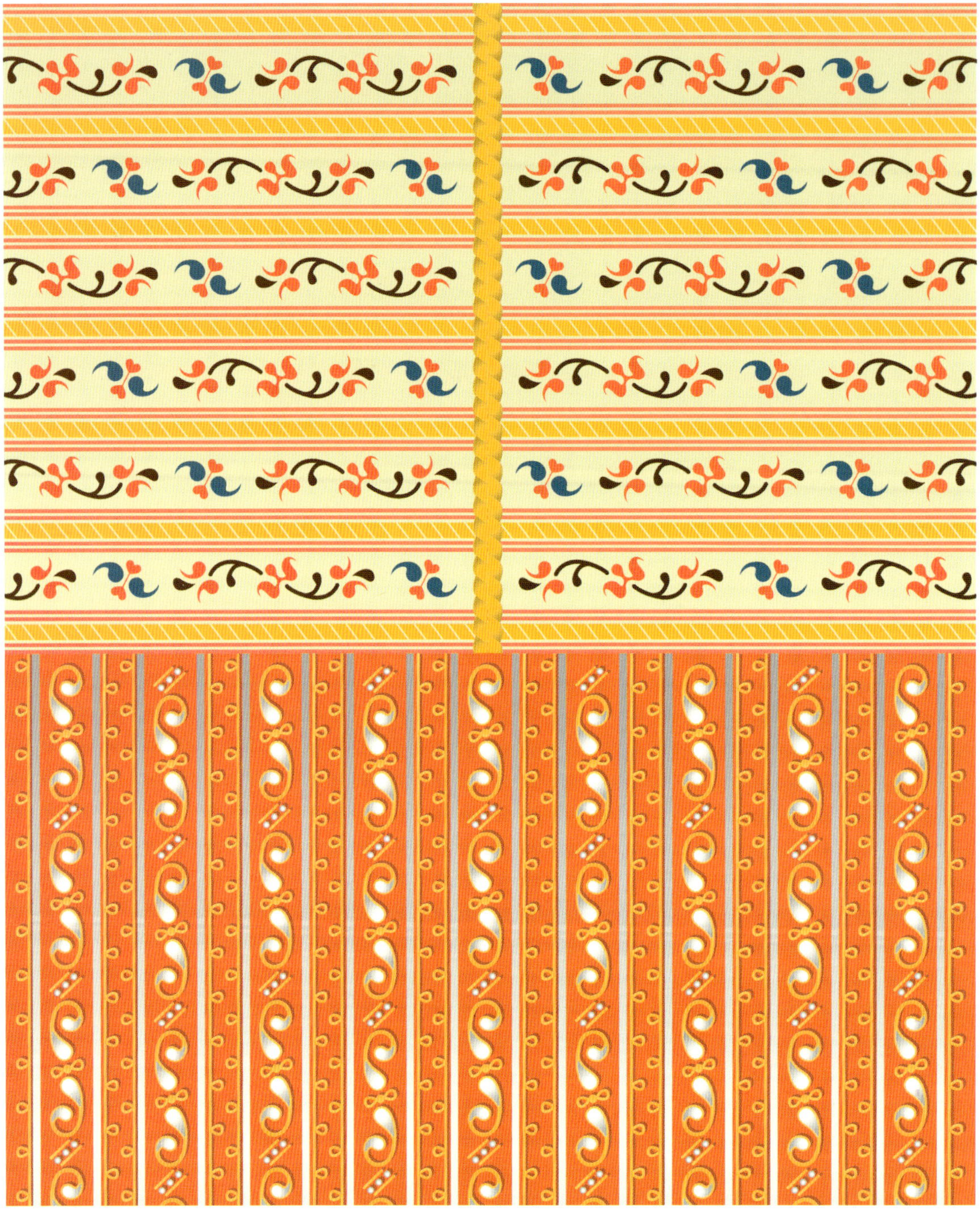

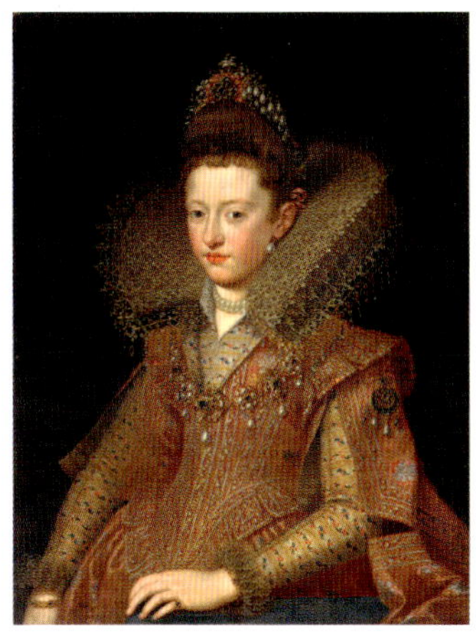

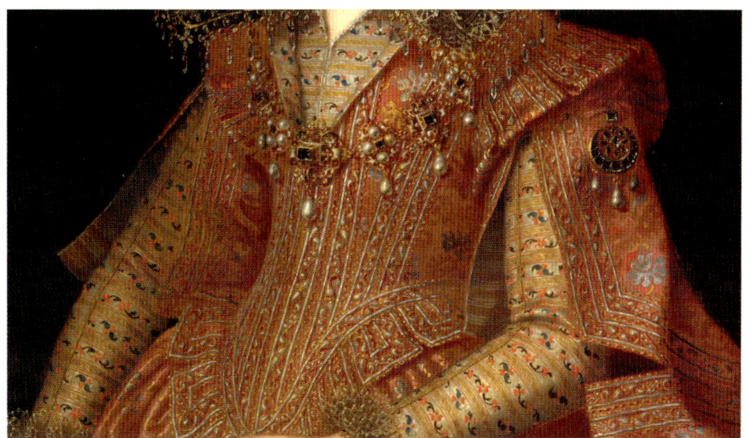

Frans Pourbus the Younger
Margherita Gonzaga, Princess of Mantua

early 1600s
The Metropolitan Museum of Art,
New York

A young Margherita Gonzaga, Duchess of Lorraine and daughter of Vincenzo Gonzaga, Duke of Mantua, poses here in a sumptuous dress with a mixture of stiffness and confidence. Perhaps the most notable feature of this painting is its extremely precise brushwork, which allows us to admire the finest details of the duchess's costume and jewelry. A close inspection of Margherita's clothing reveals that it is ornamented with an abundance of pearls: on her necklace and earrings, on her diadem, and on the brooches attached to her dress. Indeed, by the 17th century, pearls had become extremely popular adornments in Italian society. Because of their price and rarity, they were worn as demonstrations of high social rank. It was also in this period that fake pearls were invented in Italy, by mixing ground fish scales with hot wax and then pouring it into glass beads.

C 7
M 75
Y 99
K 19

C 18
M 89
Y 100
K 34

C 74
M 35
Y 59
K 50

C 11
M 12
Y 51
K 0

C 0
M 7
Y 32
K 0

C 43
M 37
Y 54
K 36

C 77
M 54
Y 45
K 59

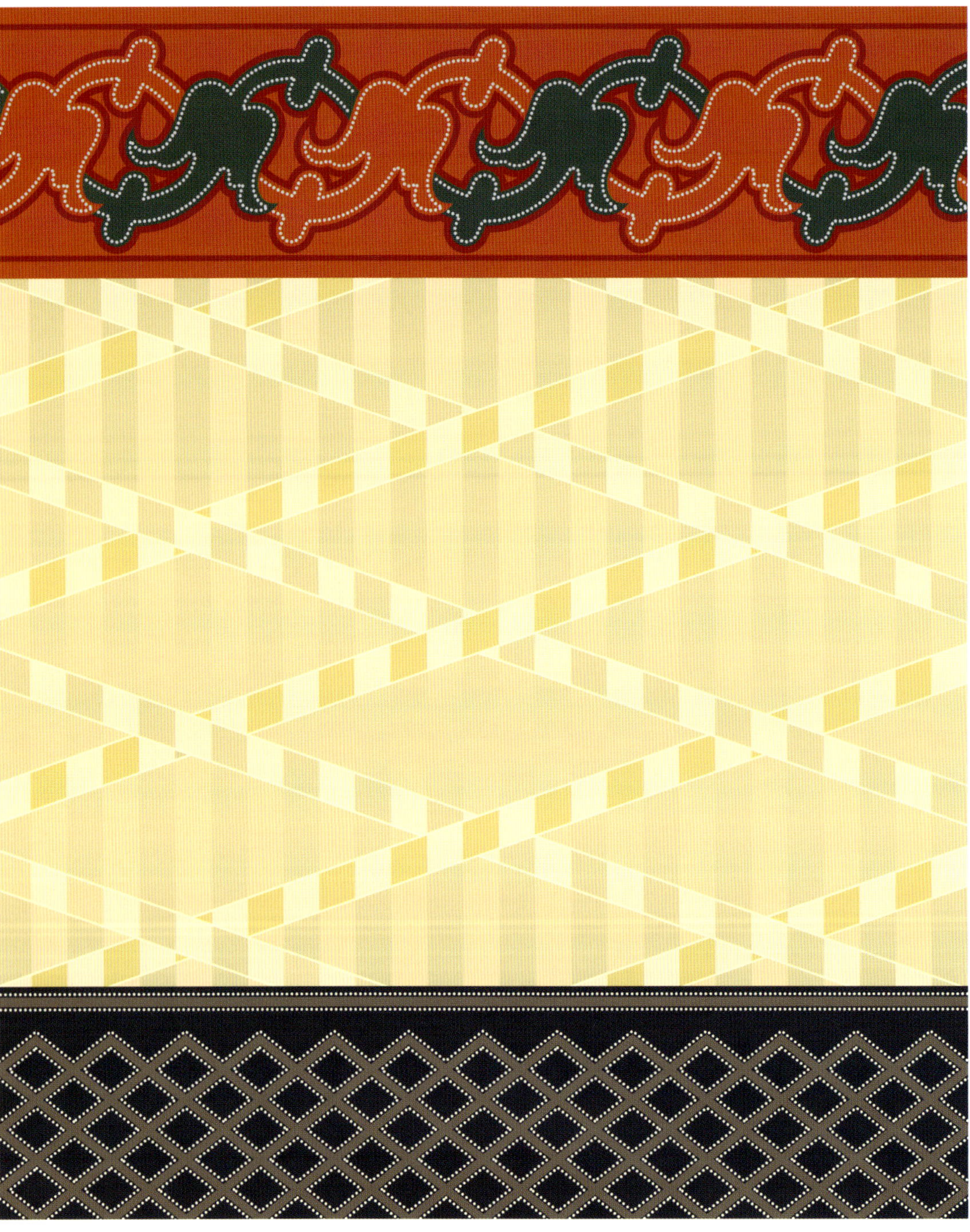

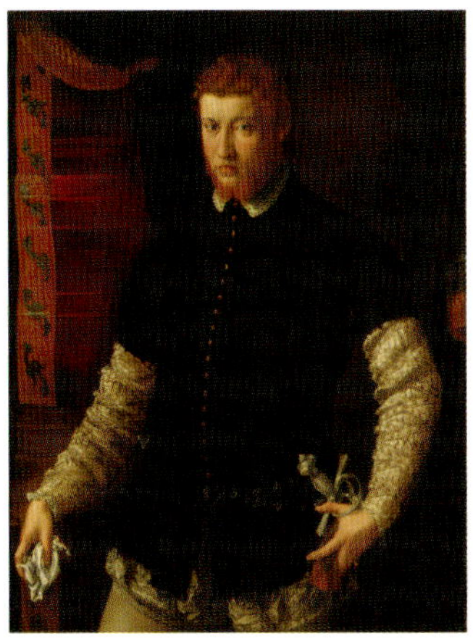

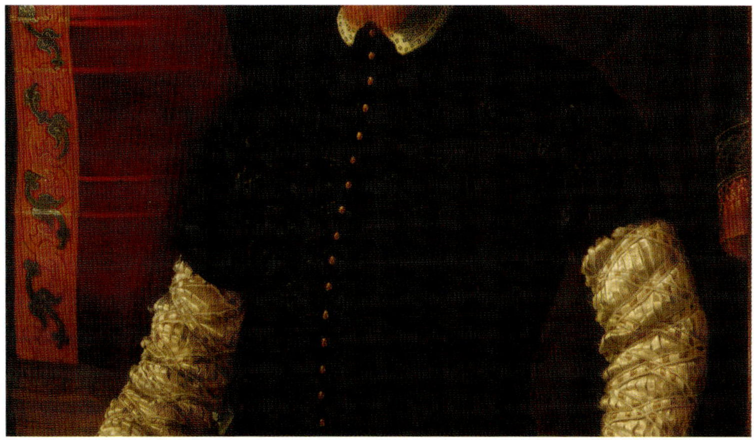

Francesco Salviati
Portrait of a Man

16th century
The Metropolitan Museum of Art,
New York

The man represented in this portrait could be a member of the Gonzaga family, as suggested by his clothing and beard. These styles were fashionable at that time in Mantua, which the Gonzagas ruled. Francesco Salviati, the Italian Mannerist painter who completed this portrait, lived and worked mainly in Florence but also produced part of his work in Rome. It is likely that this painting was done during his Roman period. The backdrop, with the decorated curtain and table, could be a fictional setting imagined by Salviati himself, or perhaps copied from his portrait of Cosimo de' Medici I. Worthy of note is the handkerchief in the subject's right hand: handkerchiefs were ubiquitous fashion items in Renaissance Italy, and they had multiple uses and meanings. In this period, the handkerchief was associated with decorous behavior. It also represented cleanliness, which in the 1500s was still a privilege of nobility and, as such, conferred dignity. Finally, it represented the aristocrats' delicate hands, which were not employed in manual labor. Depictions of handkerchiefs, together with fans, gloves, and flowers, were used in art of this period to attract attention to the hands while paradoxically highlighting how little they were used.

C 24
M 55
Y 86
K 31

C 84
M 58
Y 45
K 49

C 22
M 44
Y 73
K 20

C 84
M 48
Y 20
K 6

C 21
M 87
Y 73
K 34

C 61
M 54
Y 35
K 27

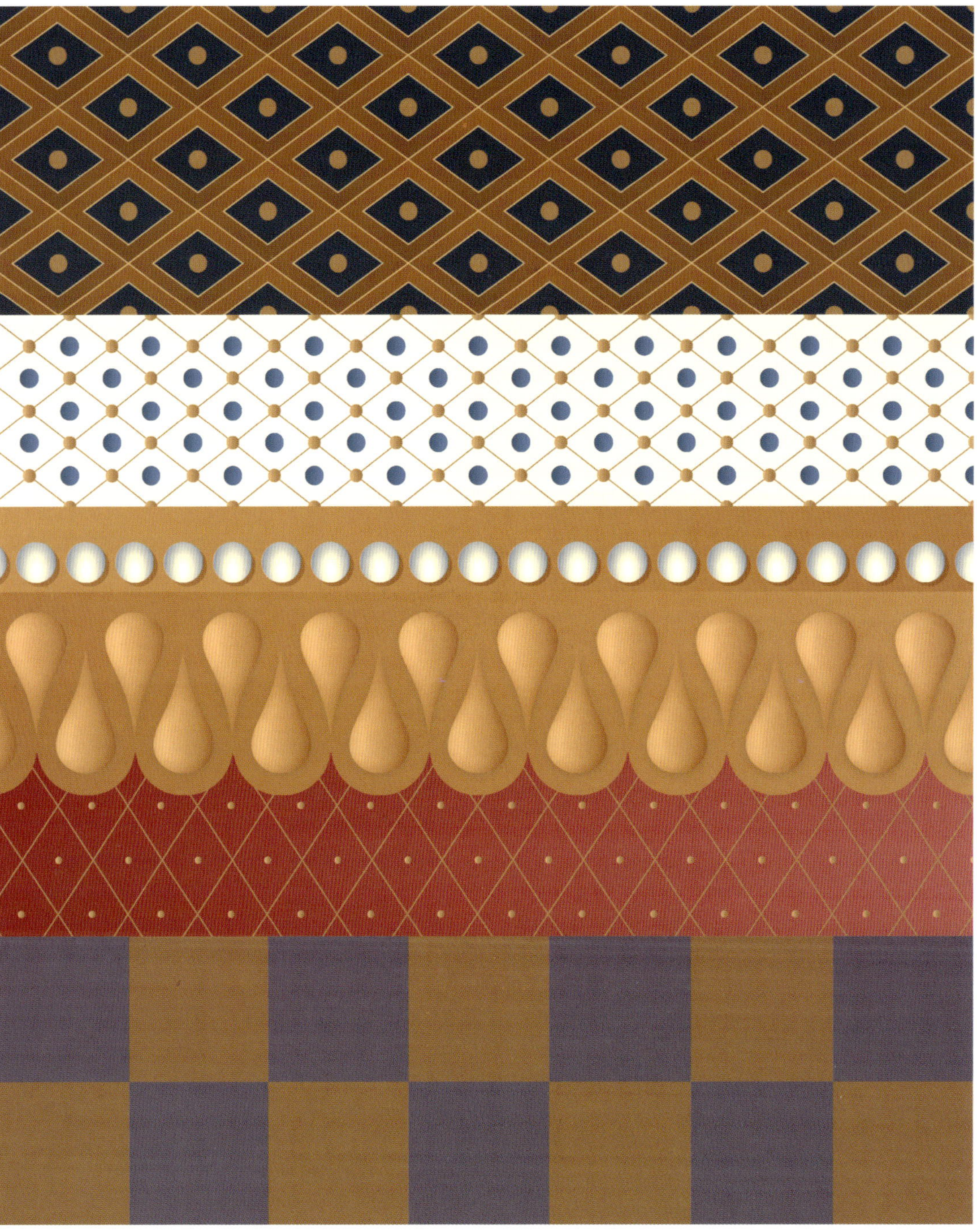

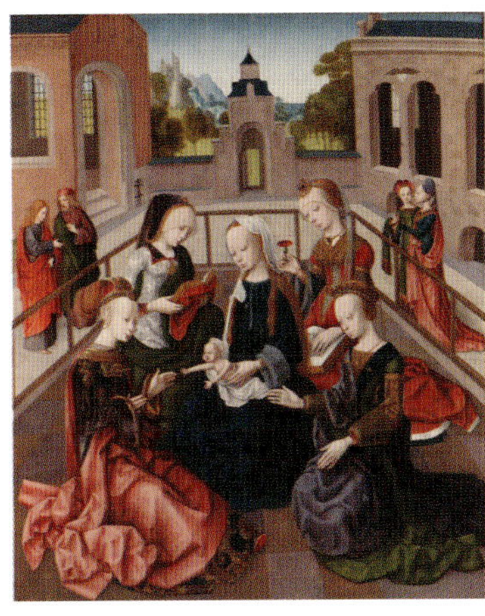

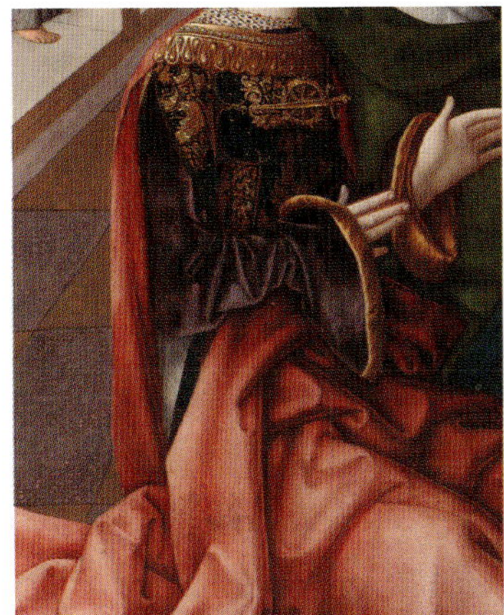

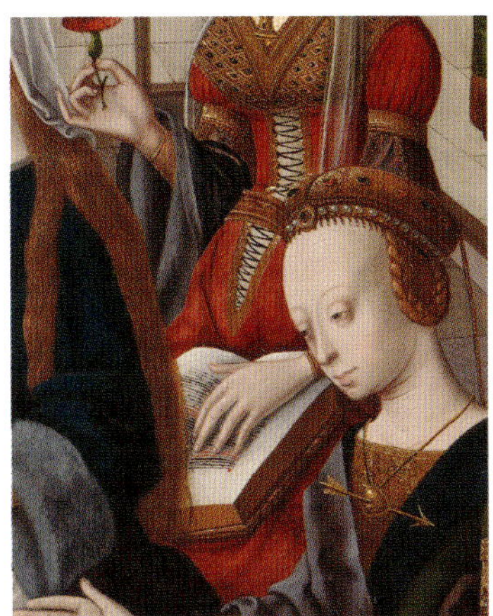

Master of the Virgo inter Virgines
The Virgin and Child with Four Holy Virgins

circa 1495–1500
Rijksmuseum, Amsterdam

The Virgin sits among four female martyrs: Saints Catherine, Cecilia, Barbara, and Ursula. With their lowered heads and half-closed eyes, they are seemingly contemplating the Virgin and her child. The only exception is Saint Catherine, who is reaching out to the infant Christ as he attempts to reach out to her, perhaps alluding to their mystic marriage. The theme of this painting is clearly that of chastity. Its anonymous creator has been dubbed the Master of the Virgo inter Virgines, Latin for "virgin among virgins." Mary and all of her companions represented here in rich draperies are virgins. They all sit within a fence, which is reminiscent of the enclosed garden, or *hortus conclusus*, a symbol of Mary's virginity. Each saint can be identified by her brooch or necklace. For example, a wheel and a sword, with which Saint Catherine was tortured, are pinned to her dress. Similarly, Ursula's necklace is adorned with the arrow that is said to have pierced her heart.

C 14
M 92
Y 100
K 17

C 20
M 51
Y 92
K 23

C 18
M 39
Y 67
K 13

C 0
M 0
Y 0
K 100

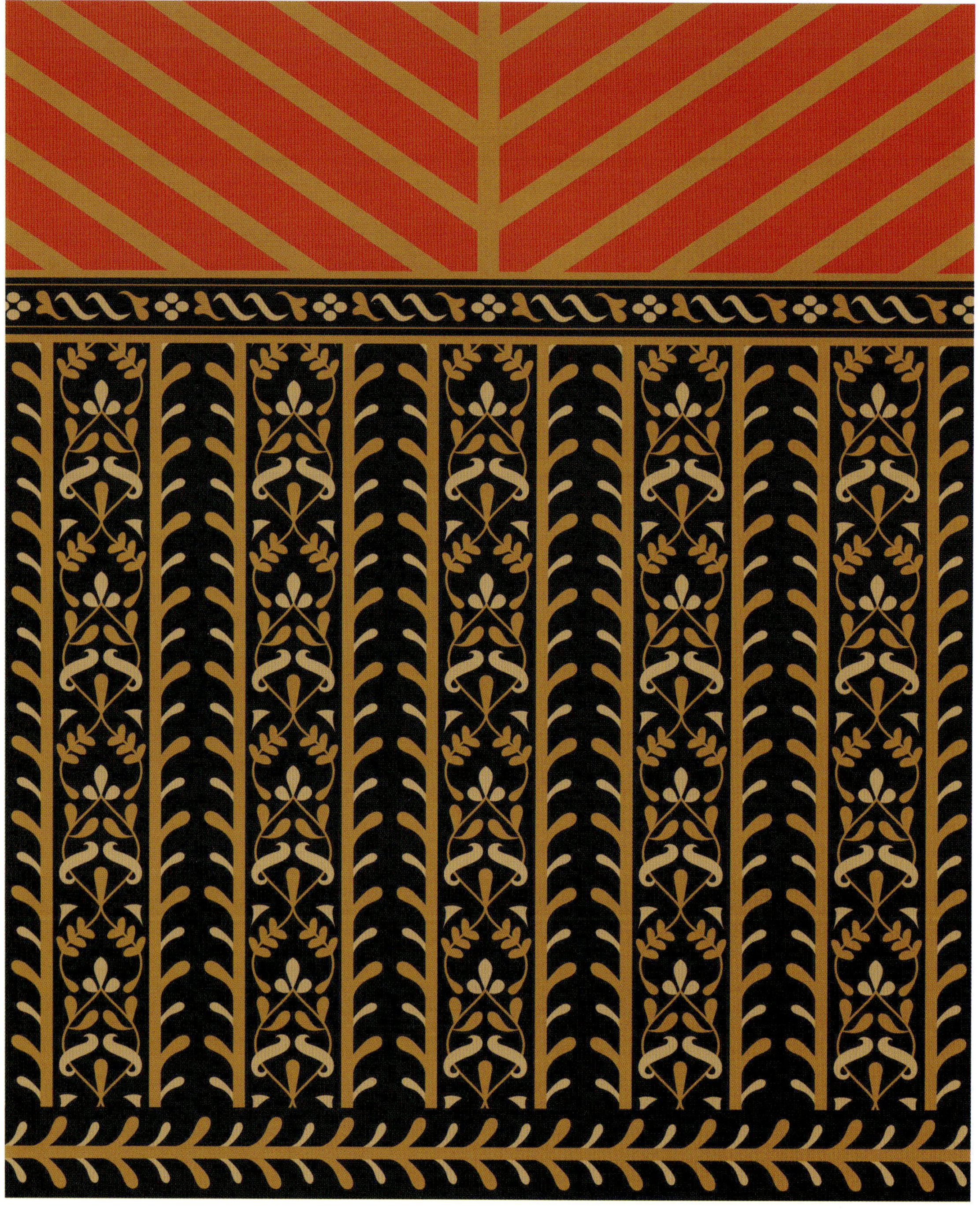

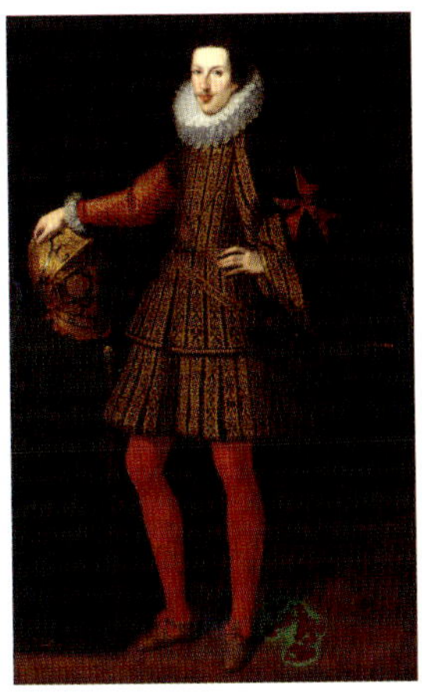

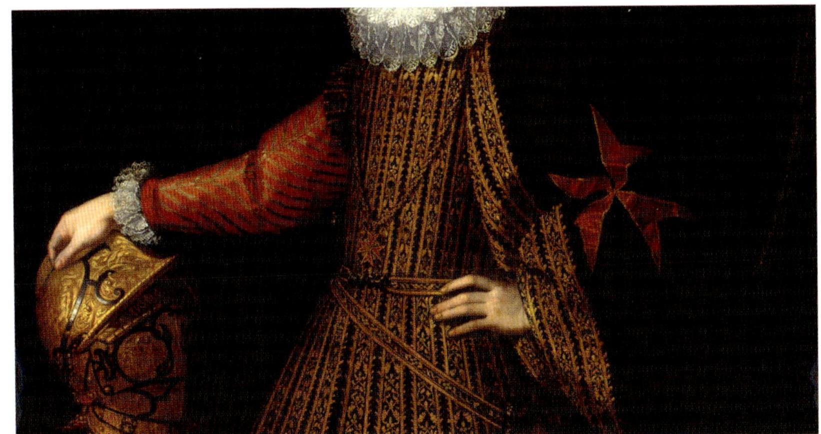

Workshop of Justus Sustermans
Cosimo II de' Medici, Grand Duke of Tuscany

1597–1681
The Metropolitan Museum of Art, New York

Cosimo II de' Medici is depicted here in noble garments by the workshop of Justus Sustermans, a Flemish painter known for his portraits of the Medici family and considered by some of his contemporaries the finest portraitist in Italy. Cosimo, born in 1590, was Grand Duke of Tuscany from 1609 to his death in 1621; it is unclear if this portrait was painted before or after he succeeded to the dukedom. Because Cosimo's health did not allow him to participate actively in the governance Tuscany, he devoted himself to the patronage of the arts and sciences. The most famous scholar supported by Cosimo's court was Galileo Galilei, his childhood tutor. The grand duke's patronage enabled Galileo to advance his controversial claims and discoveries, freeing him from teaching obligations and giving him a considerable salary. In fact, Galileo had dedicated his *Sidereus Nuncius* to Cosimo, which contained his famous and world-changing account of his telescopic discoveries.

C 12
M 2
Y 21
K 0

C 44
M 49
Y 55
K 63

C 92
M 54
Y 21
K 14

C 13
M 49
Y 75
K 21

C 12
M 27
Y 68
K 4

C 4
M 83
Y 95
K 0

C 77
M 24
Y 35
K 21

C 78
M 29
Y 89
K 39

C 15
M 5
Y 44
K 0

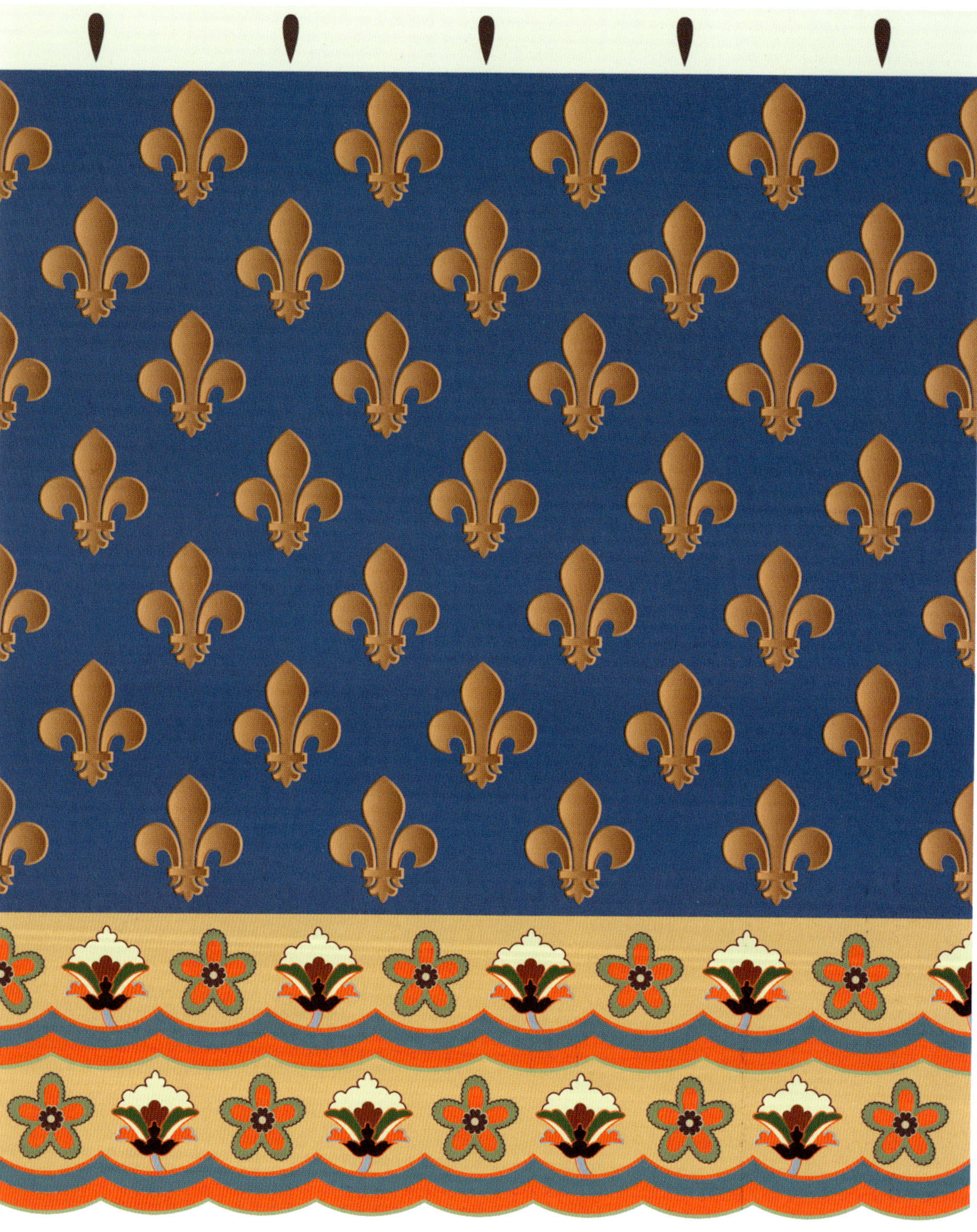

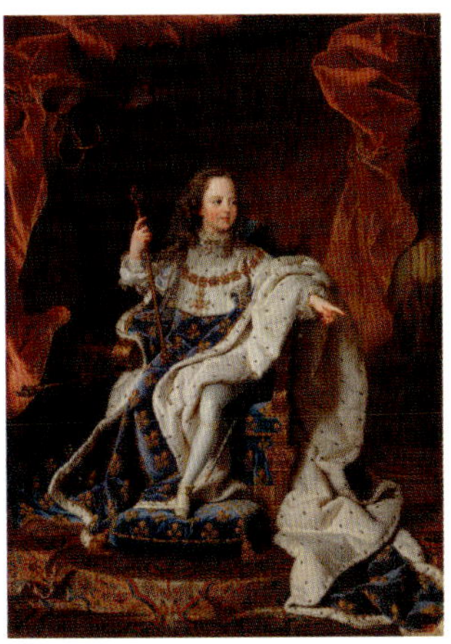

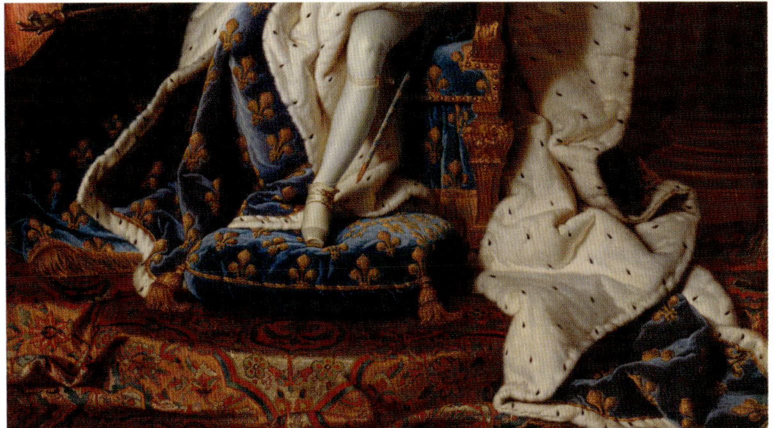

After Hyacinthe Rigaud
Louis XV as a Child

circa 1716–1724
The Metropolitan Museum of Art, New York

Hyacinthe Rigaud was a famous Baroque painter in the court of Louis XIV. His work is noteworthy in part for its accurate accounts of contemporary fashion. The painter's taste for impressive poses and displays of grandeur also secured him the esteem of the royal court. Both of these qualities are in full display in this portrait of a young Louis XV, who succeeded his great-grandfather as king of France when he was only five years old. The lifelike rendering of the fabrics conveys perfectly how the materials would feel to the touch. The proud expression and pose of the young king make him look almost adult and ready to assume the throne boldly. In reality, Louis XV became a rather indolent king. He was often manipulated by members of his court, and several of his mistresses exercised significant political influence through him. Historians identify his ineffectual rule as one of the factors that contributed to public frustration with the inadequacy of royal authority, an exasperation that ultimately led to the French Revolution in 1789, only fifteen years after Louis XV's death.

C 0
M 46
Y 100
K 16

C 90
M 25
Y 100
K 61

C 0
M 83
Y 56
K 33

C 0
M 85
Y 68
K 51

C 83
M 29
Y 26
K 51

C 0
M 12
Y 38
K 0

C 100
M 28
Y 66
K 67

C 51
M 28
Y 71
K 41

C 22
M 100
Y 34
K 62

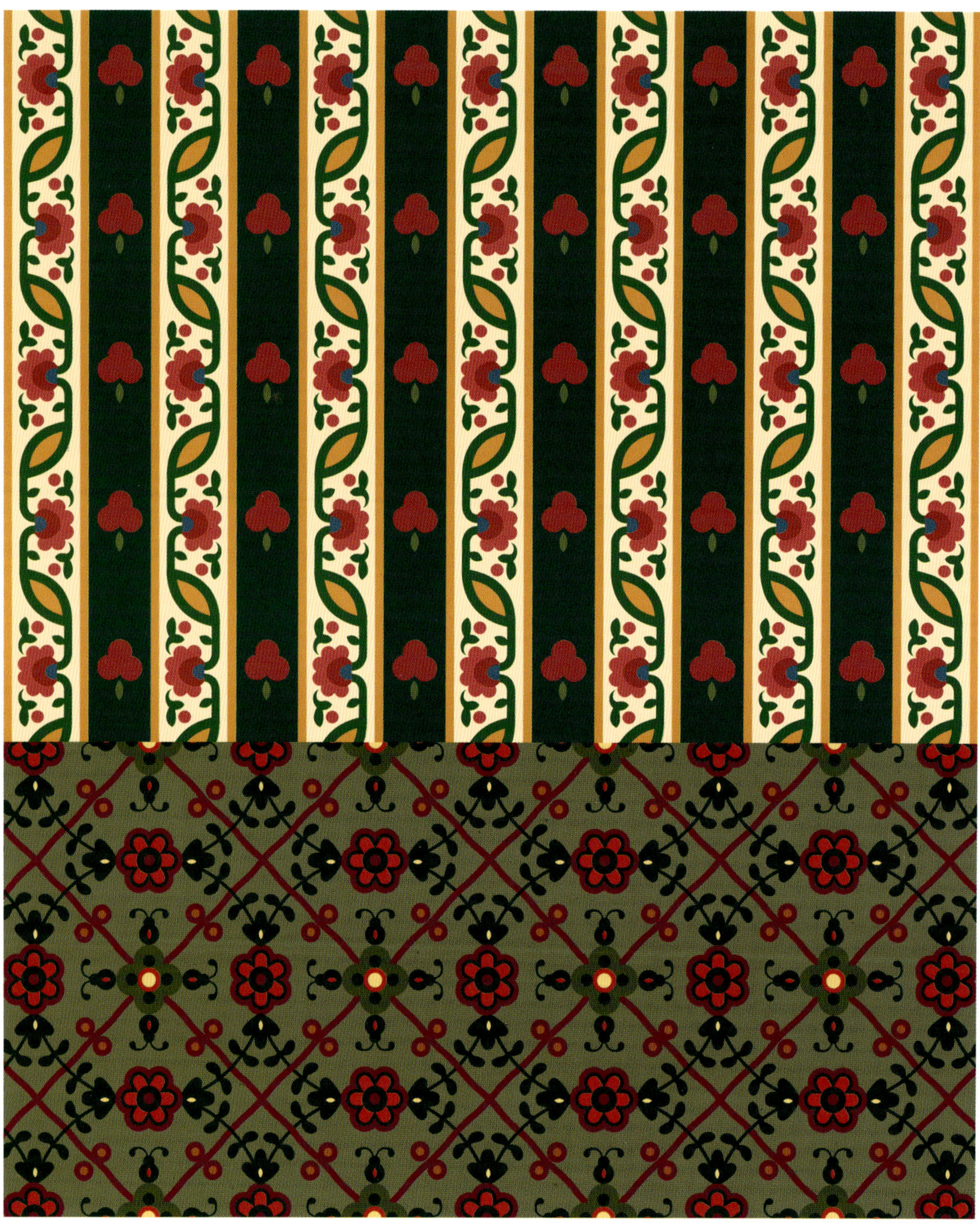

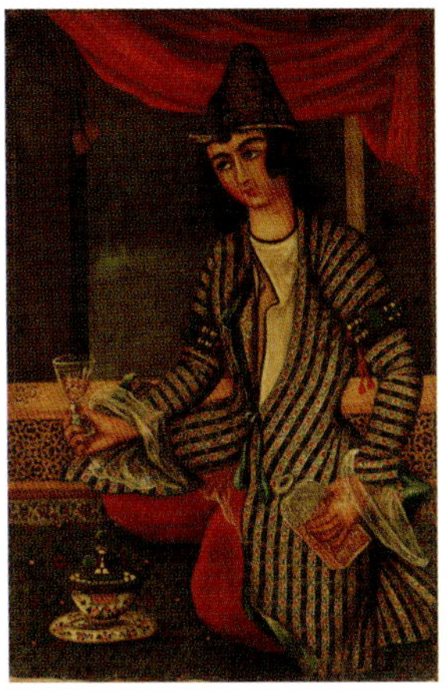
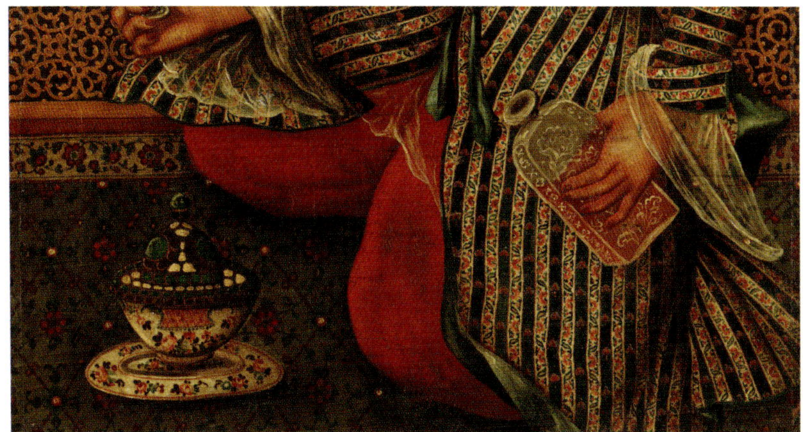

Anonymous
Portrait of a Young Man

early 19th century
The Metropolitan Museum of Art,
New York

This 19th-century Iranian painting depicts an androgynous-looking man, with painted nails, drinking something that could be either alcohol or tea. Indeed, alcohol consumption was fairly widespread in Iran during this period. During the Qajar dynasty in the late 18th and the 19th century, Iranian society underwent a significant amount of westernization. The allure of cultural exoticism, however, traveled in both directions: while Islamic cultures of this time began to adopt Western innovations in many fields, including the visual arts, many Europeans were collecting Islamic objects and adopting Islamic styles. It was during this period that Muhammad Ghaffari opened Iran's first academy of fine arts after studying in Paris, Florence, and Rome. For Iranian artists, it was utterly modern to adopt the Western technique of oil painting and depict scenes of everyday life, both of which are done in this painting. The inscription on this painting has been translated as "the humblest of painters, Ahmad, 12," and humility was widely practiced in Iranian Islamic arts of that time. A common, albeit somewhat disputed, theory claims that Islamic artists would purposefully make mistakes in the repetition of arabesques to display their humility and belief that only God could produce perfection.

C 30
M 65
Y 91
K 33

C 69
M 55
Y 59
K 51

C 64
M 64
Y 64
K 78

C 33
M 81
Y 71
K 56

C 67
M 41
Y 49
K 14

C 29
M 31
Y 63
K 0

C 17
M 58
Y 71
K 13

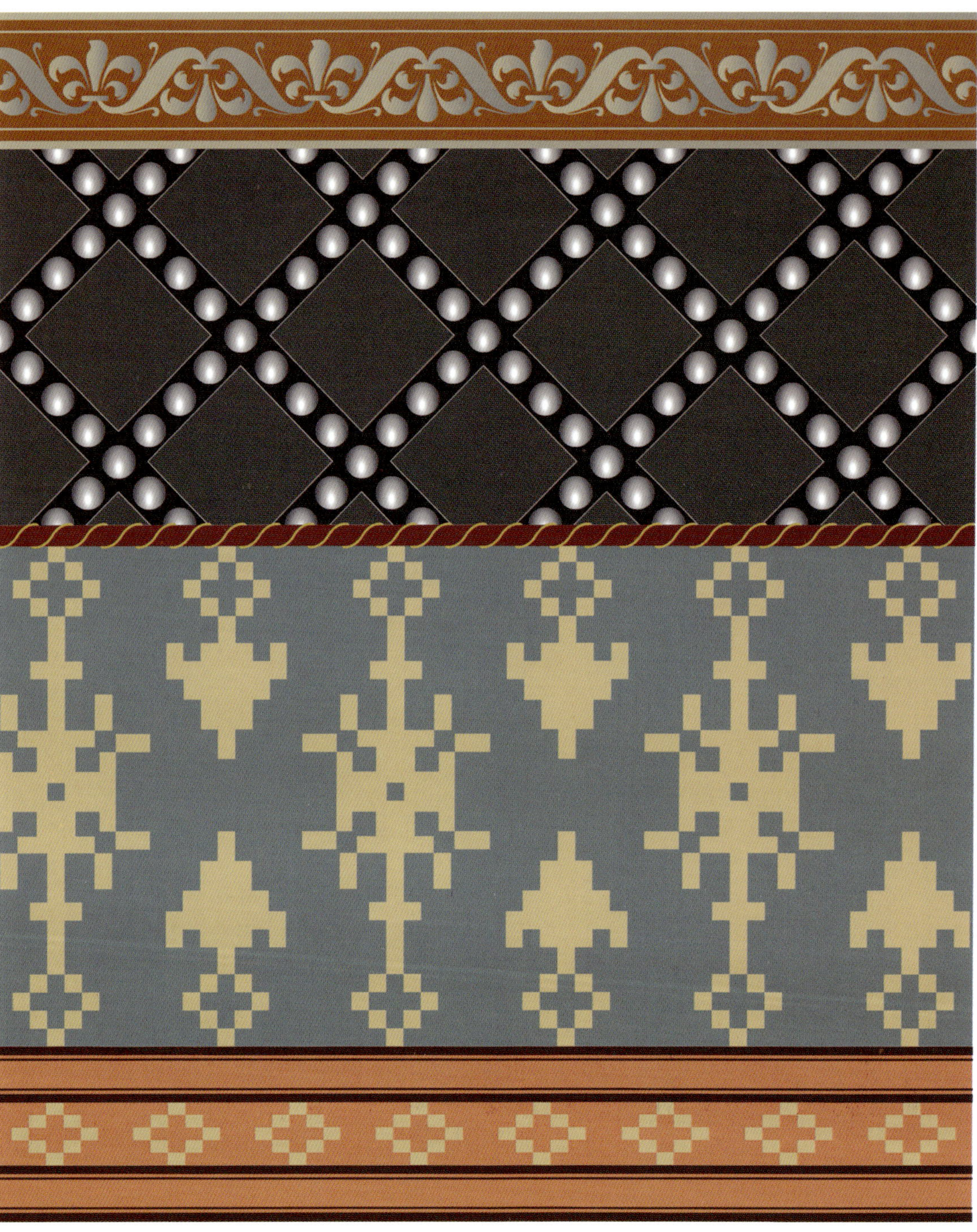

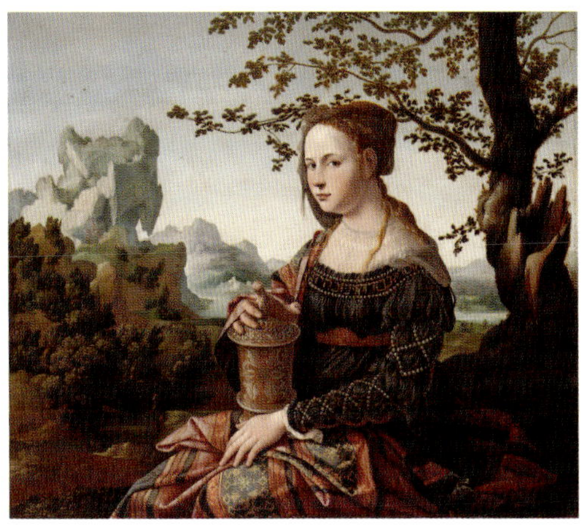

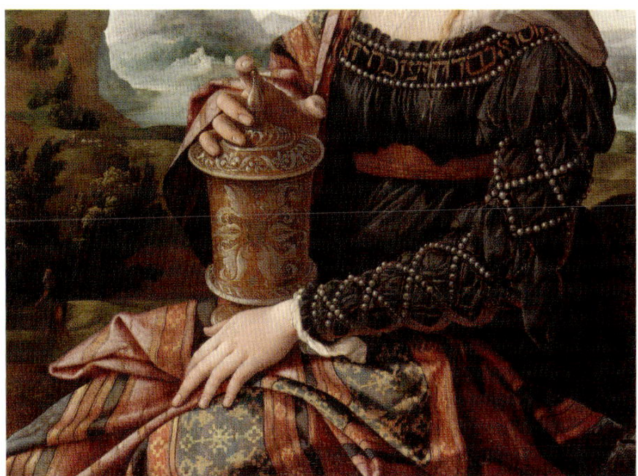

Jan van Scorel
Mary Magdalene

circa 1530
Rijksmuseum, Amsterdam

Mary Magdalene is portrayed here in a seductive manner, luxuriously dressed as a contemporary Venetian courtesan. Jan van Scorel chose to depict Mary Magdalene in these garments to reference her past as a prostitute. The tree on the right could also metaphorically refer to the story of her life as a repentant sinner: the old growth is rotten and dead, whereas the new branch flourishes, representing her new life after her redemption by Christ.
Van Sorel was responsible for introducing the Italian High Renaissance to the Netherlands and was well known for his masterful representations of textiles.
This is especially evident in the cloth draped upon Mary Magdalene's legs, which resembles Oriental textiles in texture and motif.
In fact, an Orientalist style had emerged in Venice around the turn of the 16th century, when Oriental fabrics were either imported or reproduced by local artisans.

C 78
M 44
Y 33
K 4

C 21
M 77
Y 92
K 24

C 14
M 78
Y 89
K 6

C 25
M 29
Y 41
K 0

C 0
M 0
Y 45
K 0

C 16
M 16
Y 51
K 0

C 70
M 47
Y 42
K 16

C 16
M 12
Y 25
K 0

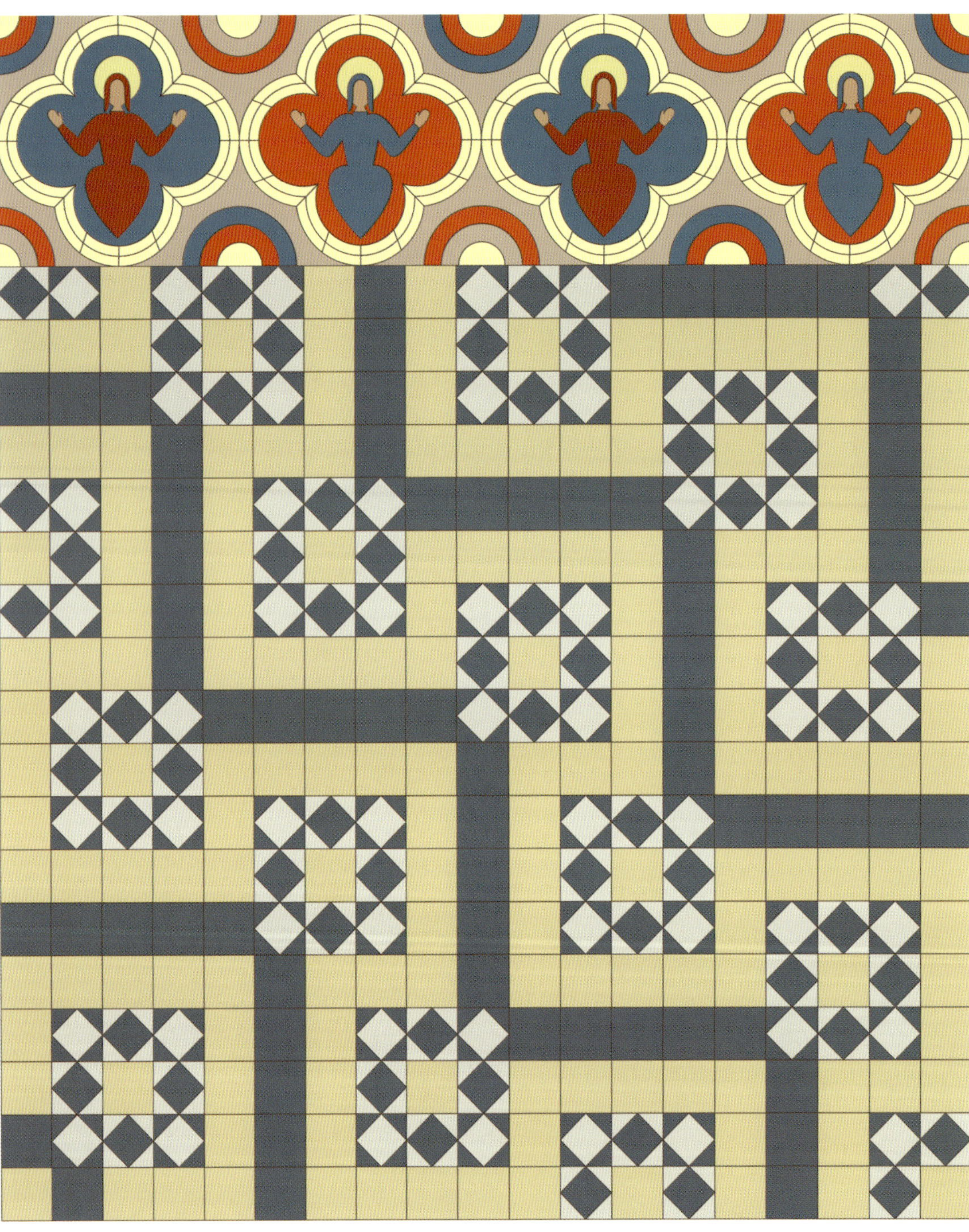

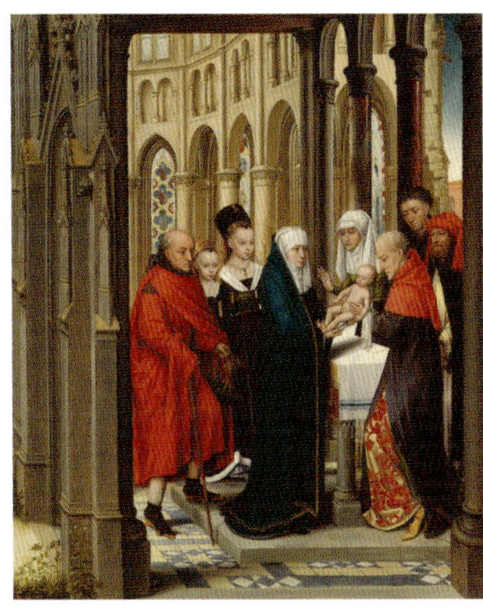

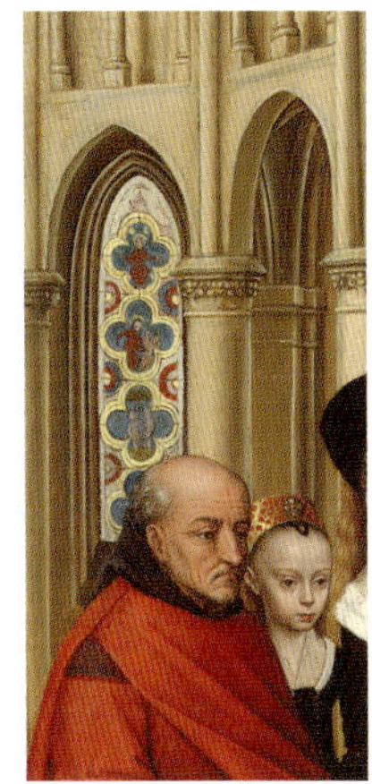

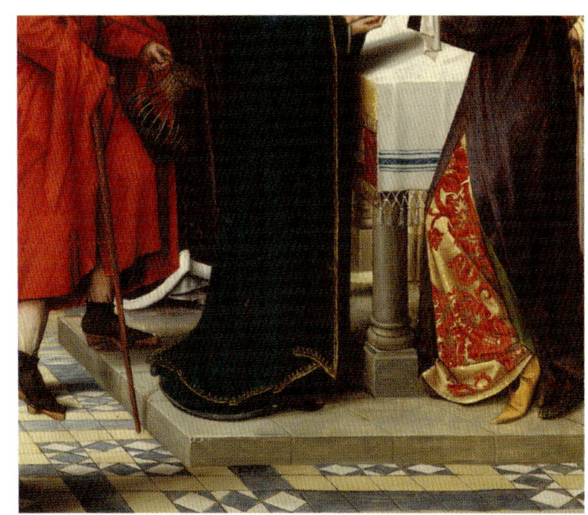

Master of the Prado
Adoration of the Magi
The Presentation in the Temple

circa 1470–1480
National Gallery of Art, Washington

Apart from the lavish representation of patterns and floor tiles, the most remarkable aspect of this painting is perhaps the miniaturistic precision with which the subjects' faces are represented. In particular, the two young girls' pensive and absorbed expressions make them extremely real and relatable. The subjects of this painting, dressed in Dutch clothes and with the typical clogs attached to their rich velvet shoes, might have been family members of this altarpiece's sponsor. The artist plays with architecture of a distinctly Dutch Gothic style, defining both open and closed spaces with pinnacles and pointed arches.
The identity of the painter is unknown, but this painting may have been produced by someone in Rogier van der Weyden's workshop, as it reveals a familiarity with Rogier's mature work. Above the heads of the two young girls, a stained-glass window with four different scenes is depicted. The three that we can clearly see show Christ in majesty, the creation of Adam and Eve, and the tree of knowledge in the Garden of Eden.

C 11
M 33
Y 89
K 7

C 20
M 38
Y 93
K 25

C 48
M 7
Y 18
K 0

C 14
M 52
Y 95
K 20

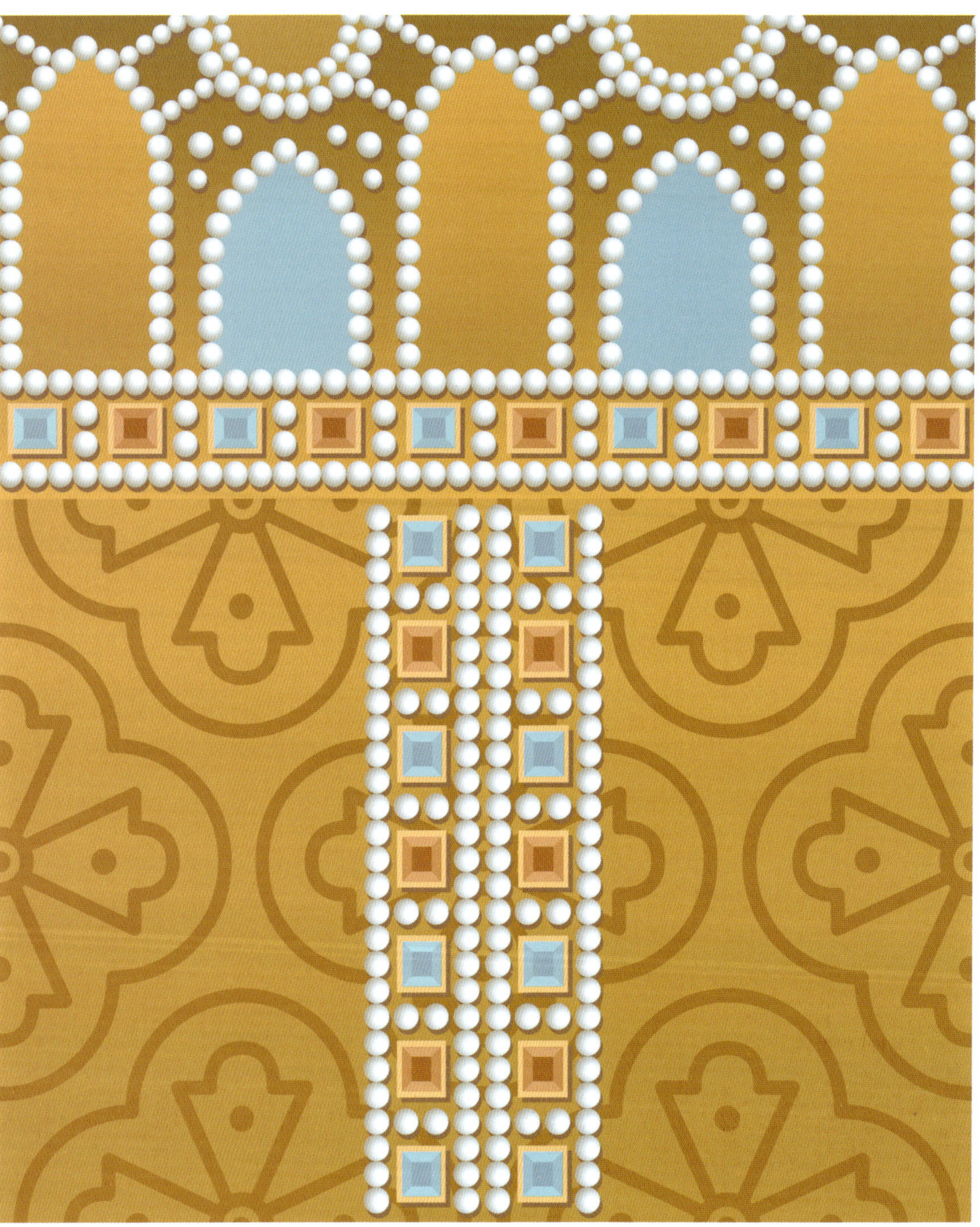

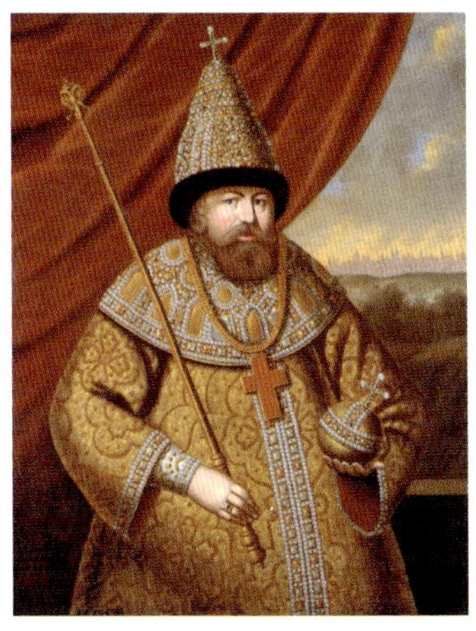

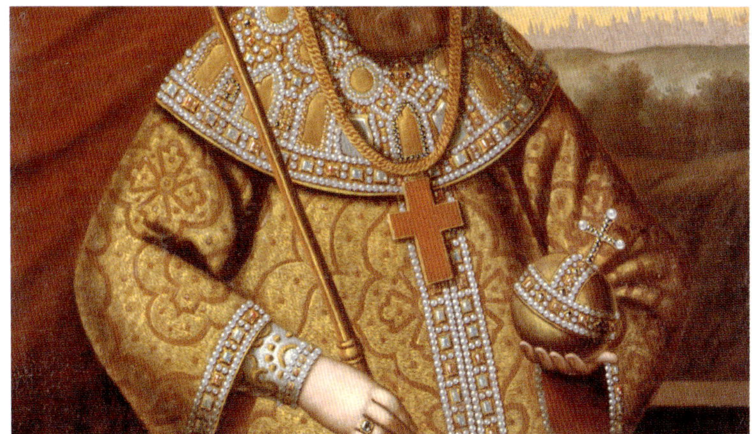

Anonymous
Alexei Mikhailovich, Tsar of Russia

17th century
Nationalmuseum, Stockholm

Alexei Mikhailovich, also known as Alexis of Russia, was the second Russian tsar of the Romanov house. His father, Michael, died when Alexei was a child, so Alexei received his education from a tutor before acceding to the throne at the age of sixteen. His contemporaries gave him the nickname "the Quietest," despite the fact that his reign was filled with social revolts and war. Alexei's reign included the Russian invasion of Poland and a war with Sweden, the Raskol (schism) in the Russian Orthodox Church, and several revolts. However, most sources agree that he was a gentle and popular ruler. He was also committed to introducing more elements of Western culture to the Russian court. Trade between Russia and Europe had started already in the 14th century, with brocade, velvet, and various kinds of silk and wool brought to Moscow from England, Italy, and France. In this portrait, we can see an example of the patterned and brightly colored fabrics used at the time in Russia. The tsar is wearing the 17th-century formal dress of his station. This "platno" is a long brocade garment with broad sleeves extending to the wrists and decorated with precious pearls. Only the tsar and priests had the right to wear the pectoral cross that is seen on Alexei in this portrait.

C 13
M 81
Y 100
K 9

C 16
M 31
Y 85
K 6

C 0
M 0
Y 0
K 100

C 22
M 52
Y 84
K 27

C 2
M 9
Y 31
K 0

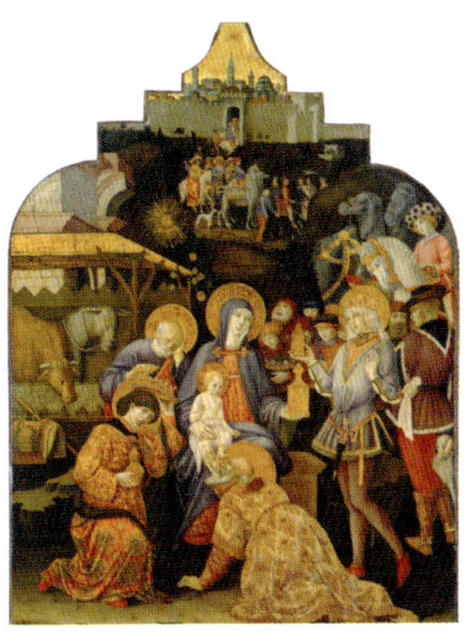

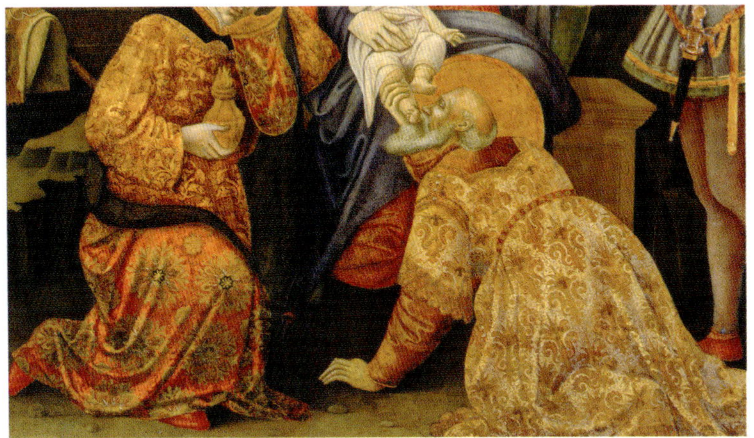

Benvenuto di Giovanni
The Adoration of the Magi

circa 1470–1475
National Gallery of Art, Washington

When we inspect this overcrowded scene closely, we can see the same characters both in the foreground and in the background at the top of the summit. This is because this painting depicts a chronological narration. What seems to be a dilapidated gate separates the past from the present, the excitement and movement of the journey from the stillness and quiet of the Magi's adoration of the infant Christ.

Here, Benvenuto already manages to approach the Renaissance ideal of realism in representation. This is achieved through an exquisite attention to detail, expressed not only in the magnificent decoration of the subjects' garments but also in the use of a wide range of facial expressions. Just a few years after he completed this painting, the artist's style changed dramatically. Perhaps the shift was already incubating around this time, when Benvenuto worked at the Siena Cathedral. There he would have seen miniatures by Liberale da Verona and Girolamo da Cremona that incorporated bright colors and manipulations of light. Benvenuto soon began to adopt these techniques, and also to experiment with the concept of spatial distortion.

C 0
M 0
Y 0
K100

C 0
M 1
Y 17
K 0

C 9
M 75
Y100
K 0

C 6
M 35
Y100
K 0

C 0
M100
Y100
K 0

C 85
M 45
Y 78
K 60

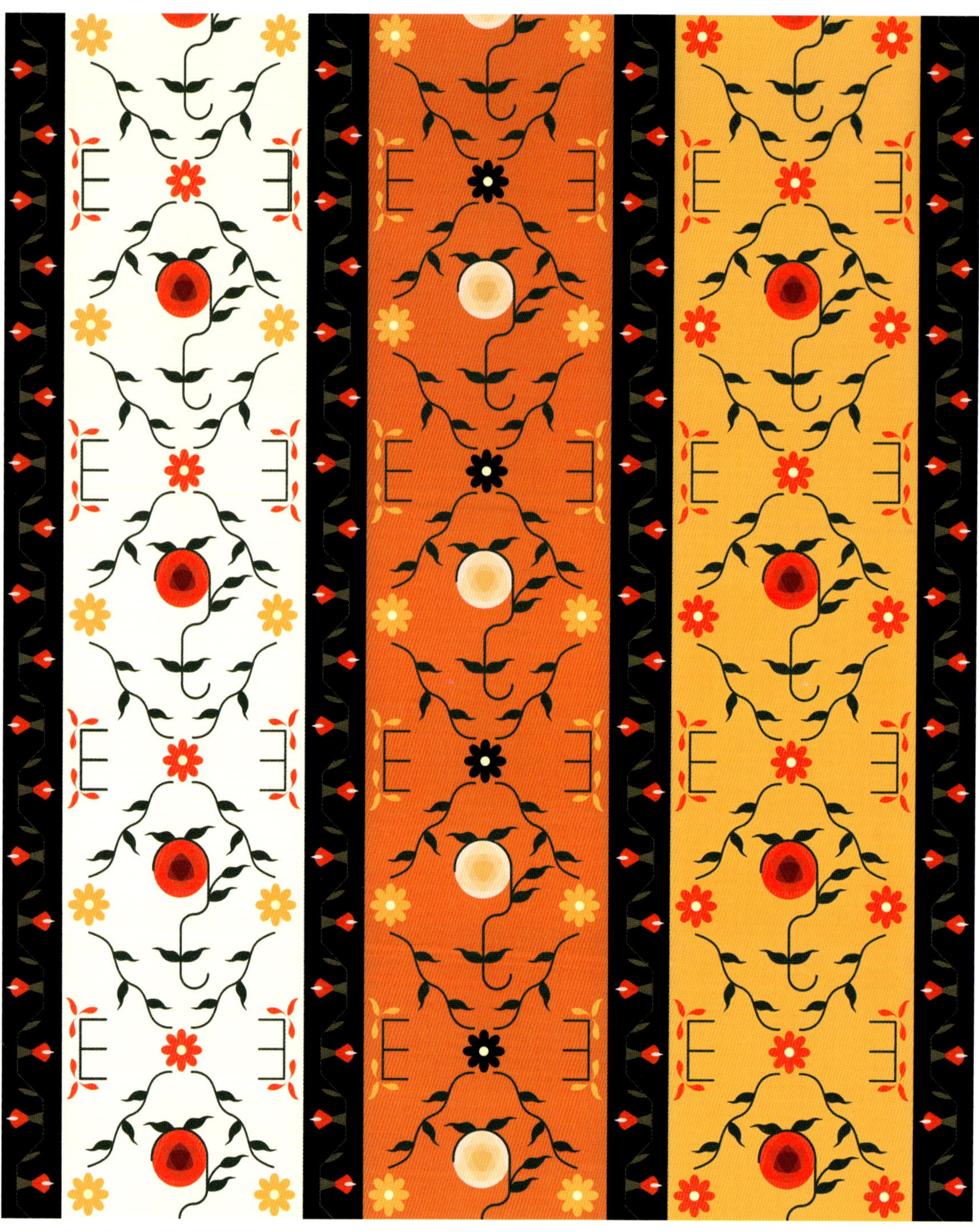

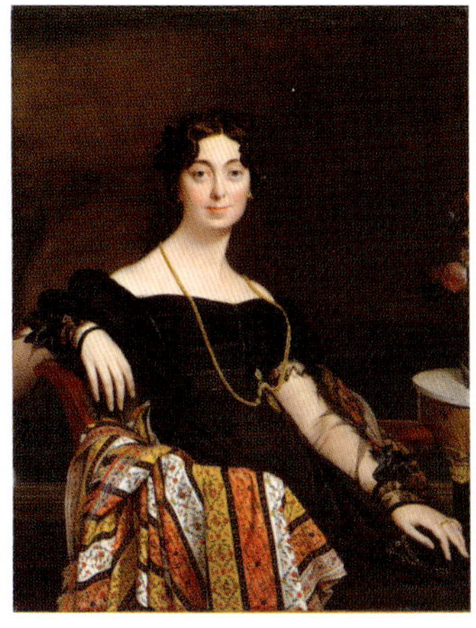
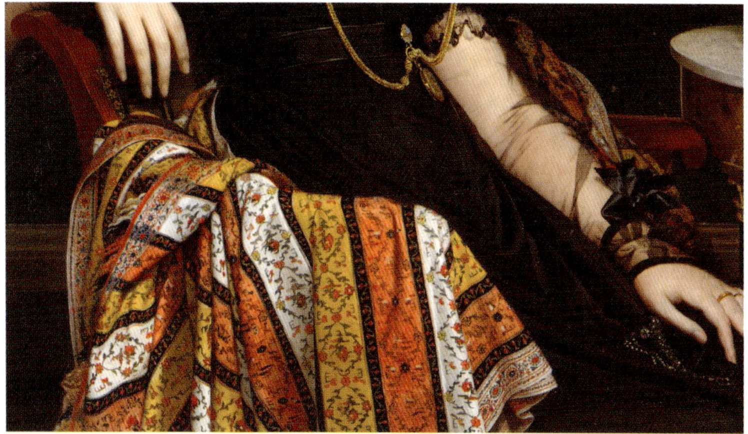

Jean-Auguste-Dominique Ingres
Madame Jacques-Louis Leblanc

1823
The Metropolitan Museum of Art, New York

Jean-Auguste-Dominique Ingres studied more than twenty different poses before finishing this portrait of Madame Leblanc. This is no surprise, as the painter was well known in the art world as a perfectionist. Like many perfectionists, however, he was also egomaniacal, insecure, and easily upset by art critics. In their critique of this painting, some commentators argued that the skin of Madame Leblanc was painted in the wrong colors: her nose looked too red, whereas the rest of her body looked as if she had no blood flowing through her veins. Other critics argued that the sitter looked like a monster with bulging eyes and sausagelike fingers, or even as if she lacked the upper part of her head. Despite such criticisms, this same painting also drew a great deal of praise. For instance, the friends Edgar Degas and Albert Bartholomé almost quarreled over who would include it in his collection. The two artists bought it along with the portrait of Monsieur Leblanc, the sitter's husband. Their initial purpose was to keep one each. Degas insisted that they not be separated and that he keep both. Bartholomé said to a friend that he lost 135,000 francs because of the excellent Madame Leblanc but that he pardoned her, since she left him for the love of Degas.

C 37
M 35
Y 92
K 35

C 0
M 34
Y 93
K 0

C 9
M 55
Y 58
K 0

C 15
M 69
Y100
K 21

C 0
M 0
Y 0
K100

C 97
M 64
Y 29
K 31

C 7
M 87
Y 99
K 22

C 4
M 56
Y100
K 0

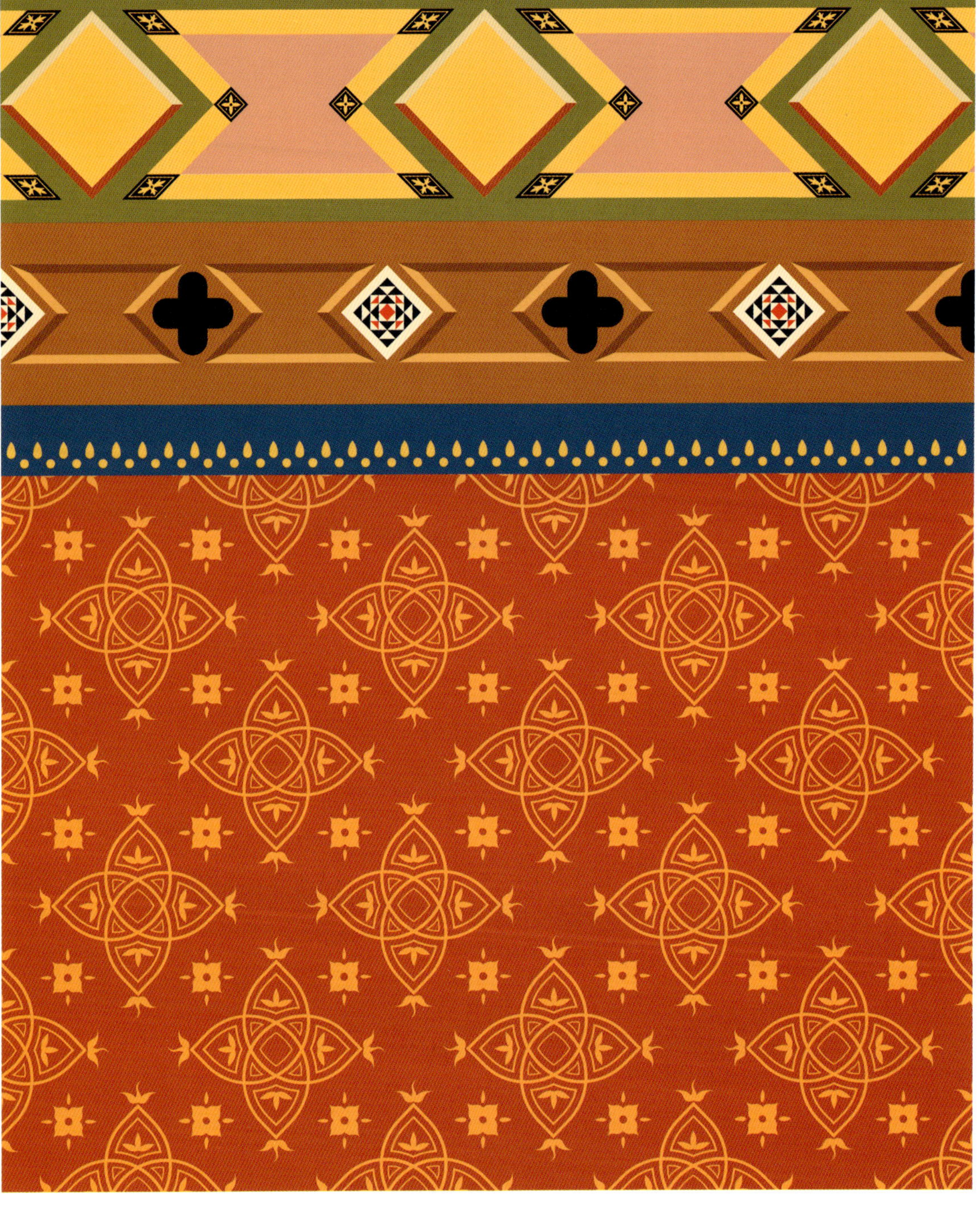

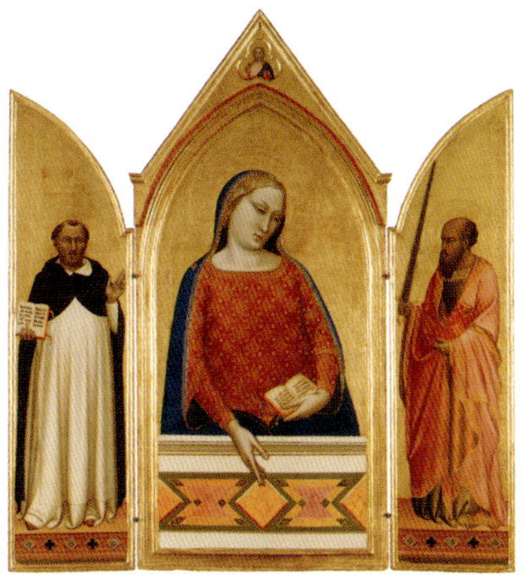
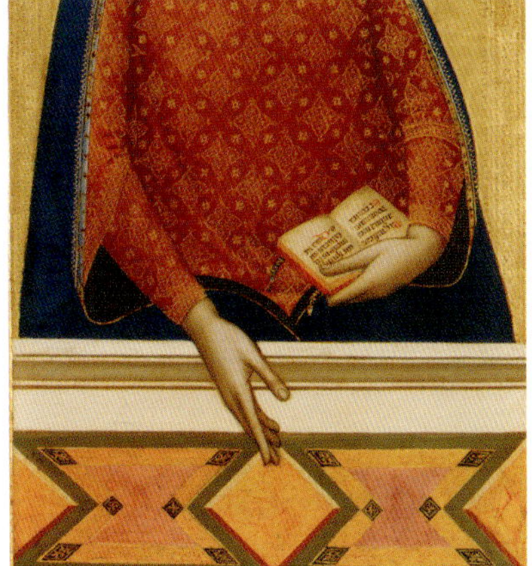
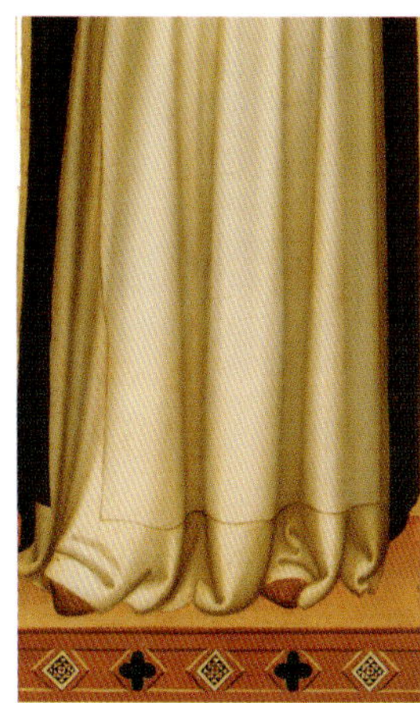

Bernardo Daddi
The Virgin Mary with
Saints Thomas Aquinas and Paul

circa 1335
The J. Paul Getty Museum,
Los Angeles

The sweet gaze of the Virgin in this work is one of the hallmarks of Bernardo Daddi's style. Daddi was one of the early Renaissance artists who broke with conventions of the previous generation of Gothic painters and strove for a more accurate depiction of reality. His art represents perhaps a sweetened version of his contemporary Giotto's style, alleviating Giotto's gravity with grace and lightness. Daddi appreciated smiling Madonnas, flowers, and draperies. In this triptych, Mary is flanked by Saints Thomas Aquinas and Paul, identified by their characteristic clothes and accessories. The artist's interest in fabrics is displayed in the richness of the Virgin's clothes. She wears a patterned dress, covered with a blue cloak painted with ultramarine or lapis lazuli, a very precious pigment at the time. Also striking is the way the Virgin's hand comes out of the circumscribed space of her parapet. It almost seems as if her hand might break out of the painting itself to reach us. By the depiction of such a simple gesture, the artist fully captures the role of Mary, whose womb is a means of reconnecting humanity and God.

C 24
M100
Y 97
K 43

C 19
M 97
Y100
K 24

C 0
M 46
Y100
K 0

C 16
M 48
Y100
K 8

C 16
M 44
Y 96
K 31

C 0
M 0
Y 0
K100

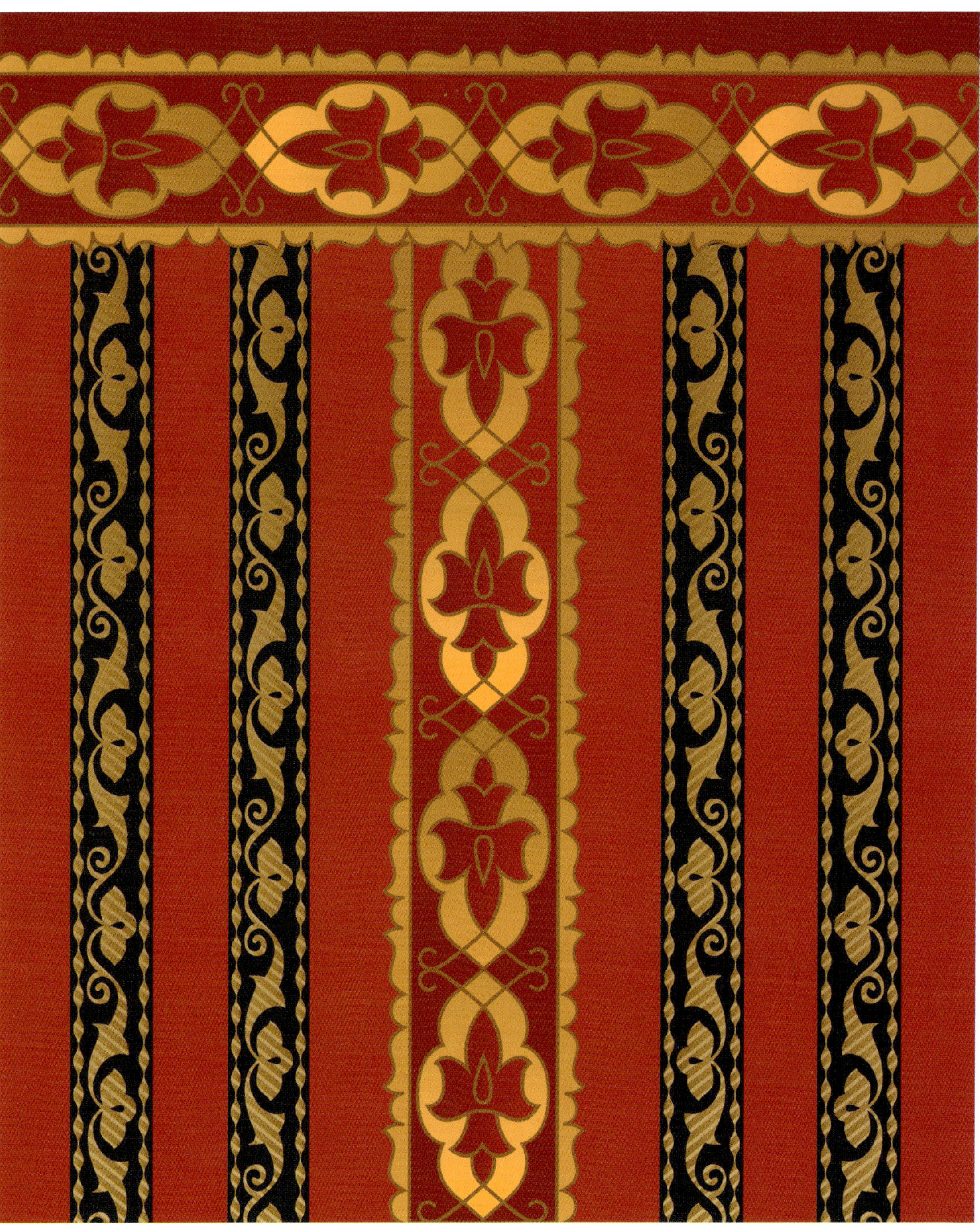

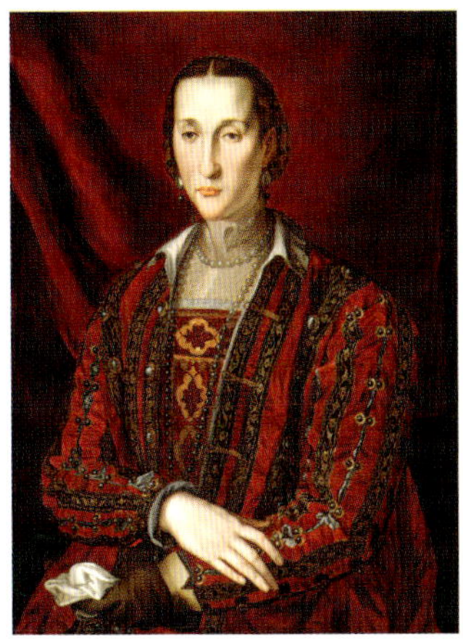

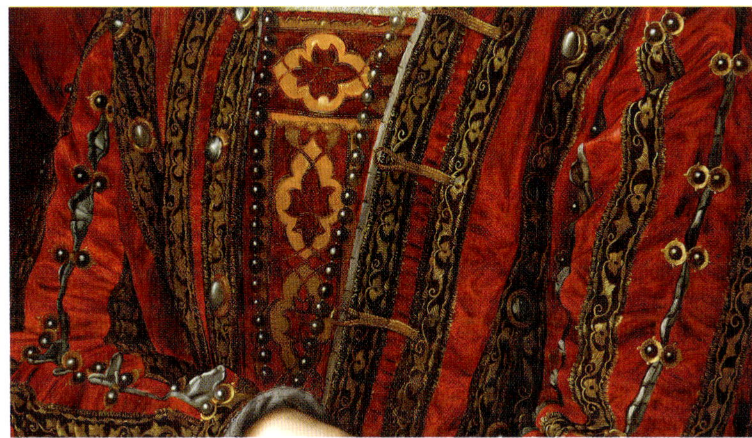

Agnolo Bronzino
Eleonora di Toledo

circa 1560
National Gallery of Art, Washington

More than six variants of this portrait have been found in Europe. Although the execution of the hand and face and the details of the rich costume would seem to be close to Bronzino's high standards of work, art historians have argued over whether this specific painting should be attributed to some other member of his workshop. The woman depicted is Eleonora di Toledo, a Spanish noblewoman who married Cosimo I de' Medici. She is considered the first modern "first lady."

Eleonora and Cosimo's marriage was a powerful and long-lasting alliance, in which both exerted a considerable influence on Florence and on each other. Although Eleonora, a Spaniard, was initially unpopular in Florence, she eventually gained acceptance through a public relations effort promoted by her husband. Astonishingly for the era, Cosimo remained faithful to her throughout their marriage. Eleonora, besides becoming a strong female role model of the time, was a fashion icon who regularly employed ten gold and silver weavers to work on her apparel. Perhaps these fine clothes helped to disguise her sickly appearance, as she suffered from both a severe calcium deficiency and malaria. The signs of Eleonora's ill health are already evident in this painting, which is likely to have been completed when she was near the end of her life.

C 62
M 52
Y 68
K 60

C 24
M 89
Y100
K 24

C 82
M 61
Y 43
K 39

C 24
M 40
Y 78
K 16

C 24
M 16
Y 36
K 0

C 0
M 0
Y 0
K100

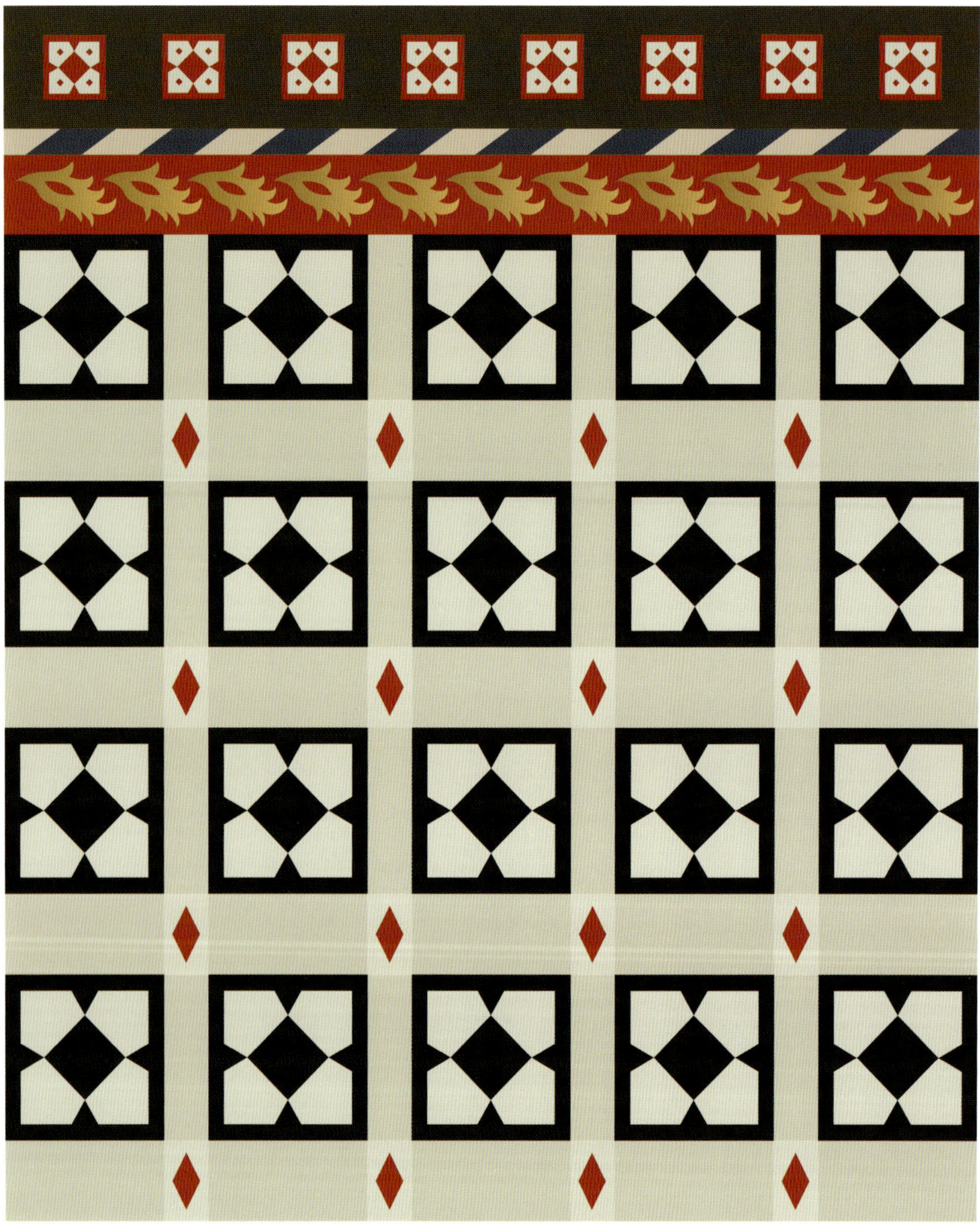

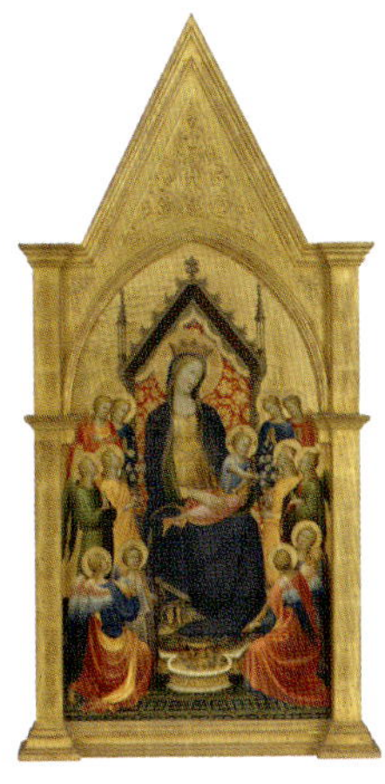
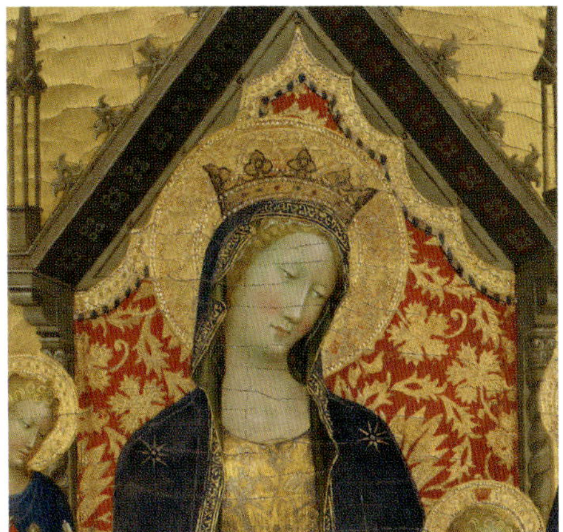
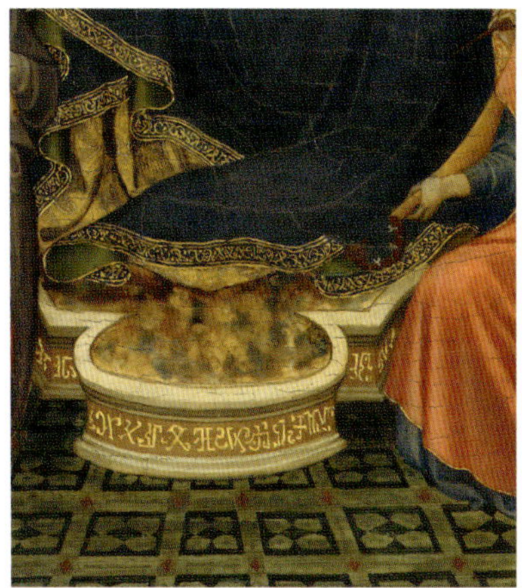

Gherardo Starnina
Madonna and Child with Musical Angels

circa 1410
The J. Paul Getty Museum,
Los Angeles

The Gothic style spread throughout Europe between 1380 and 1450. It was known as "art courtois" for its attempt to represent the aesthetics of court life, with its arabesques and golden ornaments. This Madonna and Child by Gherardo Starnina is a fine example of this artistic style. The materials and patterns of the Virgin's brocaded gown, the throne, and the floor tiles are all portrayed in rich detail. The angels' poses and the colors of their garments also demonstrate the love for symmetry that characterized this epoch. Gold leaf is used everywhere, from the background and halos to the clothing and furniture. The infant Christ interacts with his classic attributes: his left hand is wrapped around a goldfinch, a symbol of his crucifixion, while his right hand touches the lilies that an angel holds, a symbol of purity.

C 44
M 25
Y 32
K 5

C 22
M 82
Y 93
K 18

C 46
M 49
Y 96
K 49

C 17
M 80
Y 93
K 7

C 0
M 0
Y 0
K100

C 18
M 36
Y 80
K 6

C 36
M 66
Y 71
K 49

C 65
M 55
Y 69
K 60

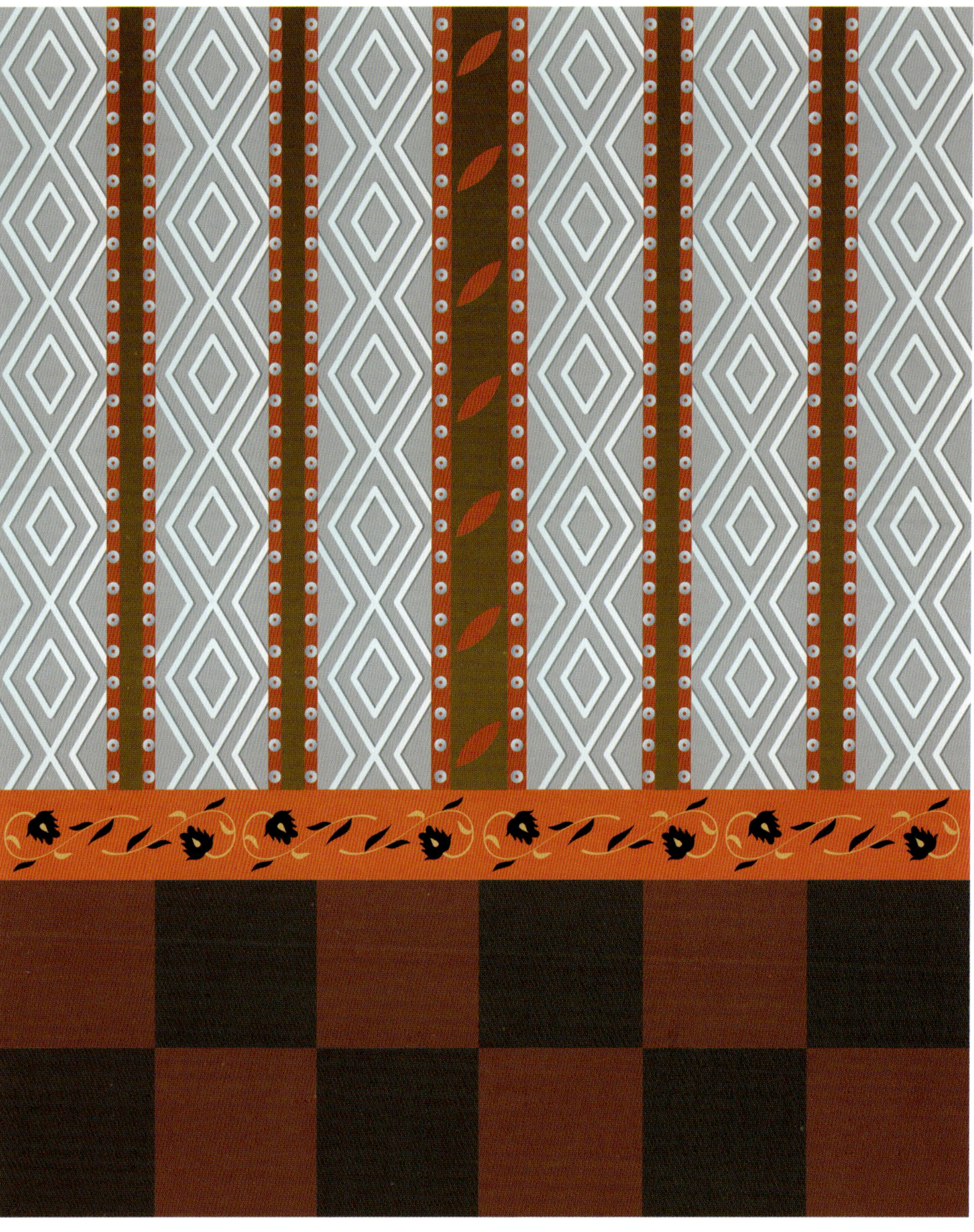

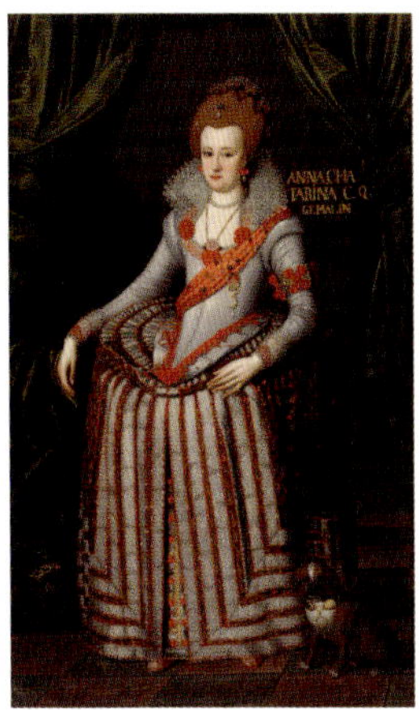

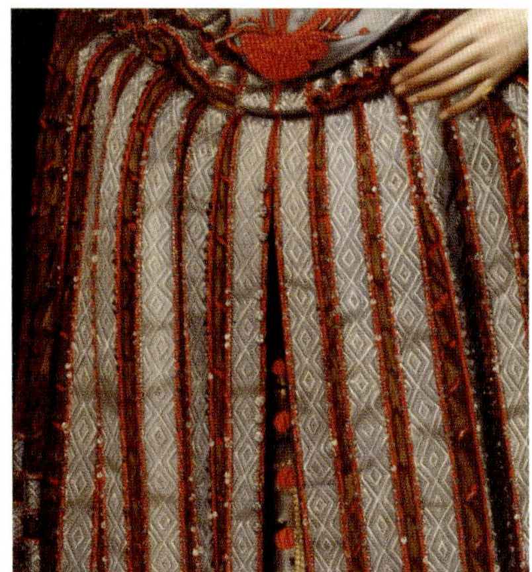

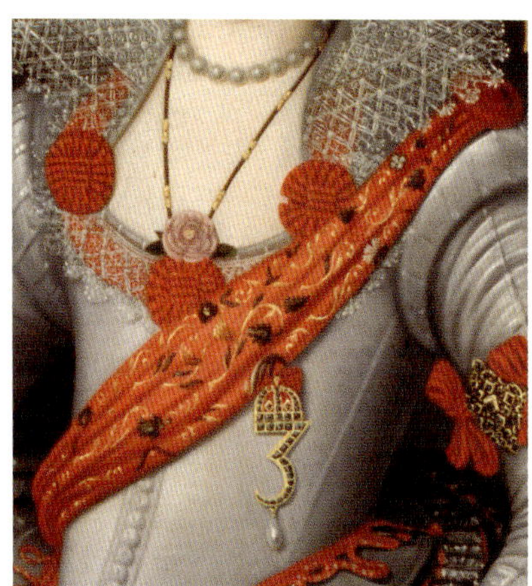

Remmert Petersen
Anna Katarina

16th century
Nationalmuseum, Stockholm

Anne Catherine of Brandenburg is portrayed here in rich garments, with an extremely wide gown and an inverted cone-shaped corset in keeping with the style of the time. Anne Catherine became queen of Denmark and Norway through her marriage to Christian IV of Denmark, who is remembered as one of the most ambitious, popular, and proactive Danish kings. Not much information about Anne Catherine is available, although we know that she became popular during her husband's reign for her modesty and piety. However, there are doubts as to whether she actually wielded any power or influence in court and whether her marriage to the king was a happy one. They married when she was twenty-two and he was twenty, a year after he ascended to the throne. Their first child was stillborn, but the couple had another six children, three of whom died at a young age. While she seems to have happily accompanied the king on his travels, she also had to deal with his several mistresses, including her chamberwoman, Kirsten Madsdatter, with whom Christian IV had one of his several illegitimate sons. The court painter Remmert Petersen was known to be a respectable and wealthy man.
He worked for the king for forty-five years, and his records show that he was repeatedly paid by the court for his portraits long after he had handed them over.

C 72
M 33
Y100
K 45

C 71
M 20
Y 60
K 18

C 0
M 0
Y 0
K100

C 11
M 82
Y 77
K 23

C 7
M 52
Y100
K 15

C 0
M 5
Y 31
K 0

C100
M 92
Y 8
K 0

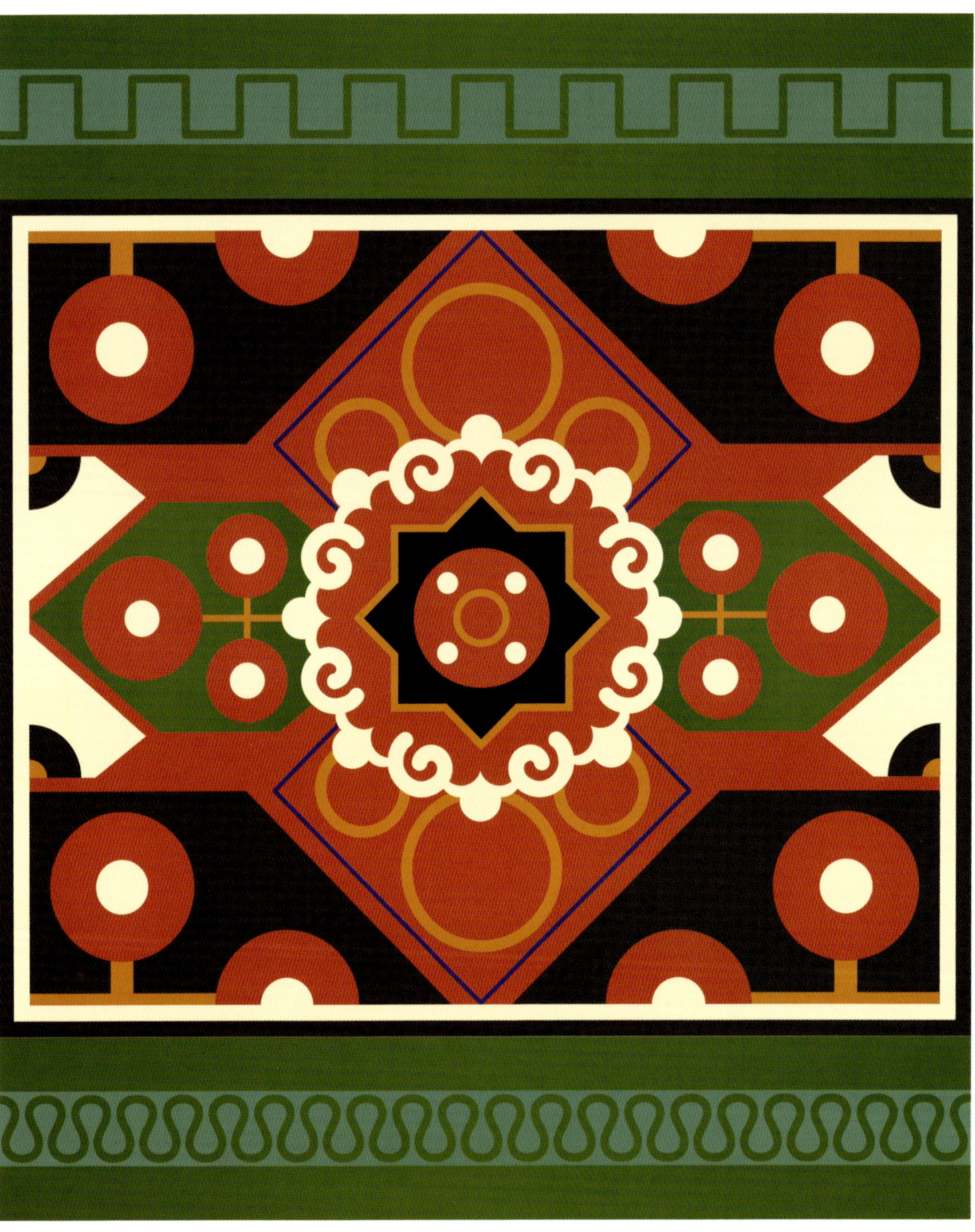

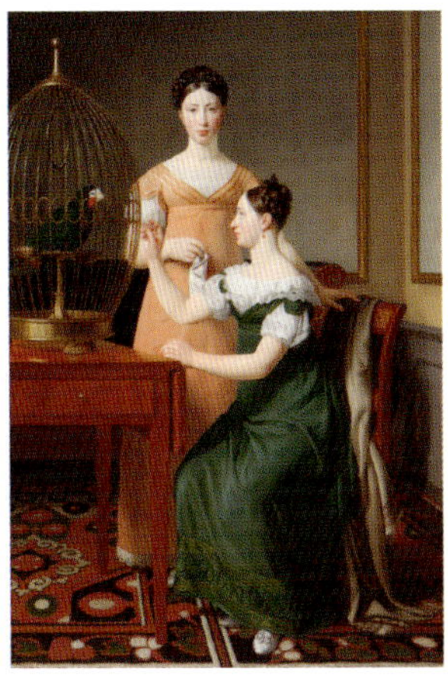

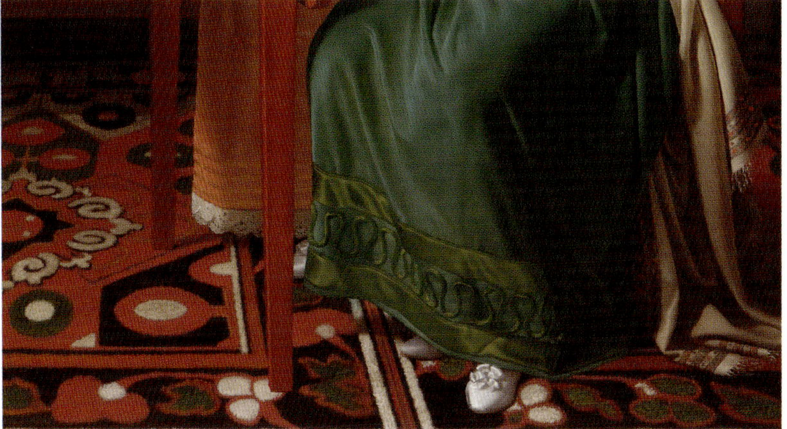

Christoffer Wilhelm Eckersberg
Mendel Lavin Nathanson's Elder Daughters, Bella and Hanna

1820
SMK National Gallery of Denmark, Copenhagen

Around 1820, Christoffer Wilhelm Eckersberg, often referred to as the father of Danish painting, was in high demand as a portraitist of Copenhagen's aristocracy and middle class. It was at this time that Mendel Levin Nathanson, his greatest patron, commissioned him to paint two large family portraits. Nathanson, an economics writer and editor, had become well known in Denmark for his successful efforts to advance equality for the country's Jewish population. In this painting, Nathanson's elder daughters, Bella and Hanna, are portrayed in different poses, yet somehow still look incredibly alike. Sobriety and elegance characterize both the sisters and the room's furnishings. The parrot in the cage could be interpreted as an allusion to the sisters' longing to leave their safe yet claustrophobic home environment.

C 56
M 29
Y 38
K 16

C 34
M 15
Y 19
K 0

C 10
M 3
Y 14
K 0

C 71
M 50
Y 44
K 49

C 14
M 45
Y 85
K 33

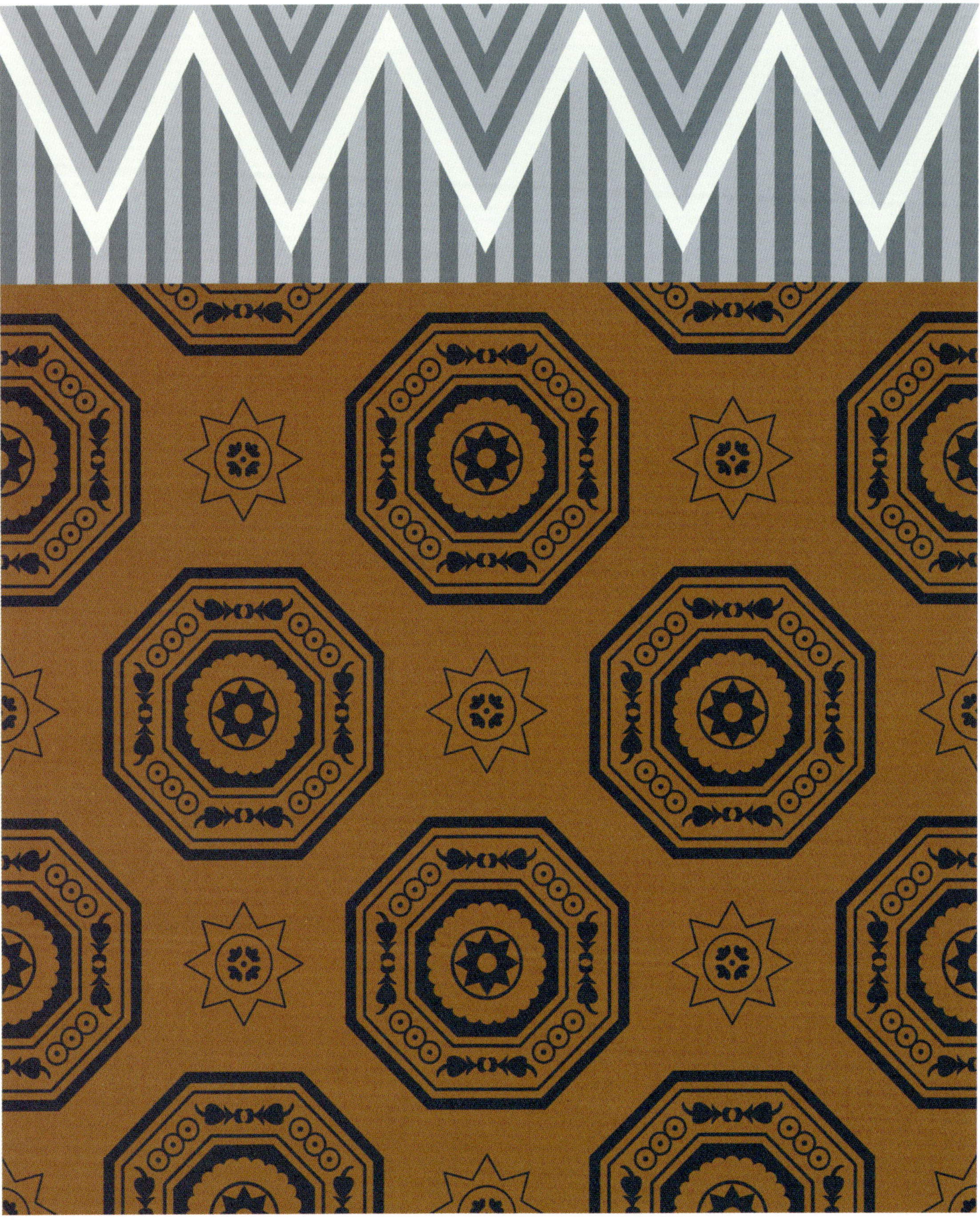

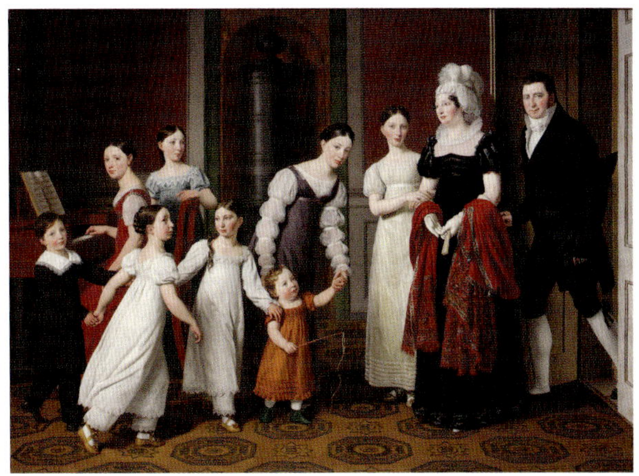
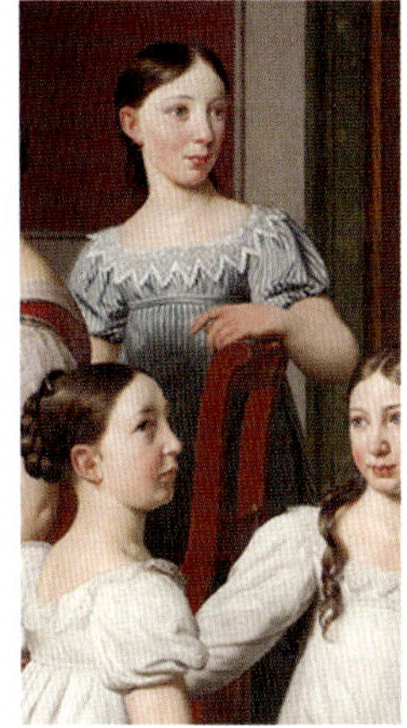
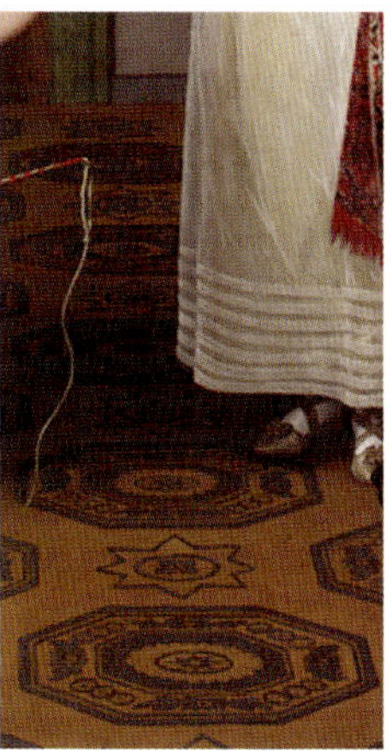

Christoffer Wilhelm Eckersberg
The Nathanson Family

1818
SMK National Gallery of Denmark, Copenhagen

This is one of the two paintings that Mendel Levin Nathanson, a Danish writer and editor, commissioned from Christoffer Wilhelm Eckersberg after the artist's return from his studies in France and Italy. In this family portrait, Eckersberg's meticulous composition and arrangement of the subjects immediately catch the eye—techniques that he learned in France during his apprenticeship with Jacques-Louis David. Eckersberg's attention to detail also allows him to masterfully convey the patterns, texture, and quality of fabrics. The artist deliberately chose to avoid a still pose in favor of depicting an everyday scene, attempting to capture the numerous family members in movement. In particular, the portrait depicts Mr. Nathanson entering the room, which arouses curiosity and excitement among most of his children. All of the family members are elegantly dressed in expensive clothes, although it is Mrs. Nathanson's attire above all that demonstrates the high social status of the family.

C 0
M 52
Y 87
K 24

C 0
M 0
Y 0
K100

C 14
M 91
Y 84
K 39

C 0
M 99
Y 92
K 77

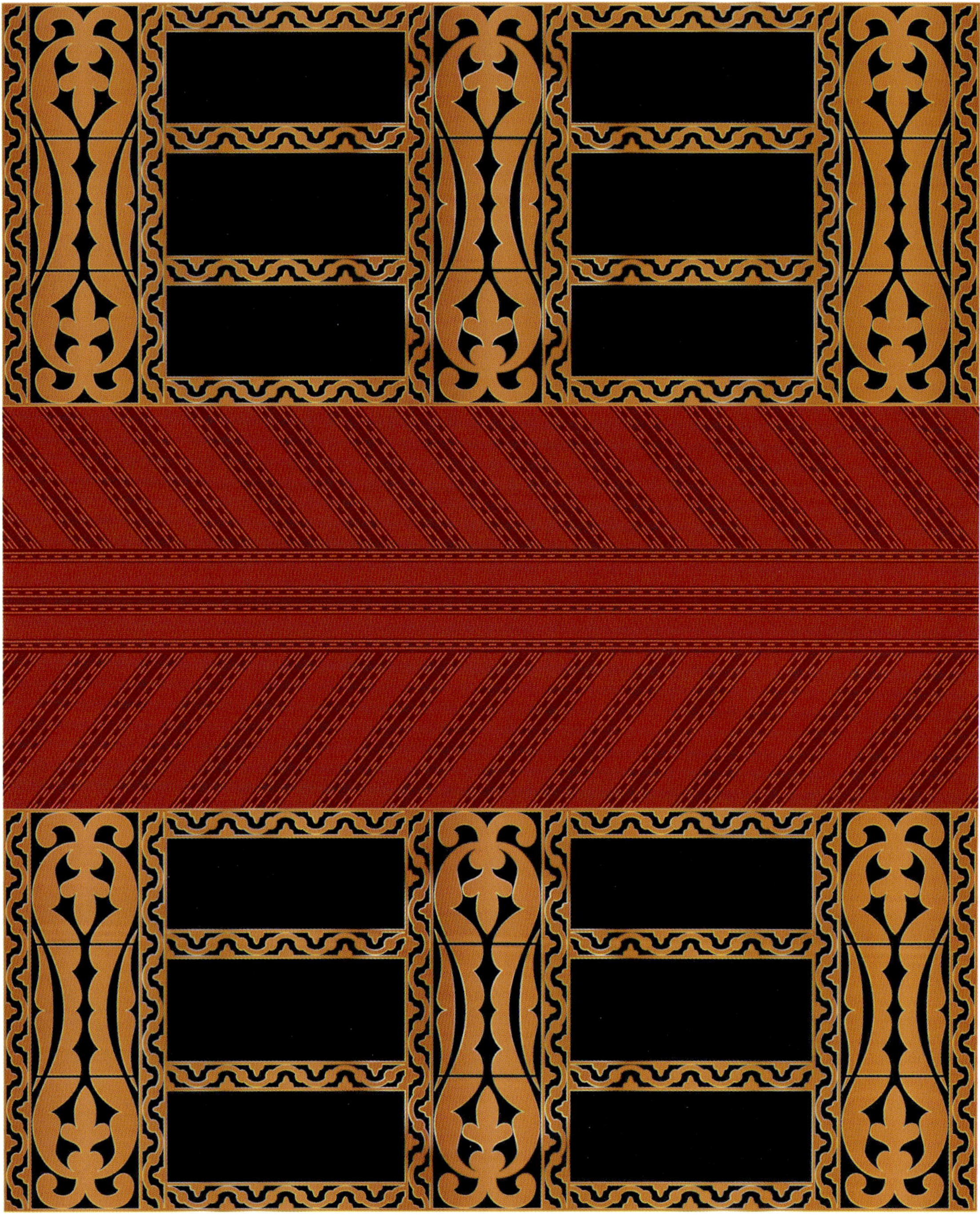

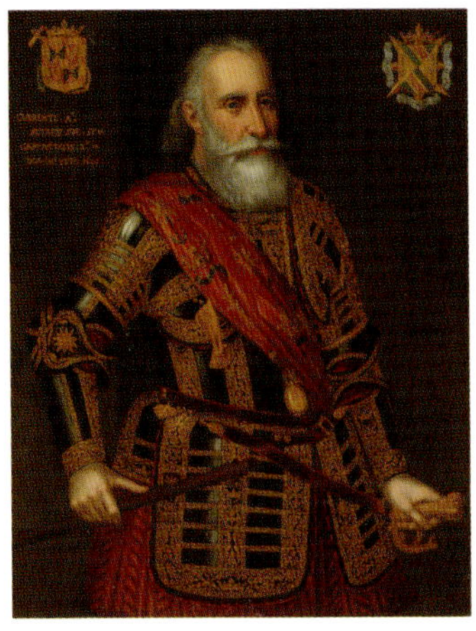

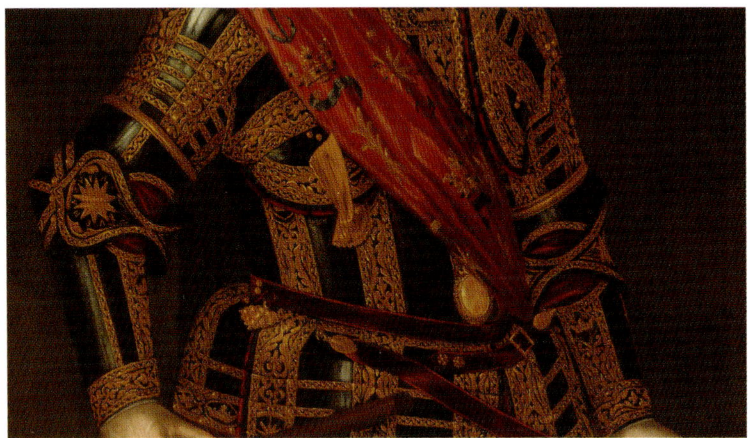

Anonymous
Portrait of Francisco Hurtado de Mendoza, Admiral de Aragon

1601
Rijksmuseum, Amsterdam

Francisco Hurtado de Mendoza was given supreme command of the Spanish army in the late 16th century. He was considered a generous general, but according to a contemporary source, "his pride and hard mind made him hated, and his bigoted piety often became an object of mockery of his subordinates." At this stage in his career, Hurtado de Mendoza was focused on a single task—to carry out a campaign against the Dutch. After several attacks made in vain, Hurtado led his Spanish troops to meet the Dutch on the dunes of Nieuwpoort beach on July 2, 1600. Thousands of soldiers fell on both sides, but the Dutch won narrowly. The Spanish admiral was captured and made a prisoner of war. Surprisingly, this portrait was painted one year into his captivity. Dressed in full regalia, he seems anything but a prisoner. Perhaps it was especially thanks to "his pride and hard mind" that he managed to keep his dignity in front of the Dutch.

C 34
M 46
Y 96
K 34

C 0
M 0
Y 0
K100

C 60
M 56
Y 84
K 76

C 18
M 14
Y 58
K 13

C 44
M 32
Y 36
K 14

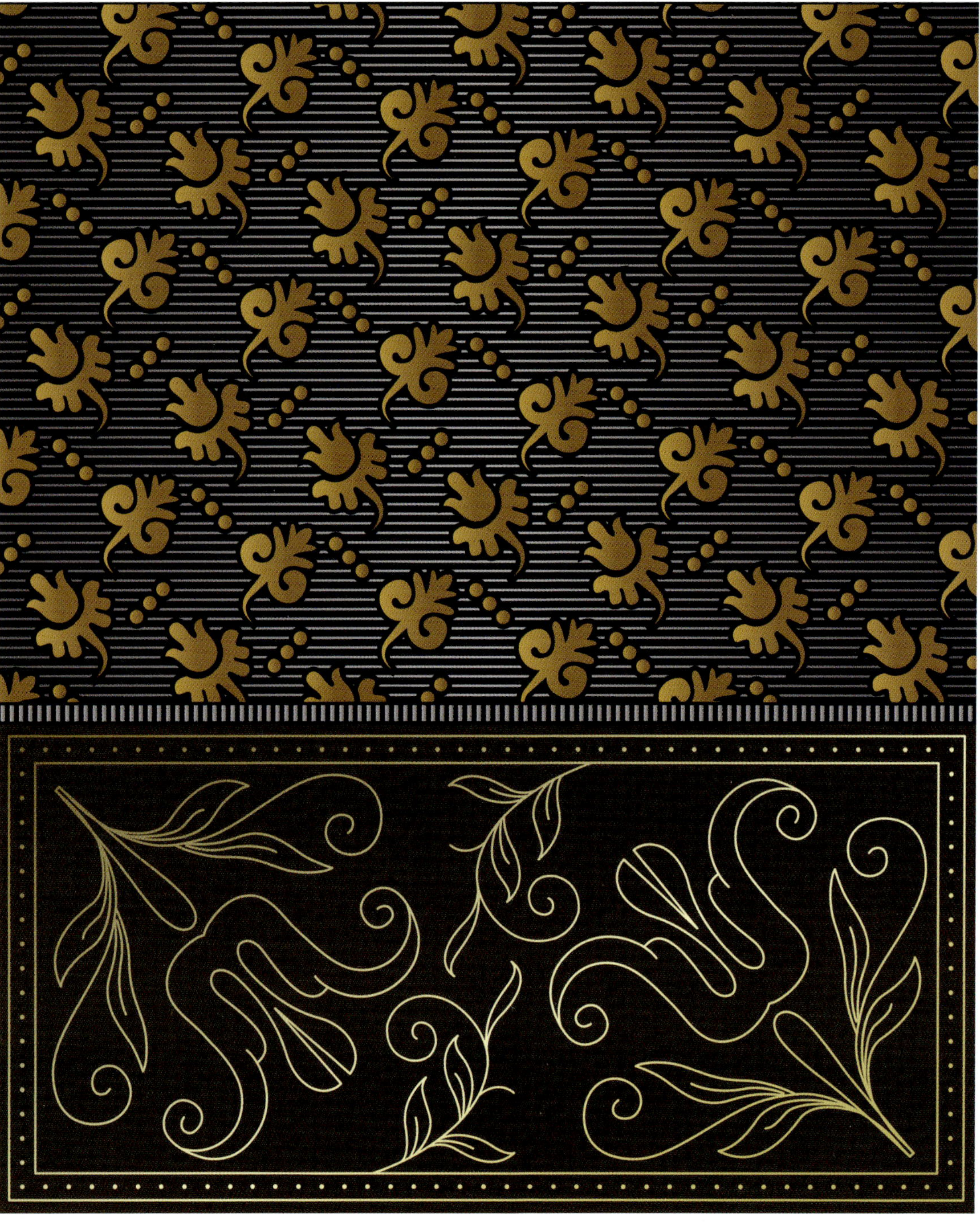

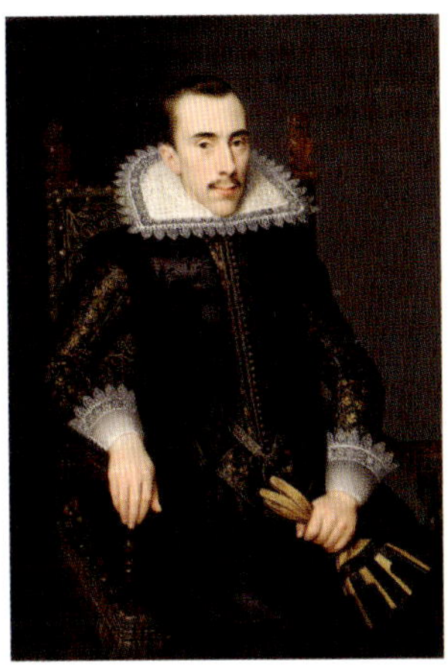

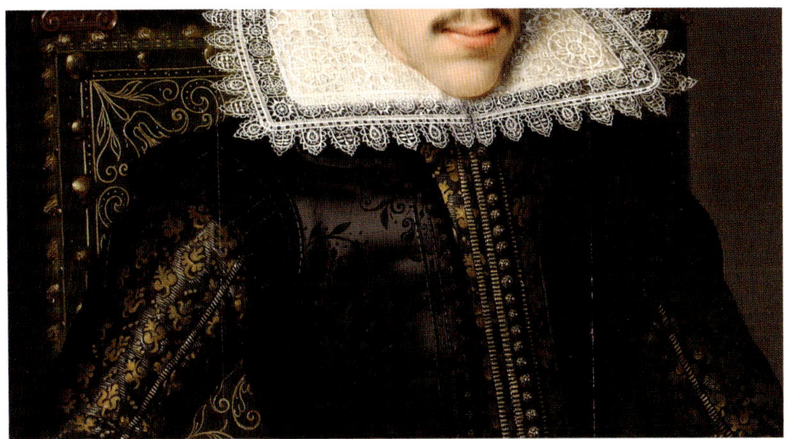

Salomon Mesdach
Portrait of a Man,
possibly Walterus Fourmenois

1620
Rijksmuseum, Amsterdam

The subject of this painting may have belonged to a successful family of textile traders, the Courten-Fourmenois, residing in England and the Netherlands. The family's flair for textiles is evident in the rich and elaborate garments worn by the man in the portrait, as well as in the intricate chair back. Between 1617 and 1630, the Courten-Fourmenois family commissioned a series of portraits from an artist whose identity was uncertain well into the 19th century. The painter has now been recognized as Salomon Mesdach, a relatively unknown artist whose work was probably sponsored by the family. Although the identity of the painting's subject is also somewhat uncertain, there seem to be enough clues to identify him as Walterus Fourmenois, brother of the better-known Catharina Fourmenois. He was described by his brother-in-law as "worshipping nothing," although it is unclear what exactly this means.

C 6
M 6
Y 27
K 0

C 0
M 0
Y 0
K100

C 5
M 28
Y100
K 5

C 13
M 93
Y 96
K 24

C 29
M 93
Y 83
K 65

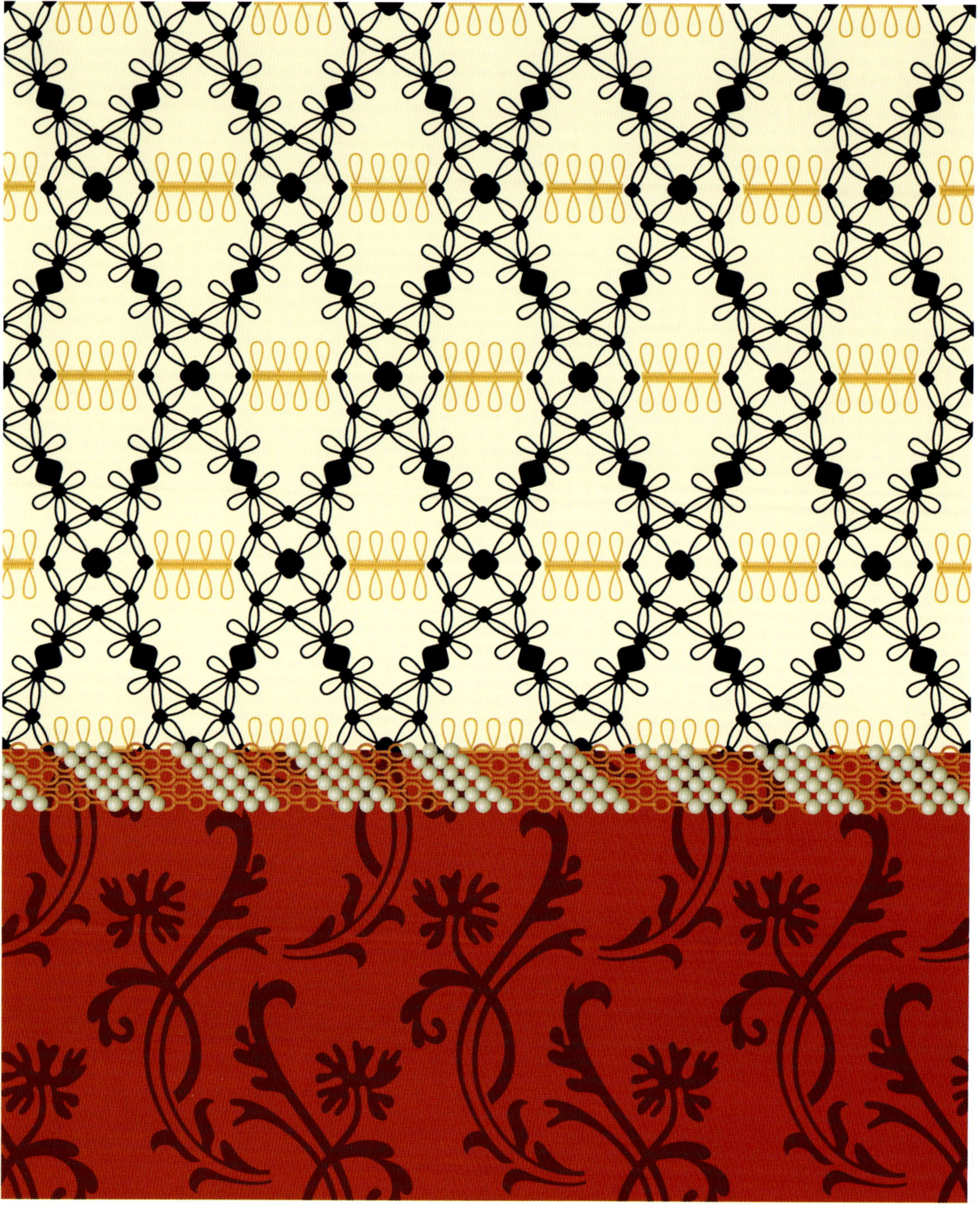

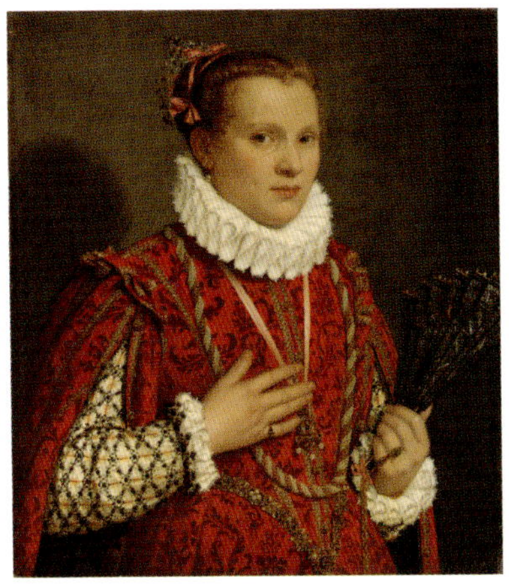

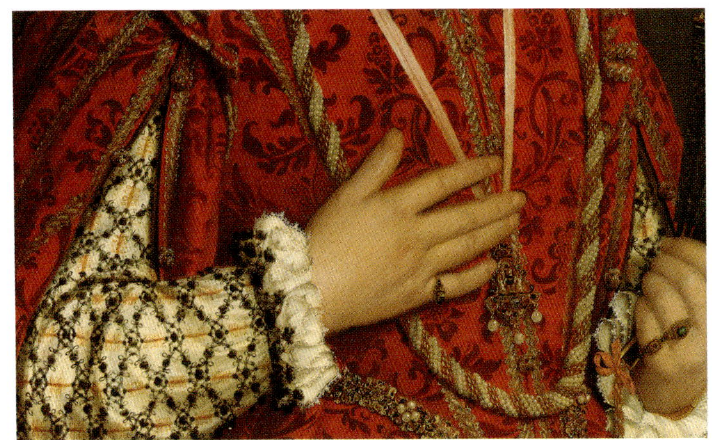

Giambattista Moroni
Portrait of a Young Woman

1560–1578
Rijksmuseum, Amsterdam

During the Renaissance, strict sumptuary laws were enacted that dictated what different members of society could wear. This would allow social groups to be distinguished from one another, and those who did not obey would be fined. In Bergamo, where the painter Giambattista Moroni spent most of his career, a law of 1540 prohibited the use of gold and other precious decorative ornaments. This law had a statute specifically relating to fans, which could only have bone handles. In this painting, Moroni and his subject do not seem to have followed this particular city ordinance, as the woman everywhere draped in gold: from the richly decorated red brocade dress and its sleeves to the large belt on her waist and the pendant of her necklace. Folding fans like the one depicted in this portrait had started to replace fixed fans throughout Europe in the 16th century. The fashion trend started in Italy, although it is likely that the innovation had found its way from the East. Such fans were an important and often opulent fashion accessory, specifically used as a status symbol and carried by both men and women.

C 15
M 77
Y 100
K 31

C 14
M 35
Y 69
K 8

C 33
M 35
Y 57
K 24

C 63
M 53
Y 72
K 70

C 18
M 89
Y 100
K 37

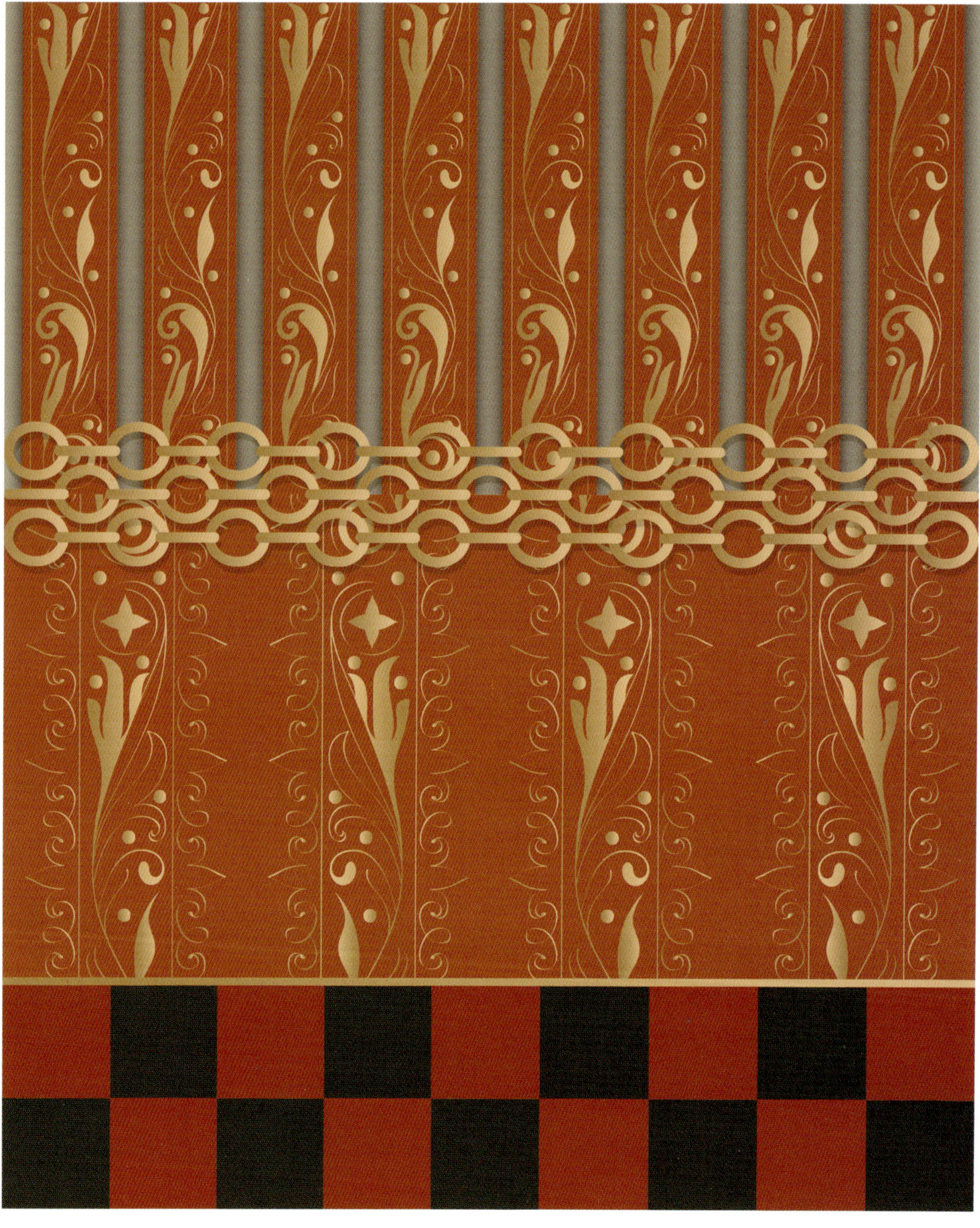

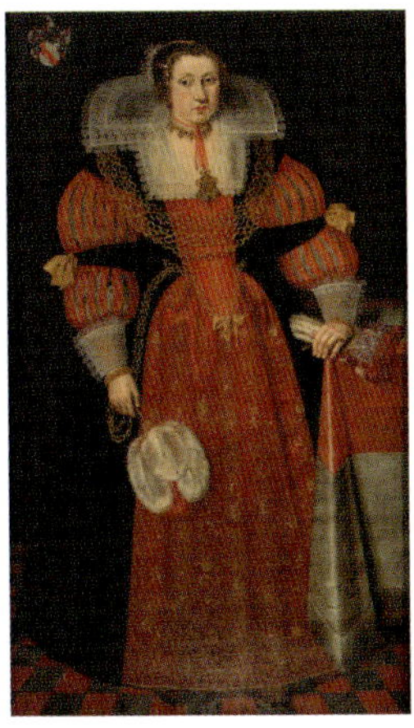

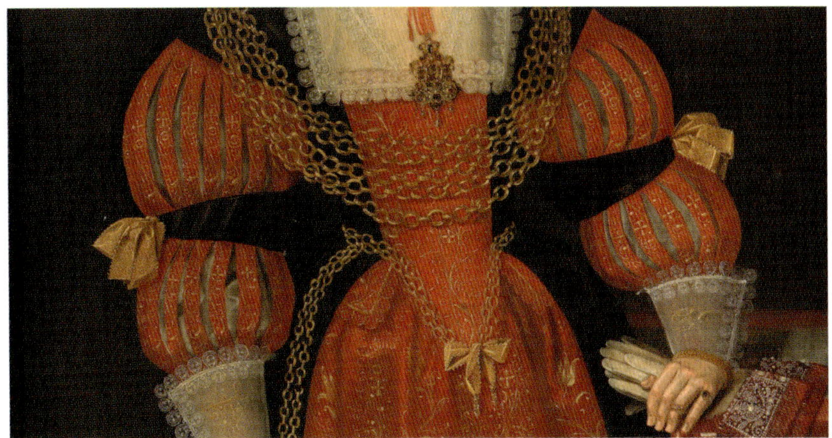

L. J. Woutersin
Portrait of Sophia de Vervou

1630
Rijksmuseum, Amsterdam

This painting of Sophia de Vervou represents a specific style of early Dutch portraiture that flourished at the beginning of the 17th century. This style observes a specific type of decorum and impersonality that Karel Mander had described in his didactic poem on the art of painting. In this example, the expression of the woman is quite aloof, formal, and unsmiling. Portraits of this period were often used to communicate status, religious attitudes, and family identity—hence the family crest in the top left corner. However, the painter seems to break with one common portrait convention of the time. Typically, men's hands were portrayed in assertive gestures, whereas women's were shown in more passive ones. However, Sophia de Vervou's hands, despite holding feminine objects such as a feather fan and richly decorated gloves, convey a sense of assertiveness, as do her overall figure and posture.

C 16
M 13
Y 41
K 0

C 15
M 30
Y100
K 13

C 24
M 97
Y100
K 54

C100
M 65
Y 25
K 29

C 16
M 80
Y 70
K 31

C 55
M 45
Y 53
K 45

C 24
M 97
Y100
K 54

C 27
M 71
Y100
K 48

C 39
M 43
Y 91
K 53

C 55
M 54
Y 80
K 75

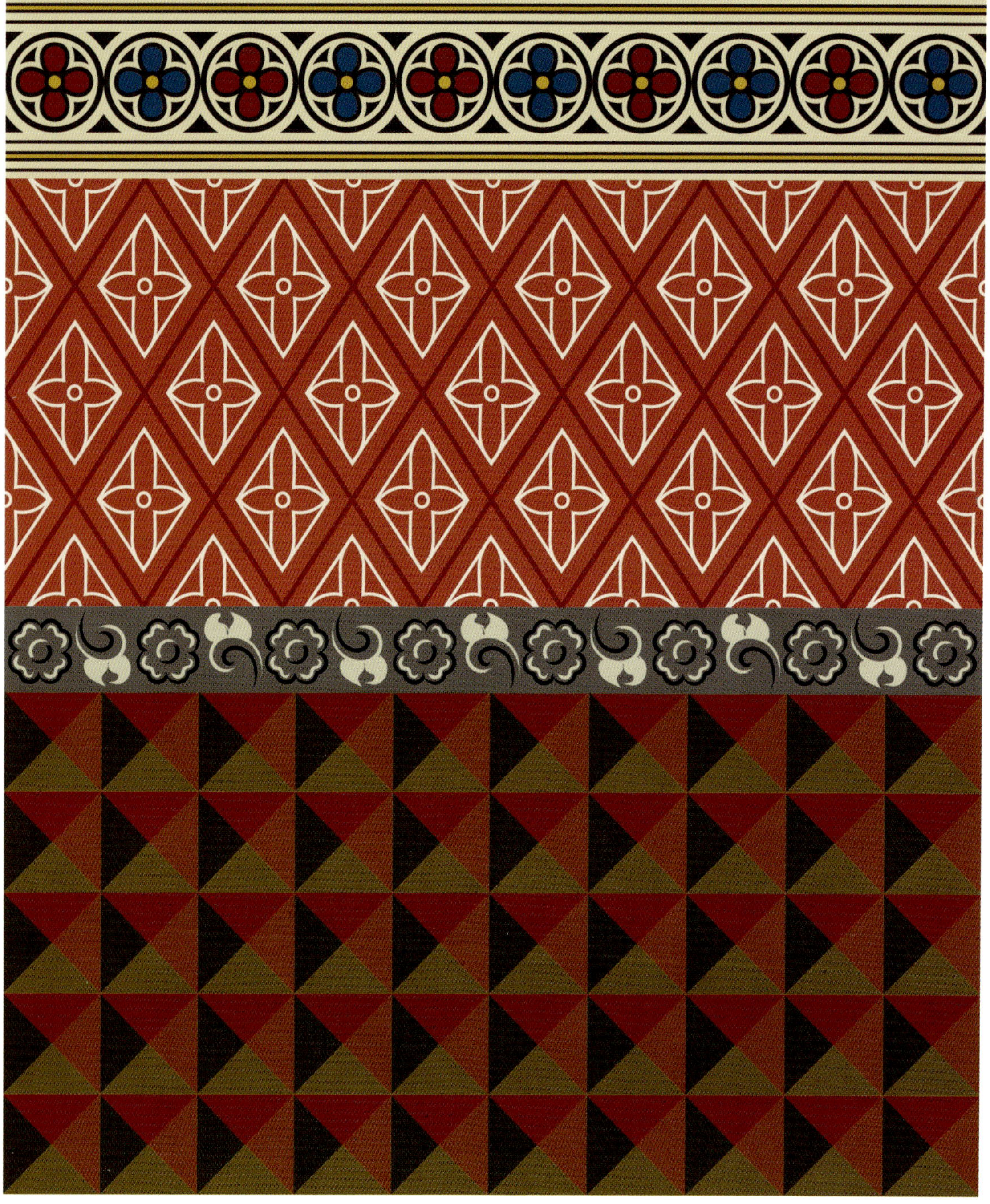

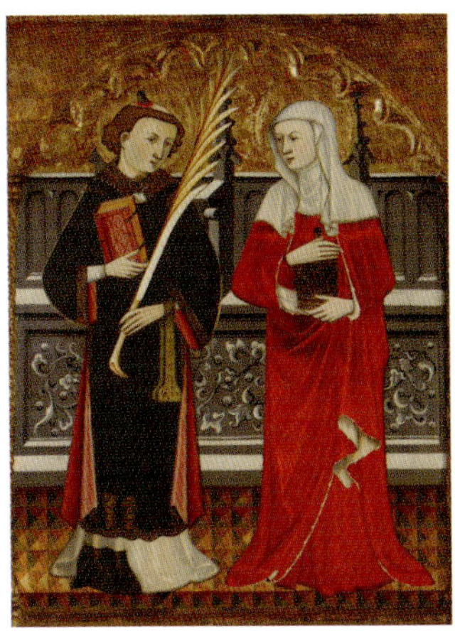 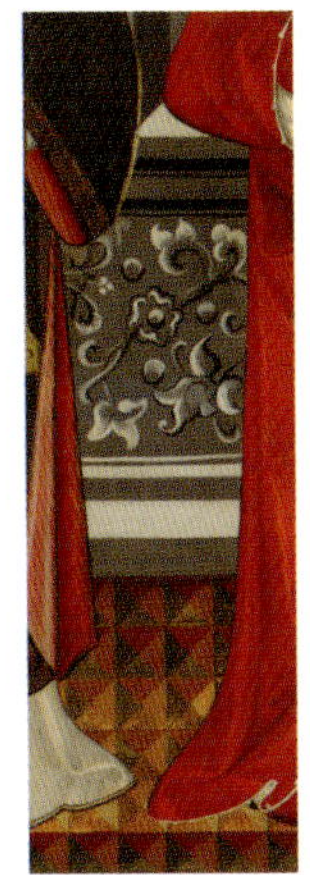 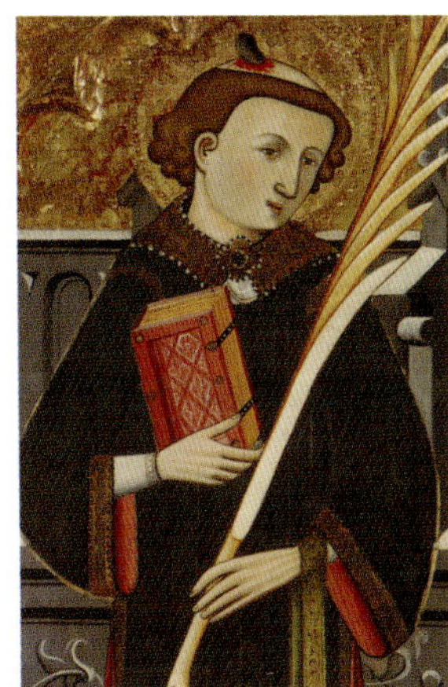 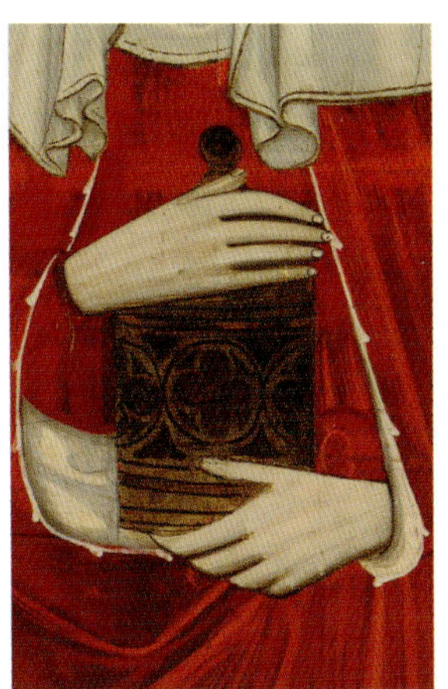

Pere Vall
Saint Stephen and Saint Mary Magdalene

circa 1400
Indianapolis Museum of Art at Newfields

Pere Vall is one of the very few identifiable artists active during the early 15th century in Catalonia. He must have been fairly popular at the time, as many of his paintings have been found in the region. Vall's work is characterized by the portrayal of unusual stories from the sacred texts, which make his paintings quite original. Here, Saint Stephen stands next to Saint Mary Magdalene in an environment characterized by Gothic architecture, perhaps in front of a church stall. Saint Stephen is traditionally venerated as the first martyr of Christianity. He was brought to trial by the Jewish authorities, who had accused him of blasphemy, and was stoned to death. Here, Vall portrays him with the symbol of his martyrdom: a stone stuck in his bleeding head. By his side, Saint Mary Magdalene stands veiled in a red tunic, holding the vessel of ointment she used to anoint of Jesus. Despite the conservative nature of his work, Vall used unique compositional devices to obtain interesting chromatic effects. In this painting Vall employs colored floor tiles that seem to constitute both the floor and the wall without any allusion to depth or perspective.

C 26
M 22
Y 44
K 0

C 22
M 78
Y 76
K 15

C 3
M 9
Y 51
K 0

C 37
M 33
Y 56
K 14

C 69
M 77
Y 90
K 78

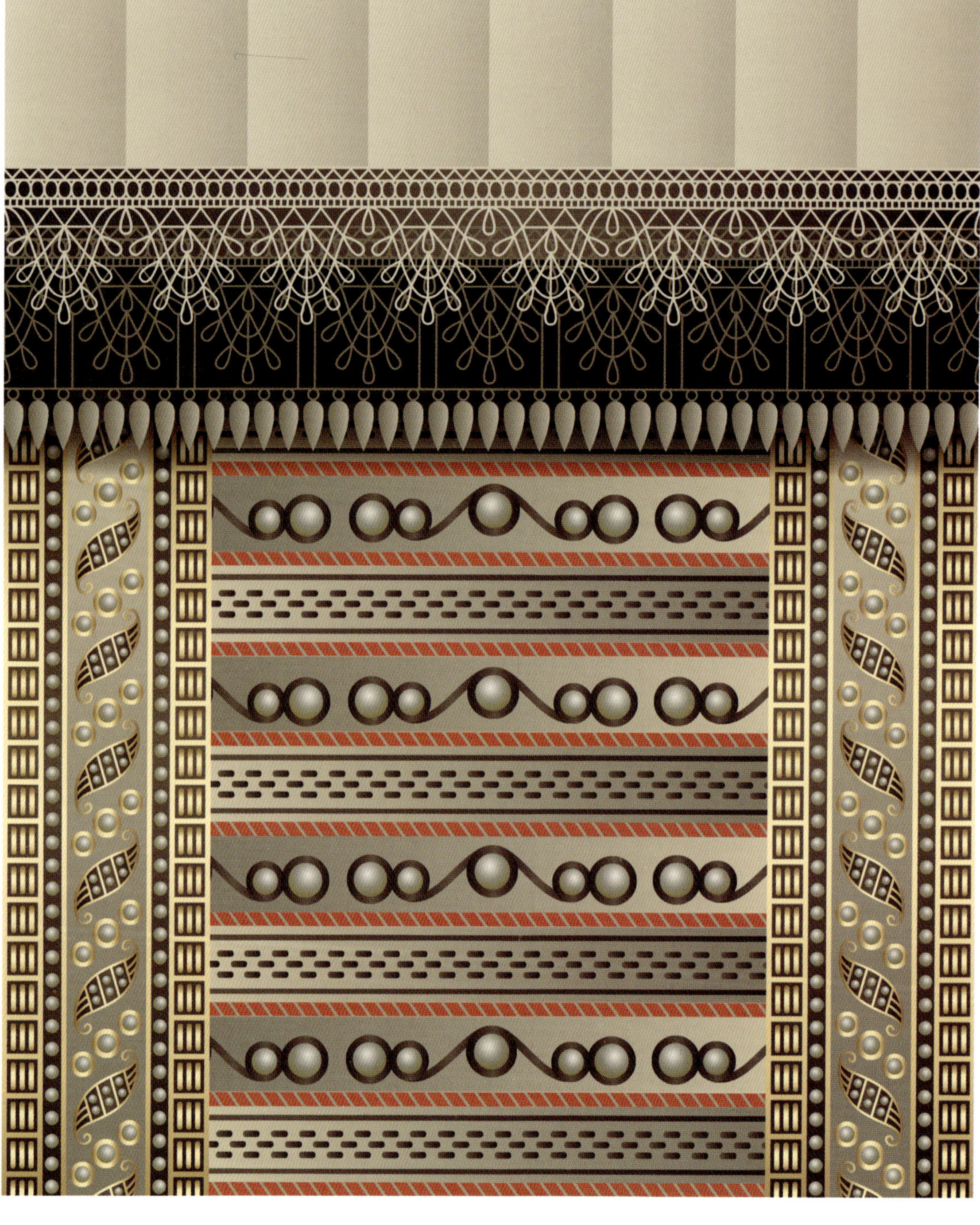

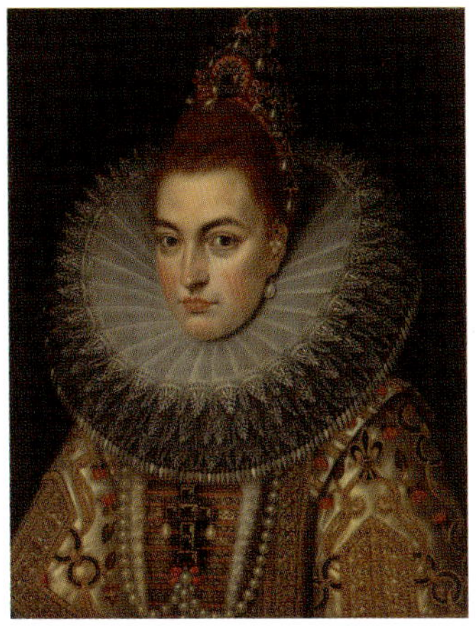

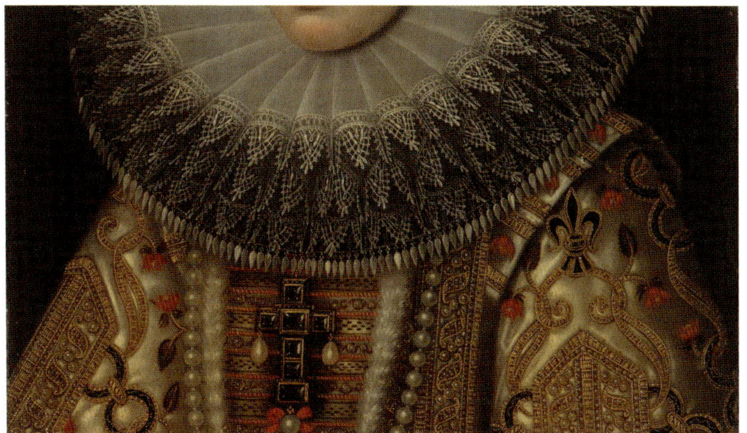

Workshop of Frans Pourbus the Younger
Isabella Clara Eugenia, Consort of Archduke Albert VII

circa 1600
Rijksmuseum, Amsterdam

Isabella Clara Eugenia of Spain, here portrayed in an ivory-colored dress decorated with red rosettes, a large ruff, and many pearl decorations, was the daughter of Philip II of Spain. Isabella married her second cousin Albert VII, Archduke of Austria. The couple, known as "the Archdukes," ruled the Spanish Netherlands on behalf of the Spanish crown. Their reign was a key period in the history of the Spanish Netherlands. The couple fueled the development of a South Netherlandish identity, and during their reign, the visual arts became a powerful tool for achieving this goal. In fact, the Archdukes' patronage of many artists resulted in the beginning of a golden age and the creation of the Flemish Baroque style. One of the key features of works by Frans Pourbus the Younger, the Flemish artist whose workshop produced on this portrait, was the placement of his subjects against plain monochromatic backdrops, as we can see here.

C 63
M 58
Y 63
K 49

C 27
M 20
Y 41
K 0

C 19
M 13
Y 38
K 0

C 67
M 44
Y 49
K 16

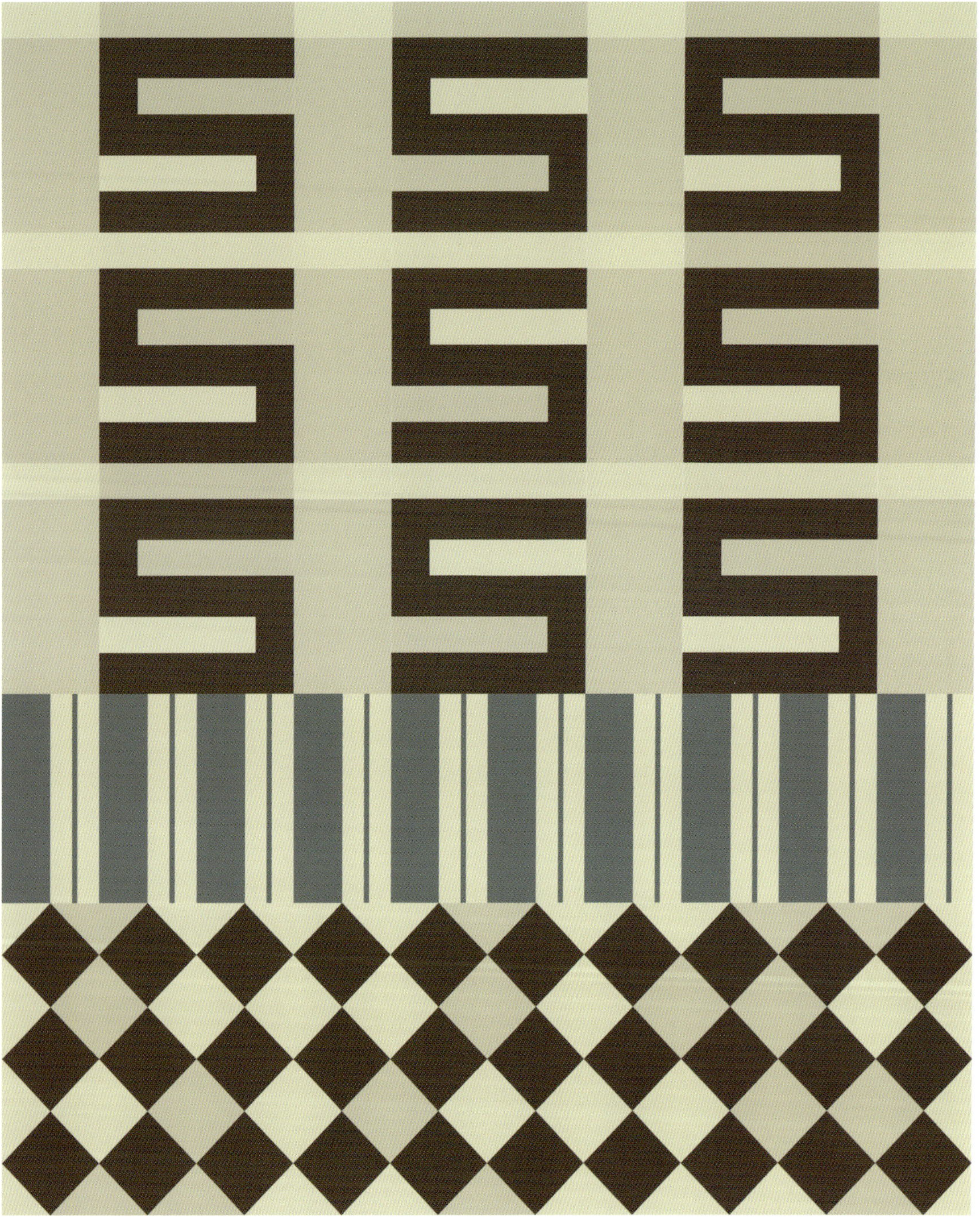

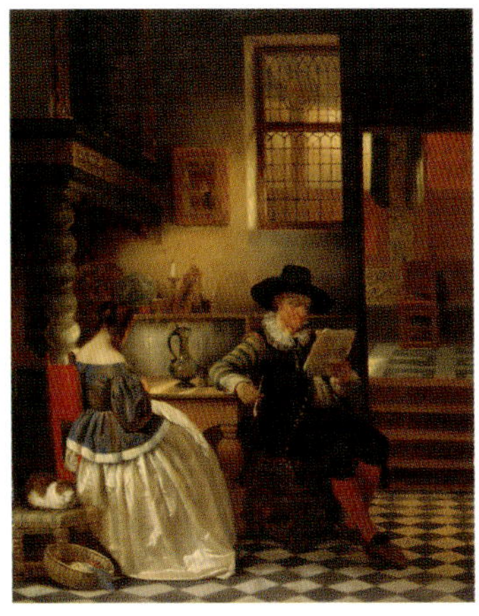

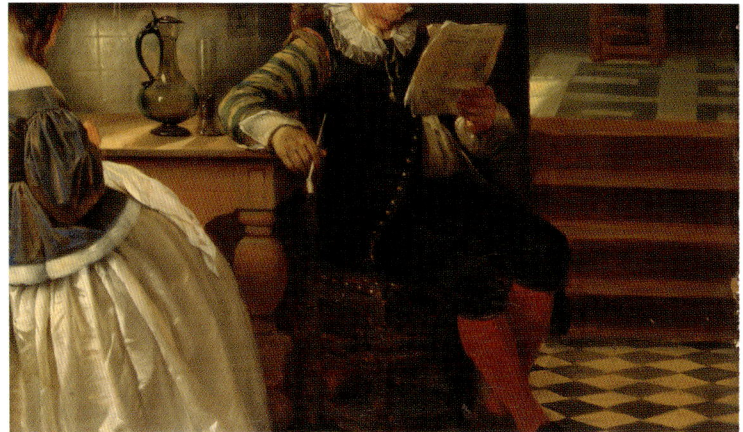

Henri Leys
Seventeenth-Century Interior

1838
Rijksmuseum, Amsterdam

The first remarkable thing to note is that this 17th-century interior scene was very accurately painted by a 19th-century artist. Henri Leys, a pioneer of the Realist movement in Belgium, gained a significant reputation at home and abroad for his history and genre paintings, especially for the high level of accuracy in his reconstruction of the past and his precise depiction of historical costumes and architecture. Critics also praised the realism of the poses and facial expressions of his subjects. These skills are evident in his depiction of this calm scene of daily domestic life. Leys conveys a sense of intimacy present in the air. He captures the ease with which the subjects sit next to each other, facing in opposite directions and carrying out their own activities. A cat sleeps on a chair next to them. We do not know whether the two subjects are husband and wife or father and daughter. However, it is apparent that they must be family from the way they sit calmly without interacting at all.

C100
M 79
Y 48
K 69

C 16
M 25
Y 61
K 9

C 8
M 9
Y 2
K 0

C 25
M 20
Y 13
K 0

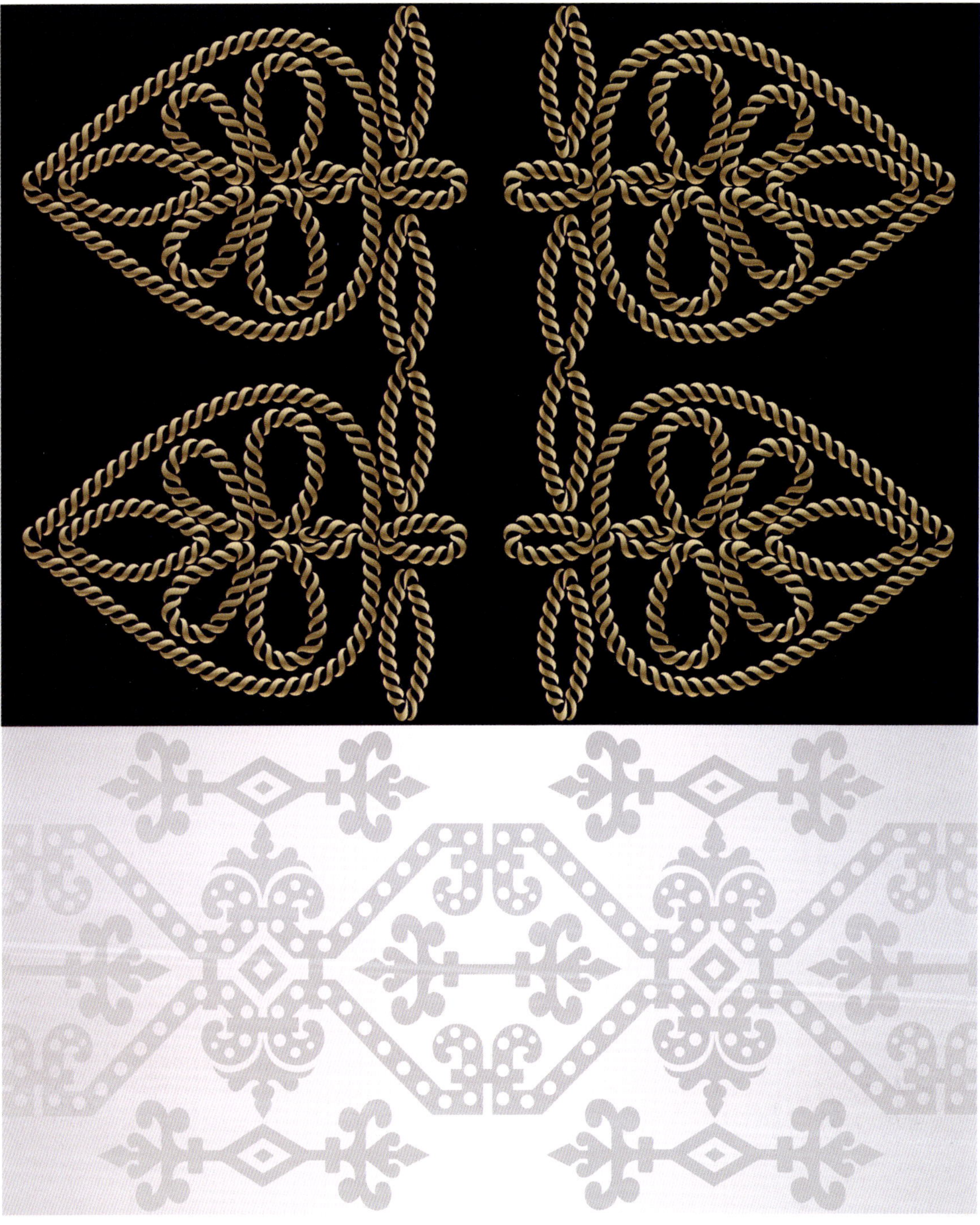

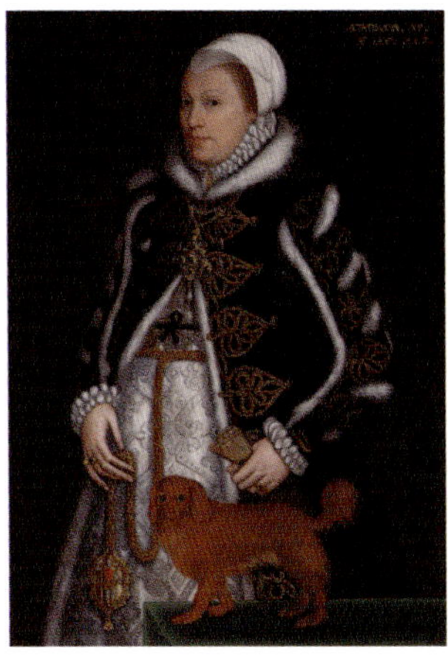

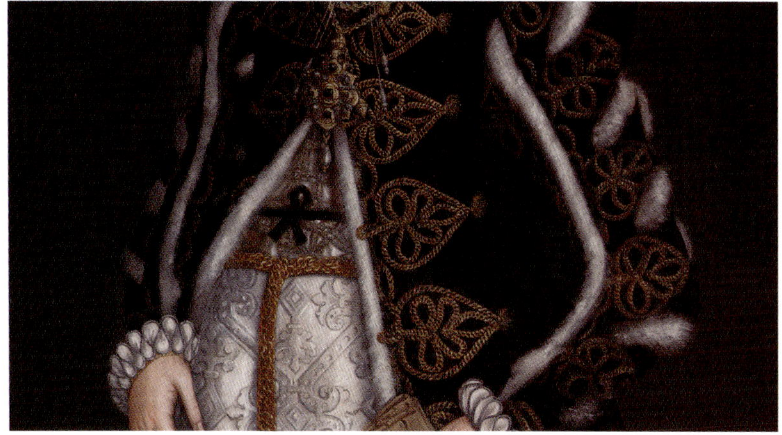

Anonymous
Katherine Knollys, née Carey

1562
Yale Center for British Art, New Haven

The richly dressed subject of this portrait is Katherine Carey, whose married name was Knollys. She is dressed as a member of the English court: velvet, fur, gold, brocades, ruffs, and jewelry convey her high social rank. It is still unknown whether Katherine was the illegitimate daughter of King Henry VIII. Her mother was in fact Mary Boleyn, who had a short-lived affair with the king before her own sister Anne Boleyn married him and gave birth to the child who would become Queen Elizabeth I. Henry VIII never acknowledged Katherine, and Queen Elizabeth never recognized her as her half sister. However, Katherine was the queen's favorite among her first cousins and was made the chief Lady of the Bedchamber. Some historians have come up with evidence at least supporting the theory of Katherine's royal paternity. Henry VIII bestowed royal grants on William Carey, Mary Boleyn's husband, potentially following Carey's acknowledgment of the child as his own. Katherine was also given an opulent funeral by Queen Elizabeth. The funeral documents were found at Westminster Abbey together with those of several queens and kings. She was the only nonroyal person in the group.

C 33
M 45
Y 82
K 41

C 17
M 25
Y 64
K 6

C 13
M 74
Y 90
K 8

C 61
M 39
Y 79
K 41

C 37
M 34
Y 53
K 23

C 21
M 22
Y 43
K 5

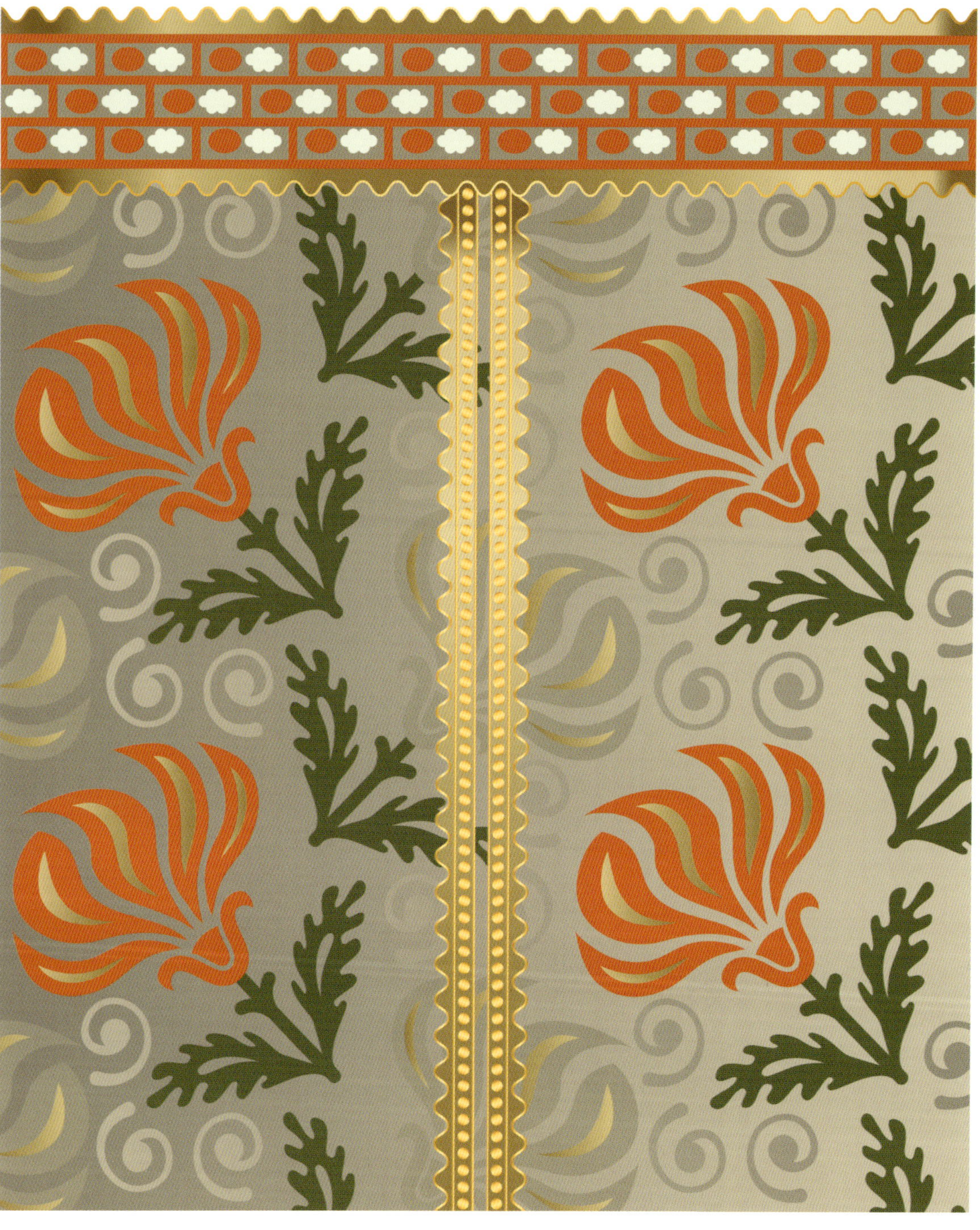

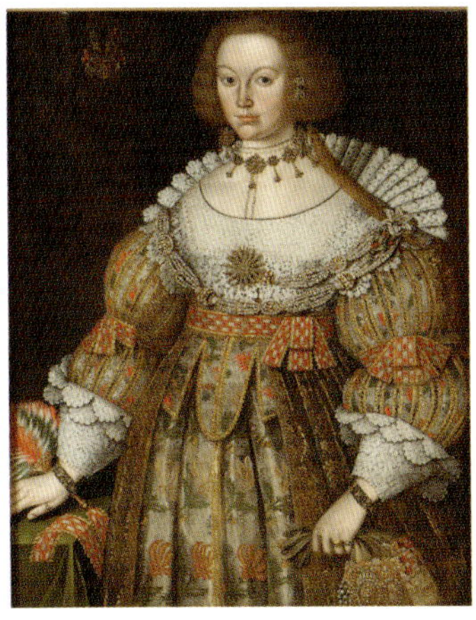

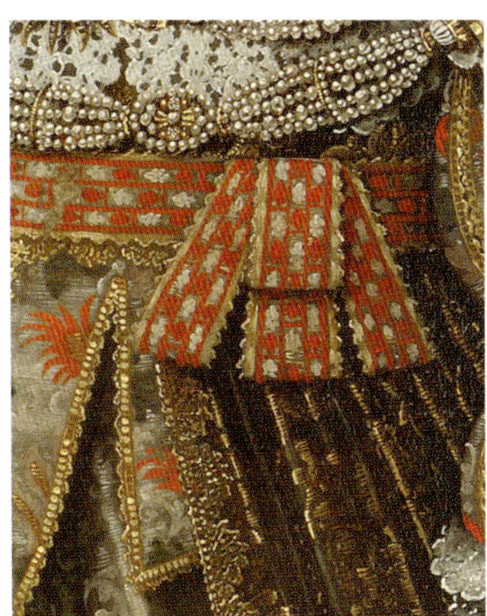

Anonymous
Beata von Yxkull

1640
Nationalmuseum, Stockholm

The richly dressed woman depicted in this portrait is Beata von Yxkull, a Swedish baroness who lived in the mid-17th century. Her husband was Councillor of State Erik Karisson Gyllenstierna of Ulaborg. Erik owned an estate called Pintorp, but after his death Beata renamed it Eriksberg Castle. Beata von Yxkull has been remembered almost solely as the supposed real-life inspiration for the legend of "Pintorpafrun" (the Lady of Pintorp), a Swedish tale that recounts the actions of a cruel wife who lived at the Pintorp estate and plagued the lives of her servants and villagers. Because of her actions, she was punished by the devil and transformed into a ghost to haunt Pintorp. Beata von Yxkull and Mrs. Anna Karlsdotter, both of whom survived their husbands and managed their estates, were the two most famous women thought to perhaps be the fabled Pintorpafrun. However, there are no sources that confirm that Beata von Yxkull was cruel and unfair or otherwise link her to this legend.

C 0
M 0
Y 0
K100

C 31
M 34
Y 64
K 33

C 43
M 36
Y 50
K 51

C 26
M 24
Y 48
K 10

C 36
M 29
Y 69
K 23

C 50
M 49
Y 63
K 72

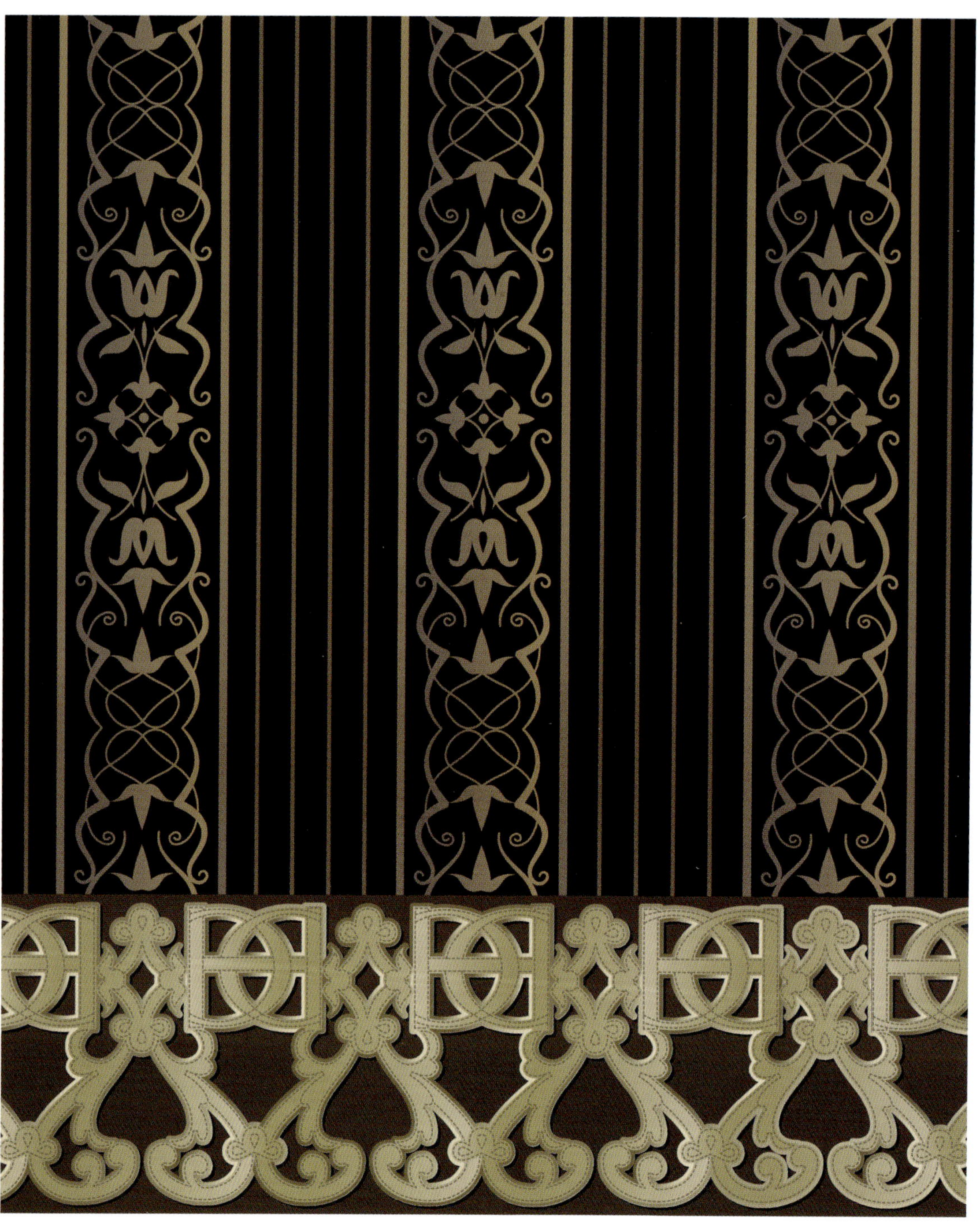

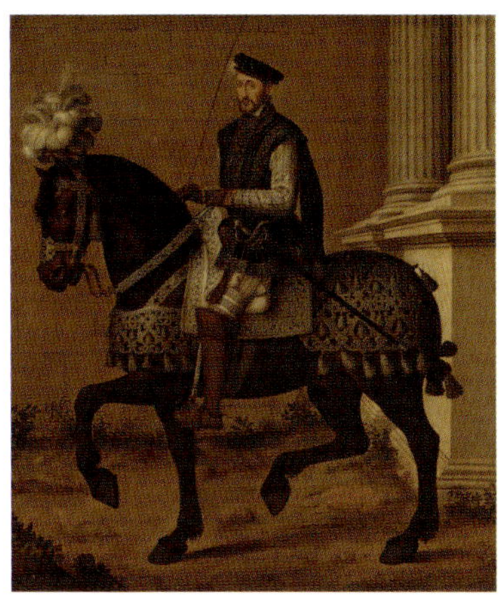

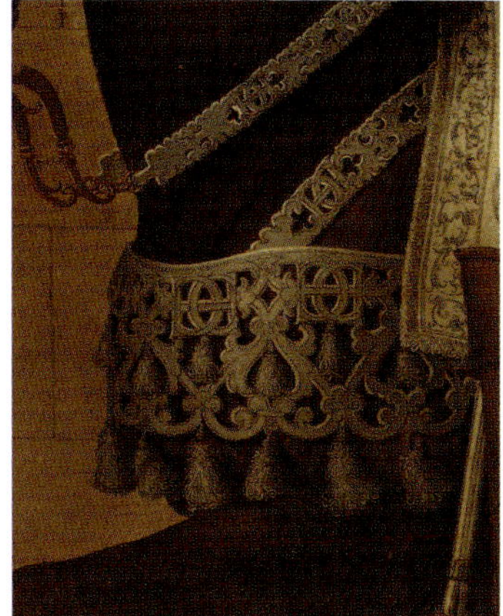

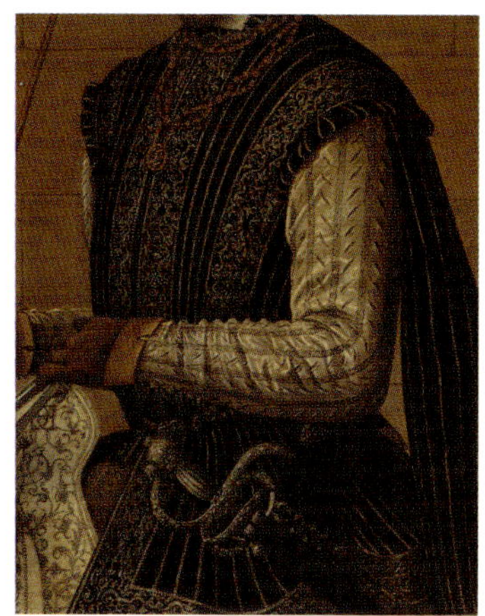

Workshop of
François Clouet
Henry II, King of France

16th century
The Metropolitan Museum of Art, New York

This is the only existing large equestrian portrait of Henry II, the king to whom we owe an early conception of patent law. Henry II had in fact developed the idea of requiring inventors to publish a description of their work in exchange for a limited-time monopoly on its use. Henry II was also very fond of riding: he was an avid hunter and participant in jousts and tournaments and ultimately met his end after he was wounded in the eye by a piece of a shattered lance during a joust. A quote from a 1558 poem, possibly referring to this work, describes a large painting depicting "Henrici equitantis domi" (Henry riding at home). This could mean that Henry is riding literally "at home" in his own courtyard or that he is riding "in civilian dress." It is unclear whether this painting was completed before or after the king's death. This is because Henry's head seems to be based on a portrait drawing of the king from about 1553, whereas the pose of the horse resembles those of the equestrian portraits of his father, Francis I. This painting, remarkable for its meticulous finish and accurate depiction of patterns, was once attributed to the court painter François Clouet.

C 21
M 96
Y 96
K 39

C 20
M 31
Y 75
K 11

C 13
M 20
Y 54
K 0

C 49
M 58
Y 76
K 75

C 14
M 90
Y 94
K 25

C 62
M 37
Y 66
K 40

C 20
M 9
Y 27
K 0

C 0
M 0
Y 8
K 0

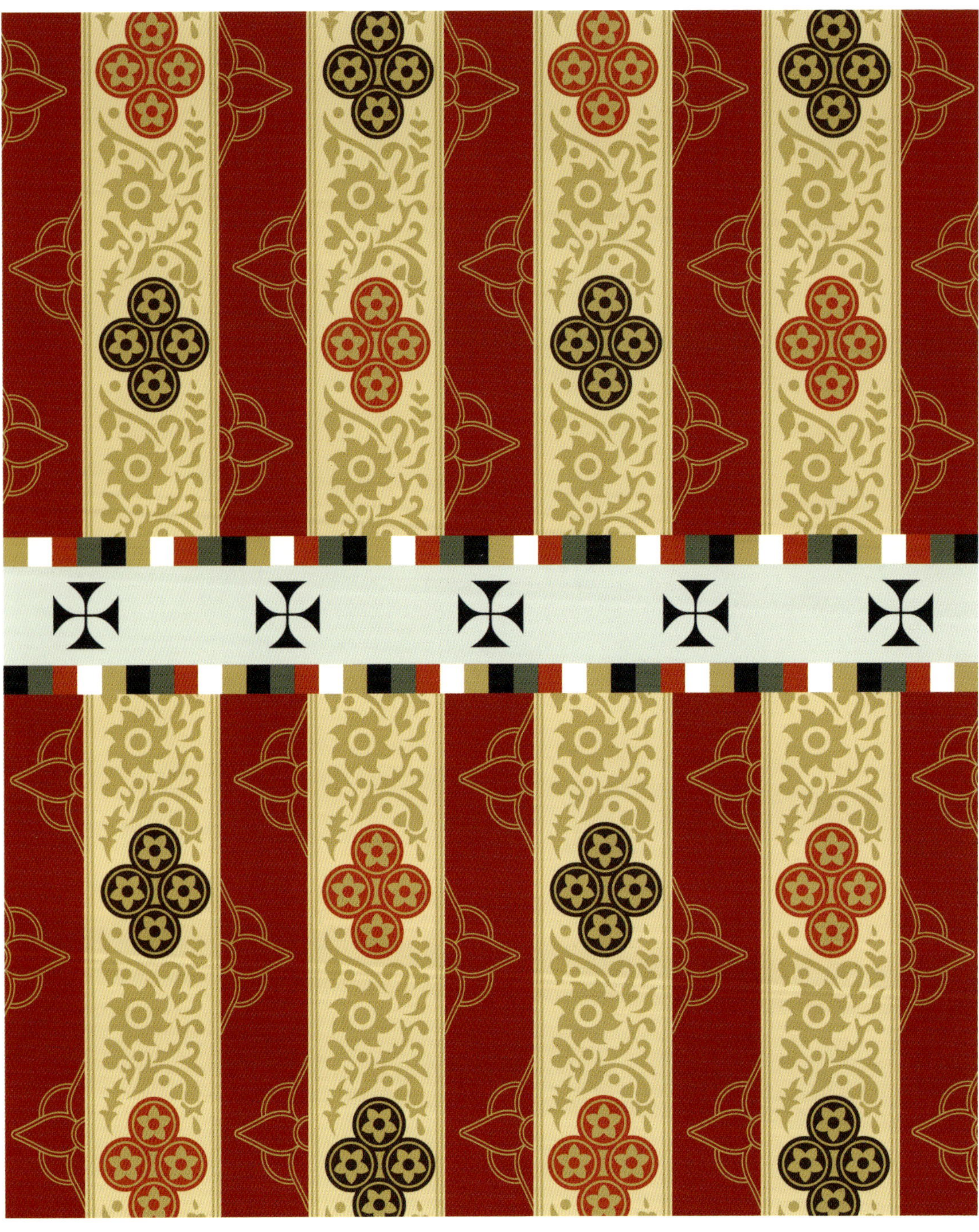

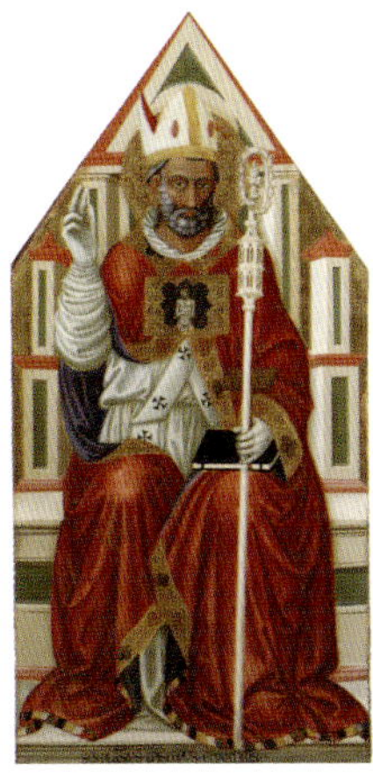

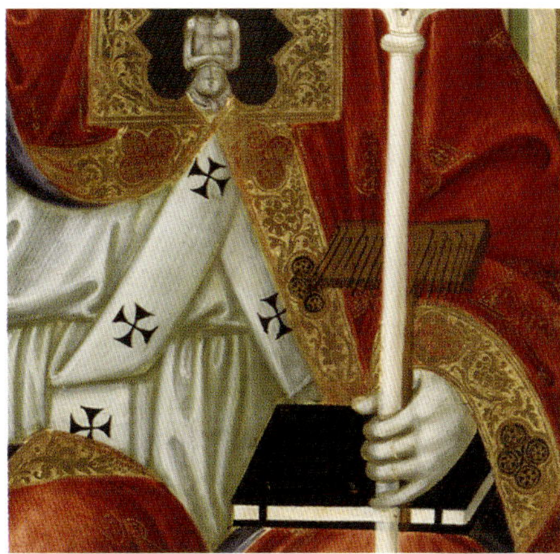

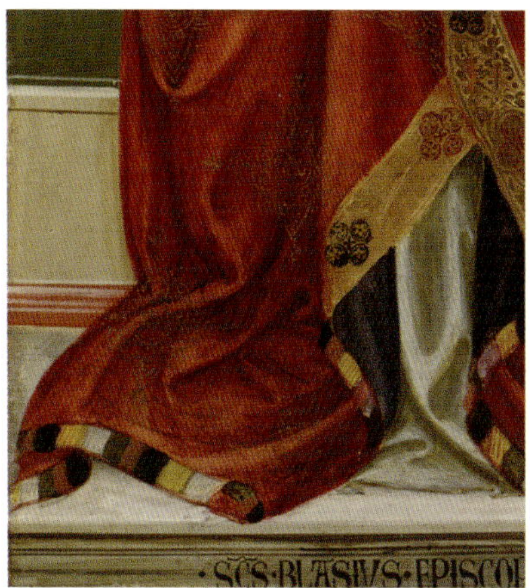

Bicci di Lorenzo
Saint Blaise

circa 1445
Indianapolis Museum of Art at Newfields

Saint Blaise was a 4th-century physician who became bishop of Sebaste in historical Armenia and then a martyr. Interestingly, this painting seems to represent Blaise's ethnicity accurately—a rarity, as Western art usually portrays religious subjects with Western features. Bicci di Lorenzo, a 15th-century artist who inherited his father's rich and flourishing workshop in 1405, was in fact not attracted to the artistic ideals of the Renaissance. Instead he maintained a large output of works in a conservative style, with the help of partnerships and collaborations with other painters. In this painting, Saint Blaise sits on a geometrically decorated throne, holding a crosier and wearing priestly clothes. A wool comb rests on his forearm, a symbol of his martyrdom. According to the *Acta Sanctorum*, on the day of his martyrdom Saint Blaise was beaten, attacked with iron combs, and beheaded. Because of the manner in which he died, he was made patron saint of wool combers.

C 86
M 54
Y 40
K 67

C 12
M 92
Y 100
K 2

C 4
M 6
Y 29
K 0

C 51
M 61
Y 71
K 73

C 10
M 21
Y 85
K 3

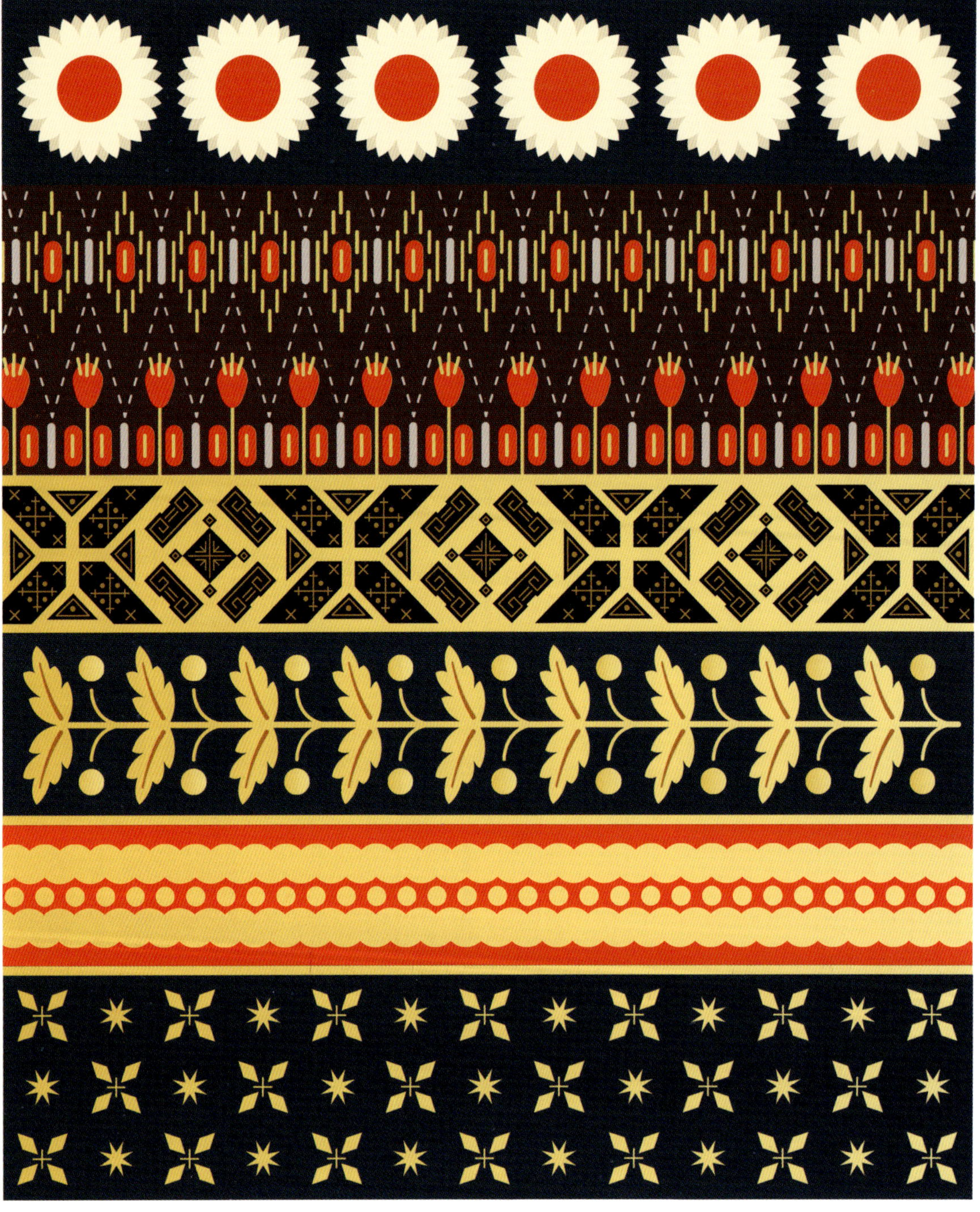

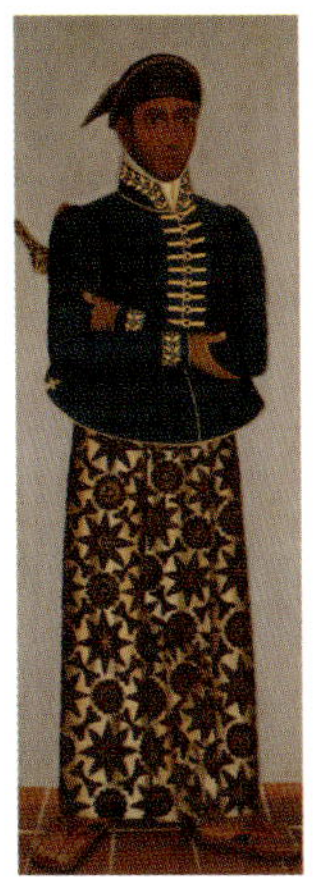
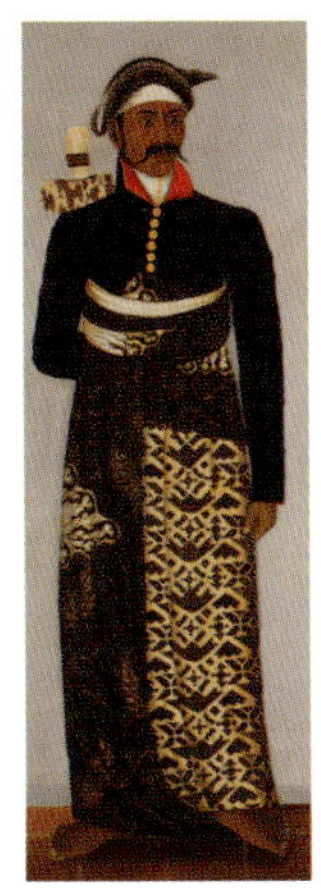
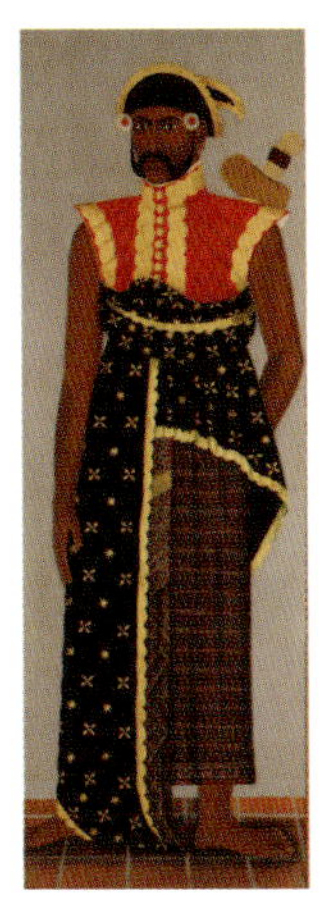
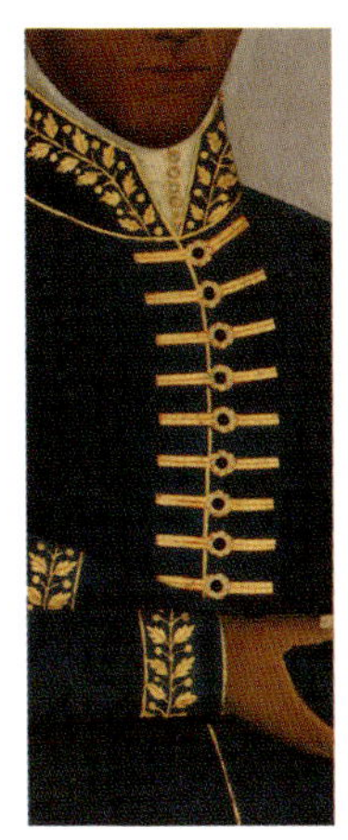
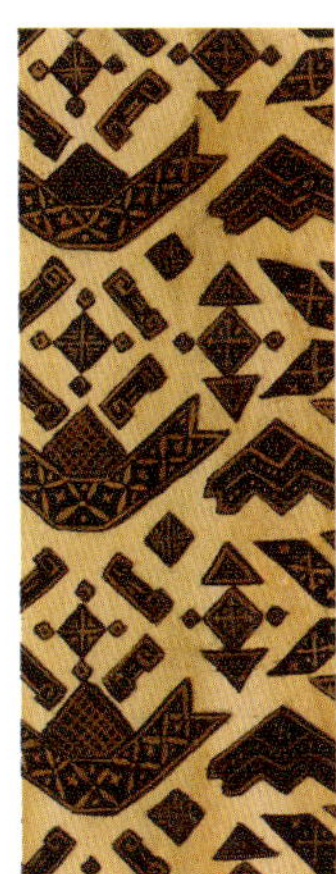
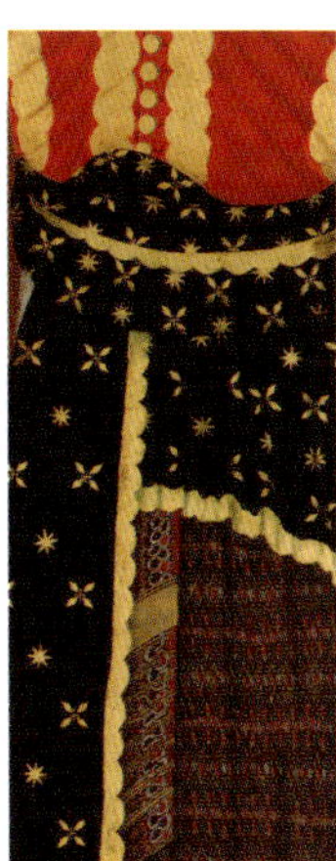

Anonymous
Javanese Court Officials

circa 1820–1870
Rijksmuseum, Amsterdam

This series of paintings aims to represent "types" of court officials in Indonesia, and as such they are not quite portraits. Each man's garments are represented in extreme detail, as they indicate his rank and status and also enabled researchers to locate these court officials to Java and Madura, Indonesia. Not only the garments but also the paintings themselves are a unique mix of indigenous and Western traditions. For example, while the style of the paintings is more typically Indonesian, Western perspective and three-dimensionality are also employed. Researchers suggest, however, that this series is likely to have been painted by non-Western artists. This is mainly because European artists usually portrayed Indonesians as adversaries, colonial subjects, or "innocent" primitives. Here, they are just men in the context of their society's hierarchy.
There are two theories as to what the purpose of these paintings could have been: they might have been ordered by a Western client interested in indigenous cultures, or they might have been some kind of prototouristic promotional materials.

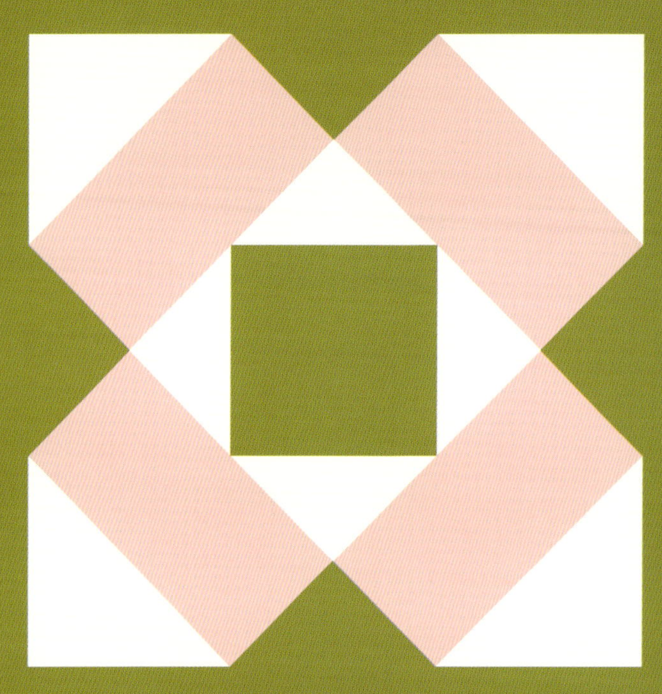

VISUAL INDEX

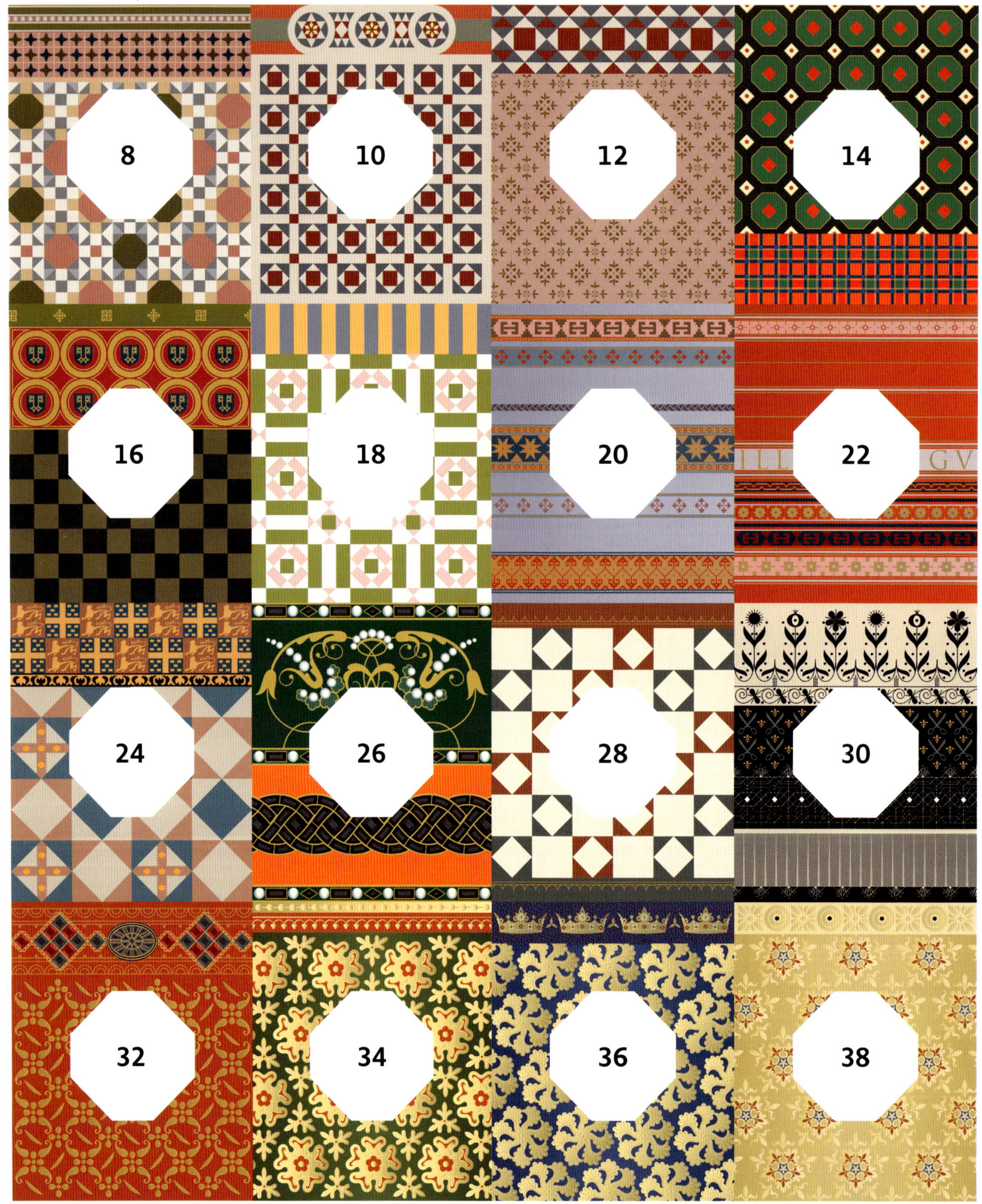
8
10
12
14
16
18
20
22
24
26
28
30
32
34
36
38

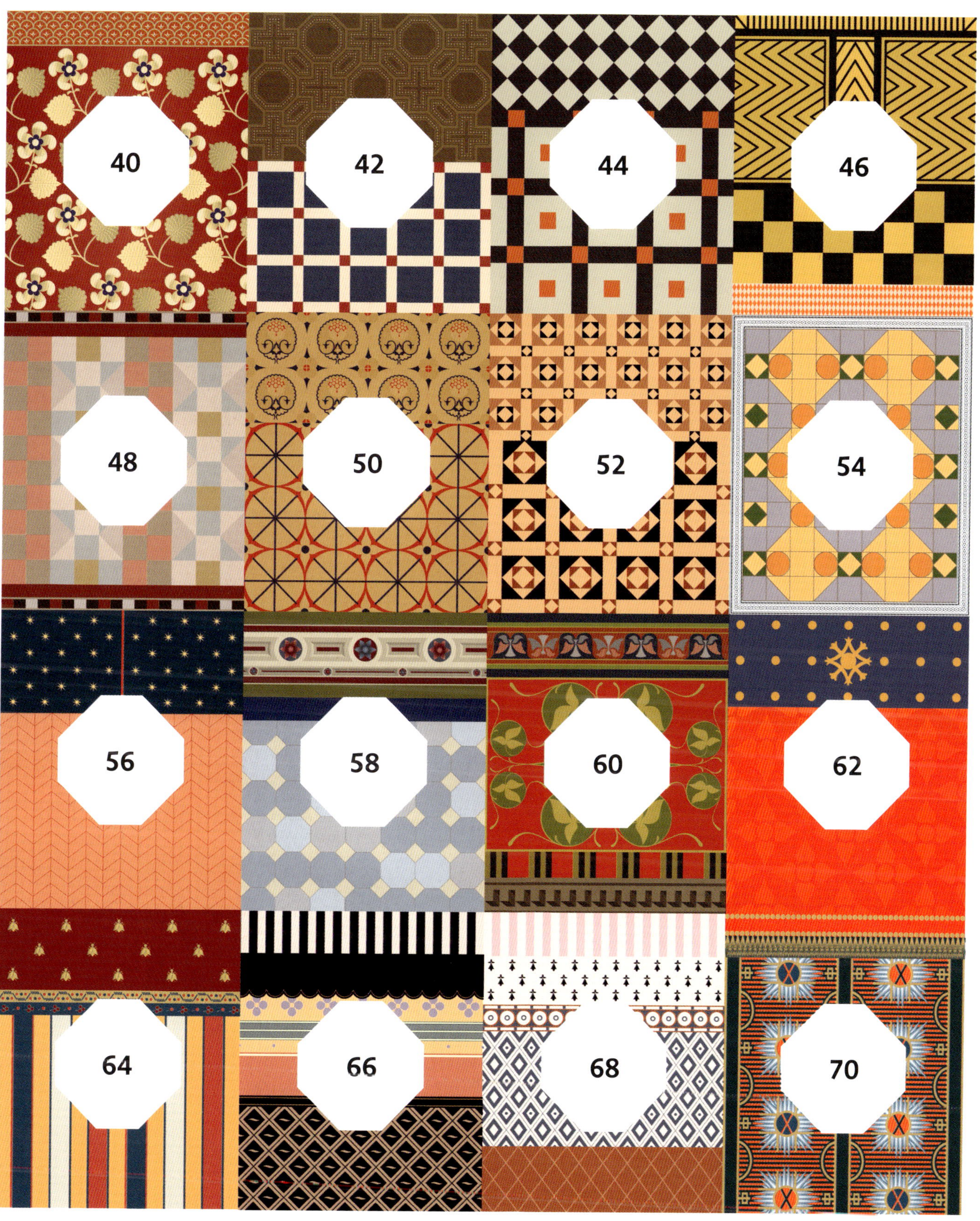

40
42
44
46
48
50
52
54
56
58
60
62
64
66
68
70

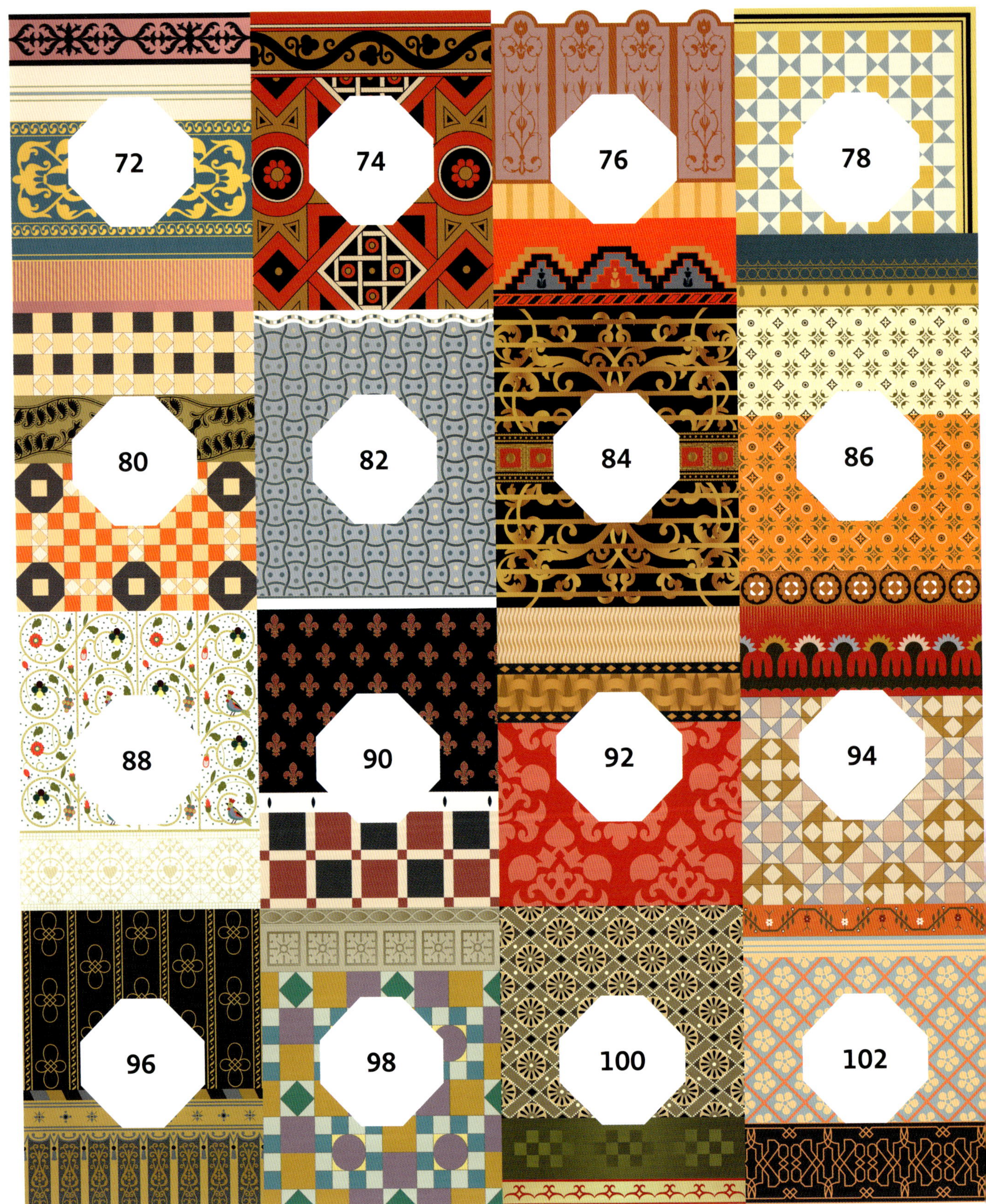
72
74
76
78
80
82
84
86
88
90
92
94
96
98
100
102

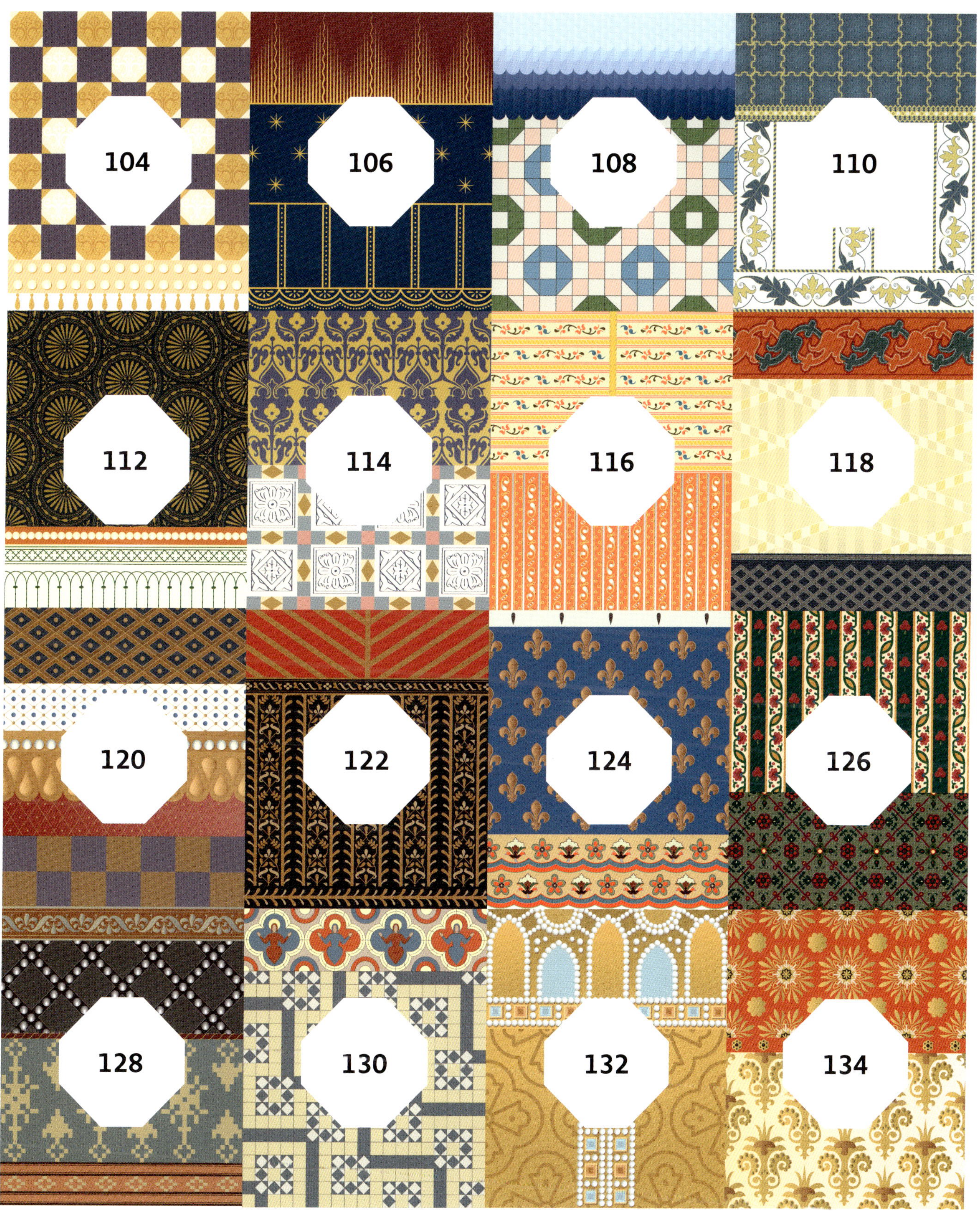
104
106
108
110
112
114
116
118
120
122
124
126
128
130
132
134

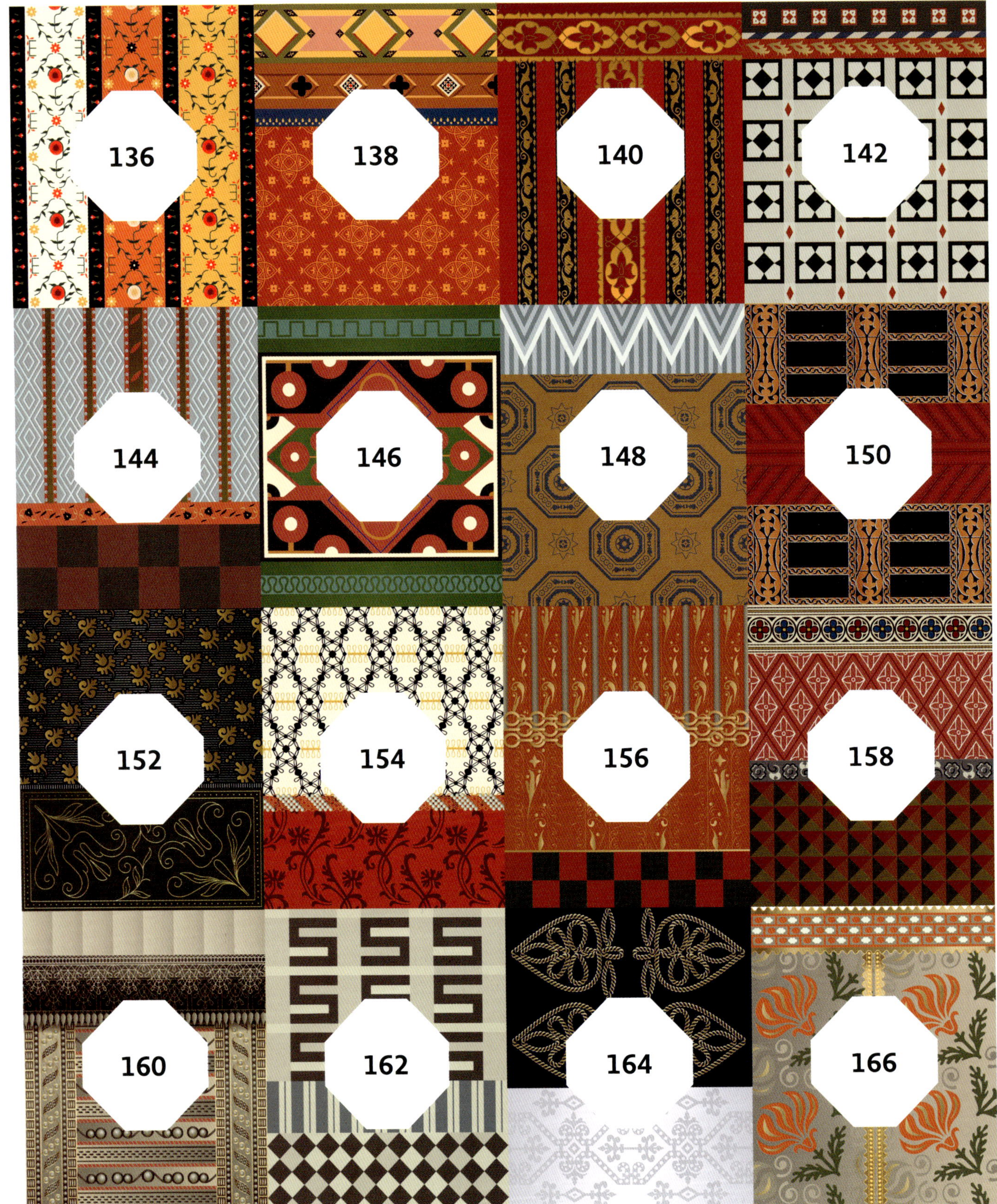
136
138
140
142
144
146
148
150
152
154
156
158
160
162
164
166

168
170
172

CREDITS

Images courtesy of Rijksmuseum, Amsterdam

p. 9 Geertgen tot Sint Jans (workshop of), *The Holy Kinship*, ca. 1495
Oil on panel, 54 × 41⅝ in. (137.2 × 105.8 cm)

p. 27 Anonymous, *Portrait of a Woman (previously identified as Queen Elizabeth I)*, 1550–74
Oil on panel, 17¼ × 12⅝ in. (43.7 × 32.2 cm)

p. 29 Master of the Salem Altar, *The Annunciation*, 1490–1510
Oil on panel, 40⅝ × 36¾ in. (103.3 × 93.4 cm)

p. 31 Anonymous, *Portrait of Trijntje Tijsdr van Nooij*, 1631
Oil on panel, 48⅜ × 35⅜ in. (123 × 90 cm)

p. 33 Frans Pourbus the Younger (workshop of), *Portrait of Margaret of Austria, Consort of Philip III*, ca. 1600
Oil on copper, 11¼ × 8⅞ in. (28.5 × 22.5 cm)

p. 43 Bartholomeus van Bassen, *Interior with a Company*, 1622–24
Oil on panel, 28 × 39⅞ in. (71 × 101.2 cm)

p. 47 Wybrand de Geest, *Portrait of a Boy with a Kolf Club*, 1631
Oil on panel, 45⅜ × 33½ in. (115.4 × 85.3 cm)

p. 49 Master of the Amsterdam Death of the Virgin, *The Death of the Virgin*, ca. 1500
Oil on panel, 22⅝ × 30¼ in. (57.5 × 76.8 cm)

p. 51 Fra Angelico, *Madonna of Humility*, ca. 1440
Tempera on panel, 29⅛ × 20½ in. (74 × 52 cm)

pp. 67, 69 Geertgen tot Sint Jans (circle of), *The Tree of Jesse*, ca. 1500
Oil on panel, 35⅜ × 23⅞ in. (89.8 × 60.6 cm)

p. 91 Frans Pourbus the Younger (workshop of), *Marie de' Medici, Consort of Henry IV, King of France*, 1590–1620
Oil on canvas, 112¼ × 85⅞ in. (285 × 218 cm)

p. 103 Pieter Aertsen, *The Adoration of the Magi*, ca. 1560
Oil on panel, 66 × 70⅞ in. (167.5 × 180 cm)

p. 121 Master of the Virgo inter Virgines, *The Virgin and Child with Four Holy Virgins*, ca. 1495–1500
Oil on panel, 48½ × 39¾ in. (123.1 × 101.1 cm)

p. 129 Jan van Scorel, *Mary Magdalene*, ca. 1530
Oil on panel, 26 × 30 in. (66.3 × 76 cm)

p. 151 Anonymous, *Portrait of Francisco Hurtado de Mendoza, Admiral de Aragon*, 1601
Oil on canvas, 38⅛ × 30 in. (97 × 76 cm)

p. 153 Salomon Mesdach, *Portrait of a Man, possibly Walterus Fourmenois*, 1620
Oil on panel, 41 × 28⅜ in. (104 × 72.1 cm)

p. 155 Giambattista Moroni, *Portrait of a Young Woman*, 1560–78
Oil on canvas, 29 × 25⅝ in. (73.5 × 65 cm)

p. 157 L. J. Woutersin, *Portrait of Sophia de Vervou*, 1630
Oil on canvas, 68½ × 40⅜ in. (174 × 102.5 cm)

p. 161 Frans Pourbus the Younger (workshop of), *Isabella Clara Eugenia, Consort of Archduke Albert VII*, c. 1600
Oil on copper, 11¼ × 8⅞ in. (28.5 × 22.5 cm)

p. 163 Henri Leys, *Seventeenth-Century Interior*, 1838
Oil on panel, 24⅜ × 19⅝ in. (62 × 50 cm)

p. 173 Anonymous, *Javanese Court Officials*, ca. 1820–70
Painting, each panel 77½ × 29¼ in. (196.8 × 74.3 cm)

Images courtesy of SMK National Gallery of Denmark, Copenhagen (photo © SMK Photo/Jakob Skou-Hansen)

pp. 11, 13 Cecco di Pietro, *Virgin and Child Playing with a Goldfinch and Holding a Sheaf of Millet*, 1379
Tempera on panel, 41⅓ × 22⅞ in. (105 × 58 cm)

p. 15 Wilhelm Bendz, *The Waagepetersen Family*, 1830
Oil on canvas, 39⅛ × 34⅞ in. (99.5 × 88.5 cm)

p. 147 Christoffer Wilhelm Eckersberg, *Mendel Levin Nathanson's Elder Daughters, Bella and Hanna*, 1820
Oil on canvas, 54¾ × 39⅛ in. (139 × 99.5 cm)

p. 149 Christoffer Wilhelm Eckersberg, *The Nathanson Family*, 1818
Oil on panel, 57½ × 76 in. (146.2 × 193.1 cm)

Images courtesy of The Metropolitan Museum of Art, New York

p. 17 Hans Memling, *The Annunciation*, ca. 1465–70
Oil on panel, 73¼ × 45¼ in. (186.1 × 114.9 cm)

p. 19 Master of the Story of Joseph, *Joseph Interpreting the Dreams of His Fellow Prisoners*, ca. 1500
Oil on panel, diameter 61½ in. (156.2 cm)

pp. 21, 23, 25 Master of the Dinteville Allegory, *Moses and Aaron before Pharaoh*, 1537
Oil on panel, 69½ × 75⅞ in. (176.5 × 192.7 cm)

p. 45 Pieter de Hooch, *Interior with a Young Couple*, ca. 1662–65
Oil on canvas, 21⅝ × 24¾ in. (54.9 × 62.9 cm)

p. 53 Giovanni di Paolo, *The Annunciation to Zacharias*, ca. 1455–60
Tempera and gold on panel, 29⅞ × 17 in. (75.9 × 43.2 cm)

p. 55 Netherlandish Painter, *A Sermon on Charity (possibly the Conversion of Saint Anthony)*, ca. 1520–25
Oil on panel, 33½ × 23 in. (85.1 × 58.4 cm)

pp. 59, 61 Jean-François Montessuy, *Pope Gregory XVI Visiting the Church of San Benedetto at Subiaco*, 1843
Oil on canvas, 49¼ × 55⅜ in. (125.1 × 140.7 cm)

p. 71 Ralph Earl, *Mrs. Noah Smith and Her Children*, 1798
Oil on canvas, 64 × 85⅜ in. (162.6 × 217.8 cm)

p. 77 Lilly Martin Spencer, *Conversation Piece*, ca. 1851–52
Oil on canvas, 28¼ × 22⅝ in. (71.9 × 57.5 cm)

p. 79 Netherlandish Painters, *The Last Supper*, 1515–20
Oil on panel, central panel 47 × 33¾ in. (119.4 × 85.7 cm), left wing 47 × 16⅞ in. (119.4 × 42.9 cm), right wing 47⅛ × 17 in. (119.7 × 43.2 cm)

p. 81 Master of the Saint Barbara Legend, *Abner's Messenger before David (?); The Queen of Sheba Bringing Gifts to Solomon*, ca. 1480
Oil on panel, 36¾ × 17⅝ in. (93.3 × 44.8 cm)

p. 83 Bartolomé Estebán Murillo, *A Knight of Alcántara or Calatrava*, ca. 1650–55
Oil on canvas, 77 × 38½ in. (195.6 × 97.8 cm)

p. 85 Gaspar de Crayer, *Philip IV in Parade Armor*, ca. 1628
Oil on canvas, 72 × 46½ in. (182.9 × 118.1 cm)

p. 107 Anonymous, *The Virgin of Sorrows*, 18th century
Oil on canvas, 10¾ × 8½ in. (27.3 × 21.6 cm)

p. 109 Gerard David, *The Annunciation* (left panel), 1506
Oil on panel, 30½ × 24⅜ in. (77.5 × 61.9 cm)

p. 111 Bernardino Campi, *Portrait of a Woman*, late 1560s
Oil on canvas, 55⅝ × 38¼ in. (141.3 × 97.2 cm)

p. 117 Frans Pourbus the Younger, *Margherita Gonzaga, Princess of Mantua*
Oil on canvas, 36½ × 27¼ in. (92.7 × 69.2 cm)

p. 119 Francesco Salviati, *Portrait of a Man*, ca. 1544–48
Oil on canvas, $48\frac{1}{4} \times 36\frac{3}{4}$ in. (122.6 × 93.4 cm)

p. 123 Workshop of Justus Sustermans, *Cosimo II de' Medici, Grand Duke of Tuscany*, 1597–1681
Oil on canvas, 78 × 48 in. (198.1 × 121.9 cm)

p. 125 After Hyacinthe Rigaud, *Louis XV as a Child*, ca. 1716–24
Oil on canvas, $77 \times 55\frac{1}{2}$ in. (195.6 × 141 cm)

p. 127 Anonymous, *Portrait of a Young Man*, early 19th century
Oil on canvas, $31\frac{1}{2} \times 21\frac{3}{4}$ in. (80 × 55.2 cm)

p. 137 Jean-Auguste-Dominique Ingres, *Madame Jacques-Louis Leblanc*, 1823
Oil on canvas, $47 \times 36\frac{1}{2}$ in. (119.4 × 92.7 cm)

p. 169 Workshop of François Clouet, *Henry II, King of France*
Oil on canvas, $61\frac{1}{2} \times 53$ in. (156.2 × 134.6 cm)

Images courtesy of Open Content Program, The J. Paul Getty Museum, Los Angeles

pp. 35, 37, 39, 41 Gentile da Fabriano, *Coronation of the Virgin*, ca. 1420
Tempera and gold leaf on panel, $36\frac{5}{8} \times 25\frac{1}{4}$ in. (93 × 64.1 cm)

p. 63 Fra Angelico, *Saint Francis and a Bishop Saint, Saint John the Baptist and Saint Dominic*, late 1420s
Tempera and gold leaf on panel, left panel $20\frac{3}{4} \times 9\frac{1}{8}$ in. (52.7 × 23.2 cm), right panel $20\frac{3}{4} \times 8\frac{1}{4}$ in. (52.7 × 21 cm)

p. 65 Jacques-Louis David, *Portrait of the Sisters Zénaïde and Charlotte Bonaparte*, 1821
Oil on canvas, $51 \times 39\frac{5}{8}$ in. (129.5 × 100.6 cm)

p. 73 Bachiacca, *Portrait of a Woman with a Book of Music*, ca. 1540–45
Oil on panel, $40\frac{5}{8} \times 31\frac{5}{8}$ in. (103.2 × 80.3 cm)

p. 101 Workshop of Rogier van der Weyden, *Portrait of Isabella of Portugal*, ca. 1450
Oil on panel, $18\frac{1}{8} \times 14\frac{5}{8}$ in. (46 × 37.1 cm)

p. 139 Bernardo Daddi, *The Virgin Mary with Saints Thomas Aquinas and Paul*, ca. 1335
Tempera and gold leaf on panel, $47\frac{7}{8} \times 44\frac{1}{2}$ in. (121.6 × 113 cm)

p. 143 Gherardo Starnina, *Madonna and Child with Musical Angels*, ca. 1410
Tempera and gold leaf on panel, $36\frac{1}{4} \times 20\frac{1}{4}$ in. (92.1 × 51.4 cm)

Images courtesy of National Gallery of Art, Washington

p. 57 Andrea di Bartolo, *The Nativity of the Virgin*, ca. 1400–1405
Tempera on poplar panel, $19 \times 15\frac{1}{8}$ in. (48.3 × 36.8 cm)

p. 75 Gerard David, *The Saint Anne Altarpiece: Saint Anne with the Virgin and Child*, ca. 1500–20
Oil on panel, $93 \times 38\frac{3}{8}$ in. (236.1 × 97.5 cm)

p. 93 Agnolo Bronzino, *A Young Woman and Her Little Boy*, ca. 1540
Oil on panel, $39\frac{1}{8} \times 30$ in. (99.5 × 76 cm)

p. 113 Francesco Benaglio, *Madonna and Child*, late 1460s
Tempera on panel, transferred to canvas, $31\frac{3}{4} \times 22\frac{1}{8}$ in. (80.7 × 56.2 cm)

p. 131 Master of the Prado Adoration of the Magi, *The Presentation in the Temple*, ca. 1470–80
Oil on panel, $23\frac{1}{4} \times 19$ in. (59 × 48.1 cm)

p. 135 Benvenuto di Giovanni, *The Adoration of the Magi*, ca. 1470–75
Tempera on poplar panel, $71\frac{5}{8} \times 54$ in. (182 × 137 cm)

p. 141 Agnolo Bronzino, *Eleonora di Toledo*, ca. 1560
Oil on panel, $34 \times 25\frac{5}{8}$ in. (86.4 × 65.1 cm)

Images courtesy of Los Angeles County Museum of Art (photo © Museum Associates/LACMA)

p. 87 Luca di Tommè, *Madonna and Child with Saints Nicholas and Paul*, ca. 1370
Tempera on panel, 52¼ × 45⅛ in. (132.72 × 114.62 cm)

Images courtesy of Indianapolis Museum of Art at Newfields

p. 159 Pere Vall, *Saint Stephen and Saint Mary Magdalene*, ca. 1400
Tempera and gold on panel, 35½ × 26 in. (90 × 66 cm)

p. 171 Bicci di Lorenzo, *Saint Blaise*, ca. 1445
Tempera and gold on panel, 66⅛ × 32¼ in. (168 × 82 cm)

Images courtesy of Nationalmuseum, Stockholm

p. 133 Anonymous, *Alexei Mikhailovich, Tsar of Russia*, 17th century
Oil on canvas, 53½ × 42⅛ in. (136 × 107 cm)

p. 145 Remmert Petersen, *Anna Katarina, Princess of Brandenburg, Queen of Denmark*, 16th century
Oil on canvas, 81½ × 48½ in. (207 × 123 cm), Nationalmuseum

p. 167 Anonymous, *Beata von Yxkull*, 1640
Oil on canvas, 37¾ × 30 in. (96 × 76 cm)

Images courtesy of Yale Center for British Art, New Haven

p. 89 William Larkin, *Portrait of a Young Lady, possibly Jane, Lady Thornhaugh*, 1617
Oil on panel, 44¾ × 33 in. (113.7 × 83.8 cm), Yale Center for British Art, Paul Mellon Fund

p. 97 Daniël van den Queborne, *Sir William Drury, of Hawstead, Suffolk*, 1587
Oil on canvas, 93¾ × 61½ in. (238.1 × 156.2 cm)

p. 165 Anonymous, *Katherine Knollys, née Carey*, 1562
Oil on panel, 42¾ × 31¼ in. (108.6 × 79.4 cm)

Images courtesy of The Art Institute of Chicago

p. 95 Colyn de Coter, *Virgin and Child Crowned by Angels*, 1490–95
Oil on panel, 59¾ × 34⅞ in. (151.9 × 88.6 cm)

p. 99 Jean Hey, known as the Master of Moulins, *The Annunciation*, 1490–95
Oil on panel, 28½ × 19¾ in. (72.5 × 50.1 cm)

p. 105 Antwerp Mannerist (Master of the Antwerp Adoration group), *King David Receiving the Cistern Water of Bethlehem*, 1505–25
Oil on panel, transferred to canvas, 29 × 10⅞ in. (73.5 × 27.5 cm)

p. 115 South German, *Holy Family*, 1475
Oil on panel, 19¾ × 18¾ in. (50.2 × 47.8 cm)

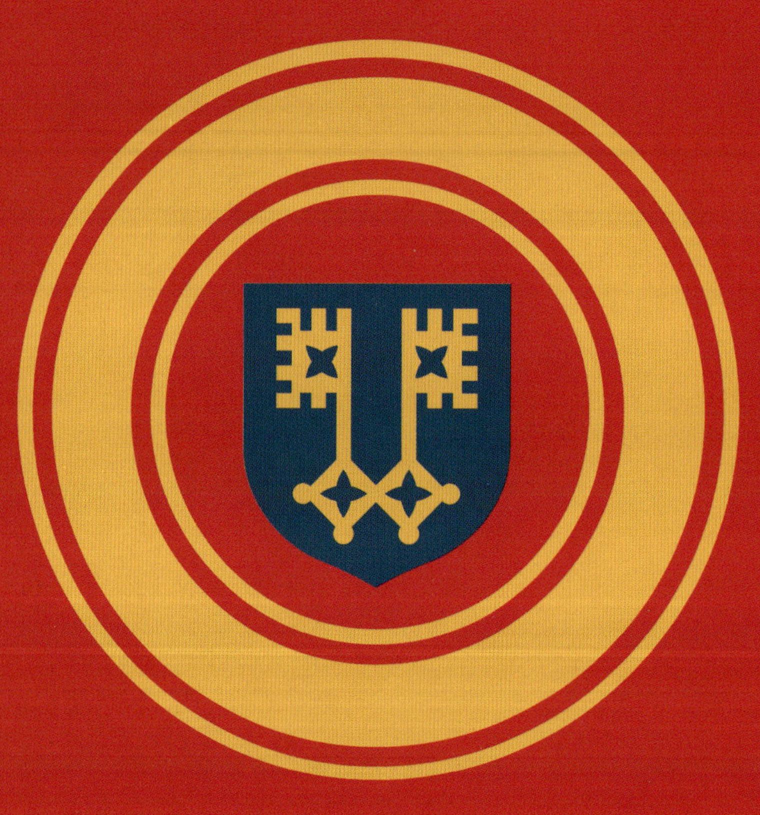

SUGGESTED READING

Argan, G. C. *Storia dell'Arte Italiana*. Milan: Arnoldo Mondadori, 2008.

Baumgartner, F. J. *Henry II, King of France, 1547–1559*. Durham, NC: Duke University Press, 1988.

Beckett, F. *Kristian IV og Malrkunsten*. Copenhagen: Lindhardt og Ringhof, 2018.

Bujis, H., and G. Luijten. *Goltzius to Van Gogh: Drawings and Paintings from the P. and N. de Boer Foundation*. Bussum, Netherlands: Thoth, 2014.

Drummond, S. *Divine Conception: The Art of the Annunciation*. London: Unicorn, 2018.

Duffy, E. *The Stripping of the Altars: Traditional Religion in England, 1400–1580*. New Haven: Yale University Press, 2005.

Elsenbichler, K. *The Cultural Politics of Duke Cosimo de' Medici*. Aldershot, UK: Ashgate Publishing, 2001.

Feinblatt, E. *The Gothic Room*. Los Angeles County Museum of Art, 1947.

Jones, S. F., and M. Wolff. *Northern European and Spanish Paintings before 1600 in the Art Institute of Chicago*. New Haven: Yale University Press, 2008.

Longworth, P. *Alexis, Tsar of All the Russias*. New York: Franklin Watts, 1984.

Marrow, D. *The Art Patronage of Maria de' Medici*. Ann Arbor: UMI Research Press, 1982.

Meakin, H. L. *The Painted Closet of Lady Anne Bacon Drury*. Abingdon, UK: Routledge, 2013.

Panofsky, E. *Early Netherlandish Painting: Its Origins and Character*. Cambridge, MA: Harvard University Press, 1953.

Shapley, F. R. *Paintings from the Samuel H. Kress Collection: Italian Schools, XVI–XVIII Century*. London: Phaidon, 1968.

Sutton, P. *Pieter De Hooch, 1629–1684*. New Haven: Yale University Press, 1998.

Zeri, F. *Behind the Image: The Art of Reading Paintings*. London: St. Martin's, 1990.

Zeri, F., and E. Gardner, E. *Italian Paintings: A Catalogue of the Collection of The Metropolitan Museum of Art*. Vol. 2, *Venetian School*. New York: The Metropolitan Museum of Art, 1973.

WEBSITES

The Art Institute of Chicago. https://www.artic.edu

Indianapolis Museum of Art at Newfields, collection site. https://www.collection.imamuseum.org

The J. Paul Getty Museum, Los Angeles. http://www.getty.edu/museum/

Los Angeles County Museum of Art. https://www.lacma.org

The Metropolitan Museum of Art, New York. https://www.metmuseum.org

National Gallery of Art, Washington. https://www.nga.gov

Nationalmuseum, Stockholm. https://www.nationalmuseum.se/en/

Rijksmuseum, Amsterdam. https://www.rijksmuseum.nl/en/

SMK National Gallery of Denmark, Copenhagen. https://www.smk.dk/en/

Yale Center for British Art. https://britishart.yale.edu

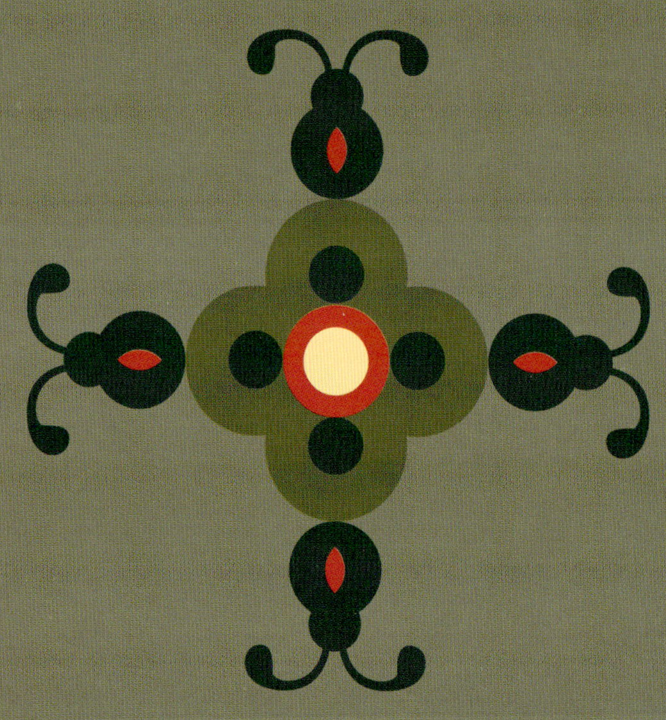

THE AUTHORS

Francesca Leoneschi is a founding member and creative director of The World of DOT, a graphic design agency in Milan specializing in illustration, typography, and editorial design, as well as logo design and branding. Francesca has a multidisciplinary training in architecture, graphics, and typography. After ten years of experience as a senior designer at Arnoldo Mondadori Editore, she joined Mucca Design in New York as art director. Her experience in New York inspired her decision to create an editorial design agency in Milan, together with her husband Iacopo Bruno. Her agency works for prominent Italian and foreign publishers. Since 2008 she has been art director of Rizzoli Libri.

Silvia Lazzaris is a freelance journalist and museum specialist based in London. She is a contributing writer for the Italian newspaper *Corriere della Sera*, and her work has appeared on the BBC World Service. Silvia also works for KCA London, where she produces content for the master planning and design of museums, galleries, and cultural destinations around the world.

Giovanna Ferraris is a graphic designer and illustrator based in Milan. After studying and working in both Milan and London, she joined the graphic design studio The World of DOT in 2010. At TWoD, Giovanna specializes in book covers, pattern design, and vector illustration. Her designs and illustrations have appeared throughout numerous books by prominent Italian publishers.

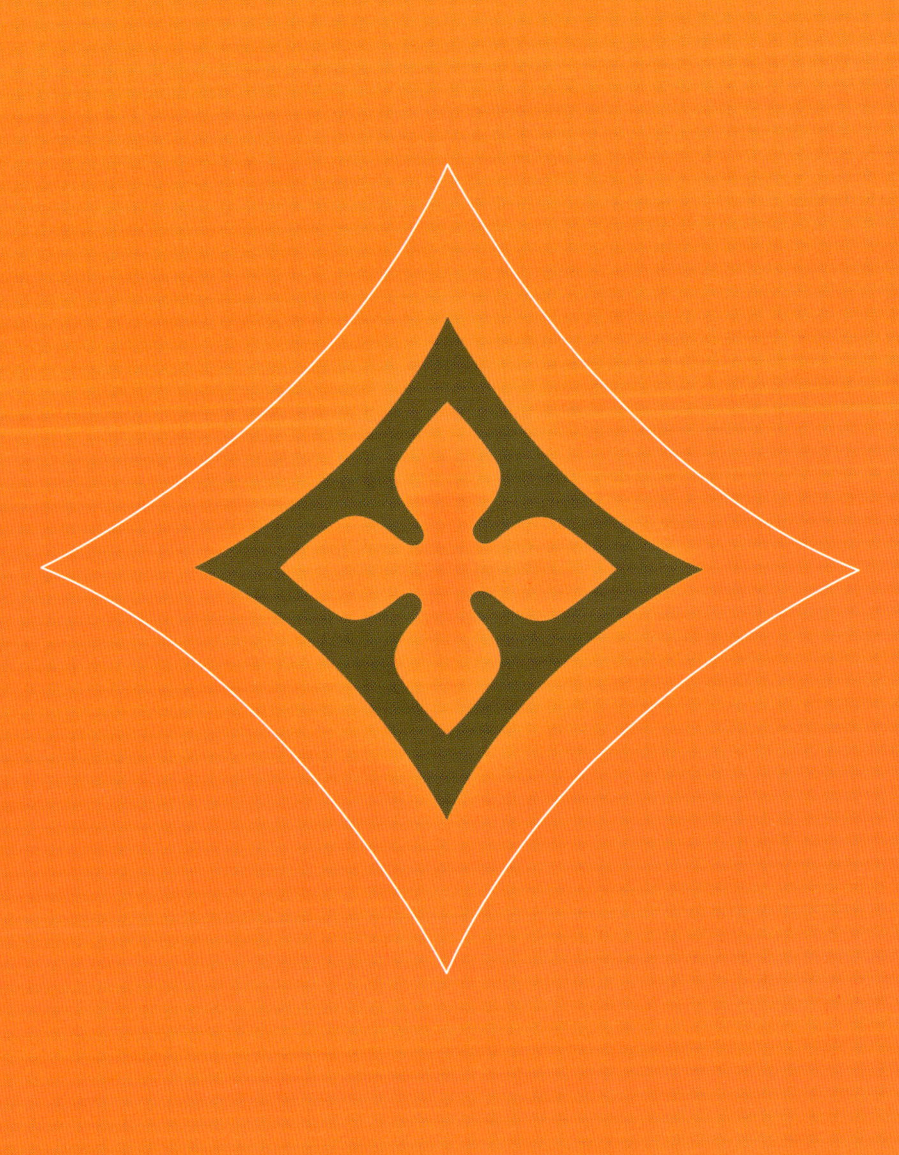

ACKNOWLEDGMENTS

We want to express our gratitude to the museums that have made part of their collections accessible online. Without your efforts to preserve and disseminate art, we could not have included any of these paintings in our book. Perhaps we would not even have been able to see many of them.

We are grateful to Balthazar Pagani, who believed in our project immediately after talking about it during a boat ride on a summer afternoon. Thank you for being such an amazing editor, as well as for your continuous help and support.

Many thanks to David Fabricant for giving us this incredible opportunity. We are proud to have been given the chance to publish with such an authoritative publisher. We are grateful for your encouragement and for your patience with managing our endless intercontinental email threads.

M. Austin Argentieri—your help was a blessing. Thank you so much for your wisdom, guidance, and care. In particular, we wish to thank you for the many hours you spent copyediting our text. You have an exceptional eye for detail. Even from the other side of the ocean, it never felt like you were far away.

We also wish to thank the wonderfully resourceful Silvia De Vecchi, the art historian whose help was invaluable to our interpretation of the paintings. Silvia, we thought we knew, but you actually taught us how to look at paintings up close.

Thanks to our partners, families, and friends, who supported us through the most challenging phases of this adventure. We would love to mention you individually, but as we are three co-authors, this would require us to fill this entire page with names. You know who you are.

We also want to send a hug to all of the members of the graphic design studio The World of DOT, for their extraordinary generosity. Thank you for bearing with us during the months that we spent on this project.

Take-away food: you fed us when we could not leave our desks. We would not have been able to do it without you.

Last but not least: thank you, old masters. You are the wonderful companions without whom this book could have never existed.

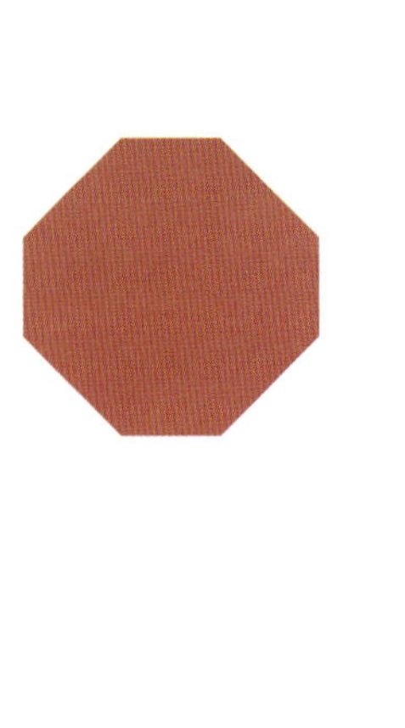

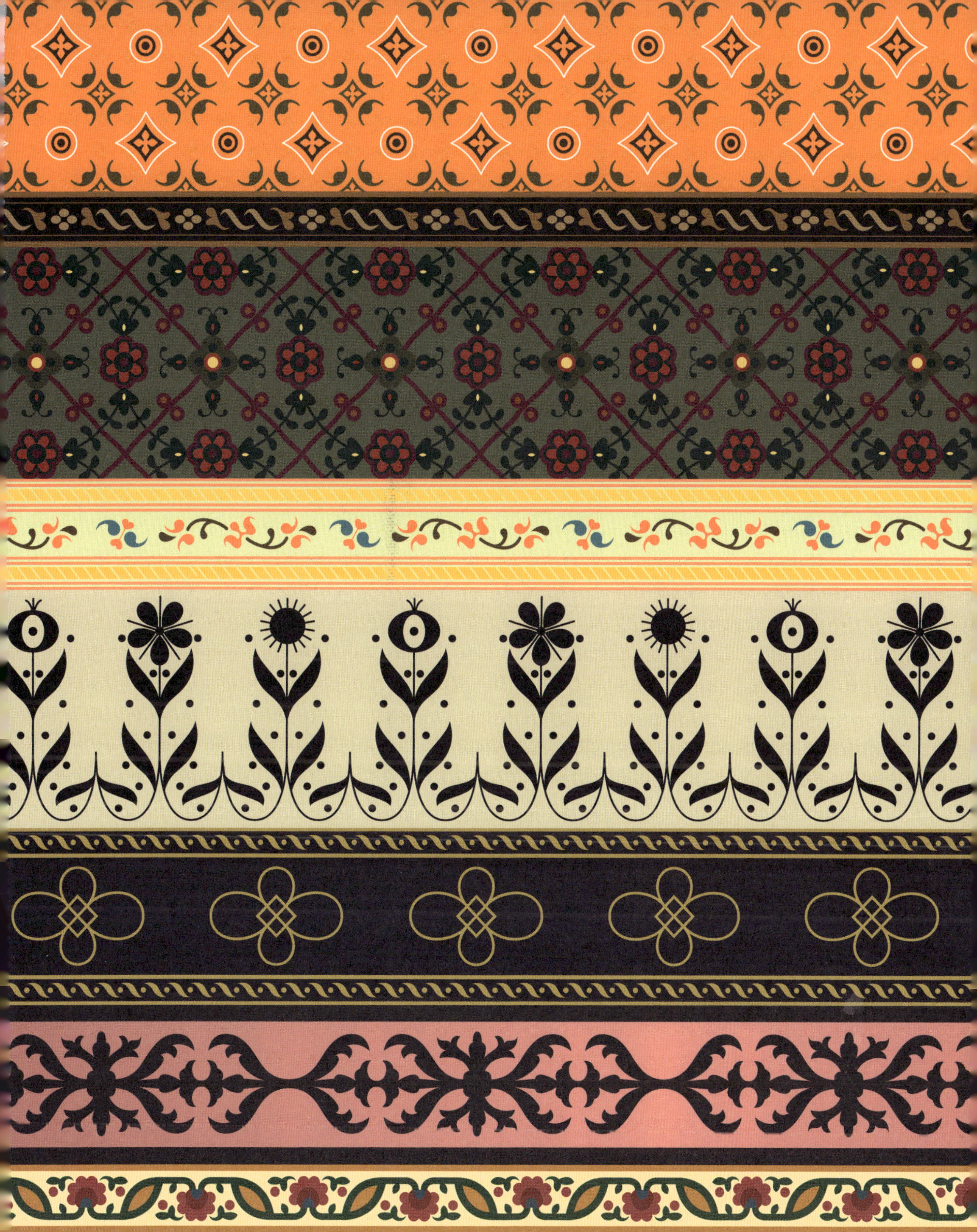

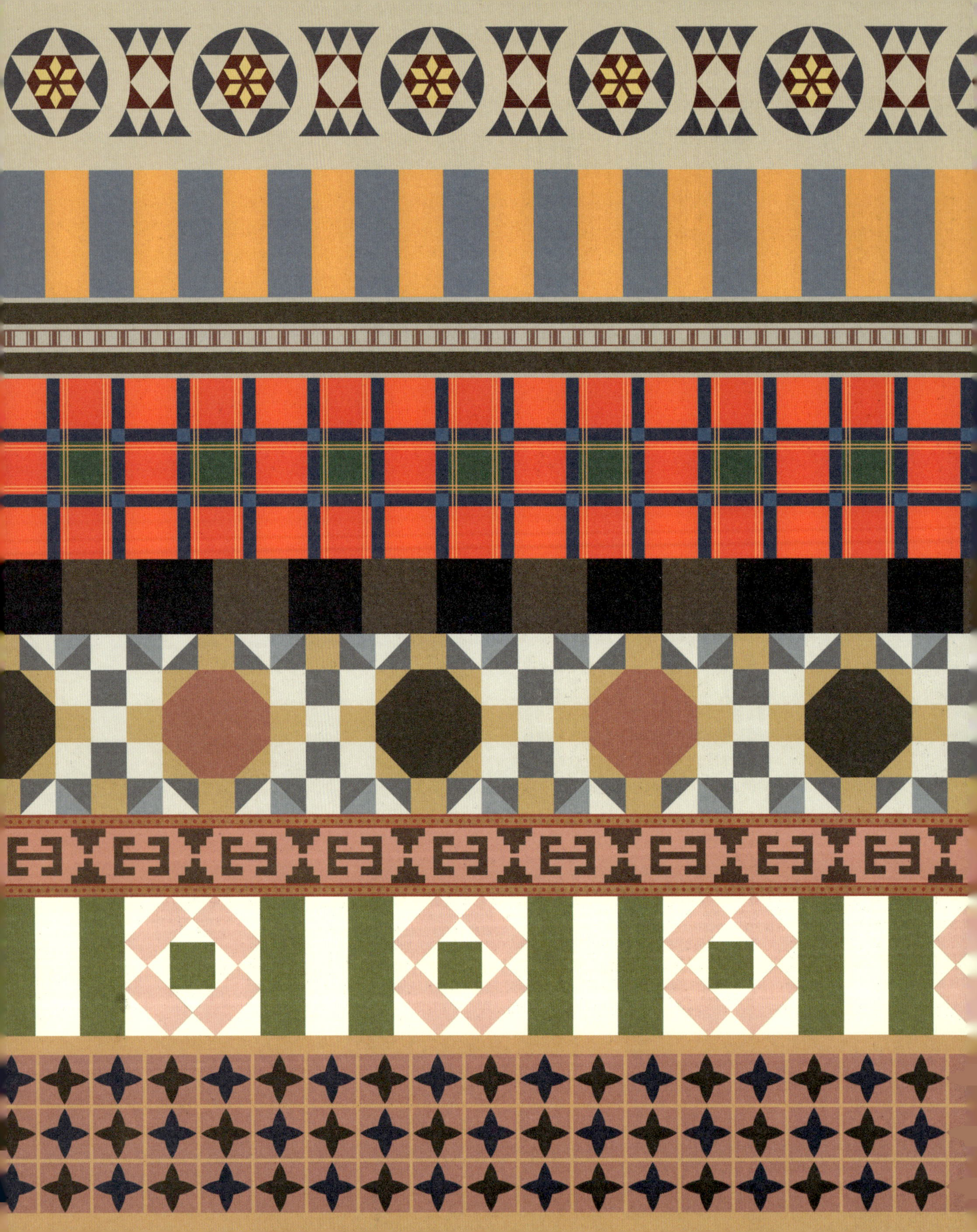